THE CALIFORNIA SEAFOOD COOKBOOK

A COOK'S GUIDE TO THE FISH AND SHELLFISH OF CALIFORNIA, THE PACIFIC COAST, AND BEYOND

by Isaac Cronin, Paul Johnson and Jay Harlow

Preface by Rick Moonen

A Herman Graf Book
Skyhorse Publishing

Skyhorse Publishing books may be purchased in bulk at special discounts for sales promotion, corporate gifts, fund-raising, or educational purposes. Special editions can also be created to specifications. For details, contact the Special Sales Department, Skyhorse Publishing, 307 West 36th Street, 11th Floor, New York, NY 10018 or info@skyhorsepublishing.com.

www.skyhorsepublishing.com

10 9 8 7 6 5 4 3 2 1

Library of Congress Cataloging-in-Publication Data is available on file.

Print ISBN: 978-1-62914-784-0

Printed in China

CONTENTS

Illustrated Species Index

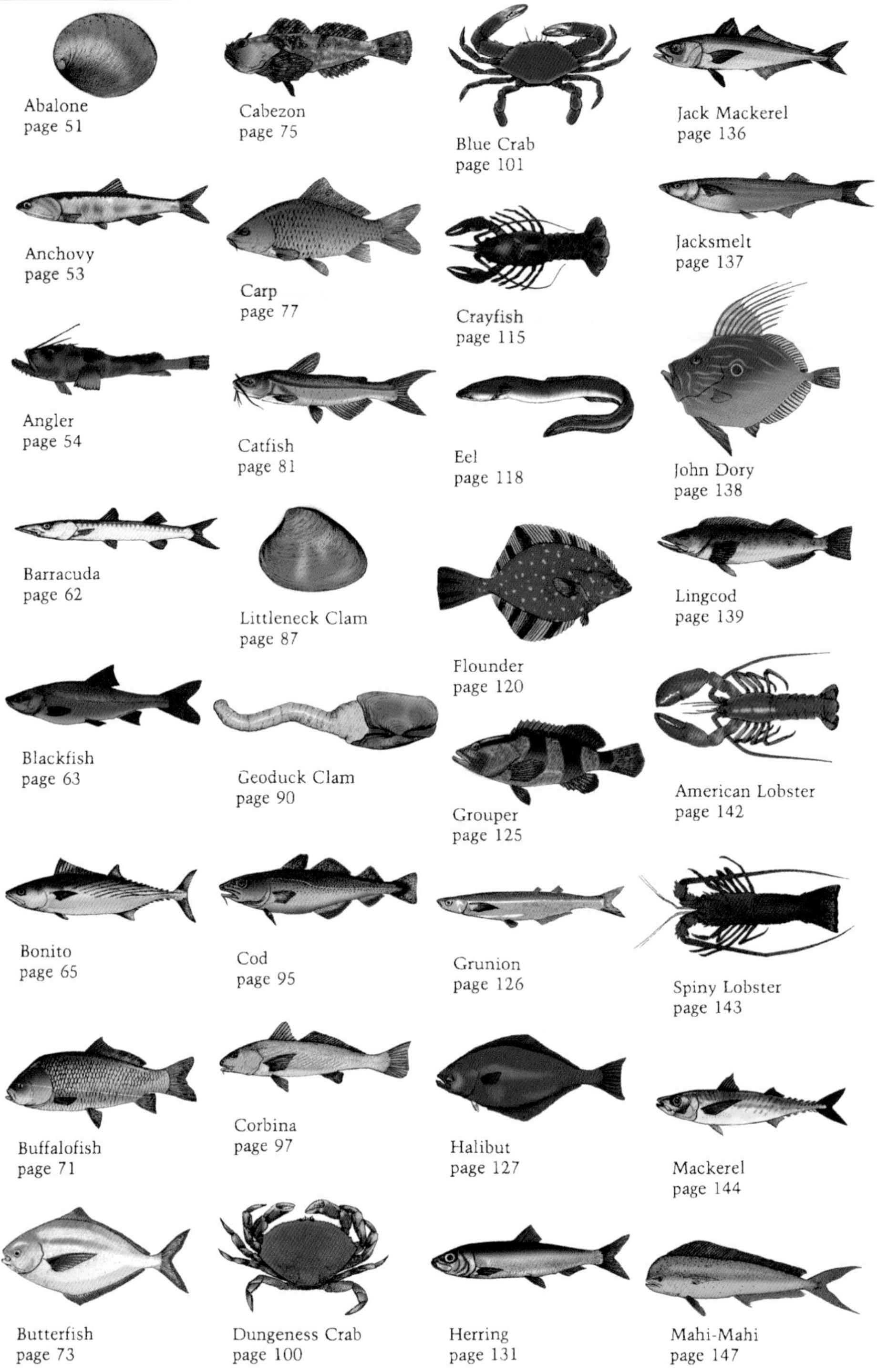

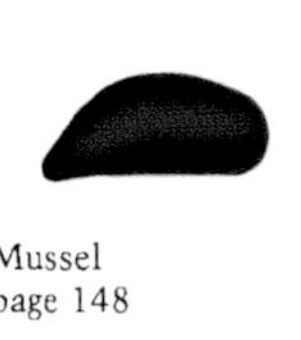

Mussel
page 148

Octopus
page 154

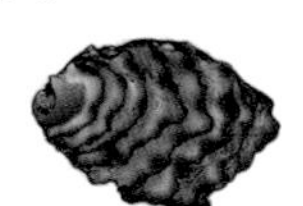

Oyster
page 156

Periwinkle
page 167

Redfish
page 168

Red Snapper
page 169

Rockfish (Bolina)
page 171

Rockfish (Goldeneye)
page 171

Rockfish (Yellowtail)
page 172

Rockfish (Bocaccio)
page 172

Sablefish
page 182

King Salmon
page 184

Silver Salmon
page 185

Sand Dab
page 191

Sea Scallop
page 193

White Seabass
page 197

Thresher Shark
page 199

Leopard Shark
page 200

Soupfin Shark
page 200

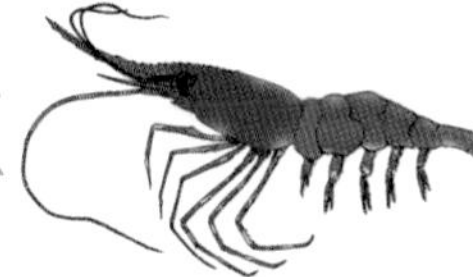

Spot Shrimp
page 204

Grass Shrimp
page 205

Skate
page 212

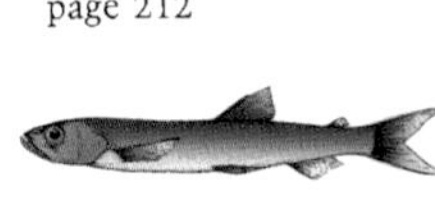

Smelt
page 213

Sole (Petrale)
page 215

Sole (Rex)
page 216

Spotted Sea Trout
page 222

Squid
page 223

Striped Bass
page 230

White Sturgeon
page 231

Swordfish
page 234

Tilefish
page 236

Rainbow Trout
page 238

Tuna (Albacore)
page 240

Wahoo
page 247

Whelk
page 248

Yellowtail
page 250

Acknowledgements

The authors would like to thank the many people who contributed to this book.

Many Bay Area restaurant chefs and other talented cooks provided recipes and specific information on culinary techniques. These include Bruce Aidells of Poulet, Somchai Aksomboon of Siam Cuisine, Carol Brendlinger of Bay Wolf, Bruce Cost, Victoria Fahey of Curds and Whey, William Marinelli, Jeremiah Tower of Santa Fe Bar and Grill and Dan Wormhoudt of Gulf Coast Oyster Bar.

A wealth of technical information was provided by various experts including many wholesale fish dealers of San Francisco and the Bay Area: Tony Porti, William Marinelli and the West Coast Aquaculture Foundation; Robert Pata and Joe Farrell of the National Marine Fisheries Service; Robert Price and Fred S. Conte of the Sea Grant Program, University of California at Davis; and Joan Eesley and Larry Marsali of the California Seafood Institute.

Seeing our words come to life through the magnificent drawings of Amy Pertschuk was a joy and an inspiration. We thank Amy for patiently bearing with us as we kept adding more and more species to the book.

Sidney Weinstein, Deborah Bruner and Tim Ware supplied invaluable editorial assistance, and Jeanne Jambu imparted clarity and elegance with her graphic design.

Although not involved in this project, the following chefs and restaurateurs have, through the years, provided culinary guidance and inspiration, and their presence is felt throughout the book: Anne Powning Haskell, Mark Miller, Jeremiah Tower and Patty Unterman.

Finally, we would like to acknowledge the support and guidance of our publisher, John Harris, who provided us with a wonderful facility in which to pursue our culinary interests, the freedom to define and organize this book according to the special demands of the subject matter, and his enthusiastic appetite at our recipe testings.

Introduction

In the fall of 1981, John Harris, our publisher, approached the three of us with an idea for a California seafood cookbook. Each of us—a food writer, a restaurant chef and a fishmonger—agreed on the need for a comprehensive culinary guide to the variety of seafood available in California. We had found that most seafood cookbooks, while they may have excellent recipes, are written from an Atlantic or Gulf Coast perspective; with very few exceptions, Pacific species are given at best passing mention. Cooks on the West Coast have had to fend for themselves in adapting Eastern recipes to locally available fish.

As we began to catalogue the varieties of seafood available in California, it became clear that we also wanted to capture the spirit of an eclectic, adventurous style of cookery which is typically Californian. Using the finest and freshest ingredients available and incorporating a wide range of ethnic influences, the chefs, caterers and cooking teachers of the Bay Area are among the best exponents of this style. Several of them came to our test kitchen during the development of this book, demonstrating techniques and contributing recipes.

However strong our enthusiasm might be for this California approach to seafood, our work would be of little use to cooks in other parts of the country if we limited ourselves entirely to local species. To avoid our own form of provincialism, we decided to test as many Atlantic and Gulf species as we could obtain, to determine which could serve as alternatives for the Pacific varieties featured in our recipes.

The California Seafood Cookbook, then, is a comprehensive guide to identifying, buying, cleaning, cutting, cooking and serving seafood available on the Pacific Coast. Part I, "A Cook's Introduction to Seafood," presents the preliminaries to cooking: techniques for judging freshness, step-by-step cleaning and cutting procedures, cooking methods and special ingredients. The heart of the book is Part II, "A Cook's Encyclopedia of Seafood." The emphasis is on species available here, whether from local waters or brought in by air, sometimes literally from around the world. Each variety is carefully illustrated so that the book can serve as a "field guide" to fish in the market.

An important feature of the recipes in the encyclopedia is the listing of alternative species, including Pacific, Atlantic and Gulf varieties. Cooks in California, for example, will find that the recipe for Sautéed Corbina with Piquant Sauce on page 98 will work equally well with some other local species such as white seabass; readers in Louisiana are advised to try it with their own redfish, and New Yorkers may freely substitute striped bass.

The recipes in this book are a personal selection and reflect many, but by no means all, of the ethnic styles to be found in California kitchens. They tend toward simple approaches to a limited number of ingredients rather than elaborate creations; they are intended to show off the food, not the cook. Because they rely on fresh, seasonal ingredients, which may not always be available, they encourage flexibility and improvisation. They draw on many cultural and culinary traditions, but are not bound to any one way of doing things. In short, they represent the way many Californians cook and eat.

We hope that our readers, in California and elsewhere, will use *The California Seafood Cookbook* in the spirit in which it was written. Researching and writing this book was a wonderful learning experience for us. There were a few disappointments along the way, but many more pleasant surprises. We hope that you will find this book useful in your own discovery of the pleasures of seafood cookery.

—Isaac Cronin, Jay Harlow,
Paul Johnson

Berkeley, California

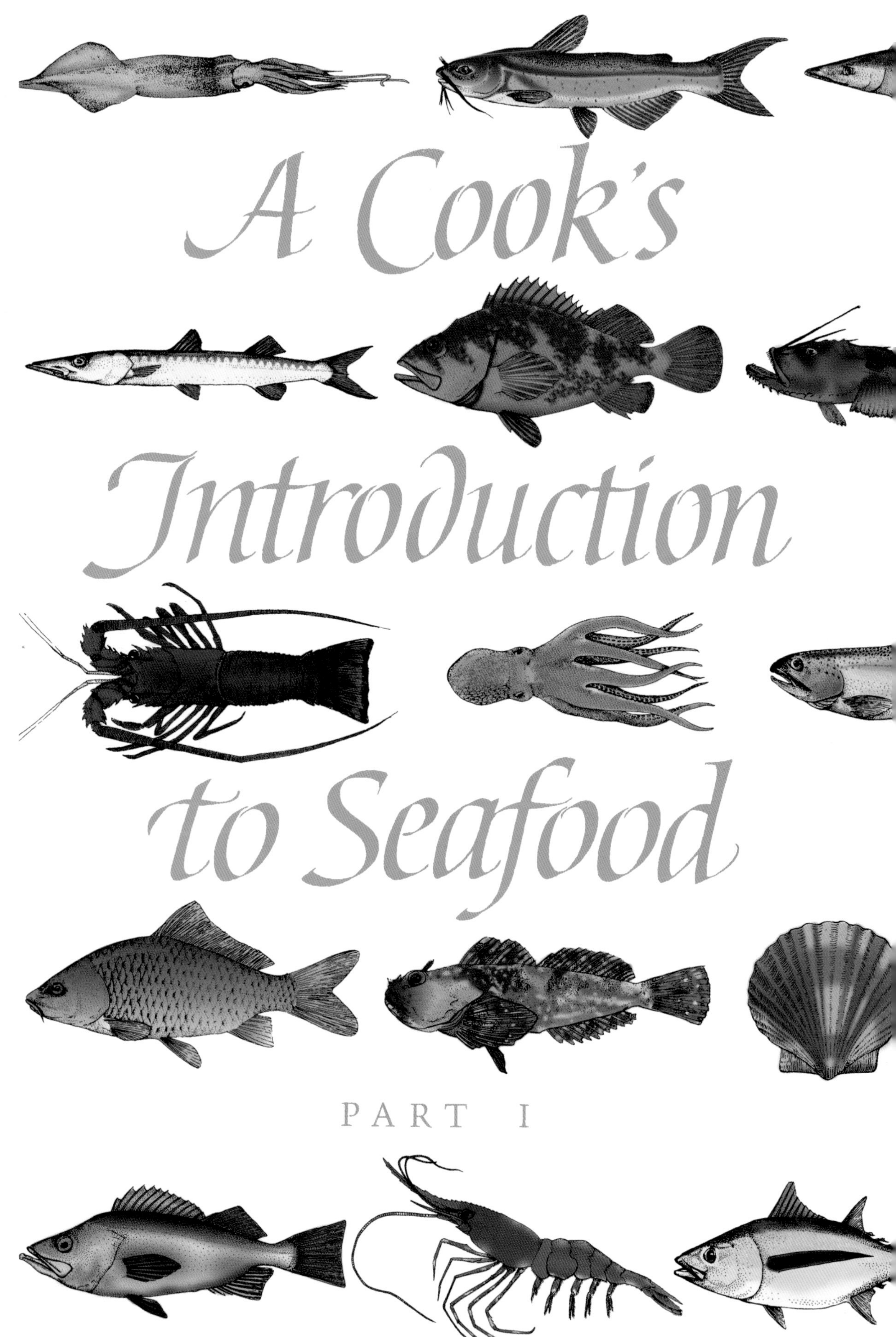

A Cook's Introduction to Seafood

PART I

AT THE FISH MARKET

A GUIDE TO BUYING FRESH SEAFOOD

SEAFOOD spoils most quickly of all foods. From the moment a fish leaves the water, bacteria which are abundant in the aquatic environment begin to break down the flesh. Cold temperatures retard this process, but even under optimal conditions seafood should be used as quickly as possible after it is caught.

The quality of seafood depends not only on how long it has been out of the water, but also on how it is handled. Certain fishing methods are rougher on seafood, rendering it more perishable. Some fishermen are very conscientious about careful

Available Forms

ROUND: The whole fish, as it comes out of the water (applies equally to flatfish)

DRESSED: Entrails removed, head intact, gills may or may not be removed

PAN-DRESSED: Dressed, head and scales removed, fins and tail may be trimmed

BLOCK: A section of a large dressed fish (primarily shark and swordfish) cut across, including skin and bone

CHUNK: An equivalent piece of a smaller fish, such as a whole salmon tail

STEAK: (a) A slice up to 2 inches thick through the body of a dressed fish, including skin and bone (salmon, seabass, halibut, etc.) (b) A slice of similar thickness, perpendicular to the bone, of a quarter or other section of a large fish (shark, swordfish, tuna), often skinless

FILET: The boneless meat of one side of a fish removed in one piece, with or without the skin; also pieces cut from a large filet or boneless meat in general

FLETCHES: Half-filets of halibut or other large flatfish, made by separating the whole filet along the seam parallel to the backbone

SLICES: Sections of a large filet or fletch (salmon, seabass, lingcod, halibut, etc.), cut diagonally or perpendicular to the bone. Usually, thicker pieces yield one per serving

SCALLOPS: Same as slices but usually thinner, two or more per serving

handling and immediate icing of their catch; others are not. Wholesalers also vary in their care of and attention to quality of their product, and retailers may mix several catches in the same batch.

With all these variables, the cook must learn to shop carefully, evaluating each fish on its own merits. Do not assume that all the fish at a given market, or even all the fish of a given species, are of the same quality. If at all possible, buy round (whole) fish (see Available Forms, page 13). It is easiest to judge the quality of fish in this form, and the head, bones and trimmings can be used for stocks. Most fishmongers will clean round fish for little or no charge if you do not wish to clean it yourself.

Selecting Seafood

Keep the following rules in mind when choosing seafood in the market:

Be flexible. It is best to go to the market with a cooking method or a general approach rather than a particular fish in mind.

Eat what is in season. This rule more than any other will insure that you are getting the best seafood available as well as the best value. Don't insist on having grilled swordfish during the height of salmon season.

Buy fish the same day you plan to cook it. Very fresh seafood will keep another day, but the quality will certainly deteriorate.

Ask the fishmonger for recommendations. After all, it is his job to know what is best. If you feel, however, that a fishmonger has recommended something because he wants to get rid of it, try another fish market.

Don't be afraid to ask for special services such as having a crab cleaned or a fish boned for stuffing. Be prepared to pay for these extras, which take time.

When placing special orders, be prepared to leave a deposit, especially if your request is at all unusual. Again, be flexible, and allow for the possibility that the fish you want may not be available on the day you want it.

Judging Freshness

The following are guidelines for judging the freshness of fish and shellfish. Important exceptions to the rules are given in parentheses.

ROUND FISH

Flesh should be firm or elastic to the touch, even to the point of *rigor mortis.* (Some fish may be so fresh that *rigor mortis* will not have set in yet.)

Odor should be clean and pleasant, like brine or fresh water, with no "fishy" smell around the gills. (Shark and skate sometimes have an ammonia smell, which should disappear with acidulation.)

Gills should be bright pink or red. (Gills of some flatfish may be darkened by mud depending upon how they were caught, but should be bright red when washed.)

Eyes should be clear and protruding. (Eyes of some deep-water fish, such as rockfish and grouper, may be cloudy due to pressure changes as they are raised from the bottom.)

Skin should be brightly colored, with scales tightly attached.

FILETS AND STEAKS

Although there are many fewer clues to freshness once a fish has been cut up, some of the above guidelines apply. Filets or steaks should have a bright, moist appearance, with no brown, yellow or pink discoloration, and a clean, fresh odor.

LIVE FISH

Freshwater species such as catfish, buffalofish, blackfish and eel are often kept alive in tanks. Choose only lively specimens.

SHELLFISH

From a cook's standpoint, shellfish fall into three main categories: crustaceans (crab, lobster, shrimp, crayfish); cephalopods (squid, octopus); and molluscs (including bivalves—clams, mussels, oysters, scallops—and univalves—abalone, whelk, periwinkles). As with fish, a clean, fresh aroma is a good indication of quality. The following are guidelines for each category:

Crustaceans

Live crustaceans should be lively, and seem heavy for their size. Shrimp, which are generally not sold alive, should have their heads firmly attached, with no blackening of the gill area just behind the head. It is not true that once a crab or lobster dies, it must be immediately discarded; it should, however, be cleaned and iced as soon as possible and cooked the same day.

Cooked crustaceans should have legs, claws and tail (if any) pulled in tightly. This is a sign that they were fresh and alive when cooked.

Cephalopods

Squid and octopus should have ivory flesh under the thin colored skin, with no discolorations.

Molluscs

Live bivalves should have tightly closed shells, or close them quickly when handled. Any which remain open are dead and should be discarded.

Univalves should also be alive, and the exposed muscle should react to the touch. To keep bivalves alive, *do not* store them in water, but keep them refrigerated and covered with a damp cloth. These intertidal species are used to being out of the water, and may keep for up to a week stored this way. (They will, of course, taste better if used promptly.) Oysters are the only bivalves which are generally stored after shucking; they should be kept in covered jars with *clear* liquid, refrigerated.

Freezing Seafood

Unless you catch more than you can use, freezing seafood is not a good idea. The connective fiber (collagen) in seafood is delicate and breaks down quickly in freezing and thawing, causing moisture and flavor loss which no cooking method or recipe can restore. And while freezing slows down spoilage of fish, it does not entirely stop it, especially when freezer temperatures are above 0°, which is the case with most home freezers.

If you must freeze seafood, observe the following guidelines:

Wrap the fish tightly and seal it well. Use a second layer of wrapping to minimize the possibility of direct contact with cold air, which will draw moisture out of the fish.

Use a freezer rather than the freezing compartment of a refrigerator if at all possible. A temperature of not more than 0° is optimal. The quicker the fish is frozen and the more even the temperature remains, the less moisture will be lost from the fish. Generally, shellfish freeze better than fish, and lean fish better than those with a higher fat content.

Thaw frozen seafood in the refrigerator until it reaches refrigerator temperature, and cook it the same day it is thawed. Never refreeze seafood that has been thawed.

TOOLS AND EQUIPMENT

THE *following is not a complete list of kitchen equipment, but rather a catalogue of the kinds of special equipment needed for fish cookery which might not be found in a home kitchen. In some cases, we are merely expressing our personal preferences. What is most important is to know the cooking characteristics of your own equipment—how it handles, how it cooks and its limitations.*

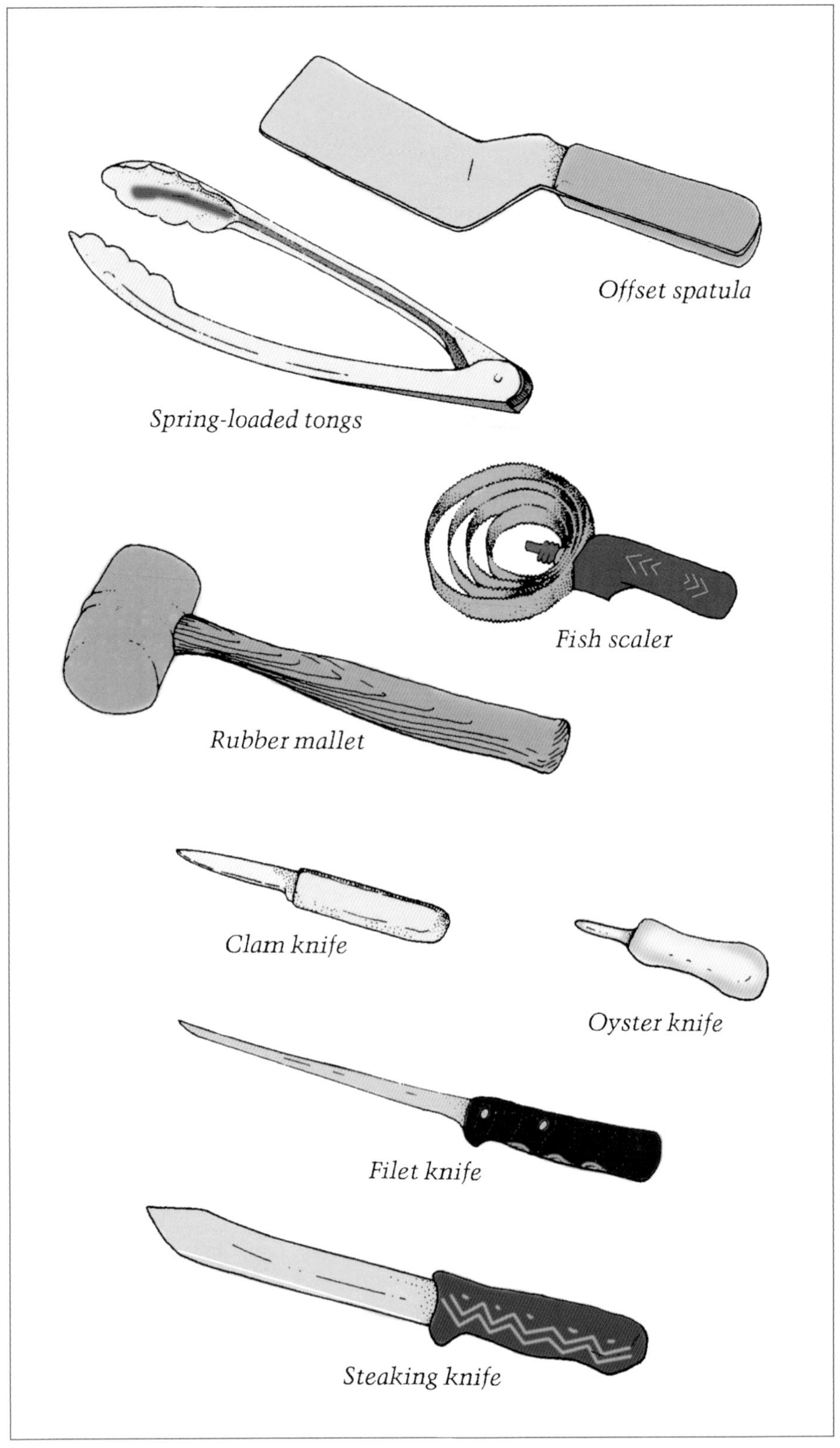
Offset spatula
Spring-loaded tongs
Fish scaler
Rubber mallet
Clam knife
Oyster knife
Filet knife
Steaking knife

Knives

In addition to the basics—*paring knife* and *French chef's knife* or *Chinese cleaver*—one type of knife is virtually indispensable when dealing with whole fish. It is called, appropriately enough, a *filet knife*. The filet knife looks like an elongated *boning knife* with a thin, flexible, tapered blade at least 7 inches long, and preferably up to 9 inches. (If the 9-inch variety is not available through normal retail outlets, try a commercial fisherman's supply store.) This knife allows for the fastest and cleanest fileting of all sizes and shapes of fish. A conventional boning knife will, of course, do the job, but will require more and shorter cuts and will tend to produce rather torn-up looking filets.

While a *Chinese cleaver* is thought of in this country primarily as a vegetable knife, it is a very useful tool for cleaning round fish, as a few minutes spent in a fish market in any Chinatown will amply demonstrate. It is also ideal for splitting fish heads for stock.

Hand Tools

We strongly recommend stocking your kitchen from commercial restaurant supply houses whenever possible. High-tech decor aside, these dealers carry tools of proven design and generally reliable quality, each designed to do a given job efficiently and for a long time. Among the hand tools especially useful for fish cookery are: an *offset spatula* with an 8-inch blade; spring-loaded stainless *tongs*, rather than the scissor-action type; and heat resistant *rubber spatulas* in a variety of sizes. Other specialized tools we found very handy in the development of our recipes are: a *tomato corer*, which looks like a tiny scoop with teeth and deftly removes the stem core; and a *lemon zester*, which removes the flavorful outer peel of citrus fruits, leaving behind the bitter white membrane.

Cookware

Very little in the way of special cookware is required for the recipes in this book. Except where noted, the material of the cooking surface (cast iron, aluminum, stainless steel, enamel or non-stick coating) is not as important as its cooking characteristics; look for fairly heavy bottoms which spread the heat evenly. Where a recipe calls for a "non-aluminum" pan, use one with a non-reactive surface such as stainless, enamel, non-stick coating or anodized aluminum. Avoid uncoated aluminum, cast iron or copper.

The *wok*, that traditional Chinese masterpiece of cooking design, no longer needs introduction in this country. In addition to its most common use for stir-frying, we found the *wok* ideal for frying and steaming fish and for tossing pasta in sauce. A 14-inch rolled steel, round-bottomed *wok* with a single wooden handle seems to us the most versatile. Complete sets of accessories are widely available, and should include a flat metal perforated tray for steaming and a semi-circular wire rack for draining fried foods.

While no home grilling equipment can quite equal the intense heat of a restaurant charcoal broiler, the same advantages of quick cooking and sealing of the fish juices can be achieved on a variety of grill types. Charcoal is the choice for a heat source, and may be contained in a home barbecue or *hibachi*. The latter provides the most compact form of heat, and can be set up on a porch or even on a windowsill planter box. Unprocessed hardwood charcoal such as *Mexican mesquite* is preferable to charcoal briquets, both in heat output and burning time and flavor.

Various indoor electric grilling systems exist, from tabletop models with rotisserie attachments to built-in stove-top grills with cast-iron artificial coals and exhaust fans. We tested several of our grilled fish recipes on the latter and found it to produce an agreeable dish, but considerably more slowly and lacking the distinctive flavor of charcoal smoke.

CLEANING AND CUTTING TECHNIQUES

The following pages contain techniques which apply to a number of species. Special techniques particular to one species are described along with the fish's entry in the encyclopedia, Part II.

*Typical Bone Structure of Round-bodied Fish**

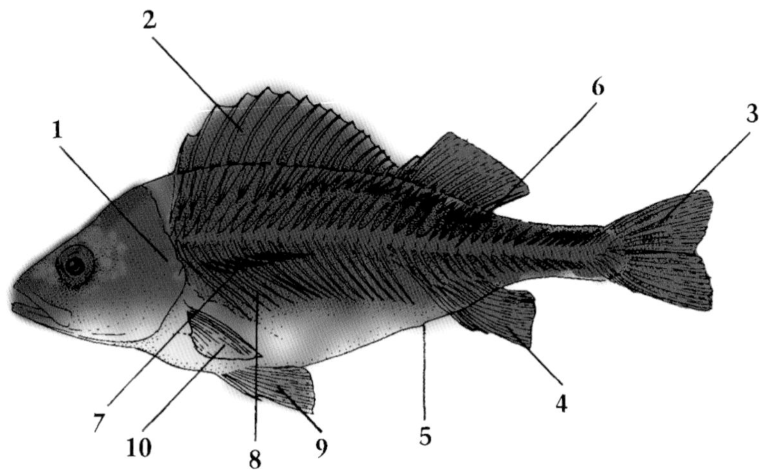

1. Operculum or gill cover	**6. Backbone (spine)**
2. Dorsal fin	**7. Pin bones (7)**
3. Tail or caudal fin	**8. Ribs**
4. Anal fin	**9. Pelvic fin (2)**
5. Vent	**10. Pectoral fin (2)**

**"Round-bodied" refers to one of two basic body shapes. "Round" is a professional term used for whole, undressed fish (see page 13).*

Familiarize yourself with the general bone structure of the two basic fish types—round-bodied and flat—before starting to work. Many of the instructions use anatomical terms to avoid confusion, e.g. "dorsal" instead of "back" or "top."

Important: Make as few cuts as possible, especially when fileting, and try to cut with long, smooth strokes. Professional cutters do this not only for the sake of speed, but to yield filets with smooth surfaces.

Typical Bone Structure of Flat Fish

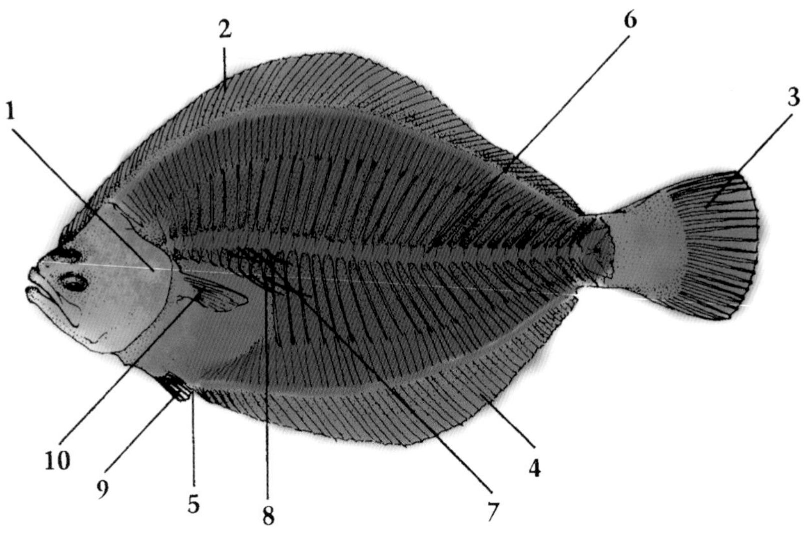

1. Operculum or gill cover	**6. Backbone (spine)**
2. Dorsal fin	**7. Pin bones (7)**
3. Tail or caudal fin	**8. Ribs**
4. Anal fin	**9. Pelvic fin (2)**
5. Vent	**10. Pectoral fin (2)**

Fileting a Round-bodied Fish

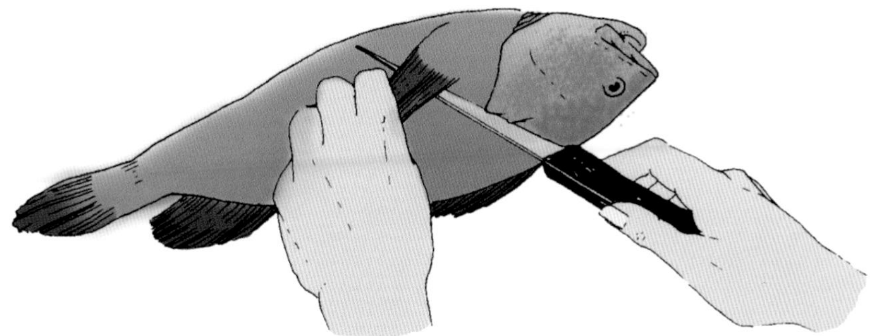

1 Place the fish on its side, dorsal fin toward you and head toward your cutting hand. Lift the pectoral fin and cut diagonally just behind the operculum toward the head. (Note that the filet extends well up into the head.) Be careful not to pierce the entrails at the belly end of the cut.

2 At the end of the first stroke, twist the knife until the edge is facing the tail and the point rests against the spine.

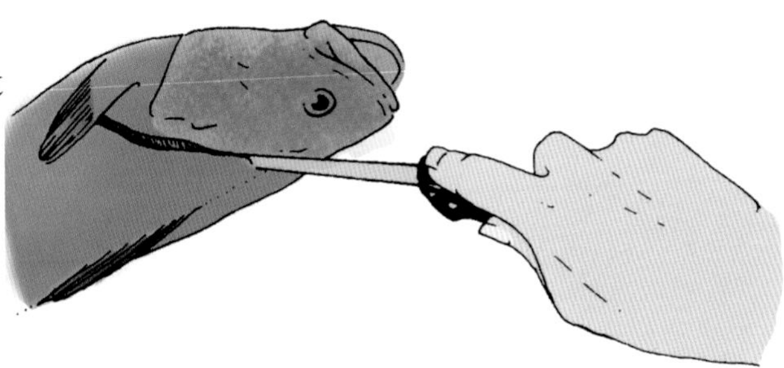

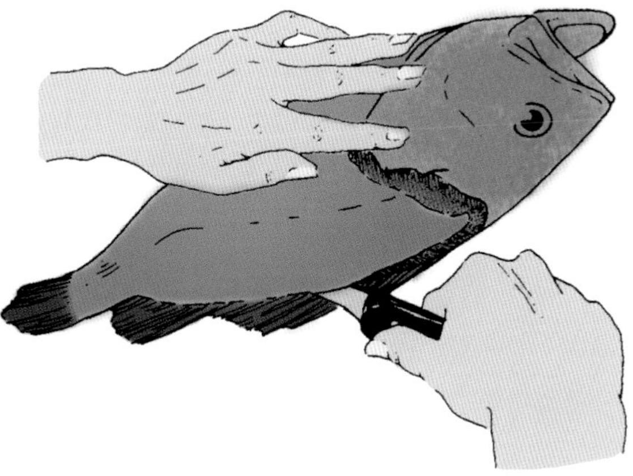

3 Probe with the tip of the knife for the backbone. Holding the blade horizontally, slide the knife along the ribs toward the tail, scraping along the bones to cut away the back side of the filet.

4 Gently peel back the filet to reveal the backbone. Sever the pin bones, but not the ribs. Slide the knife along the ribs toward the belly, again taking care not to cut into the entrails.

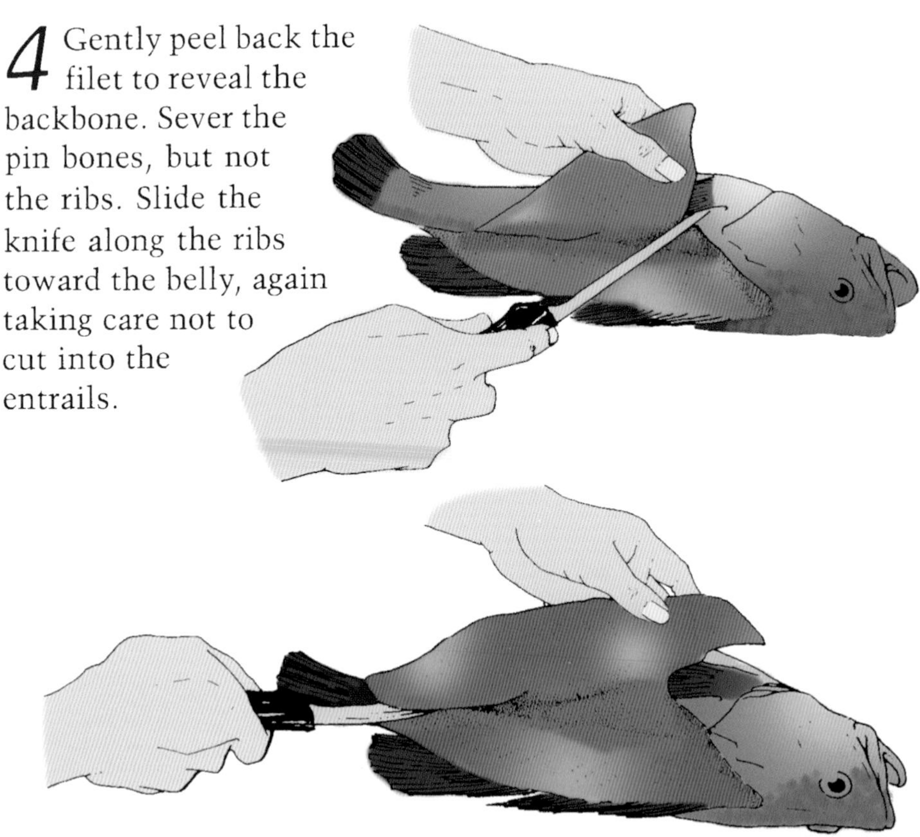

5 Continue with one smooth cut toward the tail, bending the blade flat against the bones to remove all the meat.

6 Pull the filet free and sever the skin along the anal fin. Turn the fish over, with the belly still facing away from you and the head in the opposite direction. Repeat the above steps for the other filet.

Fileting a Flatfish

Flatfish may be fileted by essentially the same process as above. Large flatfish are actually easier to filet than most round-bodied fish, as the belly cavity is more compact and the filets are larger. Halibut or other large species may also be cut into fletches by first cutting through the filet to the backbone along the lateral line, then cutting away each half filet from the bone.

Skinning Filets

Unless a recipe specifies filets with the skin on, filets should be skinned. Place the filet skin side down on the board. Hold the tail end of the skin down with a fingernail and make a shallow cut under the filet to the skin. Holding the knife at about a 10–15° angle to the board, scrape along the skin without cutting through it. Hold the skin taut and try to make one long, smooth cut. Remove the strips of soft flesh close to the fins, either by hand or with the knife.

Scaling a Fish

If a fish is to be cooked with the skin on, it is generally scaled before dressing. (Fish without scales, such as flounder and bonito, are obvious exceptions.) Small fish may be scaled with the fingertips or the back edge of a small knife. Large fish such as salmon or seabass are easily scaled with a *fish scaler* shown on page 18. With either tool, scrape from the tail toward the head to remove all the scales, and rinse the skin to remove any clinging scales. For easy clean-up, work on top of several thicknesses of brown paper or newspaper to catch the scales. After scaling, the fish may be dressed, pan-dressed or boned, as desired.

Dressing a Fish

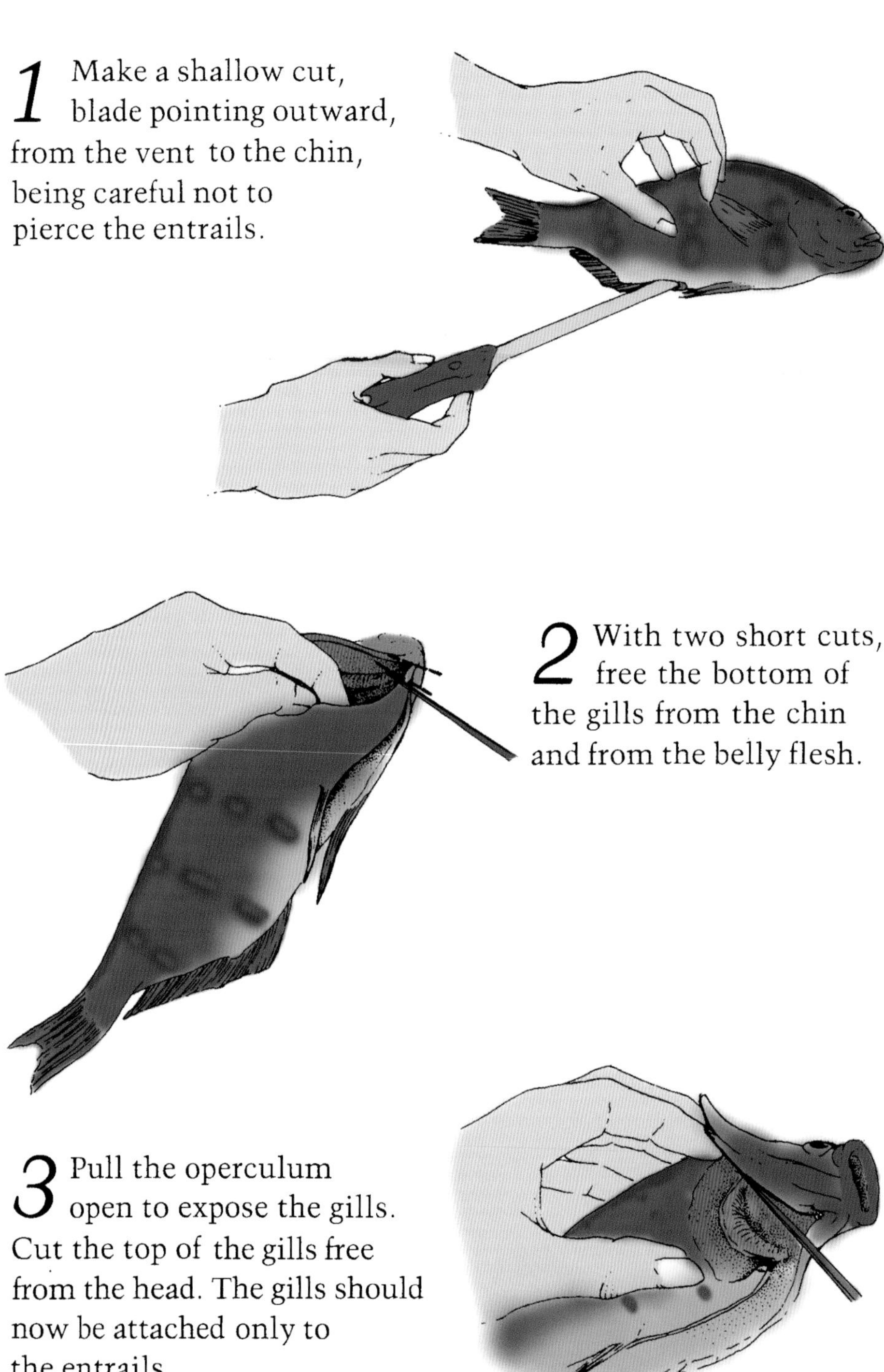

1 Make a shallow cut, blade pointing outward, from the vent to the chin, being careful not to pierce the entrails.

2 With two short cuts, free the bottom of the gills from the chin and from the belly flesh.

3 Pull the operculum open to expose the gills. Cut the top of the gills free from the head. The gills should now be attached only to the entrails.

4 Pin the gills to the board with the tip of the knife. Draw the fish away; the entrails should pull away from the body along with the gills. Remove the kidneys (the strip of reddish tissue near the backbone) and any other material left in the cavity, and rinse well.

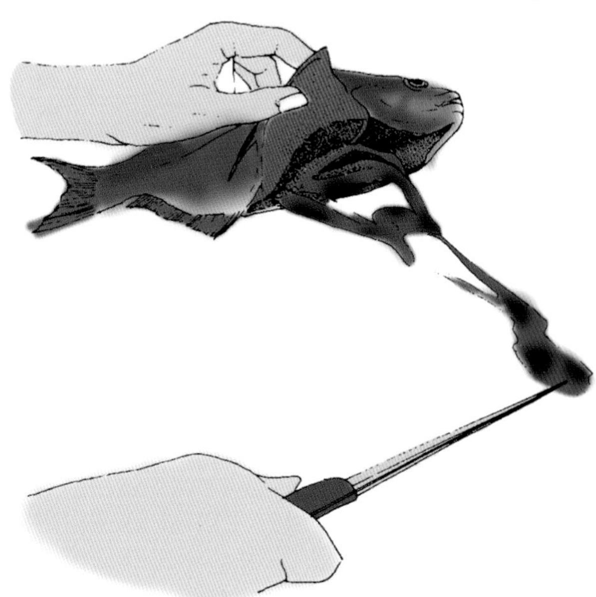

Pan-Dressing a Small Flatfish

This technique, illustrated here on a sand dab, works equally well for horizontally compressed fish such as butterfish, surf-perch and freshwater "panfish" such as bluegill. Work with a large French knife or Chinese cleaver, starting with the point of the knife on the board as if slicing vegetables.

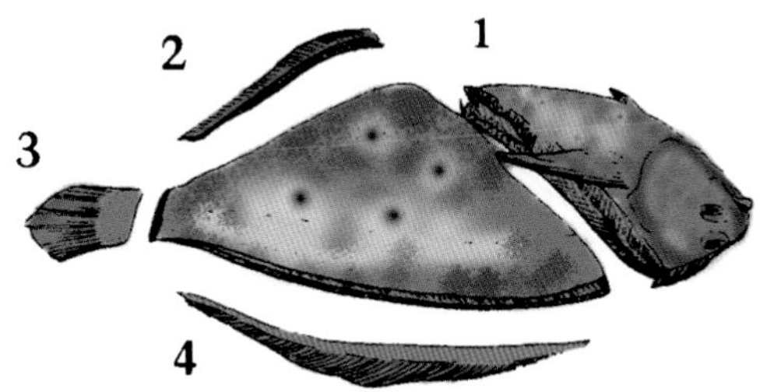

1 Start with the fish oriented as shown. Make one decisive cut from just behind the head to behind the vent, removing the head, gills and entrails in one piece. (Feel for the point where filet stops and the belly cavity begins, and cut just behind this point.)

2 Turn the fish 90° clockwise. Remove the anal fin together with the short bones which support it and the attached strips of soft flesh. Save these for the stock pot.

3 Turn the fish again and trim or remove the tail fin.

4 Turn once more and remove the dorsal fin, again with the supporting bones. What are left are the two filets attached to the backbone. Remove any traces of kidney and roe and rinse the fish well.

Steaking a Dressed Salmon

This technique is adaptable to any similarly sized and shaped fish. It produces four filet portions, two from the tail and two from near the head, as well as steaks from the central section. For the first steps, use a French knife or Chinese cleaver for best results.

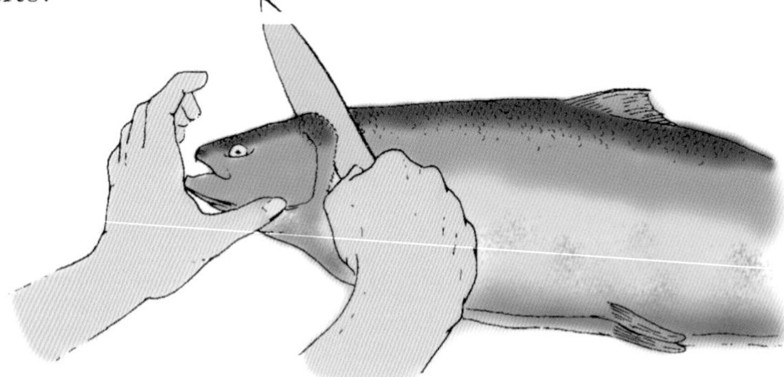

1 Cut diagonally behind the operculum, as close to the bone and as far into the head as possible.

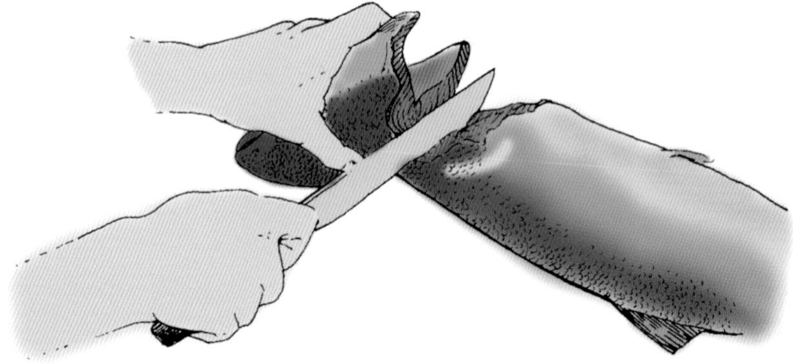

2 Turn the fish over and repeat. Sever the backbone to remove the head.

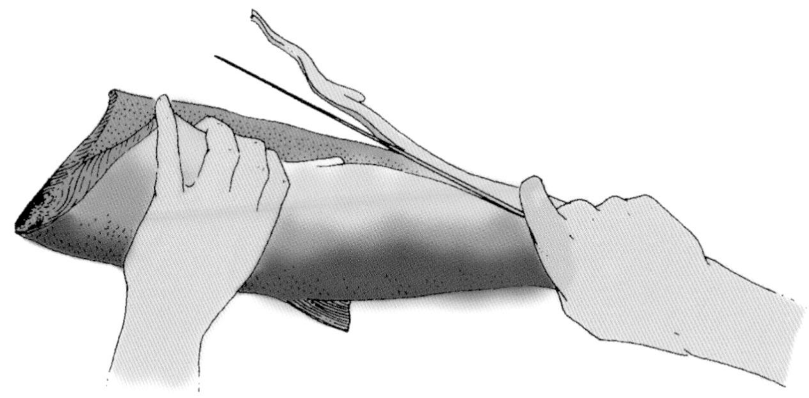

3 Trim the flap of belly flesh by about an inch, if desired. (This is the fattest and least desirable part of the meat.)

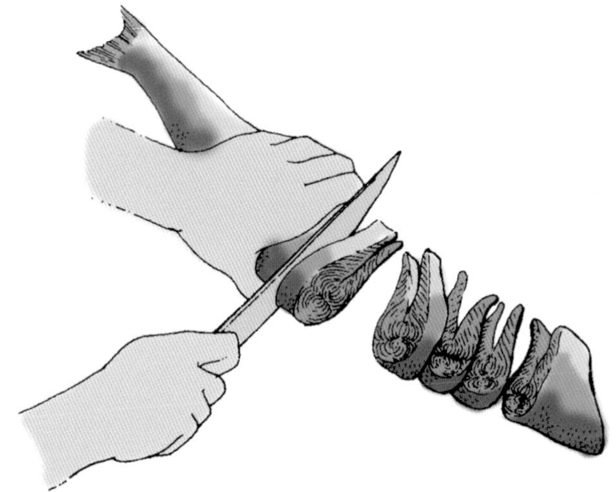

4 Using a steaking knife (see page 18) or a French knife make the first cut perpendicular to the backbone about 4 inches from the head end. Slice the fish into steaks, ¾–1½ inches thick, to approximately the point of the anal fin. If the backbone is particularly large you can force the knife through it by hitting the blade with a rubber mallet (see page 18). Filet the head and tail portions or reserve them for cooking whole.

COOKING METHODS

Dry Heat Methods

GRILLING

PROBABLY the oldest method of cooking fish, and arguably the best, is directly over a fire. In its modern version, grilling, the fish is cooked over direct heat while supported by a grill of parallel metal bars or wire. The heat source may be charcoal or wood, a gas flame or an electric heating element. The fish is cooked both by direct heat and by heat transmitted through the grill bars, which typically leave a pattern of dark searing marks on the cooked surface.

Most grilled seafood benefits from a preliminary oil-based marinade. Additional flavor can be introduced by throwing fresh or dried herbs and herb stems on the coals as the fish cooks; rosemary, thyme and wild fennel stalks are especially appropriate for this treatment. For a typical grilling procedure, see Grilled Salmon with Fennel (page 187).

The most common grilling problems are fish sticking to the grill and over- or under-cooking. To avoid these:

Oil filets or steaks which have not had a preliminary marinade, draining off excess oil to prevent flare-ups on the grill. (An exception to this rule is small pan-dressed flatfish, which seem more likely to stick if they are oiled; they are best grilled without any oil or marinade.)

Allow the pieces to warm briefly to room temperature before cooking. This allows the heat to penetrate to the center more quickly without overcooking the outside. (This advice applies to other cooking methods as well.)

Preheat the grill thoroughly. Fish will nearly always stick to a cold grill.

Work with a hot fire. Mexican mesquite charcoal or hardwood produces a hotter fire than briquets and imparts a nicer aroma.

Generally speaking, if you can hold your hand a few inches above the grill for any length of time, the fire is not hot enough. Set electric or other indoor grills to maximum heat.

Maintain the grill surface carefully during and after use. Clean the grill with a wire brush between rounds of grilling, and oil after cleaning as you would a cast-iron skillet.

Position fish carefully to minimize contact with the grill. Whether cooking whole fish or filets, place them perpendicular to the grill bars rather than parallel. Start filets skin side up for the best presentation.

Try to turn fish only once, and present the fish with the first-cooked side (bone side) up. Remember that a piece may cook more or less than halfway on the first side, and adjust the time for the second side accordingly. Avoid excessive handling of the fish. The more times a piece is moved, the more chances it has to stick. If the piece will not lift easily with tongs or the long edge of an offset spatula, let it sit another half minute or so before you try again.

BROILING

One step removed from grilling is broiling, which exposes the fish to high direct overhead heat. Almost any kind of fish filet or steak as well as small whole fish may be broiled. Lean fish, however, are prone to drying out quickly when broiled; they should be basted with an oil-based marinade or a compound butter to prevent this. Thin filets and steaks will cook through from one side, but larger pieces will generally require turning. For a detailed broiling procedure, see Broiled Sablefish with Anchovy Butter (page 183).

FRYING

Perhaps the most popular method of fish cookery in the world is frying (or "deep frying" as it is frequently and redundantly called). Many dishes which are commonly described as "fried" are actually sautéed, stir-fried or pan-fried (see pages 32–33 for a description of these techniques).

Fried foods are those which are immersed in hot fat, either vegetable or animal, and cooked without contact with the cooking vessel. Most frying involves a batter or a dry coating of flour, cornmeal or the like which seals in the flavors and juices and prevents absorption of excess fat. Properly fried foods are crisp on the outside and steaming hot inside; little or none of the cooking oil should remain on or in the food. Improperly fried foods, however, may absorb large quantities of fat and be difficult to digest, or be well-browned on the outside but only partially cooked inside.

Unless otherwise specified, all recipes for fried seafood in this book require a mild-flavored vegetable oil such as peanut or safflower. The ideal temperature for most frying is between 350° and 375°. For examples of this technique, see Sweet and Sour Fish (page 79).

Frying with consistently good results is a skill which takes practice and careful attention. The following are some common problems and ways in which to avoid them:

Greasy or soggy coating is caused by cooking at too low a temperature. Start with the oil around 375° (a fat thermometer is helpful). Avoid adding too many pieces at once; if the oil does not return to at least 325–350° quickly after the fish is added, you are frying too much at a time.

Dark coating or burnt flavor is caused by either too high a temperature or oil which has been overheated or overused. Skim any bits of batter from the oil before they burn, and discard oil which has darkened noticeably or has a burnt aroma.

Batter falling off in frying or serving is caused by applying batter to wet pieces or by excessive handling in the battering process. Dry the fish pieces before battering, and try to keep one hand dry when making the batter.

SAUTÉING

Sautéing is cooking food in a shallow pan with a small amount of fat over moderate to high heat. The heat is transmitted to the food both by the pan and by the cooking fat. Generally, pieces of food are either turned or otherwise moved during the cooking process to evenly heat all surfaces. Sauces for sautéed fish are frequently made in the pan after the fish has been cooked and removed, and may involve all or part of the cooking fat. For an example of this technique, see Sautéed Halibut with Cream and Herbs (page 128).

PAN-FRYING AND STIR-FRYING

"Pan-frying" and Oriental "stir-frying" are essentially variations on sautéing techniques. In pan-frying, relatively large pieces are cooked in a generous amount of fat and turned once. In stir-frying, the ingredients are generally cut more finely and cooked in almost constant motion. As with sautéing, recipes for either pan-frying or stir-frying frequently involve a sauce made with some of the cooking fat. For an example of these techniques, see Kung Pao Shrimp (page 208).

Stir-frying has its own set of rules. For the best results, pay strict attention to the timing and keep the following in mind:

Cut foods into uniform pieces for uniform cooking time.

Add ingredients to the wok or pan according to their relative cooking times. Be careful with chopped garlic, ginger and the like which are typically added early to flavor the oil, but which burn easily.

Keep the food pieces in constant motion to cook all surfaces evenly.

Use sufficient oil to cook all the ingredients, at least at the early stages. Excess oil may be removed before adding sauce ingredients.

BAKING

Baking is cooking wrapped or unwrapped foods in an oven, with heat ranging from moderate to high. Because of the time required to cook fish by baking, it must be enclosed somehow to prevent its drying out. This may be achieved by baking in a covered dish, entirely wrapping the fish in a package of paper or foil, or battering the fish as for frying. The first two methods are ideal for baking fish with aromatic vegetables or herbs; the steam released by the cooking fish combines with the other flavors to produce a nice sauce. For an example of this technique, see Baked Rockfish Veracruz Style (page 173). Baking in a batter, or in puff pastry or filo dough, provides an edible coating which still seals in most of the moisture and flavor. For an example of this technique, see Angler Baked in Filo (page 58).

Moist Heat Methods

BRAISING

Braising is actually a hybrid of dry and moist cooking methods. The food is first cooked quickly in oil to seal the outside flesh, then liquid is added for the remaining cooking time. Braising fish permits more exchange of flavors between the fish and sauce than does a simple sauté with sauce, but less than stewing. Braising is ideal for combining ingredients with assertive flavors, such as olives, anchovies, garlic, ginger and curry.

For a detailed braising procedure, see Braised Mackerel with Tomatoes, Rosemary and Garlic (page 145).

STEWING

Stews are combinations of foods cooked and served in liquids without the initial dry-cooking step of braising. Stewing is generally a longer and slower process than braising, and it produces a more complete exchange of flavors. Examples of stewing are California "Bouillabaisse" (page 179) and Laotian Catfish Soup (page 85).

STEAMING

Steaming is cooking in an enclosed vessel over boiling water, wine or an aromatic liquid, which is then discarded. Of all moist heat methods of cooking fish, steaming produces the best-textured flesh, although with only a slight interchange of flavors. Whole fish, steaks or filets may be steamed.

A variety of equipment may be used for steaming fish (see page 64). We recommend steaming on a plate in a wok as the most practical way to retain the liquids released from the fish in cooking. These are often the base of a sauce, along with Salmon (page 186) and Filet of Sole Stuffed with Shrimp (page 220).

"STEAMING" SHELLFISH

"Steaming" also describes a slightly different technique for cooking clams or mussels in the shell. The shellfish are placed in a saucepan with a small amount of liquid (and usually garlic and herbs), covered and brought to a boil. The shellfish cook in both the boiling liquid and the trapped steam, opening their shells when they die. The liquid released from the shells, together with the remaining cooking liquid, is then served with the shellfish or incorporated into a sauce.

POACHING

Poaching is cooking by immersion in simmering (*not* boiling) flavored liquid. Properly done, poaching produces some of the most delicate seafood dishes. The liquid may be Court-Bouillon (page 251), Fumet (page 252) or simply water flavored with wine and a few herbs.

Poaching techniques vary, except for the common rule that the liquid must never reach the boiling point. Small filets and thin steaks may be directly immersed in simmering liquid to cook in just a few minutes. Filets with a stuffing are more easily handled by placing them in the poaching pan and pouring the separately heated liquid over them. Larger pieces or whole fish are typically started in cold or lukewarm liquid which is then heated to a simmer. Large fish, such as salmon, may be wrapped in cheesecloth before cooking for ease of handling the cooked fish. For larger filets, steaks or whole fish, allow about 8 minutes per inch of thickness after the liquid begins to steam.

After poaching fish in *court-bouillon*, you will be left with a sort of weak *fumet*. Some poached fish preparations use a reduction of this liquid in the accompanying sauce. Otherwise, it may be strained and reserved for another use. Poached fish is frequently served cold with a mayonnaise (pages 257–59) or another cold sauce. For poaching procedures, see Poached Salmon (page 186) and Filet of Sole Stuffed with Shrimp (page 220).

BOILING

There are two instances where we recommend boiling seafood: cooking live shellfish, especially crab and crayfish, and blanching squid in rapidly boiling salted water for use in salads and Squid Stuffing for Pasta (page 229).

SPECIAL INGREDIENTS

An important feature of "California cuisine" is the availability of a number of special ingredients—herbs, spices, condiments and exotic vegetables often associated with a given ethnic cuisine. What follows is a selected list of the special ingredients used in our recipes, including their typical sources and recipes for possible substitutions, if any.

Achiote or **Annato seed:** The seed of a tree found in tropical America. The seeds are ground, usually with other spices, to produce a paste. Achiote is sold in Latin American groceries and in many supermarkets.

Anchovies: Canned anchovies vary widely in quality and saltiness. Most are packed in oil, but some well-stocked delicatessens carry salt-packed whole anchovies, which are more delicate in flavor. After a can of these is opened, however, they should then be stored in oil, preferably in good olive oil. When anchovies are used in slow-cooking dishes, their saltiness will permeate the dish, making additional salt unnecessary. For most other uses, however, rinse the filets of excess salt and oil before adding to the dish.

Basil: Use basil with garlic in hot butters or herb mayonnaise, or in sauces involving tomato. The dried herb is a poor substitute.

Bay: Use imported bay leaves for the most delicate flavor. The California bay laurel, a common tree in many parts of the state, yields a pungent, strong-flavored leaf which should be used sparingly.

Butter: We recommend unsalted ("sweet") butter in all recipes. If this is unavailable, remember to decrease the salt.

Celery: Celery is generally thought of as a vegetable, but the leaves from the heart are useful in a *bouquet garni*. Use with caution in making *fumet* or *court-bouillon*, as its flavor can easily dominate.

Chervil: Chervil is a delightful but relatively little-known herb which resembles a mild, sweet parsley with overtones of anise. It is only useful fresh; dried, it has almost no flavor or aroma. Use in compound butters, herb mayonnaise, or other simple sauces.

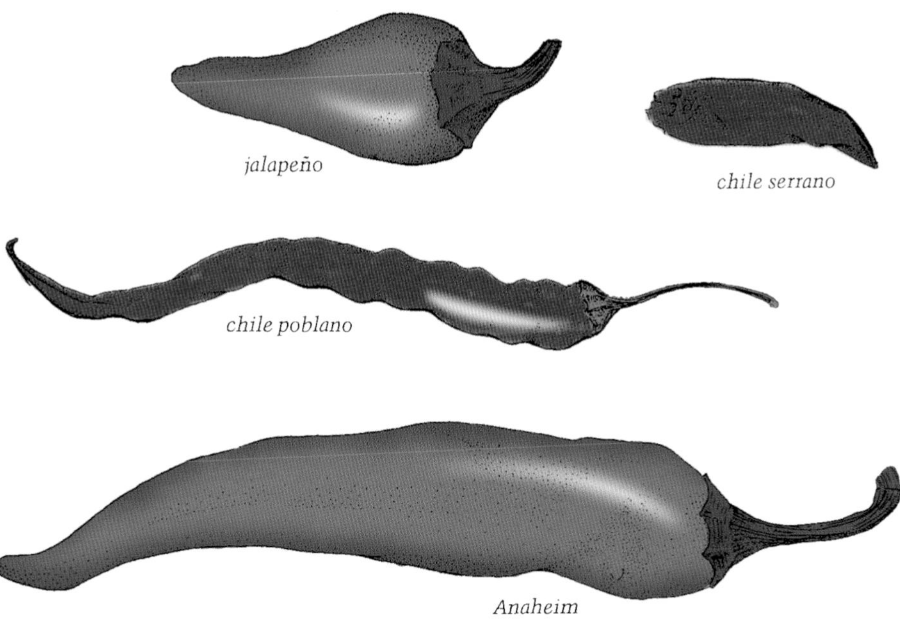

Chiles: Most of the chile varieties listed below are also available in ripened and dried form. Fresh chile peppers range widely in size and flavor, from the 6- to 8-inch mild Anaheim to the 2-inch very hot *chile serrano*. These two varieties are the most widely available. You may also find others, including the large, dark green, richly flavored *chile poblano*, the medium to hot green Fresno and yellow wax varieties, and the long slender red type sold mainly in Philippine and other Asian markets. Several recipes in this book call for whole small dried chiles; the varieties labeled *chile japonés* or *serrano seco* in Latin American markets or simply "whole red pepper" in Asian markets are appropriate. Note that "chile powder" is simply ground dried chiles while "chili powder" is a blend of chile powder and other spices such as garlic and oregano.

Chives: Use chives for a mild onion flavor in cold or hot sauces. Like all onions, they will grow stronger after cutting; avoid keeping chive sauces overnight.

Cilantro

Cilantro: Cilantro or coriander (also known as Chinese parsley) is a pungent herb grown in most of the tropical and semi-tropical regions of the world. The root is stronger than the leaves and should not be used unless the recipe specifically calls for it.

Coconut milk: An extract made from the flesh of the coconut (not the juice inside the shell), coconut milk is available canned or you can make your own. It is easiest to prepare with dry shredded coconut although grated fresh coconut makes a slightly richer milk. Combine equal parts coconut and boiling water in a blender or food processor (be careful when starting the machine so as not to scald yourself). Blend for 1 minute. Strain through a fine sieve or cheesecloth. The yield is about three-quarters of the amount of water added. You can use the same coconut twice; the second batch is often referred to as thin coconut milk.

Cooking oils: Unless a specific oil such as olive or sesame is called for, "oil" in these recipes means a vegetable oil of relatively neutral flavor. We prefer peanut, but safflower and sunflower are perfectly acceptable. Frying oil may be filtered and reserved for additional frying until it darkens noticeably or develops a cooked aroma.

Crème Fraîche: The French term for a type of thick, ripened cream with excellent cooking qualities. Its flavor is less sour than commercial sour cream with a slight nuttiness, and it is unmatched for cream-reduction sauces.

Yield: 1 cup
½ pint whipping cream
2 tablespoons cultured buttermilk

Combine the cream and buttermilk in a non-aluminum saucepan, heat to 85–90° (higher heat will inhibit the culture) and transfer to a warmed glass, earthenware or stainless bowl. Cover, place in a warm spot and allow to ripen at least 6 hours or overnight. The cream should have a texture between that of fresh cream and yogurt.

Dill: Use dill in simple hot or cold butters, as its flavor will be lost in more complicated sauces. Especially well-suited to trout and salmon.

Fennel: Fennel is a name loosely given to several related plants. Commercial bulb fennel, which is used as a vegetable, is also frequently labeled "sweet anise." Its foliage, as well as that of the wild variety, can be used as an herb in butters and marinades. The wild variety, common in coastal California, has fibrous, inedible stems which are an excellent addition to a charcoal fire, adding their fragrant smoke to that of the charcoal. Both types provide edible seeds in the fall.

Fish Sauce: Fish sauce is a clear, dark extract made from fermented salted anchovies. It is used as we would use salt in much of Southeast Asia, including Thailand, Laos, Vietnam, Cambodia and the Philippines. Fish sauce is sold at most Asian groceries and in some supermarkets. Anchovy paste is not a good substitute.

Five Spice Powder: Five spice powder is a fragrant Chinese mixture composed of black pepper, fennel seed, cinnamon, cloves and star anise. It is sold bottled or packaged in Asian groceries and in many supermarkets.

Garam Masala: *Garam masala* is an Indian spice mixture used much the same way we employ salt and pepper. It is added just before the food is served or during the last couple of minutes of cooking. Recipes for *garam masala* vary, but they usually contain cardamom, cloves, cinnamon, coriander, cumin and black pepper. *Garam masala* is sold in Indian groceries, or you can make your own using freshly ground spices in these proportions (by volume): 1 part each cumin, coriander and cinnamon; 2 parts black peppercorns; ½ part cloves; 1½ parts cardamom.

Herbs: A wide range of herbs are useful in seafood cookery. The milder herbs, such as parsley, chervil and chives, are the most useful and versatile; at least one of these appears in almost every Western recipe in this book. The milder herbs provide a background of flavor without upstaging the other ingredients. Others with more pronounced flavors are more limited in use, and are often sufficient in themselves to give a whole new dimension to a dish. Use fresh herbs whenever possible. Many are easily grown outdoors (all year in mild climates) or indoors on a windowsill. As a general rule, use a quarter to half as much dried herbs as fresh. Even with dried herbs, relative freshness is important, and they lose their potency over time. Herbs in half-empty, year-old jars are unlikely to have much flavor.

Laos Root: Laos root is an important ingredient in the cooking of Southeast Asia, particularly in Thailand and Laos. It has a strong, slightly medicinal taste. Ginger is *not* a particularly good substitute. Laos root is sold dried and in powder form (often under the name of *galangal*) in Asian groceries. To use dried Laos root, soak it in water for at least 3 hours. The powdered root has less flavor and is a second choice.

Lemongrass

Lemongrass: Lemongrass is a pungent herb of the tropics whose taste is somewhat like lemon blossoms. It is a major flavoring in much of Southeast Asia. Lemongrass is available fresh in a growing number of produce markets and in some Asian groceries. Dried lemongrass is available in health food stores and some supermarkets. The fresh is much preferable. Dried lemongrass should be soaked in water for at least 30 minutes. Lemon peel and fresh ginger together form a passable substitute.

Marjoram, Oregano: Closely related and similar in use, oregano and marjoram are primarily for dishes involving tomato, olive oil and garlic. Both are a good addition to olive oil marinades for grilled fish, and the stems and additional sprigs can be thrown on the fire for fragrant smoke.

Mirin: A sweet rice wine produced in Japan and recently in the United States, it contains 10–12% alcohol. In recipes calling for dry sherry or dry rice wine *and* sugar, you can substitute *mirin* and eliminate most of the sugar. *Mirin* is sold in Asian groceries and in some liquor stores and supermarkets.

Olive Oil: Olive oil is used in many Mediterranean-based dishes in this book. As its purpose is to add a distinctive flavor to the dish, choose an oil with some flavor, something which is lacking in many widely available, overly refined oils. Extremely fine oils labeled Virgin or Extra Virgin are now available in many markets at prices ranging from expensive to astronomical; however, a small amount of one of these mixed with a commercial brand produces a very nicely flavored oil. With some experimenting, you should be able to arrive at a delicious and reasonably priced "house blend."

Parsley: Use flat-leaved Italian parsley if a stonger flavor is desired.

Rice Wine Vinegar: Rice wine vinegar is a mild white vinegar distilled from rice wine. It is often used in Japanese cooking and can usually be substituted for distilled white vinegar in other recipes. It is sold in Asian groceries and in many supermarkets.

Rosemary: Rosemary will dominate most dishes; use with care, alone or with other assertive flavors. This herb is best for rich, flavorful fish such as mackerel, and unsurpassed as an addition to a charcoal fire.

Saké: Saké is a Japanese rice wine which contains about 16% alcohol. It is slightly sweeter than a dry European or American white wine. It can be substituted for Chinese rice wine (*Shao Hsing*) without altering the recipe. Saké is sold at Asian groceries, supermarkets and many liquor stores.

Salted Black Beans: Salted black beans are fermented and dried in Canton, the only part of China where they are used. They are the key ingredient in black bean sauce. Salted black beans are sold packaged in plastic bags in Asian groceries and in some supermarkets.

Sesame Seeds: Both white and black sesame seeds are available in this country. White sesame seeds are used as a coating for Chinese fish dishes. Sesame seeds are sold in bulk in health food stores and packaged in Asian groceries and in some supermarkets.

Sesame Oil: Sesame oil is a very powerful flavoring agent made from toasted sesame seeds and not to be confused with the cold-pressed sesame oil available in health food stores. It is not a cooking oil, but is added in small quantities just before serving, releasing its perfume as it warms with the food.

Shao Hsing Wine: *Shao Hsing* wine is a rice wine nearly as dry as western white wines. It can be used in place of saké. It is sold in Asian groceries and in some liquor stores.

Shrimp Paste: Shrimp paste is a strong, salty extract made from dried shrimp. Each country has its own version, varying greatly in saltiness and strength. In Chinese recipes try to use Chinese shrimp paste, etc. Shrimp paste is sold in Asian groceries and in some supermarkets.

Sichuan Bean Paste: Sichuan bean paste is a pungent, spicy fermented mixture usually sold under the name "chili paste with garlic" in Asian groceries. It will keep almost indefinitely if stored in the refrigerator. There is no substitute.

Soy Sauce: Soy sauce is produced in three principal grades: (1) light—labeled "light," (2) medium—which has no particular labeling and includes most soy sauce sold in this country, and (3) dark—often labeled "black." These three grades differ mostly in coloring rather than in taste. Unless otherwise noted, use medium soy sauce for the recipes in this book.

Tamarind: Tamarind is produced from the pulp of the pod of a tropical plant. Its tart flavor appears in many Southeast Asian, Indian and Latin American dishes. Tamarind is sold fresh in some specialty shops and produce markets. It is also available as a paste or extract which is added to water. Lemon juice is not a particularly good substitute since the sour taste of tamarind is distinctive. Tamarind extract keeps in the refrigerator for months.

Tarragon: Tarragon is fairly assertive, and not very compatible with other herbs. It is the essential ingredient in Béarnaise Sauce (page 257). If unavailable fresh, use whole leaves bottled in vinegar.

Thai Basil: Thai basil is a highly aromatic herb which can be transplanted if you can find somebody with plants already growing. Its flavor is something of a cross between mint and Italian basil. Use both together as a substitute for Thai basil.

Tomatoes: Tomatoes are a common ingredient in seafood dishes from the Mediterranean and the Americas. While we generally recommend using fresh produce wherever possible, the only tomatoes available for much of the year are watery, mushy and tasteless due to early harvest or mass growing techniques. When properly ripened, flavorful tomatoes are available, by all means use them. However, during the many months when fresh tomatoes are only available by the miracles of modern science, we find good canned tomatoes superior in flavor and more attractive in price. Italian tomato varieties seem to preserve the best. Better still, buy them in quantity during the peak of the season and can them yourself.

To peel and seed tomatoes: Have ready a large bowl of ice water. Cut the cores from the tomatoes and slash the skin in a cross pattern with the tip of a knife. Plunge the tomatoes into rapidly boiling water, remove them as soon as the skin begins to peel back from the cuts, and transfer them to the ice water to cool. The skins should peel away easily, leaving the barely cooked flesh intact. Slice the tomatoes in half crosswise to expose all the seeds. Gently squeeze the seeds and excess juice from the tomato halves, straining and reserving the juice if it is to be used in the recipe.

Tomatillos: *Tomatillos,* despite the name, are not related to the tomato but are a type of berry. They can sometimes be found fresh in Latin American markets, and have a papery husk covering the smooth green skin. They are widely available canned, with the confusing label "Mexican green tomatoes." There is no substitute.

Thyme: Thyme is a most useful herb, and a standard ingredient in a *bouquet garni.* There are many varieties, some with lemon or other flavors. Its agreeable flavor blends well with other herbs.

Wasabi: *Wasabi* is green horseradish powder made in Japan. It is used with soy sauce as a dip for *sushi* and incorporated into other raw fish dishes. It is sold in small tins in Asian groceries and in many supermarkets.

Watercress: Use watercress sparingly in compound butters for its peppery, slightly bitter flavor.

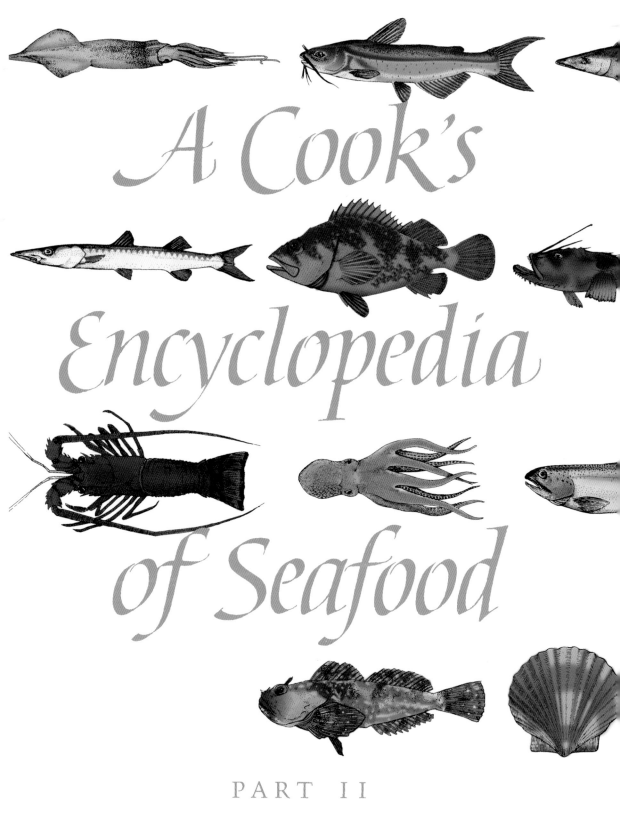

A Cook's Encyclopedia of Seafood

PART II

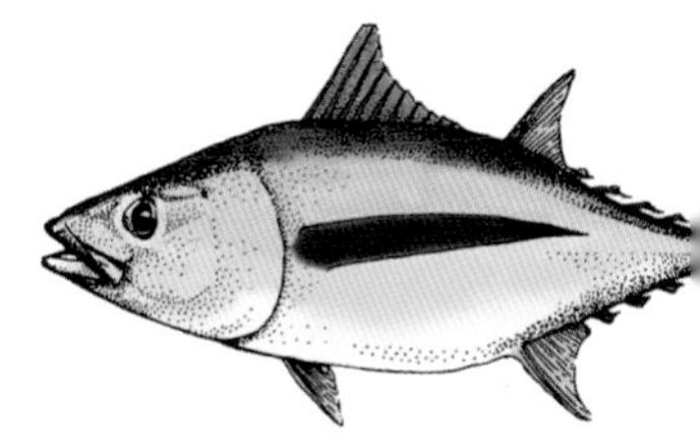

KEY TO ENCYCLOPEDIC ENTRIES

The following encyclopedic entries are concise profiles of fish typically available in the market or commonly caught by sportsmen in California. Exceptions to the listed seasons, sizes and ranges will, of course, occur. We have also listed many species available fresh in California from other regions of the country. (Where categories are not relevant to a particular species, they are left out.).

Name: *Common and Latin names follow Miller and Lea (1972).* *(See Bibliography, page 283)*

Other Names: *These are primarily other names by which the fish may be marketed; some are common fishermen's names.*

Description: *Primarily color. A description such as "blue-green fading to silver" refers to the typical pattern of shading, dorsal to ventral sides.*

Size: *Overall size range as well as normal market size are given.*

Range: *Listed south to north. Some species may occur outside the ranges given, but these represent the areas where they are typically caught.*

Season: *Again, these are typical seasons. Availability of many species depends upon water temperature and food supply, which can vary considerably from one year to the next. Commercial seasons may also be regulated by government agencies, opening and closing on short notice due to population monitoring, parasite incidence or other considerations.*

Fat Content: *Lean fish are those which carry little or no fat in the muscle tissues, storing it instead in the liver or other organs. Others contain more or less fat in the meat, ranging from about 6% in herring to over 20% in eel.*

Yield: *Unless otherwise noted, yield figures are given as a percentage of the weight of a round fish, based upon the forms recommended for cooking—steaks and filets of salmon, pan-dressed rex sole, edible portion of squid, etc.*

Available Forms: *Forms are described on page 13. When a species is available in several forms, we have listed the more common or preferred form first.*

Similar Species: *These are either related to the listed species or otherwise similar; they may or may not be suitable alternatives, as noted in each entry.*

Alternatives: *Where other species are similar enough in cooking characteristics that they may be used in all recipes for the main species, they are listed in the encyclopedic entry. See the individual recipes for other specific alternatives.*

(A), (G) and (P) are used as a quick reference guide to the geographic range of suggested alternatives—Atlantic, Gulf of Mexico and Pacific. Species exclusive to the Pacific have no special designation.

How to Locate Recipes

There are two places in this book to find recipes for a given species: first, following the species' entry in the Encyclopedia; second, in the Index where additional recipes for which a species is an *alternative* are cited under the common name.

Notes on Recipes

Please don't overcook fish! Personal tastes vary, but for our purposes fish is done when the center of the thickest part of the fish is just about to lose its translucency. Remember that a piece of fish will continue cooking for a few minutes after removal from the heat.

Cooking times are approximate. There are so many variables—size of fish, oven and grill temperatures, heat conductivity of pans and so on—that these times should be taken as general guidelines. Familiarity with your own cooking equipment is essential for the best results.

Several recipes mention the "skewer test." A thin metal or bamboo skewer is a perfect instrument for gently probing the flesh of a cooking piece of fish. Try it on a piece of raw fish, then again during the cooking process, and finally with a cooked piece to get the feel of the various stages. This technique can also be used as a test for fish baking in foil or in other situations where testing with the eye or fingertip is impractical.

Most of these recipes do not specify quantities of salt, suggesting instead "salt to taste." Increasing awareness of the health risks of too much sodium has caused us to adjust our thinking on proper levels of salt. Our own tastes have been shifting somewhat in recent years to less reliance on salt for flavoring the foods we eat. Bear in mind also that many of the ingredients used throughout this book (anchovies, olives, capers, soy sauce, fish sauce and so on) contain substantial salt and are sufficient to flavor the dishes in which they appear.

Most of the recipes allow 4–6 ounces of fish per serving as main courses. They may, of course, be adjusted up or down according to personal preferences. Many of the Asian recipes also give a yield in terms of side-dish servings, where the dish is one of several courses in a meal.

All of the recipes have been written for 4 servings unless this number is inappropriate. Large-scale productions such as Crab Gumbo (page 113) are most likely to be served at a large gathering rather than at a small family dinner. The variety of fish required for our Bouillabaisse (page 179) makes it difficult to prepare on a small scale. On the other hand, where the recipe is difficult to increase beyond 2 servings, such as Warm Cabbage Salad with Angler (page 60), the recipe is given for the smaller number.

Alternative species have been suggested whenever appropriate. They have been chosen for their basic similarity in flavor, texture or cooking characteristics. However, we are not suggesting that you will get identical results, only that you need not rule out a recipe just because a particular fish is unavailable.

We have included recommendations for side dishes, garnishes or vegetable accompaniments in some cases but we have not tried to present whole menus, which we leave to the reader. Similarly, we have not given specific suggestions for wines or other beverages other than the general guidelines in the section Wine and Seafood (pages 276–77).

CALIFORNIA SEAFOOD A–Z

ABALONE

(Haliotis spp.*)*

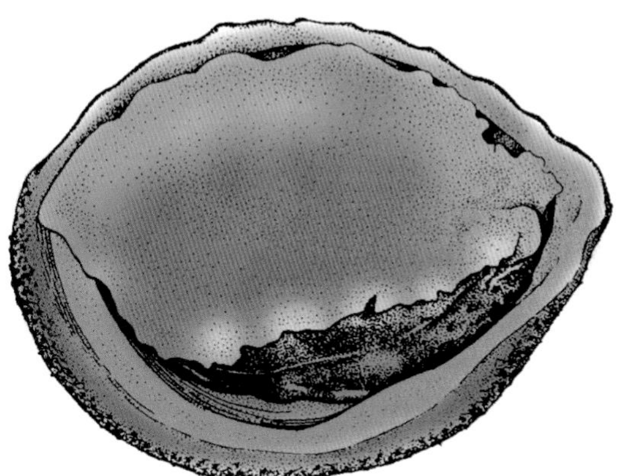

Description: *Univalve. Outside of shell usually encrusted with barnacles, inside of shell iridescent shades of pink, blue and green.*

Size: *5¾–8 inches legal minimum, depending on species.*

Range: *Highest concentrations of edible species found along the coasts of Japan, Australia and California.*

Season: *Highly regulated. Sporadically available May–March.*

Fat Content: *Low.*

Yield: *If overall live weight is over 1 pound, yield is 50% meat with an additional 25% usable trim.*

Available Forms: *Live, tenderized steaks.*

Black, red and green abalone are the most commonly available live varieties. Abalone is rapidly disappearing due to overfishing and natural predation. However, it is being aquacultured and may make something of a comeback. California abalone cannot be shipped out of the state in any form; abalone available elsewhere comes from Mexico and Japan.

Abalone is very tough and must be pounded before cooking. Pounded steaks are usually floured or dipped in egg and sautéed over very high heat for 20–30 seconds per side. Longer cooking will toughen the meat. Like whelk, abalone makes excellent Ceviche (page 70).

To Clean Abalone

Pry the meat out of the shell, severing the connector muscle as if shucking a clam (page 89). (A large spoon works well.) After prying the meat out, scrub the outer edges to remove the black coating. (If you prefer, you may cut the edges off although you will lose a good deal of meat.) Cut thin steaks by slicing across the muscle, or strips by slicing with the grain. Pound the pieces with a mallet or the side of a cleaver until tender but not shredded.

Abalone in Oyster Sauce

This Thai-style sauté features two spring treats—abalone and asparagus. Both cook at about the same rate which makes the dish easy to prepare.

Alternatives: *Whelk (A,P), geoduck*

Serves 4–6 as a side dish

2 tablespoons oil

1–2 tablespoons chopped garlic

2 teaspoons chopped ginger

2 tablespoons Chinese oyster sauce

2 teaspoons fish sauce (page 40)

2 tablespoons water

½ pound abalone meat, pounded and cut into narrow strips 1½ inches long

1 pound asparagus, cut into 2-inch lengths

¼ cup loosely packed cilantro

1 teaspoon cornstarch dissolved in 1 tablespoon water

Sauté the garlic and ginger in oil in a wok or heavy skillet until nearly cooked. Add the oyster sauce, fish sauce and water. Bring to a boil. Add the abalone and asparagus. Cook over high heat for about 3 minutes or until the asparagus is tender. One minute before the dish is done, add the cilantro and stir the ingredients thoroughly. Pour in the cornstarch mixture. When the sauce thickens, remove the skillet from the heat. Serve over rice.

ANCHOVY

(Engraulis mordax)

Description: *Blue-green fading to silver.*	**Fat Content:** *High.*
Size: *4-5 inches.*	**Yield:** *50% filet.*
Range: *Pacific coast.*	**Available Forms:** *Round.*
Season: *Fall-Winter.*	

The Pacific anchovy catch is now only a fraction of its peak of earlier years due to a combination of overfishing and environmental influences. Most of today's catch is preserved for commercial use as a favorite bait for salmon fishing.

Fresh anchovies are, however, occasionally available. Their soft flesh has a moderate-to-pronounced flavor similar to herring and sardines, to which they are related. The extreme saltiness associated with preserved anchovies is part of the canning process, not an inherent characteristic of the fish.

Pan-dressed anchovies may be grilled or floured and fried. (To pan-dress anchovies or similar small fish, simply grasp the head and twist, drawing the entrails away with the head.) Larger anchovies are suitable for most herring recipes (pages 132–35).

ANGLER

(Lophius americanus)

Other Names: *Goosefish, monkfish, lotte.*

Description: *Loose, scaleless skin. Variegated brown to black fading to light grey.*

Size: *2–50 pounds (larger fish more desirable).*

Range: *New England coast. Also Mediterranean and eastern Atlantic.*

Season: *Year-round, especially fall-winter.*

Fat Content: *Low.*

Yield: *50–60% filet from tail.*

Available Forms: *Whole or boneless tail.*

This exceedingly ugly but delicious fish is well-known around the Mediterranean and along our Atlantic coast, and is becoming more popular and available fresh in the west. Its name comes from its unique method of attracting prey by "angling" with a small appendage on top of its head as "bait." Only the tail is generally marketed, the huge head being discarded at sea.

Angler flesh is dense and firm with a mild, sweet flavor which has been compared to lobster. (In fact, shellfish make up an important part of its diet.) Angler is suitable for almost any cooking method, and is nearly indispensible in *bouillabaisse.* Its large single bone makes a particularly rich and gelatinous stock.

To Filet an Angler

1 Remove the loose outer skin from the tail. Trim the dorsal fin if desired. (Note: For grilled butterfly filets, also remove all of the thin membrane under the skin, or it will shrink in cooking and distort the filet.)

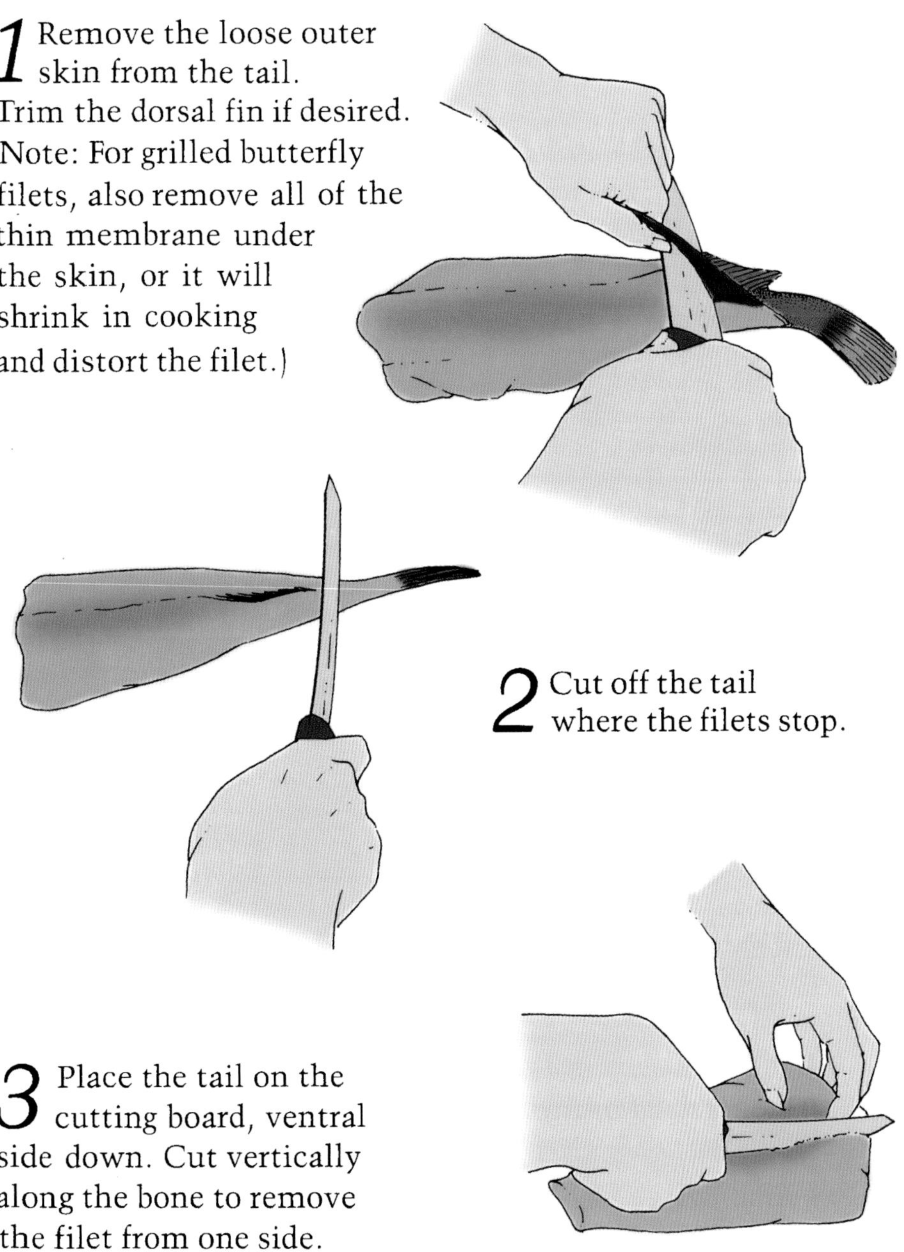

2 Cut off the tail where the filets stop.

3 Place the tail on the cutting board, ventral side down. Cut vertically along the bone to remove the filet from one side.

4 Repeat on the other side of the bone. Reserve all the bones, skin and trimmings for the stock pot.

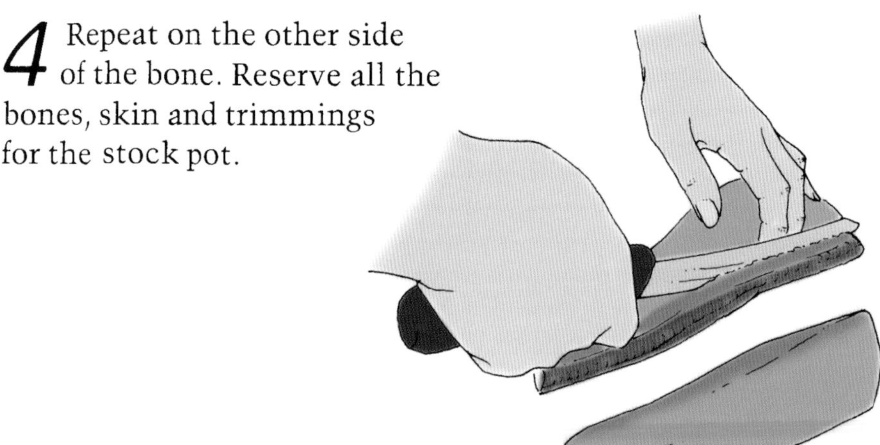

To Butterfly Angler Filets

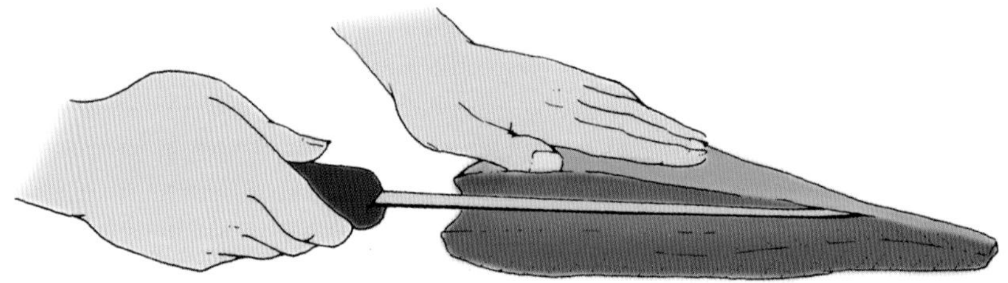

1 Place a filet on the board, ventral side down and bone side vertical. Holding the knife horizontally about ⅜ inch above the board, cut from the outside toward the bone side, to within ¼ inch of cutting through the filet.

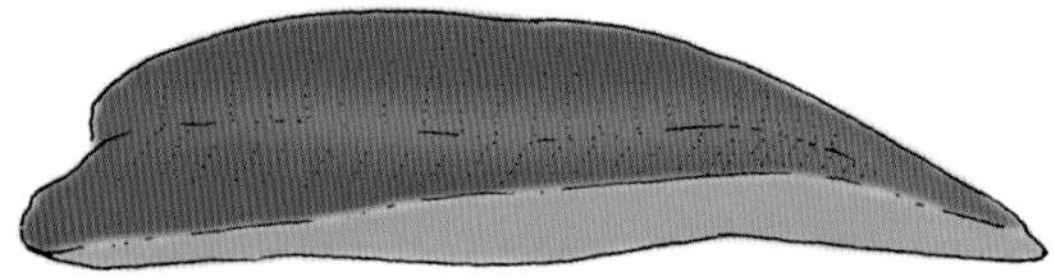

2 Unfold the upper part of the filet until the bone side is flat against the board. If this part of the filet is still quite thick, make a second cut in the same plane, again to within ¼ inch of the outer surface, and unfold the remaining part. Continue the process until the entire filet is reduced to the thickness of the original ¾-inch cut.

Grilled Angler Filet

Because of its dense flesh, angler must be cut into thin pieces to grill easily. The best technique is the continuous butterfly cut described on the previous page. An alternative method is to slice the filet crosswise into ⅜–½-inch pieces and grill them on skewers.

Serves 4

4 6-ounce filets
Olive oil
Fresh herbs
Salt and pepper to taste

Marinate the cut filets in olive oil and fresh herbs. Grill until done by the skewer test. Serve with Beurre Blanc (page 253) or another delicately flavored sauce.

Baked Angler with Sicilian-Style Stuffing

Serves 4

A 1½-pound piece of angler

Stuffing

¼ cup bread crumbs
¼ cup raisins
2 tablespoons chopped parsley
2 tablespoons chopped capers
2 tablespoons pine nuts
3 cloves chopped garlic
1 tablespoon olive oil
1 tablespoon lemon juice
Tomato slices for garnish

Preheat the oven to 350°.

Cut the angler butterfly style.

Combine the stuffing ingredients. Spread the stuffing across the fish. Roll the fish around the stuffing, wrap tightly in foil and bake for 25 minutes or until the fish is cooked.

To serve, slice across the roll. Garnish with tomato pieces.

Angler Baked in Filo

Carol Brendlinger

This wonderful combination of crisp filo, firm fish, mushroom filling and an aromatic tomato sauce was contributed by Carol Brendlinger of Oakland's famed Bay Wolf restaurant.

Alternatives: *Grouper (A,G,P), fancy rockfish* *Serves 4*

Duxelles

4 tablespoons butter

½ pound mushrooms, chopped

½ cup chopped shallots

¼ cup cream

½ cup parsley

Salt and pepper to taste

Melt the butter in a skillet. Add the other ingredients and cook over low heat for about 15 minutes.

Tomato Sauce

2 tablespoons olive oil

½ cup chopped shallots

1 teaspoon each fresh thyme, oregano and tarragon or *¼ teaspoon each of dried*

1 cup dry white wine

5 large tomatoes, peeled, seeded and chopped

Heat the oil in a heavy saucepan. Add the shallots and herbs. Sauté briefly, add the wine and simmer until the wine is completely evaporated. Add the tomatoes. Simmer for 3 minutes. Set aside until just before the fish is cooked.

Angler in Filo

1 pound angler, cut into 12 ¾-inch slices

2 tablespoons olive oil

¼ pound butter, melted

8 sheets filo pastry (widely available fresh and frozen)

Preheat the oven to 450°.

Sauté the fish in olive oil until it is about two-thirds cooked.

Lay down one sheet of filo. Brush the entire surface lightly with melted butter. Cover it with a second sheet of filo and repeat the brushing. Overlap three pieces of fish at the center of the end of the pastry nearest you. Top with about 2 tablespoons of the *duxelles* mixture. Fold over the two sides of the filo to the center. Brush the folded edges with a little butter to make them stick. Roll up the package and seal it with a little more melted butter. Repeat this procedure for the other three packages. Bake for 10 minutes, or until the pastry is golden brown.

Just before the fish is cooked, reheat the tomato sauce to the simmering point. Spoon it onto a warm serving platter or individual plates. Arrange the pastries on top of the sauce and serve.

Angler Salad

Alternatives: *Lingcod, skate* *Serves 4 as a first course*

1–1½ tablespoons vinegar

Salt and pepper to taste

⅓–½ cup olive oil

1 pound angler filet, poached and chilled

1 medium red or green bell pepper, seeded and julienned

3–4 scallions, sliced

2 tablespoons or more capers

Leaf lettuce

In a salad bowl, combine the vinegar, salt and pepper. Add the oil, combine thoroughly and correct seasoning. Slice the fish into thin slices or large julienne. Toss the fish in the dressing with the peppers, scallions and capers. Serve on large lettuce leaves.

Warm Cabbage Salad with Angler

Serves 4 as a first course *Serves 2 as a main course*

4–6 ounces angler filet

1 tablespoon vinegar (sherry, red wine or rice wine)

Large pinch salt

A generous grating of black pepper

4 cups finely shredded red cabbage

1 teaspoon chopped garlic

6 tablespoons olive oil

Have all the ingredients at room temperature.

Cut the angler into crosswise slices or strips about ½ inch thick.

Warm a stainless or other heatproof bowl. Combine the vinegar, salt and pepper in the bowl. Toss the cabbage in this mixture. Correct the seasoning and keep warm.

Sauté the fish pieces and garlic in oil until just done. Pour the hot oil and fish over the cabbage, toss thoroughly and serve on warmed plates.

Angler Stuffing for Pasta

Use this forcemeat to fill ravioli, tortellini and other similar pasta.

Alternatives: *Lingcod, cabezon* *Yield: Enough for 30–36 ravioli*

1 pound angler filet
Olive oil
1 yellow onion, chopped
1 tablespoon chopped garlic
1 tablespoon chopped parsley
2 tablespoons bread crumbs
½ teaspoon dried thyme or *1½ teaspoons fresh*
Salt and pepper to taste

Chop the fish finely with a knife or in a meat grinder or food processor. If using a food processor, be careful not to reduce it to a paste. The chopped fish should be the texture of finely ground beef.

Sauté the onion and garlic in olive oil until soft. Add the remaining ingredients and cook just until the fish loses its raw color. If the fish gives off a large amount of liquid, strain it back into the pan to reduce, adding another teaspoon or so of bread crumbs to absorb the liquid. Add to the stuffing.

Season the mixture to taste, and allow it to cool before filling the pasta.

PACIFIC BARRACUDA

(Sphyraena argentaea)

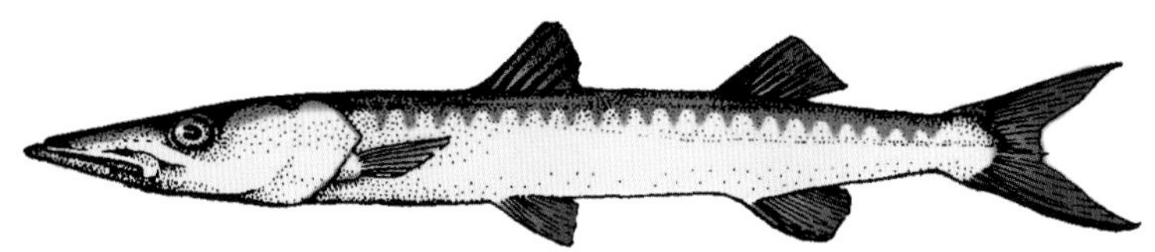

Other Names: *California Barracuda.*

Description: *Dark brown fading to blue then silver.*

Size: *4–8 pounds.*

Range: *Primarily southern California coast.*

Season: *Spring–fall.*

Fat Content: *Moderate.*

Yield: *33% filet.*

Available Forms: *Pan-dressed, filet.*

While the great barracuda *(S. barracuda)* may have toxic flesh, the Pacific variety is perfectly edible and is sporadically available in West Coast markets. Like mahi-mahi, wahoo and other similarly flavored and textured fish, it takes well to grilling and broiling. Serve with a full-flavored sauce such as Wasabi Butter (page 255) or Fresh Tomato Salsa (page 262).

BLACKFISH

(Orodan macrolepododus)

Other Names: *Black trout, Sacramento blackfish, hardhead, Chinese "steelhead."*

Description: *Black or dark grey fading to silver. Small scales.*

Size: *2-4 pounds.*

Range: *Large lakes and slow-moving brackish waters of the Sacramento and San Joaquin rivers. Has been introduced into southern California where it is aquacultured.*

Season: *All year.*

Fat Content: *Low.*

Yield: *40% filet.*

Available Forms: *Live, round, dressed, pan-dressed.*

Blackfish is the live fish most commonly available in California. It is transported in tank trucks to Chinese markets where it swims in oxygenated water with catfish and carp. Blackfish has a delicate, mild flavor. It is rarely eaten by Caucasians because the Chinese almost never suggest it to their non-Asian customers for fear they will have trouble with the small, fine bones. Care is necessary, but the blackfish is worth it. It is almost always steamed whole.

Steamed Blackfish with Ham

Pork is frequently used as a flavoring in Chinese seafood recipes, especially for freshwater fish. Use a fine-flavored ham such as Smithfield, Westphalian or *prosciutto* for the best results.

Alternatives: *Catfish* *Serves 4 as a main course*

A 2-pound blackfish, dressed
8 thin slices ginger
8 thin slices ham, 2 inches long by ¾ inch wide
¼ cup loosely packed cilantro
2 tablespoons dry sherry or *rice wine*
2 tablespoons soy sauce
½ teaspoon white pepper
½ teaspoon cornstarch dissolved in 1 tablespoon water
2 teaspoons sesame oil

Preheat the steamer, which may be a wok with a steaming rack, a stockpot with a perforated insert and a cover, or any other covered vessel which will hold the fish on a plate over the steaming liquid. Be sure to start with plenty of water in the steamer to ensure that it will not boil dry while the fish is cooking.

Extend the belly cavity of the fish by cutting about a third of the way from the vent to the tail, so that the fish will lie flat on the plate. Make four cuts perpendicular to the backbone on either side of the fish. Insert a piece of ginger and a piece of ham into each cut. Place the fish, belly side down, on a plate and surround it with the cilantro. Combine the wine, soy sauce and pepper, pour over the fish and steam until the thickest part of the flesh is done by the skewer test.

Remove the fish to a heated serving platter, draining the sauce into a saucepan. Bring the sauce to a boil and add the cornstarch mixture. As soon as it thickens, pour over the fish, sprinkle with sesame oil and serve.

BONITO

(Sarda chiliensis)

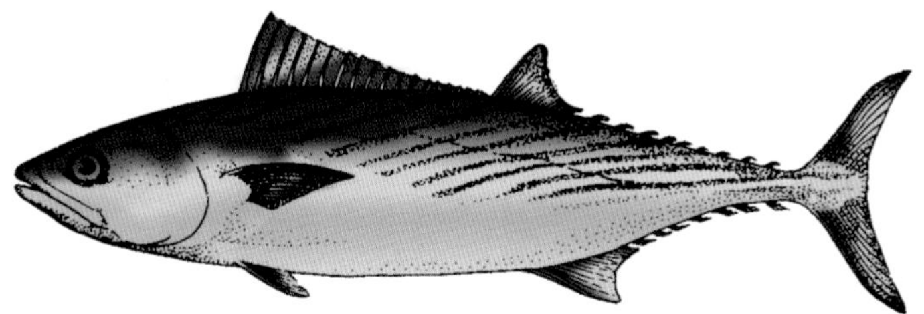

Other Names: *Bonita.*

Description: *Steel blue fading to grey. Black oblique stripes.*

Size: *5 pounds and up.*

Range: *Baja to southern California.*

Season: *Late fall–early summer.*

Fat Content: *Moderate.*

Yield: *50% filet.*

Available Forms: *Round, filet.*

One of the most reasonably priced members of the tuna family, bonito is widely available in season. It has a moderate to pronounced flavor and is very easily fileted. The Japanese use dried bonito (in the form of *dashi*) as a basis for soups and sauces. Smaller fish can be used whole in recipes for mackerel, and larger filets or steaks are suitable for any tuna recipe. Bonito makes delicious Ceviche (page 70).

Alternatives: Other tunas, larger mackerel (A,P), yellowtail, other jacks.

Bonito Sauce for Pasta

This is a simple, delicious pasta sauce which illustrates the tuna family's affinity for the tomato.

Serves 2

1 tablespoon olive oil

1½ pounds fresh tomatoes, peeled, seeded and chopped or *2 cups canned tomatoes, chopped*

1 shallot, finely chopped or *½ medium yellow onion, finely chopped*

1 tablespoon chopped parsley

1 teaspoon fresh thyme or *¼ teaspoon dried thyme*

1–2 tablespoons chopped garlic

½ pound bonito, cut into ¾-inch slices or cubes

¼ cup dry white wine

¼ cup concentrated chicken stock (reduce a regular stock by half)

½ pound fresh or dried pasta, such as linguine, tagliarini or *spaghetti*

A generous grating of black pepper

Salt to taste

In a pot large enough to hold the sauce and the pasta (a wok is ideal), cook the tomatoes, shallot, parsley, thyme and garlic in olive oil until the tomatoes soften. Add the bonito, white wine and chicken stock. Simmer until fish is cooked through. (For fresh pasta, the sauce should be quite liquid. For dried pasta, reduce the sauce further; the dried pasta will not absorb as much liquid.) Correct the seasoning.

Cook the pasta in boiling salted water, drain and toss it in the pot with the sauce.

Serve in heated bowls, with ground black pepper to taste.

Bonito Baked Provençal Style

The combination of flavors is similar to the previous recipe, but here the fish appears as the main ingredient.

Serves 4

2 tablespoons olive oil

1–1½ pounds bonito filets, skin on

4 tomatoes, peeled, seeded and roughly chopped or *1 cup canned tomatoes, chopped*

2 teaspoons fresh thyme or *½ teaspoon dried thyme*

2–3 canned anchovy filets, rinsed and roughly chopped

12 whole Niçoise or other black olives, pitted and chopped

½ cup dry white wine

Preheat oven to 425°.

Oil a baking dish, preferably one which can be brought to the table. Place the filets in the dish, skin side down. Scatter the rest of the ingredients over the filets. Cover with a lid or seal with aluminum foil. Bake for 15–20 minutes. If there is any excess liquid in the pan, ladle it into a saucepan, reduce and pour over the fish before serving.

Serve the fish from the baking dish, or carefully transfer the filets to a heated serving plate with the tomato sauce on top.

Grilled Bonito with Chinese Soy Marinade

Serves 4

¼ cup soy sauce

2 tablespoons white vinegar

2 tablespoons dry sherry

1 inch ginger, sliced thin

2 teaspoons finely chopped garlic

1 teaspoon cornstarch dissolved in 1 tablespoon water

4 6–8-ounce bonito filets, skin on, from two 1½-pound fish

Cilantro or toasted sesame seeds for garnish

Combine the soy sauce, vinegar, sherry, ginger and garlic. Marinate the filets in the soy mixture for at least 30 minutes in the refrigerator.

Strain the marinade into a small saucepan. Bring to a boil, add the cornstarch mixture and remove from heat as soon as the sauce thickens. Grill the filets skin side up for 2 minutes per side or until just done, basting generously with the sauce.

Serve the bonito accompanied by any remaining sauce, garnished with sprigs of cilantro or toasted sesame seeds.

Stir-Fried Bonito Indonesian Style

Serves 4 as a main dish

1 pound bonito filets, skinned and cut in 1-inch slices

Cornstarch

¼ cup oil

1 medium yellow onion, finely chopped

1 inch ginger, chopped

1-2 tablespoons chopped garlic

2-3 fresh serrano, jalapeño *or other small hot chiles, seeded and finely chopped*

1 tablespoon tamarind paste (page 43) dissolved in 3 tablespoons water

2 tablespoons white vinegar

2 tablespoons water or chicken stock

2 teaspoons soy sauce

2 teaspoons sugar

Cilantro for garnish

Dust the bonito lightly with cornstarch.

Fry the fish in hot oil. When brown, remove the pieces from the pan. Pour off all but 2 tablespoons of the oil. Add the onions, ginger, garlic and chiles. Sauté until the onions are transparent. Add the tamarind mixture, vinegar, water or stock, soy sauce and sugar. Cook for 1 minute, stirring frequently. Return the bonito to the pan for a few seconds until reheated.

Garnish with cilantro and serve with rice.

Ceviche

Many people think of this Latin American standard as raw fish. "Cold-cooked" would be a better description. The lime juice "cooks" the seafood, transforming the protein in the same way that heating it does. This preparation can be used for almost any saltwater shellfish or fish (an exception is salmon—see An Ounce of Prevention, page 281).

Alternatives: *Rockfish, halibut, scallops, oysters, whelk, abalone*

Serves 4 as an appetizer

½ pound of bonito filets, cut into 1-inch cubes

Lime juice to cover the fish, approximately ¼ cup

1 or 2 fresh serrano, *Fresno or other hot chiles, seeded and chopped*

2 tablespoons chopped cilantro

1 tomato, peeled, seeded and chopped

Salt to taste

Thin slices of red onion or scallion for garnish

In a small stainless or glass bowl, combine the fish, chiles and cilantro. Cover with lime juice, tossing the fish to moisten pieces evenly. Cover and refrigerate at least 1 hour. Fifteen minutes before serving, add tomato and salt to taste. Garnish with onion or scallion slices.

Ceviche can be served in glasses, on a bed of greens or in avocado halves.

BUFFALOFISH

(Ictiobus cyprinellus)

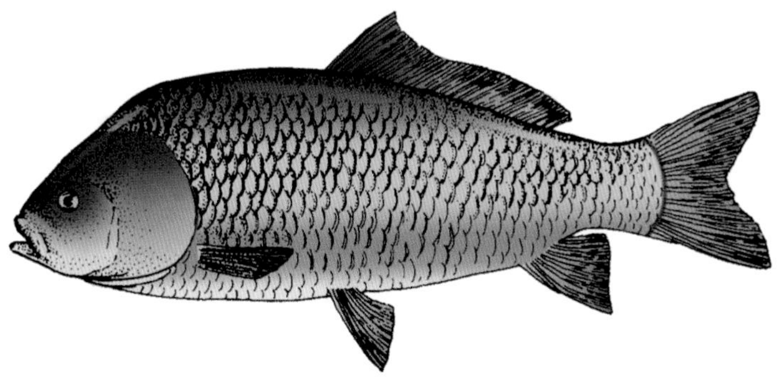

Other Names: *Lake buffalo, blue buffalo, bigmouth buffalo.*

Description: *Dark brown or blue fading to pale olive.*

Size: *3–12 pounds.*

Range: *Rivers and lakes of north-central and south-central United States.*

Season: *All year.*

Fat Content: *Moderate.*

Yield: *25% filet.*

Available Forms: *Live, round, pan-dressed, halved, filet.*

A favorite in the South, buffalofish is sold in markets which cater to lovers of freshwater fish. It is frequently available live, especially in Chinese fish markets. The meat has a firm texture and a mild, sweet flavor.

Baked Buffalofish with Creole Sauce

Creole sauce has come to mean just about anything with tomatoes and cayenne. Without making any claims to authenticity, we think this is a very good version.

Alternatives: *Grouper (A,G,P), snapper (A,G), lingcod, rockfish* *Serves 4*

1 tablespoon olive oil

1 tablespoon butter

1 small yellow onion, julienned

2 small bell peppers, roasted, peeled and julienned

3 scallions, chopped

4-6 cloves garlic, chopped

2 medium tomatoes, peeled, seeded and chopped, juice reserved or *1 small can peeled tomatoes with juice*

1 bay leaf

1 teaspoon capers

¼ cup green sliced green olives

½ teaspoon paprika

Cayenne to taste

Zest of 1 lemon

¼ cup dry white wine

1–1½ pounds buffalofish filet

Sauté the vegetables in oil and butter until soft but not browned. Add all but the fish and simmer for at least 30 minutes; the flavor will improve with up to 3 hours of slow cooking. Correct the seasoning.

Preheat oven to 400°.

Place the fish in a deep baking dish or ovenproof casserole and cover with the sauce. Bake with lid on for 12–15 minutes.

Serve over rice with Tabasco or another hot sauce on the side.

PACIFIC BUTTERFISH

(Peprilus simillimus)

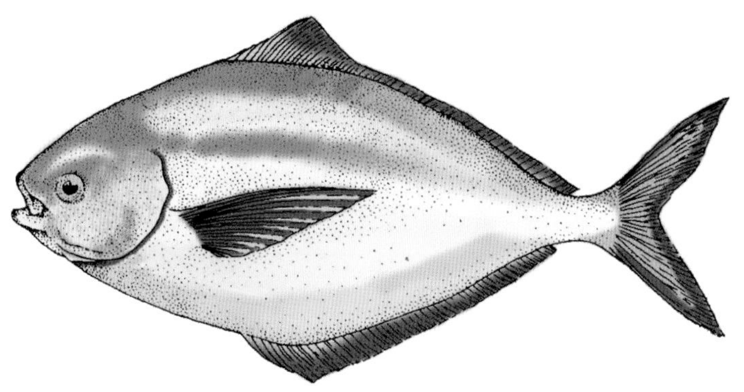

Other Names: *California pompano.*

Description: *Metallic silver, greenish above. No scales.*

Size: *Under 1 pound.*

Range: *Pacific coast, primarily southern California.*

Season: *Spring and summer.*

Fat Content: *Moderate.*

Yield: *60–70% pan-dressed.*

Available Forms: *Round.*

There is no unambiguous name for this fish. It is not related to the Florida pompano or to the Pacific sablefish (a fish generally marketed as butterfish in West Coast markets). Whatever you choose to call it, this fish has moderately flavored, soft flesh that is best suited to dry-heat cooking in a batter. Its tender skin will not survive either grilling or sautéing without a coating.

Pan-Fried Butterfish

Serves 2–3

1 pound butterfish
1 cup all-purpose flour
1 egg
1 cup fine cornmeal
4 tablespoons oil
Salt and pepper to taste

Pan-dress the fish. Rinse thoroughly and pat dry.

Dip the fish first in flour, then in egg and finally in cornmeal. Shake off any excess meal. Fry in the oil until golden brown. Turn and brown the other side.

Serve with lemon wedges and Tartar Sauce (page 259).

CABEZON

(Scorpaenichthys marmoratus)

Description: *Variable. Mottled green to red.*

Size: *3–10 pounds.*

Range: *Baja to Alaska.*

Season: *All year.*

Fat Content: *Low.*

Yield: *20% filet.*

Available Forms: *Round, filet.*

A commercial fish of minor importance, cabezon is the largest member of the sculpin family. It is frequently caught by sport fishermen.

The flesh of cabezon is fairly firm and mild in flavor, and can to be used in much the same way as angler. The roe of cabezon is poisonous.

Thai Fish Cakes

Somchai Aksomboon

Somchai Aksomboon, owner and chef of Berkeley's wonderful Siam Cuisine restaurant, provided this recipe. It is one of the most popular appetizers in many American Thai restaurants. The Red Curry Paste, which is the key ingredient, may be prepared ahead of time.

Alternatives: *Other sculpins, lingcod, rockfish* *Yield: 18 cakes*

1 pound of cabezon filets, cut into 1-inch slices

1½ tablespoons Red Curry Paste (page 266)

1 tablespoon fish sauce (page 40)

¼ cup string beans, thinly sliced crosswise

Oil for frying

Thai Sweet and Sour Dipping Sauce (see below)

Chop the fish in a food processor or grind finely in a meat grinder. In a bowl, mix the fish together with the curry paste and fish sauce. Add the string beans and combine.

Heat oil to 350°. Form the fish mixture into cakes about ½ inch thick and 2 inches in diameter. Fry the cakes until dark brown, but not burnt. They are done when they float to the top. Serve with the following sauce.

Thai Sweet and Sour Dipping Sauce

¼ cup white wine vinegar

¼ cup sugar

Scant ½ teaspoon salt

2 tablespoons cucumber, peeled and cut into ¼-inch dice

2 teaspoons roughly chopped roasted peanuts

1 jalapeño or other medium hot fresh chile, chopped

Combine the vinegar, sugar and salt in a saucepan. Bring to a boil, remove from the heat and allow to cool. Just before serving, add the cucumber, peanuts and chile.

CARP

(Cyprinus carpio)

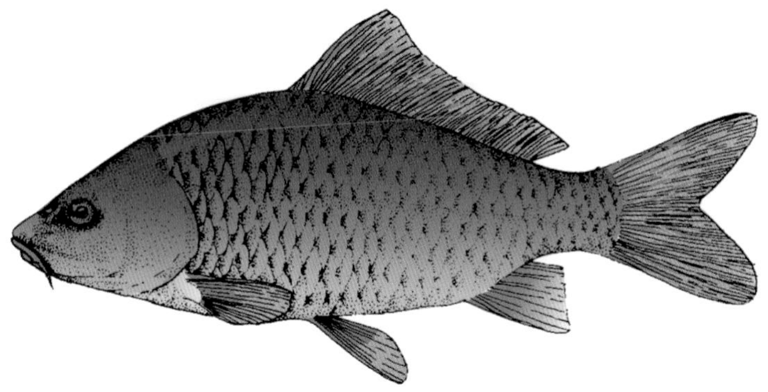

Description: *Gold to olive brown fading to pale yellow. Red highlights. Coarse scales.*	**Season:** *All year.*
	Fat Content: *Moderate.*
Size: *2–3 pounds.*	**Yield:** *25% boneless meat.*
Range: *Aquacultured in many states.*	**Available Forms:** *Live, pan-dressed, chunk.*

Carp was the first fish to be aquacultured, some 2500 years ago in China. Because it is easily raised, this species will become more important here as a food fish in the years to come. Carp is primarily associated with Asian and central European recipes but it is actually one of the most versatile freshwater fish. Its flaky, white, mild-flavored flesh is ideal for frying, baking in a sauce or braising, especially in combination with other freshwater fish such as catfish and eel.

Aquaculture

An important part of the future of seafood may be the age-old technique of *aquaculture*, the practice of raising fish and shellfish under controlled conditions. The Chinese began rearing carp in maintained ponds 2500 years ago, and today a substantial part of the fish eaten in Asia is aquacultured. American aquaculturists are responsible for most of the trout sold in our markets, and for increasing amounts of catfish, crayfish and oysters. Other species are coming into major production, and are occasionally available in our markets: freshwater prawns, carp, pan-sized coho salmon, Sacramento blackfish and tilapia, an introduced Asian species. Research is under way on aquaculture of American lobster, striped bass, sturgeon, abalone and clams.

Aquaculture includes a variety of techniques, from simple protection and maintenance of oyster beds to total artificial environments. All methods, however, have the common aim of increased food yield per acre of water. Publicists and popular writers like to describe a rosy future for aquaculture, with 6- to 8-fold production increases over the next 20 years. Still, aquaculture is not without its problems, both economic and technological. Competition for water and land is stiff; also, water is a difficult growing medium to manage, as disease organisms can spread rapidly through dense populations of fish and shellfish.

Still, aquaculture will play a growing role in supplying seafood for Americans and the rest of the world. In addition to broadening the range of choices of seafood, aquaculture can reduce the dependence on certain overfished wild stocks, and in some cases help to replenish wild populations.

Sweet and Sour Fish

Bruce Cost

Bruce Cost teaches Chinese cooking, having studied for many years with Virginia Lee, a leading authority on Chinese food. Many of his recipes come from the Shanghai region, which favors rich, complex sauces. Bruce is currently working on a ginger cookbook.

Alternatives: *Fancy rockfish, black sea bass (A), striped bass (A,G,P)*

Serves 6 or more as a side dish
Serves 2–3 as a main course

A 2–2½-pound carp, dressed

1 egg, beaten

Salt

½ cup cornstarch

4 dried black mushrooms (the common Chinese variety)

1 small yellow onion, peeled and cut into quarters

3 thin slices ginger

5 cloves garlic, cracked and peeled

2 fresh red sweet or hot peppers, cut into 1-inch dice

2 scallions, cut into 1-inch lengths and then shredded lengthwise

6 pickled shallots or pickled scallions (available in Asian groceries)

1½ cups water

¾ cup sugar

½ cup red wine vinegar

2 teaspoons dark soy sauce

2 teaspoons light soy sauce

1 teaspoon salt

2½ tablespoons cornstarch dissolved in ¼ cup water

Oil for frying

Cilantro for garnish

Extend the belly cavity from the vent almost to the fin. Place the fish belly side down on the cutting board. Press down hard on top of the head of the fish with the heel of your hand to crack the head open. The fish can then be cooked and served in an upright position. Make deep diagonal cuts almost to the backbone at 1-inch intervals from gill openings to tail.

Blend the egg and salt. Rub this mixture over the fish and into the cut surfaces. Spoon a couple of tablespoons of cornstarch into a sieve and sift it over the fish. Rub it in well and let it stand for 15 minutes. Repeat this procedure 3 or 4 times, rubbing in the cornstarch each time.

Meanwhile, soak the mushrooms in hot water for 15 minutes. Drain, squeezing to extract the moisture. Cut off and discard the stems. Cut the caps in two and set aside in a mixing bowl with the onion, ginger, garlic, peppers, scallions and pickled shallots.

Combine water, sugar, vinegar, soy sauces and salt in a saucepan and bring to a boil, stirring to dissolve the sugar; lower the temperature and keep warm.

Heat oil to near smoking (400°) in a large wok or heavy pot. Cook fish over high heat for 10–15 minutes. The fish should be golden-brown but still adhere well to the bones. Drain off the excess oil and place on a large platter. (The fish may be cooked to this point several hours ahead. Just before you are ready to serve, fry the fish again, cooking for about 5 minutes, drain and place on a large platter.)

Heat ¼ cup of oil in a wok or skillet and add the mushrooms and other reserved vegetables. Stir fry for 1 minute then add the sugar/vinegar mixture. Bring to a boil. Add the cornstarch mixture and cook until clear. Pour the sauce over the fish and serve, garnished with cilantro.

CATFISH

(Ictalurus punctatus)

Other Names: *Channel catfish.*

Description: *Dark grey fading to white. Irregular black spots.*

Size: *1–3 pounds. Larger in the wild.*

Range: *Widespread throughout North America. Aquacultured in many states.*

Season: *All year.*

Fat Content: *Moderate.*

Yield: *50% filet.*

Available Forms: *Live, round, pan-dressed, filet.*

Without a doubt, catfish is one of the fish of the future. Tens of millions of pounds are grown annually, yet the supply falls short of the rapidly growing demand. Catfish take well to aquaculture, adapting easily to crowded conditions as long as the water is clean and well oxygenated.

Until recently, cultural prejudice has kept many Americans from trying catfish which has traditionally been thought of as a "trash fish." Now, however, catfish is being consumed outside its narrow regional and ethnic market as more people discover its fine cooking qualities.

Catfish has a flaky, moist texture and a mild, agreeable fresh-water flavor. It is well-suited to frying, sautéing, steaming or braising.

Alternatives: *Blackfish.*

To Skin a Catfish

Because of the toughness of its skin, catfish must be skinned before cooking. There may be more than one way to skin a catfish, but this one works well. It is also suitable for eel.

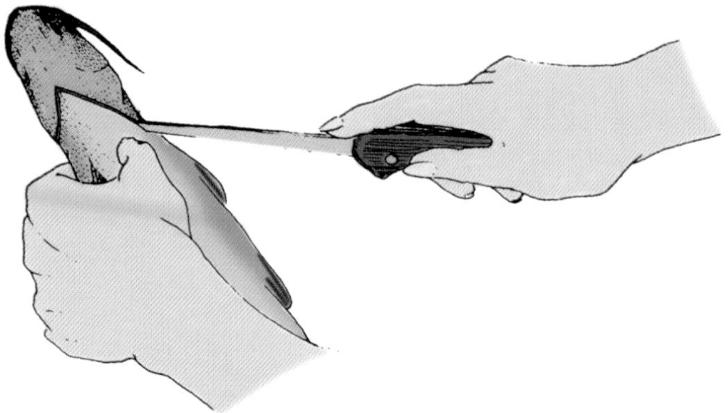

1 Make a V-shaped incision just through the skin, starting from the top of the head and down behind the operculum.

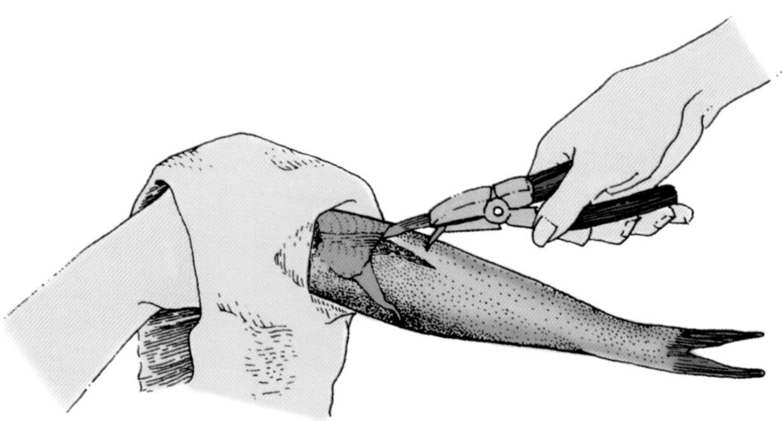

2 Wearing a glove or using a towel to protect your hand from the barbed "whiskers," hold the fish by the head, grasp a flap of skin with pliers and pull the skin away towards the tail. (A helpful device, if you have many catfish or eels to skin, is a board with an exposed nail protruding from one end; impale the fish head on the nail to hold the fish while you pull the skin off.)

Catfish in Red Curry Sauce

Somchai Aksomboon

Alternatives: *Rockfish, tilefish (A), grouper (A,G,P)*

Serves 4 as a side dish
Serves 2 as a main course

2 tablespoons Red Curry Paste (page 266)

4 tablespoons oil

2 cups coconut milk (page 39)

½ teaspoon salt

1 teaspoon sugar

3 tablespoons fish sauce (page 40)

A 2-pound pan-dressed catfish, cut into 1-inch steaks

1 tablespoon Thai basil leaves or *substitute Italian basil and mint leaves*

1–3 fresh hot chiles, finely chopped

Heat the curry paste in oil. Stir and cook for 2 minutes. Add ¼ cup of the coconut milk and the fish sauce. Simmer slowly for 2 minutes to release the flavor of the curry. Then add salt, sugar and the rest of the coconut milk. Bring to a boil and as soon as the sauce boils, add the fish. Do not stir the fish until the sauce returns to a boil. Chai, who likes his fish without even a hint of a fishy taste, says that if you disturb the fish before the sauce boils, it will acquire a strong aroma. Simmer the fish until done, about 5 minutes. Let the dish sit for at least 15 minutes (or as long as overnight in the refrigerator) so the curry flavor will permeate the fish. Reheat, without boiling. Just before serving, add the basil leaves and chiles. Serve over rice.

Fried Catfish Chinese Style

The Chinese love catfish, which they prefer to buy live. In Hong Kong, many restaurants have tanks full of swimming catfish. This practice has been transplanted to America where certain Cantonese fish markets and restaurants offer live catfish.

Serves 4

¼ cup dry sherry or rice wine
½ teaspoon five spice powder (page 40)
1 pound catfish filets
1 egg white
2 tablespoons cornstarch
1 cup white sesame seeds
Peanut oil for frying

Marinate the filets for 30 minutes in the sherry and five spice powder. Beat the egg white and cornstarch together. Dip filets into the egg mixture, then coat with sesame seeds.

Heat the oil to 350° in a wok or deep-fryer. Fry the filets until golden brown. Drain on paper towels.

Serve with Green Chile Sauce (page 264) or Fresh Cilantro Chutney (page 265).

Fried Catfish Southern Style

To minimize the slight freshwater flavor of catfish, soak the filets in buttermilk for 15 minutes or more. Drain slightly. Roll the filets, still wet with the buttermilk, in seasoned cornmeal until well coated. Fry or pan-fry the filets in butter, oil or bacon drippings until golden brown. Serve with lemon wedges and Tartar Sauce (page 259) or Creole Mayonnaise (page 257). Fried catfish is traditionally served with hush puppies which are small sticks of fried cornbread batter.

Laotian Catfish Soup

This is a recipe from *Traditional Dishes of Laos* by Phia Sing (Prospect Books, London, distributed by the University Press of Virginia). Laotian food is almost unknown in America although quite a few of the recent immigrants from Asia come from Laos. Laos is landlocked but rich in freshwater aquatic life. As is the case throughout Southeast Asia, catfish is an important Laotian food source.

Serves 4 as a first course

- *1 fresh* jalapeño or *Fresno chile, seeded*
- *1 small Japanese-style eggplant*
- *3 shallots, unpeeled*
- *1 whole head of garlic*
- *3 cups chicken stock* or *water*
- *½ pound catfish filets, cut into 1-inch squares*
- *Juice of 1 lime*
- *1–2 teaspoons fish sauce (page 40)*
- *½ cucumber, peeled, seeded and cut into ½-inch dice*
- *Finely chopped cilantro*
- *Lime wedges for garnish*

Grill the chiles, eggplant, shallots and garlic over a fire or under the broiler. When they are nicely browned, remove their skins and pound them together in a mortar or purée in a food processor.

Poach the fish in the chicken stock until cooked. Remove to individual warmed bowls. Stir the puréed vegetables into the poaching liquid. Bring to a boil and remove from the heat. Add lime juice, fish sauce, cilantro and cucumber to the soup. Ladle the liquid over the fish. Serve immediately, accompanied with lime wedges.

Thai Sour Fish Soup

Somchai Aksomboon

Alternatives: *Cheap rockfish, sablefish, sculpin*

Serves 4 as a first course

4 shallots, peeled and left whole

1 stalk fresh lemongrass or *1 teaspoon dried lemongrass, finely chopped*

1 quart water

1 teaspoon peppercorns

2 tablespoons fish sauce (page 40)

2 tablespoons cilantro

1½ teaspoon tamarind paste (page 43) dissolved in 2 tablespoons water

½ teaspoon shrimp paste (page 43) (optional)

¼ pound catfish filets, cut into 1-inch slices

Cilantro for garnish

Simmer 3 of the shallots and the lemongrass in the water for 10 minutes. In the meantime, pound the other shallot, the cilantro and the peppercorns in a mortar. Add this paste, the fish sauce, the tamarind mixture and the optional shrimp paste to the soup stock. Simmer for 10 minutes. Add the fish slices and cook until done. Serve immediately, garnished with cilantro.

CLAM—HARD-SHELL

Pacific Littleneck

(Prothaca staminea)

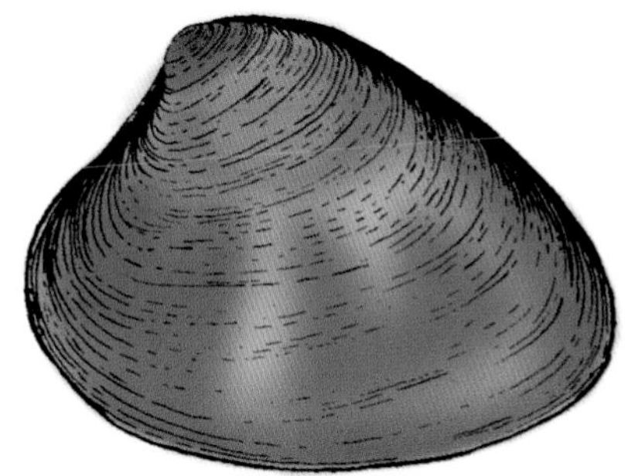

Other Names: *Rock clam, painted clam.*

Description: *Similar to Atlantic hard-shell, but smaller in size.*

Size: *Average 10 per pound.*

Range: *Humboldt Bay to Alaska. Commercially harvested from the California-Oregon border north.*

Season: *All year. Better in colder months.*

Fat Content: *Low.*

Yield: *25% meat.*

Available Forms: *Live, smoked.*

Similar Species: *Manila clam* (Tapes phillippinarium), *is a dark, triangular shaped clam, running about 15 per pound.*

Atlantic

(Mercenaria mercenaria)

Other Names; *Littleneck, cherrystone, quahag or quahog are market terms for the same species. Littleneck are the smallest, quahag the largest.*

Description: *Bivalve. Chalky grey to manila brown.*

Size: *12 per pound to 1 per pound.*

Range: *Atlantic coast. Main commercial grounds are in southern New England.*

Season: *All year. Better in colder months.*

Fat Content: *Low.*

Yield: *15-30% meat. Better yield from smaller clams.*

Available Forms: *Live, shucked, smoked.*

The hard-shell clam species mentioned above are representative of hundreds of closely related species which are often mixed together and sold under a variety of names.

Eastern hard-shells are usually shucked and eaten on the half-shell; western varieties are tougher and not as well suited to this treatment. Clams should be cooked as little as possible as they quickly become tough. (There are always a few stubborn clams in each batch which refuse to open quickly. To avoid overcooking the others, remove clams as they open. The stubborn ones may also be opened with a knife, but away from the pot as the shells might be full of mud.) Hard-shell clams can be steamed, braised or grilled in the shell. Once opened, they can be stuffed. Any of the mussel recipes in this book are appropriate for hard-shell clams.

To Shuck a Clam

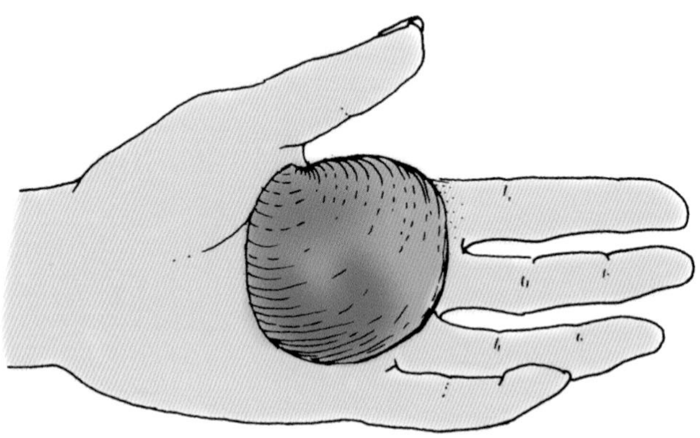

1 Hold the clam securely in the palm of your left hand, with the notched side toward your thumb. Work over a bowl to catch spilled juices.

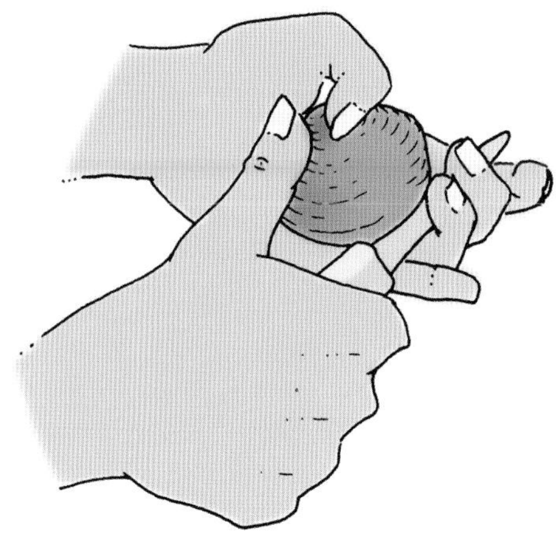

2 Position the thin edge of a *clam knife* (page 18) or a sturdy but slightly dull paring knife along the seam between the two shells. Squeezing with the fingers of your left hand, force the knife between the shells.

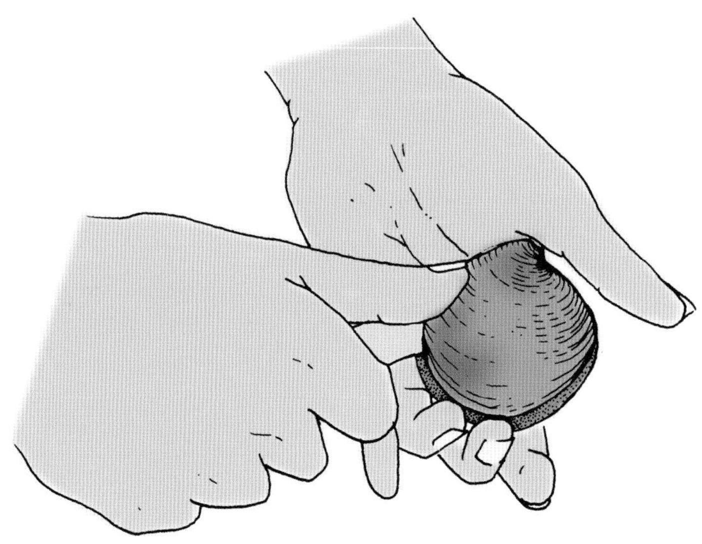

3 Continue working the knife between the shells towards the hinge until you can pry the shells apart.

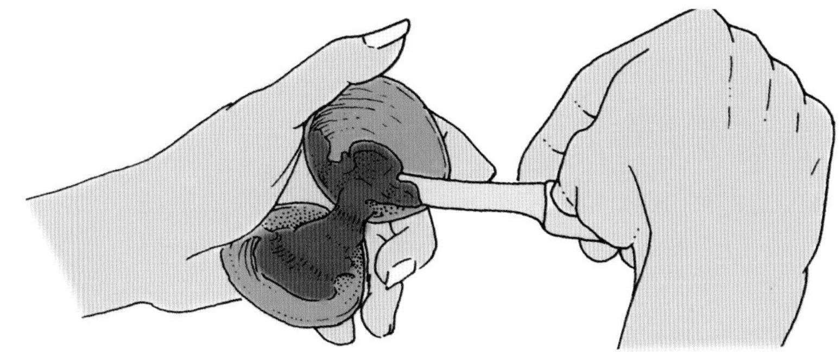

4 Sever the connecting muscles (two per shell), separate the shells and arrange the clam on the half-shell. Spoon any reserved juice into the shell.

Note that this method, although it is the fastest, cuts through part of the clam meat. If you wish to keep the meat intact, carefully work the tip of the knife up against the inside of the upper shell before separating the shells.

CLAM—SOFT-SHELL

(This accepted description is somewhat misleading; the shells of these species are actually thin and brittle, not soft.)

Geoduck

(Panopea generosa)

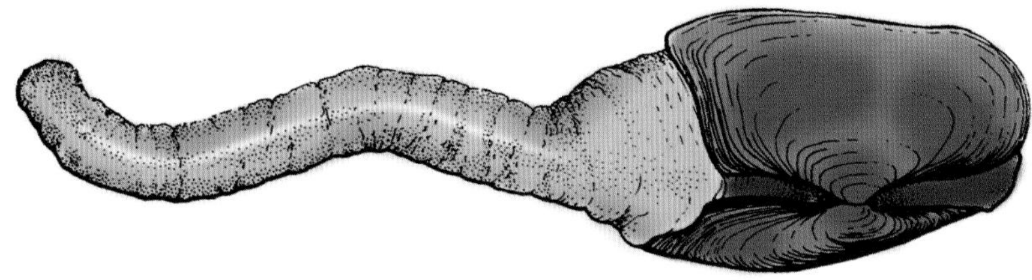

Description: *Bivalve. Large neck protruding up to a foot from the shell.*

Size: *Generally harvested at 2–4 pounds. Largest intertidal mollusc.*

Range: *Washington and British Columbia.*

Season: *Most widely available October–April.*

Fat Content: *Low.*

Yield: *70%.*

Available Forms: *Live.*

Geoduck (pronounced gooey-duck) is delicious raw as *sashimi* or marinated in Ceviche (page 70). Sliced, pounded and sautéed, it resembles abalone. It also makes a wonderful chowder.

To Clean a Geoduck

Remove it from the shell with a knife. Dip the neck into hot water for 30 seconds and peel back the skin. Cut away and discard the entrails. Slice diagonally into thin strips.

Other Soft-Shell Clams

Steamer clams *(Mya arenaria)* of the East Coast are sometimes available on the West Coast. They can be steamed in the shell or shucked and sautéed, and are delicious marinated in a vinaigrette dressing.

Razor clams *(Siliqua patula*—Pacific species; *Enis directus*—Atlantic species) are primarily sport species. Long and narrow, they resemble a folded straight razor. Treat them as you would steamer clams.

Clams in Black Bean Sauce

Bruce Cost

Serves 6 or more as a side dish *Serves 4 as a main course*

2 tablespoons salted black beans (page 42)

2 tablespoons dry sherry or *rice wine*

3 tablespoons oil

1 tablespoon chopped garlic

2 teaspoons chopped ginger

4 pounds hard-shell clams, in the shell

½ cup clam broth

½ teaspoon soy sauce

1 teaspoon sugar

1 teaspoon cornstarch dissolved in 1 tablespoon water

Coarsely chop the beans and soak them in the sherry for at least 30 minutes.

Steam the clams open and reserve the broth.

Sauté the garlic and ginger in oil in a heavy skillet or wok. When the garlic and ginger begin to color, add the clams, clam broth, soy sauce, sugar and the bean mixture. Stir-fry for 2 minutes, coating all the clams with the sauce. Add the cornstarch mixture and continue stirring. When the sauce thickens, remove from the heat and serve immediately.

Clams with Lemon in Oyster Sauce

Bruce Cost

Lemon peel is a fairly common ingredient in Cantonese cooking although it is not often seen in American-style Cantonese dishes.

Serves 4 as a side dish *Serves 2 as a main course*

24 medium clams

2 cups water

1 tablespoon shredded ginger

2 small fresh hot chiles, shredded

1 tablespoon shredded lemon peel

1 tablespoon grated lemon peel

1 tablespoon salted black beans (page 42)

2–4 cloves garlic, chopped

1 tablespoon dry sherry

1 tablespoon soy sauce

2 tablespoons Chinese oyster sauce

1 teaspoon sugar

4 tablespoons oil

1 tablespoon cornstarch mixed with 3 tablespoons water

Cilantro for garnish

Scrub the clams.

Bring 2 cups of water to a boil in a wok or large pot. Add the clams, cover and steam just until they open. Immediately remove them to a bowl filled with ice water to stop the cooking. Save the clam broth. Drain the clams.

Combine the ginger, hot chiles and the shredded lemon peel.

Chop the black beans and combine with the garlic and sherry.

Combine the reserved clam stock, soy sauce, oyster sauce, grated lemon peel and sugar.

Heat the oil in a wok or large skillet. Add the ginger mixture, stir 10 seconds and add the black bean mixture. Cook 30 seconds and add the clam stock-soy sauce mixture. When the sauce boils, add the cornstarch mixture. Cook until thickened, then add the clams. Stir until clams are heated and coated with the sauce. Serve the clams in their shells with the sauce. Garnish with cilantro.

Clam Sauce for Pasta

Although this dish is delicious with any pasta, the thinner cuts such as linguine or tagliarini are most suited to seafood sauces. Of course, fresh pasta is preferable to the dried variety.

Serves 4 as a first course *Serves 2 as a main course*

2 pounds clams
½ cup white wine
1 tablespoon or more chopped garlic
2 tablespoons butter
1 tablespoon chopped parsley
½ pound fresh or dried pasta
Salt and pepper to taste

Combine all ingredients except pasta in a skillet with a tight lid. Cover, bring to a boil and steam until clams open. Meanwhile, cook the pasta, drain well and toss with the clam sauce.

Serve in shallow bowls with clams arranged on top in their shells. Sprinkle with additional chopped parsley, if desired.

PACIFIC COD

(Gadus macrocephalus)

Other Names: *True cod.*

Description: *Brown or grey with browish spots above. Paler below.*

Size: *5–10 pounds.*

Range: *Oregon to Bering Sea.*

Season: *All year.*

Fat Content: *Low.*

Yield: *40% filet.*

Available Forms: *Filet.*

This is the only true Pacific representative of the cod family. Rock cod, lingcod and black cod are all local names for unrelated species. For this reason, this species is often marketed here as "true cod." It is nearly identical to the Atlantic variety, with only minor anatomical differences.

Cod, with its white, flaky, very mild flesh, is a versatile food fish, suitable for grilling, broiling, frying, baking, poaching and stewing. It may be freely substituted in recipes for rockfish, lingcod, sablefish or any other mild-flavored white fish.

Fish Chowder with Leeks

This recipe is neither a New England nor a Manhattan chowder. If leeks are not available, the white parts of scallions may be used; yellow onions are not a good substitute. Although this recipe is recommended for cod, any mild, lean white fish will do. Very soft varieties such as sablefish or smaller soles will more or less disappear into the soup, and are therefore less desirable.

Alternatives: *Rockfish, sculpin, lingcod, halibut, larger flatfish*

Serves 8

2 tablespoons butter

½ cup thinly sliced leeks (the white and pale green parts—save the tops for stock)

2 large (about 1 pound) new potatoes, scrubbed or peeled, cut into ½-inch dice

1 quart Fumet (page 252)

2 cups milk or half-and-half

1 pound cod filets cut in bite-sized pieces

Salt and pepper to taste

2 tablespoons chopped parsley or 1 tablespoon chervil

In a large saucepan, melt the butter and cook the leeks gently until soft, about 5 minutes. Add the potatoes and liquids, bring to a boil and simmer until potatoes are tender, about 15 minutes. Add the fish and simmer just until it is done; remember that the fish will continue to cook in the soup, even when removed from the heat.

Season to taste with salt and pepper. Just before serving, stir in the herbs. Serve in shallow soup bowls with a good crusty bread.

CORBINA

(Menticirrhus undulatus)

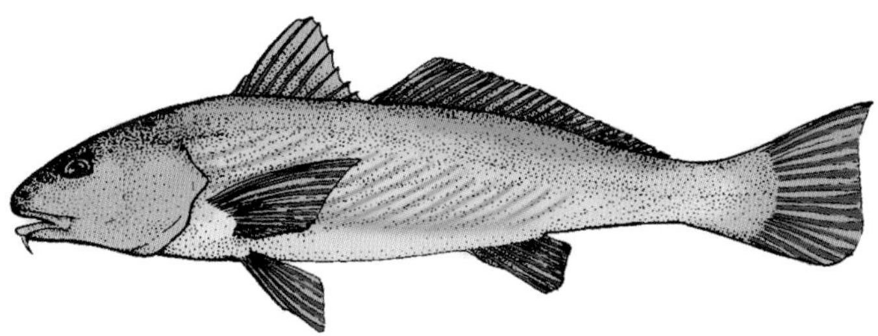

Other Names: *Corvina.*

Description: *Uniform metallic grey with gold highlights.*

Size: *3–7 pounds.*

Range: *Southern California and Baja California coasts.*

Season: *Spring–summer.*

Fat Content: *Moderate.*

Yield: *33% filet.*

Available Forms: *Round, pan-dressed, filet.*

This small West Coast representative of the croaker family has firm, fairly rich flesh with a moderately pronounced flavor. It is well suited to grilling, broiling and steaming.

Alternatives: *Seabass (P), striped bass (A,P), drum, redfish, sea trout, snapper, grouper (A,G).*

Sautéed Corbina with Piquant Sauce

Serves 4

1½ pounds corbina filet

Salt

Coarsely ground black pepper

2 tablespoons olive oil

1 teaspoon chopped garlic

2 teaspoons sherry vinegar or *red wine vinegar*

Cut the filet into 4 serving pieces. Season with a little salt and a generous amount of pepper. In a large skillet, sauté the fish in olive oil over moderate to high heat until done. Transfer the filets to a heated serving platter or individual plates. Sauté the garlic in the remaining oil, but do not brown. Off the heat, add the vinegar (carefully—it will splatter). Return to the heat for a few seconds to evaporate some of the vinegar and pour the sauce over the fish.

Serve with steamed or boiled new potatoes with butter and parsley.

Corbina Steamed in Lettuce

This is one of the best uses for iceberg lettuce.

Serves 4 or more as a first course   *Serves 2 as a main dish*

¾ pound corbina filet
2 tablespoons soy sauce
2 tablespoons dry sherry
6–8 slices ginger
1–2 cloves garlic, chopped
Outer leaves of iceberg or butter lettuce (see below)

Slice the filet across the grain into 1-ounce pieces. Marinate the fish pieces in the soy sauce, sherry, ginger and garlic for 30 minutes.

Peel off enough lettuce leaves to wrap the fish pieces, tearing the large leaves into several pieces if necessary. Blanch the leaves in rapidly boiling water for a few seconds and rinse them in cold water and drain. Wrap each piece of fish in a leaf, forming a tight envelope. Steam on a plate with any remaining marinade until the fish is done, about 5–8 minutes.

CRAB

Dungeness Crab

(Cancer magister)

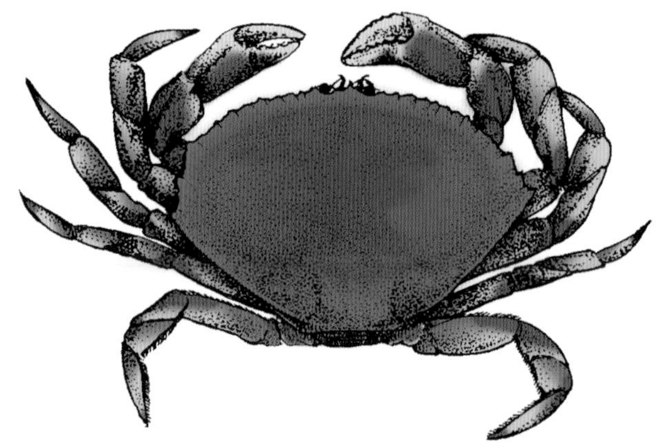

Other Names: *Market crab, common crab.*

Description: *Reddish brown to purple above, cream to yellow below when raw. Brick red to orange when cooked.*

Size: *1½–3 pounds and up.*

Range: *Baja California to Alaska. Most common from central California north.*

Season: *October–May.*

Fat Content: *Low (in meat).*

Yield: *25% meat.*

Available Forms: *Live, cooked, fresh meat.*

This is the main commercial crab on the West Coast, and is a symbol to many of Fisherman's Wharf in San Francisco. Much of the catch is frozen for sale in the off season.

The Dungeness crab population seems to fluctuate on a cycle of about seven years. A large population supports the growth of a parasite which feeds on the crab's eggs. Peak populations of the parasite follow crab peaks by several years, reducing the crab population until the egg supply in turn diminishes and cannot support the parasite population.

Blue Crab

(Callinectes sapidus)

Other Names: *Soft-shell crab.*

Description: *Dark blue to dark green with blue or cream mottling above, cream below. Light to dark orange above, white below when cooked.*

Size: *3½–7 inches across, 2 per pound hard-shell, 4–6 per pound soft-shell.*

Range: *South Atlantic coast to New Jersey; Gulf of Mexico.*

Season: *All year, local seasons depend on water temperature.*

Fat Content: *Low (in meat).*

Yield: *20% meat from hard-shell.*

Available Forms: *Live, picked or lump meat.*

The blue crab is the major commercial species on the Atlantic and Gulf coasts and is second only to shrimp in volume of the catch.

As this crab grows, it periodically sheds its shell to grow a larger one. In this stage it is known as a soft-shell, and is especially good eating. Experienced crabbers can spot "busters," or crabs about to molt, and keep them apart from the rest of the catch. As soon as the crab has shed its shell, it must be transferred immediately to fresh water or it will begin to harden.

Soft-shell blue crabs are widely available frozen, and occasionally appear fresh in our area. Soft-shells are usually fried, sautéed or broiled, and the whole crab is eaten, soft outer layer and all. Hard-shell blue crabs are also available live by air freight from the East Coast and may be treated just like the Dungeness crab.

Other crab species of commercial importance are the Alaska king and snow crabs, and the Florida stone crab. These species are generally available as frozen legs or in bulk form, either frozen or canned.

Two of the easiest ways to cook crab are boiling and steaming. Both methods yield moist, firm meat as long as the crab is not overcooked. A 2–2½-pound Dungeness crab will cook in 10–12 minutes immersed in boiling water, and in 12–15 minutes in a steamer over boiling water. In any case, crab is cooked when the shell turns red.

Cracked crab may be served warm or cold. For warm crab, serve with a hot butter sauce such as Lemon-Garlic Butter (page 255), or with one of the chutneys or dipping sauces on pages 264–65. Cold crab is best with one of the mayonnaise sauces, especially Creole Mayonnaise (page 258).

For an attractive presentation of whole crab, arrange the legs and claws in a lifelike pattern around the body meat, and cover the body with the shell.

To Clean a Cooked Dungeness Crab

No matter how you intend to serve a cooked crab, the cleaning procedure is the same.

1 Hold the crab from underneath. Grasp the top shell by the edges and pull it up and away from the body. Do not discard the shell.

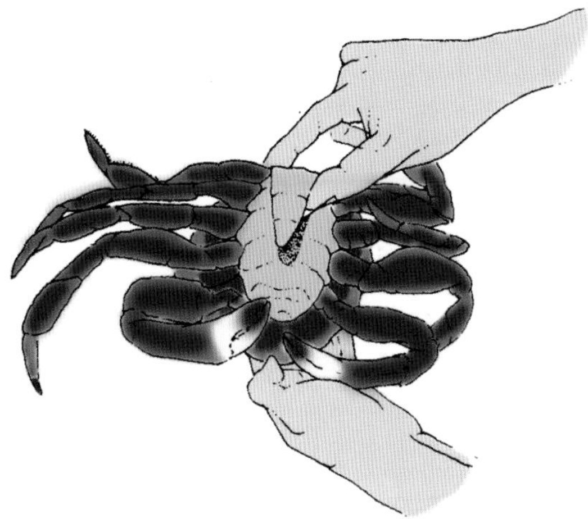

2 Turn the crab over. Lift the "breastplate," a roughly triangular piece of shell, being careful of the soft spines hidden underneath. Remove these together with the breastplate, and discard.

3 Looking at the upper side of the crab again, remove and discard the gills ("dead men's fingers") on either side of the body above the legs. Remove and discard the intestine, a firm white crooked piece along the center of the back.

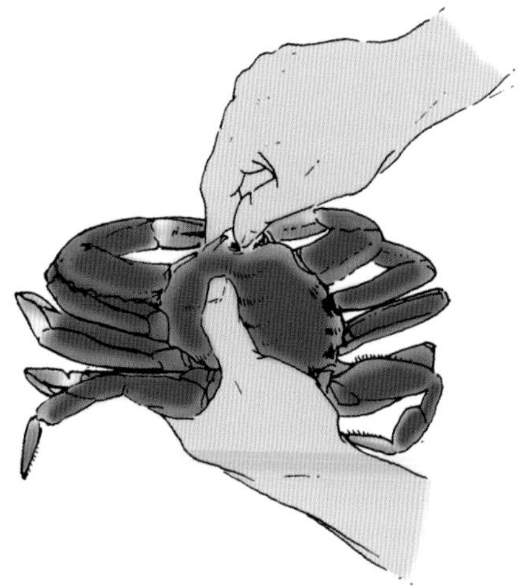

4 Remove and discard the mouth parts. The body cavity will be full of a soft, white to yellow mass of fat and edible organs collectively known as "butter." This is a delicious and essential ingredient in many crab dishes. Remove and reserve the butter. Rinse any remaining matter from the body of the crab, which should now be just shell and meat.

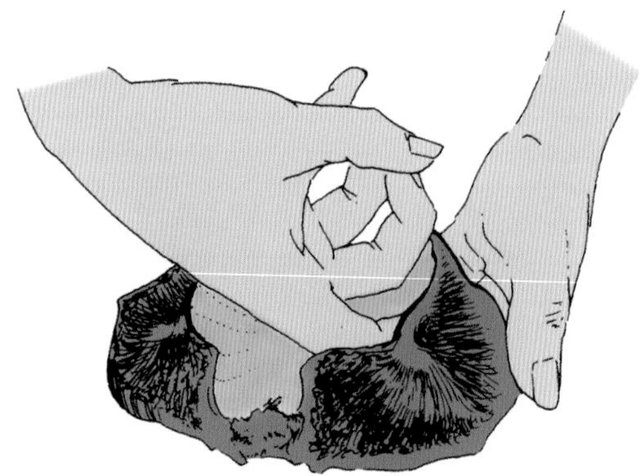

5 Reach into the corners of the shell for any more butter. Rinse the shell if it is to be used in presentation.

To Crack a Cooked and Cleaned Dungeness Crab

Cracking the crab in the kitchen prior to serving makes eating the crab an easier and less messy business at the table. The legs may be separated from the body, which is then served whole or in halves; alternatively, the body may be cut into pieces, each attached to a leg, as shown on page 107.

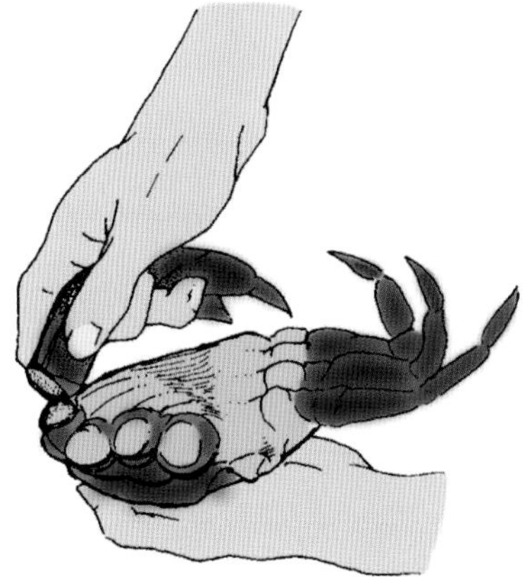

1 To remove the legs, hold the body, grasp each leg as close to the body as possible, and twist to separate the leg from the body.

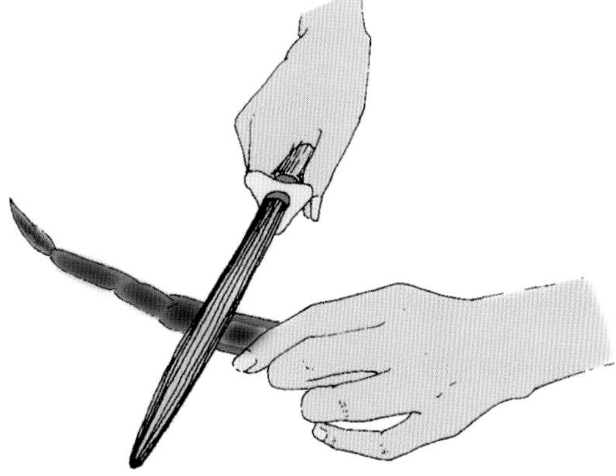

2 Crack each leg and claw section with a mallet, a sharpening steel or the back of a heavy cleaver, being careful not to mash the meat inside.

To Kill and Clean a Crab

Use this technique for grilling, stir-frying or any other method where precooked crab is not appropriate. Refrigerate the live crab for several hours before preparing it to render it a bit more docile.

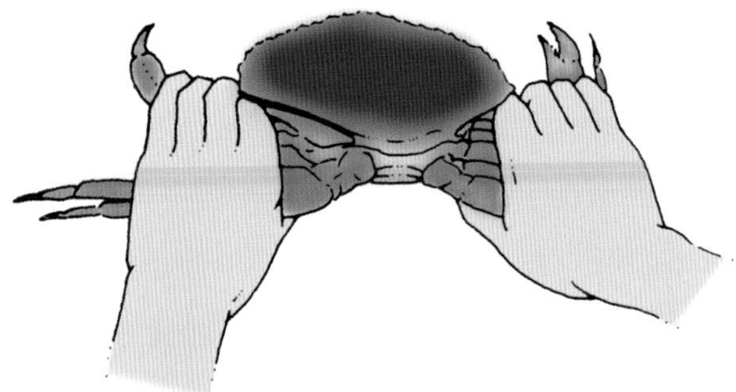

1 Approach the crab from behind. Grasp all four legs and the claw on each side near the body, being careful to avoid the powerful claws.

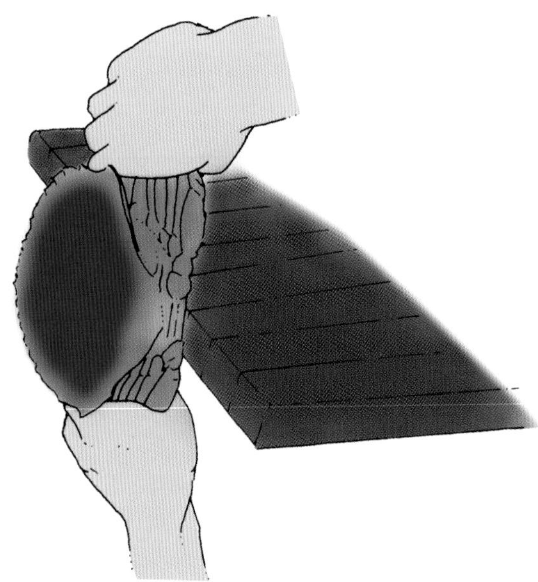

2 Using a sharp edge of a sink, tabletop or cutting board, crack the underside of the shell down the middle with one sharp blow, stunning the crab.

3 Draw both sets of legs together in one hand, grasp the shell with the other hand and pull the body out of the shell. The crab may now be cleaned by the same method for a cooked crab.

4 *Or*, if the crab is less lively and the shell is not being used for presentation, the crab may be split with a knife, shell and all, and cleaned by the same method.

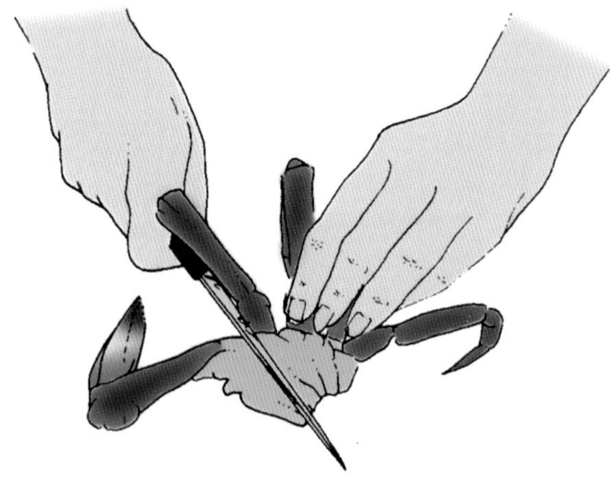

5 **For Sautéing or Stir-Frying:** Cut each half of the body into sections with each section attached to a leg. Crack each leg before cooking.

6 **For Grilling:** Leave the crab halves intact or partially split; crack the legs before marinating, while still attached.

Grilled Crab

Serves 2

1 inch thinly sliced ginger

¼ cup olive oil

1 tablespoon chopped garlic

1 tablespoon chopped parsley

½ teaspoon coarsely ground black pepper

2 serrano or other hot green chiles, chopped

1 2–2½-pound live crab, halved and cracked

¼ cup butter

Combine the ginger, oil, garlic, parsley, black pepper and chiles in a bowl. Add the crab pieces. Toss and refrigerate for at least 1 hour. Strain the marinade, reserving the vegetables for the dipping sauce and the liquid for basting the crab. Grill the crab 3–4 minutes per side, depending on the heat of the fire. Baste with the marinade liquid. Meanwhile, melt the butter in a saucepan. Add the reserved vegetables. Simmer for 5 minutes. Serve with the crab.

Green Crab Enchiladas

Serves 4 (8 enchiladas)

1 pound tomatillos, *husks removed,* or *1 large can of* tomatillos, *drained (page 44)*

2 tablespoons oil

4 serrano, *Fresno or other hot fresh chiles, seeded and finely chopped*

1–2 tablespoons chopped garlic

¼ cup chopped cilantro

2 cups crab meat, (about 1 pound)

8 corn tortillas

Oil for frying (about ⅛ cup)

½ cup sour cream or *Crème Fraiche (page 39)*

½ cup grated jack, Swiss or other mild cheese

Preheat oven to 400°.

Cover the *tomatillos* with cold water. Bring to a boil and cook until soft, but not mushy. They will turn olive green when done. Drain the *tomatillos* and transfer them to a bowl. Mash them with a wooden spoon or potato masher. (If using canned *tomatillos,* just drain and mash them.)

In a large skillet, sauté the chiles and garlic in 2 tablespoons of oil. After 1 minute, add the *tomatillos.* Turn down the heat and simmer for 20 minutes, stirring frequently. Remove from heat and add the cilantro.

Combine the crab meat with enough sauce to moisten it, about ½ cup. Taste and adjust seasoning. Set aside.

In a small skillet, fry the tortillas in ¼ inch of oil until soft, about 30 seconds, and drain on paper towels.

Spoon a little sauce into the bottom of a baking dish big enough to hold the enchiladas in one layer. Divide the crab mixture into 8 portions. Spread one across the center of each tortilla. Roll the tortillas and place them, seams down, in the baking dish. Pour the remaining sauce over the enchiladas. Top each enchilada with a dollop of sour cream (thinned with a little milk if necessary). Sprinkle with cheese and bake for 10 minutes. Serve immediately.

Yellow Curried Crab

Thai curries come in three colors and three levels of spiciness. Red curries, made with dried red chiles, are the hottest. Green curries, prepared with fresh chiles, are in the middle and yellow curries are not hot at all.

Serves 6–8 as a side dish *Serves 4 as a main dish*

3 tablespoons oil

1 medium yellow onion, chopped

1 teaspoon chopped ginger

1 tablespoon chopped garlic

3 tablespoons oil

1 teaspoon mild curry powder

1½ cups chicken stock

1 teaspoon fish sauce (page 40)

1 pound crab meat

2 red potatoes, peeled and cut into ½-inch dice

Sauté the onions, ginger and garlic in oil until the onions are soft. Add the curry powder and cook another minute. Add the stock and fish sauce. Bring to a boil, add the crab and potatoes, and simmer until the potatoes are cooked, about 6–8 minutes. Serve over rice.

Cioppino

Cioppino is said to have been created by San Francisco's fishing community using the local Dungeness crab and rockfish. Other fish and shellfish are often included in the tradition of all fisherman's stews. It can be prepared with blue crab or any other variety.

Serves 8

1 2½-pound live crab

1½ pounds tomatoes, peeled, seeded and chopped with skins, seeds and juice reserved or *1 large can Italian plum tomatoes, juice reserved*

2 quarts Fumet (page 252)

8 clams

1 or more cups dry white wine

2 tablespoons chopped parsley

2 tablespoons or more chopped garlic

2 bay leaves

1 teaspoon fresh herbs such as thyme or oregano or *¼ teaspoon dried*

16 mussels, debearded

1 pound rockfish filets (or any firm white fish)

Salt and pepper to taste

¼ cup Rouille (page 261)

Clean and crack the crab, reserving the shell. Add the tomato peels and seeds or juice and the crab shell to the *fumet*. Simmer 30 minutes and strain. Place the clams in a large, heavy pot or casserole. Add the *fumet* and, if necessary, white wine to cover the clams. Add the bay leaves, parsley, garlic, tomatoes and herbs. Cover and bring to a boil. Add the mussels and crab. Simmer 3–4 minutes until clams and mussels are open. Add the rockfish and cook 2–3 minutes more.

Serve immediately in heated soup bowls accompanied with hot French bread and *rouille*.

Braised Crab

Alternatives: *Lobster* *Serves 4*

2 tablespoons butter

2 tablespoons olive oil

2 2-pound live crabs, cleaned and cracked, fat reserved

2 tablespoons or more chopped garlic

¼ cup chopped parsley

1 tablespoon fresh thyme

Black pepper to taste

1½ cups dry white wine

¼ cup Fumet (page 252)

2 tomatoes, peeled, seeded and diced

In a wok or large skillet, heat the butter and olive oil. Add the crab and sauté over a high flame for 2 minutes. Add the garlic, herbs, wine, *fumet,* crab fat and pepper. Cover and cook at highest heat until shell is red, about 3 minutes. Remove the crab to a warm serving plate. Reduce the sauce at least by half over high heat. Toss the tomatoes in the sauce.

Arrange the crab legs on a heated serving platter or individual plates in a lifelike pattern. Pour the sauce over the crab, garnishing with the tomatoes.

Crab Gumbo

"Gumbo" encompasses a whole range of Louisiana recipes that are thickened with either okra or filé powder. Some include chicken or sausage as well as seafood. Our recipe is an all-seafood version based on crab stock, but feel free to improvise!

Serves 8

1 2½-pound live crab or *8 blue crabs*

1 pound whole prawns or shrimp

3 pounds tomatoes, peeled, seeded and chopped, juice and skins reserved

2 tablespoons flour

2–3 tablespoons butter

1 large bell pepper, diced

2 onions, diced

2 tablespoons or more chopped garlic

½ teaspoon cayenne

2 bay leaves

1 sprig fresh thyme or *½ teaspoon dried*

Zest of 1 lemon

1 pound rockfish filet or *any firm white fish*

2 tablespoons filé powder

Salt and pepper to taste

In a large kettle or stockpot, steam or boil the crab, reserving the cooking liquid. Cool the crab quickly in ice water and drain thoroughly. Clean the crab, reserving the fat. Add the cleaned shell back to the pot, and set the crab aside. Shell the shrimp and add the shells and heads to the pot. Add the tomato skins, seeds and juice, bring to a boil, simmer for at least 30 minutes and strain.

In a pot big enough to hold all the ingredients, melt the butter and add enough flour to absorb the butter and form a thin paste. Cook this *roux* over gentle heat, stirring frequently, until it is a golden brown. Stir in the crab fat. Add the bell pepper, onion, garlic and cayenne and cook for a few minutes until the onion and pepper soften. Add the stock, herbs, lemon zest and tomatoes and simmer for 30 minutes.

Meanwhile, separate and crack the crab claws and legs, devein the shrimp if desired and cut the rockfish into bite-sized pieces. Add the fish and shellfish and the filé powder to the pot during the last 5 minutes or so. Do not boil after this point, or the filé powder will become bitter and stringy. Simmer until the fish and shrimp are just done and correct the seasoning.

Serve the gumbo in bowls over rice. Pass additional filé powder and Tabasco or another hot pepper sauce if desired.

(Note: This dish can be made with precooked crab as well. Simply start the stock with water or a mild *fumet* in place of the crab cooking liquid.)

Stir-Fried Crab

Alternatives: *Lobster*

Serves 4 or more as a side dish
Serves 2 as a main course

2 tablespoons salted black beans (page 42)

2 tablespoons sherry or *rice wine*

A 2–2½-pound live crab, cleaned, cut into serving pieces and cracked, fat reserved

Cornstarch

3 tablespoons oil

2 tablespoons chopped garlic

2 tablespoons chopped ginger

2 tablespoons soy sauce

2 teaspoons sugar

¼ cup water

4 scallions, trimmed into 1-inch lengths and then cut in half

1 teaspoon cornstarch dissolved in 1 tablespoon water

Cilantro for garnish

Coarsely chop the black beans and combine with the sherry. Let the mixture stand for 30 minutes.

Dip the cut ends of the crab legs and claws into cornstarch.

Heat the oil in a wok or heavy skillet. Stir-fry the garlic and ginger for 30 seconds; do not brown. Add the crab pieces and toss thoroughly. Add the soy sauce, sugar, water, scallions and reserved crab fat. Cook over high heat until the crab is done, 2–3 minutes. Add the cornstarch-water mixture, and cook until the sauce thickens. Garnish with cilantro and serve.

CRAYFISH

(Astacus pacifasticus)

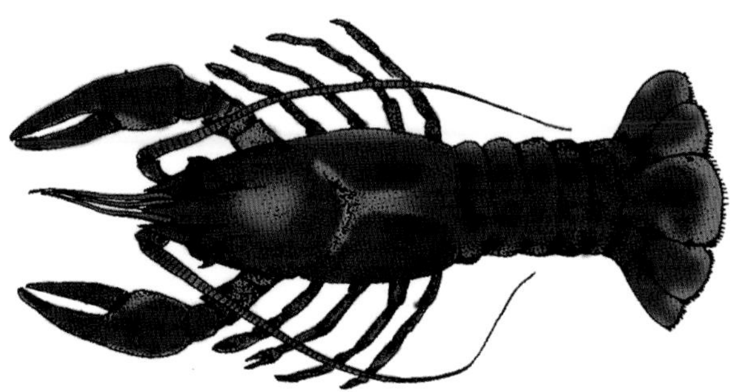

Other Names: *Crawfish, crawdad.*

Description: *Reddish brown when alive. Bright red when cooked.*

Size: *2–8 ounces.*

Range: *Rivers and estuaries of North America.*

Season: *Varies locally with water conditions. Generally spring-early fall in California.*

Fat Content: *Low (in meat).*

Yield: *15–20% meat.*

Available Forms: *Live, whole cooked.*

Similar Species: *Louisiana crayfish* (Procambarus *spp.*) *are generally flown in during the winter months.*

An important ingredient in Creole and Cajun cooking, these small freshwater crustaceans are found on every continent except Africa. They are highly regarded in Europe, but relatively unknown in much of North America. However, as lobster becomes prohibitively expensive, many Americans are discovering its delicious little cousin.

Crayfish are easily aquacultured. The current production is primarily in Louisiana, which exports thousands of tons of crayfish to Europe annually. Even California's small commercial harvest is largely exported.

Hot or cold, crayfish are best eaten with the fingers. Most of the meat is in the tail, but the delicious fat in the head should not be missed.

Crayfish Boil

This traditional Louisiana feast is ideally served outdoors. The crayfish should be eaten with the fingers so that the head, which is full of delicious fat, can be enjoyed along with the meaty tail. If you are eating indoors, cover the table and provide bowls for the shells.

Serves 4–6

1 gallon water
2 cups red wine
3 onions, chopped
3 scallions, chopped
½ cup chopped parsley
3 stalks celery, chopped
½ package shrimp boil spices (sold in most supermarkets)
Garlic to taste (at least 8 whole cloves)
Cayenne to taste (at least 1 teaspoon)
Salt and pepper to taste
2 pounds new potatoes, unpeeled
3 pounds live crayfish

Bring all the ingredients except for the crayfish and potatoes to a boil in a large pot. Simmer 30 minutes. Add the potatoes and cook 5 minutes. Add the crayfish and cook until done, about 8 minutes more.

Serve the crayfish and potatoes hot or chilled, accompanied with a spicy mayonnaise such as Creole Mayonnaise (page 258) or Aioli (page 259).

Crayfish Bisque

Serves 4 as a first course

1½ pounds live crayfish
1 bay leaf
½ cup diced celery
1 cup diced onion
¼ cup butter
Pinch cayenne
1 tablespoon fresh thyme
3 cups milk and 1 cup cream or 2 cups milk and 2 cups half-and-half
Salt and white pepper to taste
Chopped chives for garnish

Boil the crayfish in water for about 7–8 minutes with the bay leaf and half the vegetables. Cool and reserve ½ cup of the cooking liquid. Shell and devein the crayfish, reserving the fat and shells. Chop the meat finely, combine it with the fat and set aside.

Chop the heads and shells with a knife or food processor. Heat the butter and cayenne in a large saucepan. Sauté the remaining vegetables gently until soft. Add the shells and debris, thyme and reserved liquid. Simmer 15–20 minutes. Strain the liquid into a smaller saucepan. Add the milk and cream, bring to a simmer and add the crayfish meat and fat. Remove from heat, season with salt and pepper, and ladle into individual serving bowls. Garnish with chopped chives.

EEL

(Anguilla anguilla)

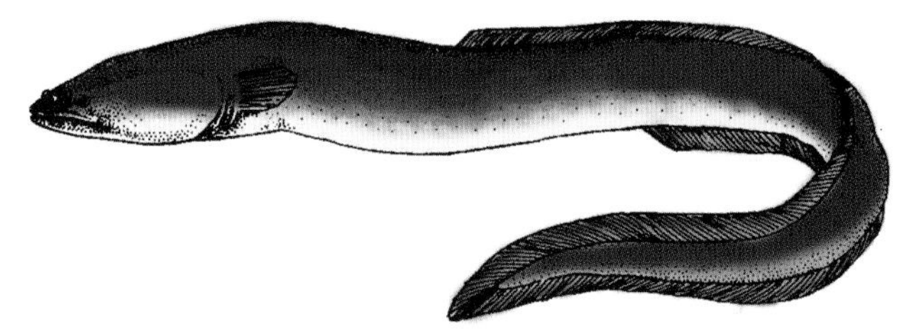

Description: *Dark green to black, fading to yellow.*

Size: *To 3 feet.*

Range: *Coastal and inland waters of the northern Atlantic coast.*

Yield: *About 70% meat.*

Fat Content: *High.*

Season: *Sporadically available all year.*

Available forms: *Live, dressed, smoked.*

Eel is a favorite food in Europe, but is generally ignored by Americans. In their natural habitat, eel breed in salt water and live either in shallow coastal waters or in fresh water. In many countries, eel is aquacultured in fresh water. Unfortunately, they are expensive to raise because eel will eat only fish protein.

Eel can be stewed or grilled with excellent results. Teriyaki Sauce (page 264) makes a wonderful marinade.

To Skin an Eel

Like catfish, eel has tough skin which should be removed before the meat is cooked. See directions for skinning a catfish (page 82).

Eel Stewed in Red Wine

Serves 3–4

2 tablespoons olive oil
1 yellow onion, chopped
1–2 tablespoons chopped garlic
1 pound eel, cleaned and cut into 2-inch lengths
1 cup canned tomatoes with juice, chopped
2 cups red wine
2 cups Fumet (page 252)
1 ounce pine nuts
1 tablespoon chopped parsley
1 tablespoon vinegar
Salt and pepper to taste

Sauté the onion and garlic in oil in a casserole or heavy saucepan large enough to hold all the ingredients. When the onions are translucent, add the eel and toss the pieces in the oil. Add the remaining ingredients. Cover and simmer slowly for 30 minutes. Serve over rice or with French bread.

FLOUNDER

Starry Flounder

(Platichthys stellatus)

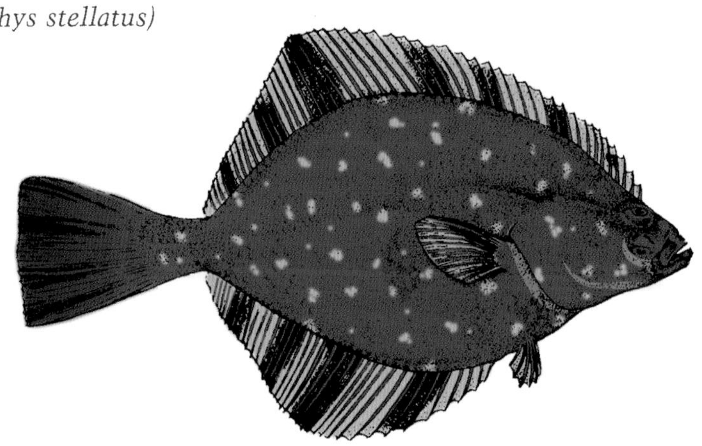

Description: *Dark brown to black with rough skin above. Creamy to white below. Orange-white and black stripes on fins.*

Size: *1–6 pounds. Smaller fish are milder in flavor.*

Range: *Central California to Alaska.*

Season: *All year, especially winter months.*

Fat Content: *Low.*

Yield: *40% filet.*

Available Forms: *Round, filet.*

Winter Flounder

(Pseudopleuronectes americanus)

Other Names: *Lemon sole (smaller fish only).*

Description: *Rust-brown mottled with black above.*

Size: *1–2 pounds. Occasionally to 5 pounds.*

Range: *Atlantic coast. Chesapeake Bay to southern Canada.*

Season: *Fall to spring.*

Fat Content: *Low.*

Yield: *40% filet.*

Available Forms: *Filet, round.*

Summer Flounder

(Paralichthys dentatus)

Other Names: *Fluke.*

Description: *Mottled grey-brown to olive-green above.*

Size: *2–5 pounds and up.*

Range: *Atlantic. Carolinas to New England.*

Season: *Summer.*

Fat Content: *Low.*

Yield: *50% filet.*

Available Forms: *Round, filet, steak.*

Perhaps no fish is a better example of the maxim "familiarity breeds contempt." Because of the wide availability of flounder, it seems mundane to most restaurants and their patrons. However, with its delicate but distinctive flavor and agreeable texture, starry flounder is certainly in a league with the more popular Pacific flatfish. Flounder filets can be freely substituted in any sole recipe. Pan-dressed flounder may be grilled or baked, with the skin adding a characteristic flavor. Filets with the skin attached are tricky to grill as they tend to curl. Skinless filets are suitable for sautéing, poaching and, if on the large side, broiling. Choose a delicate sauce such as Beurre Blanc (page 253) or a cream-based sauce.

Alternatives: *Petrale or other soles.*

Broiled Flounder Filets with Herb Butter

Some appropriate fresh herbs are suggested below. One or two is plenty; too many herbs become confusing. Pungent herbs such as rosemary, oregano or tarragon are not suitable for the delicate taste of flounder.

Serves 4

4 tablespoons softened butter

2 tablespoons chopped fresh herbs such as parsley, thyme, watercress, chervil, chives or basil

Salt and pepper to taste

Juice of ½ lemon

1–1½ pounds flounder filets

Preheat the broiler.

Blend the butter, herbs, salt, pepper and lemon juice. Arrange the filets skin side down on a buttered roasting pan. Spread the herb butter on top of the filets and broil close to the heat until just done.

Transfer the filets to warm plates and drizzle with any butter remaining in the pan.

Flounder Baked with Fresh Herbs

This is one of the simplest and least caloric ways to use flounder, and also a delicious one. Herbs suggested on page 122 are also appropriate here.

Serves 4

1–1½ pounds flounder filets
Salt and pepper to taste
Juice of ½ lemon
1–2 tablespoons chopped fresh herbs

Preheat oven to 500°.

Season the fish with salt, pepper and lemon juice. Spread with a generous layer of chopped herbs. Place filets skin side down on a flameproof platter or shallow baking dish. Cover tightly with foil. Bake until just done by the skewer test, about 5–8 minutes. Serve with lemon wedges.

Grilled Herb-Stuffed Flounder in Grape Leaves

Once again, flounder and fresh herbs are combined. In this recipe, however, these delicate flavors are a foil to the more aromatic grape leaves and charcoal-grilled flavor. This dish was originally conceived as a main dish, with whole filets stuffed and wrapped in lettuce or other large leaves. But the flounder that day turned out to be very small, we had grape leaves on hand and somehow the idea of fish *dolmas* came to mind. This dish may be made in advance as an appetizer to an outdoor barbecue.

Serves 8 as an appetizer

2–3 cloves garlic

¼ cup chopped fresh herbs such as parsley, basil, thyme or chives

Juice of 1 lemon

1½–2 pounds flounder filets

24 bottled grape leaves, drained, stems trimmed

Press the garlic into a small bowl, add the herbs and lemon juice and combine.

Divide the filets into 1-ounce pieces, roughly rectangular. (If some of the filets are large, the thick end can be sliced in half horizontally.)

Flatten the grape leaves, dull side up and stem end toward you on the board. Place a piece of filet spread with the herb mixture on each leaf and roll it into a cylinder. Starting with the base of the leaf, wrap the leaf around the rolled filet, tucking in the sides of the leaf like the flaps of an envelope. The roll should be a tight bundle with only the point of the leaf opposite the stem showing. Chill the rolls until ready to grill. (These can be assembled several hours ahead of time.)

Oil the rolls lightly and grill until the leaves are well marked but not burnt. Serve on platters to be eaten with the fingers.

GROUPER

(Family *Serranidae*)

Other Names: *Sea bass, various species names.*

Description: *Deep-bodied with projecting mandibles. Color varies according to species.*

Size: *Smaller species in 2–3-pound range. Larger species to several hundred pounds.*

Range: *Worldwide in tropical and temperate waters.*

Season: *Sporadically all year.*

Fat Content: *Low.*

Yield: *30–40% filet, depending on size.*

Available Forms: *Round, filet, steak.*

This large cosmopolitan family includes many important food fishes. Although some are found off the Pacific coast, most grouper are flown in from the eastern United States or New Zealand. All species are likely to be marketed as grouper or seabass. The relatively rare giant seabass *(Stereolepsis gigas)* of the Pacific coast, while unrelated, is also marketed as grouper.

The firm, lean flesh of the grouper falls somewhere between halibut and the basses in flavor and texture, and is suitable to the same cooking methods as these varieties. Smaller filets and tail portions are easily grilled or broiled; larger sections may be cut into steaks or diagonal slices up to an inch thick for the same treatments, or may be stuffed and baked with Oyster Stuffing for Fish (page 166). Grouper is also a good choice for soups and stews.

GRUNION

(Leuresthes tenius)

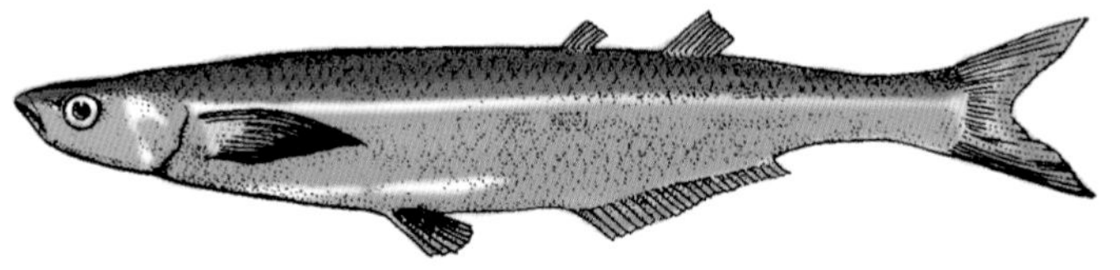

Description: *Green fading to silver. Black lateral line.*

Size: *3-6 ounces.*

Range: *Southern California.*

Season: *Summer.*

Fat Content: *Moderate.*

Available Forms: *Sport fish only.*

The grunion is a small member of the smelt family which spawns above high tide in the light of the full moon. A sport fish, it can only legally be taken by hand; no nets or other equipment are allowed.

Grunion may be cooked in the same manner as jacksmelt or whitebait although it should be boned if eaten whole.

HALIBUT

Pacific Halibut

(Hippoglossus stenolepis)

Description: *Greenish brown above.*

Size: *10-100 pounds and up.*

Range: *Pacific Ocean from southern California north.*

Season: *Highly regulated and local. Primarily winter.*

Fat Content: *Low.*

Yield: *Up to 65% filet.*

Available Forms: *Pan-dressed, steak, filet, fletch (half filet).*

California Halibut

(Paralichthys californicus)

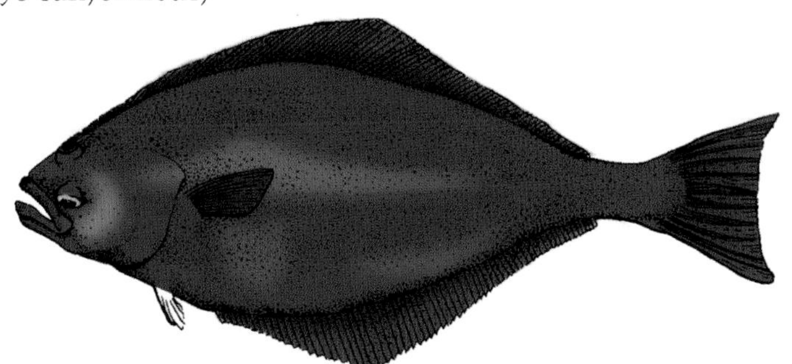

Description: *Olive green to black above. White or variegated below. Right-eyed nearly as often as left-eyed.*

Size: *5–35 pounds.*

Range: *Baja to central California.*

Season: *All year.*

Fat Content: *Low.*

Yield: *65% filet.*

Available Forms: *Round, filet, fletch, occasionally steak.*

Of the two local halibut species, the larger Pacific variety is slightly preferable and considerably scarcer. Both are excellent if not overcooked. The dense, mild and slightly sweet flesh of halibut is excellent for grilling, broiling and sautéing. Serve with a compound butter (pages 254–55), Fresh Tomato Salsa (page 262) or Green Chile Sauce (page 264).

Alternatives: *Greenland halibut (A), grouper (A,G,P).*

Sautéed Halibut with Cream and Herbs

Alternatives: *Snapper, grouper (A,G,P), sole, flounder (A,P) fancy rockfish* *Serves 4*

1–1½ pounds halibut filet

2 tablespoons butter

1 teaspoon chopped shallots

1 teaspoon lemon zest

1 tablespoon chopped fresh herbs such as parsley, chervil, chives, thyme, tarragon or dill

1 cup Crème Fraîche (page 39) or *whipping cream*

Salt and white pepper to taste

Cut the halibut into serving pieces. Thin tail filets may be cut straight across; filets over an inch thick are best cut diagonally into slices or scallops.

Melt half the butter in a skillet large enough to hold all the pieces. Sauté the fish gently until just short of done and transfer to hot plates or a serving dish. (The fish will finish cooking on its own.) If the butter in the pan has browned, discard it.

Add the remaining butter to the pan with the shallots and lemon zest. Cook without browning for a minute or so. Add the herbs and *crème fraîche* and a pinch of salt and pepper. Bring to a boil, reduce by half and correct the seasoning.

If the fish has cooled noticeably, return it to the pan briefly to reheat. Otherwise, pour the sauce over the fish and serve, accompanied by a colorful assortment of steamed vegetables.

Variations

This technique can be used for a wide variety of fish (see above for alternatives). It also lends itself to many sauce variations:

Use ginger and lime or orange zest in place of the shallots and herbs; garnish with julienned scallions.

A scant teaspoon of tomato paste or a tablespoon of fresh tomato sauce will produce a pale pink *sauce aurore.* Omit the lemon zest and stick to the milder herbs in this case.

Soak a few saffron threads or a pinch of powdered saffron in the cream for an hour or so, and omit the herbs.

Add 2 tablespoons mashed or puréed avocado to the cream sauce just before serving in place of the herbs and lemon zest. Heat but do not cook or the avocado will become bitter. Garnish with lime zest.

Salt-Grilled Halibut

Salting fish before grilling is a typically Japanese technique, used to draw out any strong flavors. Any fish suitable for grilling may be salt-grilled. Milder fish such as halibut are salted the least, while stronger fish such as salmon or mackerel are more heavily salted.

Serves 4

1–1½ pounds halibut steaks or filets

Salt

Sliced raw vegetables such as carrots and cucumbers for garnish

Dipping Sauce

4 tablespoons soy sauce

2 tablespoons lemon juice or rice vinegar

Cover the steaks on both sides with a thin layer of salt. Refrigerate for one hour. Combine the soy sauce and lemon juice. Set aside.

Grill the steaks until done by the skewer test. Serve the fish with the dipping sauce, garnished with slices of raw vegetables.

Steamed Halibut in Nori *Seaweed*

Nori, a Japanese seaweed which is shredded and dried in sheets, is best known as the wrapping for rolled *sushi.* It also makes a delicious wrapping for steamed fish, imparting a characteristic flavor and aroma to mild fish. *Nori,* which is extremely nutritious, is available in Asian markets.

Alternatives: *Grouper (A,G,P), snapper (G), the basses (A,G,P), fancy rockfish*

Serves 4

1–1½ pounds halibut filet

1 teaspoon wasabi *powder (page 44)*

Water

4 sheets nori *(8–10 inches square)*

Dipping sauce for Salt-Grilled Halibut (page 129)

Choose a thick piece of halibut if possible; an inch or so is ideal. Blend the *wasabi* with enough water to form a smooth paste. Slice the filet crosswise into serving pieces. Fold the thin pieces cut from the tail in half to form a thicker portion. Spread one side of each piece with a small amount of the *wasabi* paste.

Sprinkle a sheet of *nori* with just enough water to make it pliable. Place a piece of fish, bone side down, diagonally across the middle of the sheet. Fold the sheet around the fish, forming an envelope. Repeat for the other pieces of fish. Steam the packages on a plate, about 8 minutes per inch of thickness. Serve with rice and the dipping sauce.

PACIFIC HERRING

(Clupea harengus pallasii)

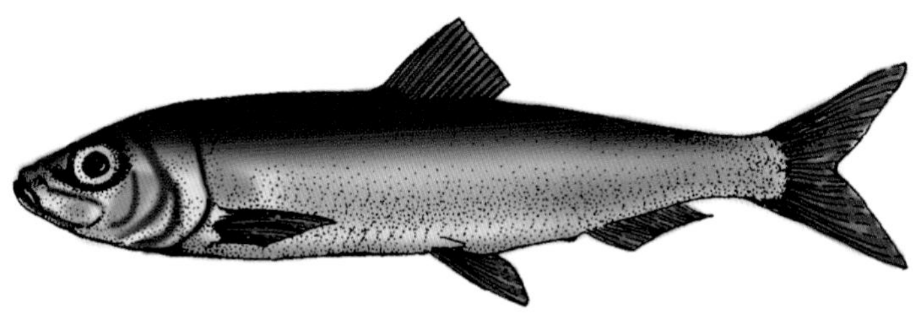

Description: *Silvery blue-green fading to white. Loose scales.*

Size: *2–4 per pound.*

Range: *Pacific coast. Northern Baja California north.*

Season: *Late fall–early winter, while spawning.*

Fat Content: *High.*

Yield: *50% filet.*

Available Forms: *Round, pickled, salted, smoked.*

San Francisco Bay is a major spawning ground for the Pacific herring. Most of the catch is sent to Japan where the roe is a high-priced delicacy, making the brief herring season a lucrative one for the Northern California fishermen. A small amount of the catch stays here and is available locally.

Herring's moderate to pronounced flavor and soft texture make it ideal for pickling, but it may also be cooked when fresh.

Herring, like other rich fish, takes well to grilling. A preliminary marinade of olive oil, salt, pepper and herbs complements the charcoal flavor nicely. Fresh or dried thyme, rosemary, oregano or marjoram are good choices for herbs. Allow ¾–1 pound of whole fish per person.

Whole herring roes may be cured in brine according to the general procedure for Caviar (page 232); use a 15% salt solution and omit cutting open the egg sac.

To Clean and Bone Herring

To clean herring, make a slit from the vent to below the jaw with a paring knife. Remove the roe from females (the yellow sac filling most of the belly cavity) and reserve. Cut through the backbone just behind the head, grasp the head and pull the head and entrails away from the body. Remove the dark strip along the backbone and rinse the cavity well. Rub away scales under running water with fingertips.

To bone a herring, especially if you are going to stuff or grill it, place the fish belly side down on the board. Press down from the top, forcing the two filets apart. Turn the fish over and peel the backbone away from the filets, leaving them attached to the skin and tail.

Baked Herring with Tomatoes and White Wine

Serves 4

2 tablespoons olive oil

2 tablespoons chopped garlic

½ yellow onion, julienned

1 pound tomatoes, peeled, seeded and chopped or *2 cups canned peeled tomatoes, drained and chopped*

½ teaspoon fresh (or *¼ teaspoon dried) oregano, thyme or marjoram*

2½–3 pounds herring, round

¼ cup white wine

Salt and pepper to taste

Sauté the garlic and onion in oil until soft but not browned. Add the tomatoes and herbs and cook until most of the liquid is evaporated. Season to taste.

Clean the herring, leaving the backbones in. Place them in a single layer in a baking dish. Add the wine and the tomato sauce, cover, and bake 12–15 minutes or until filets pull away from bones easily. Remove the fish to a warm serving dish;

reduce the sauce if it is too watery, and pour over the fish. Serve with plain or saffron-flavored rice.

Grilled Stuffed Herring Brochettes

Alternatives: *Anchovies, whitebait* *Serves 4*

2 pounds herring, cleaned and boned

Olive oil

Lemon wedges for garnish

Bread Crumb Stuffing

3 tablespoons olive oil

¼ cup chopped garlic

¼ cup chopped parsley

¼ cup bread crumbs

¼ cup Parmesan or *Romano cheese, grated*

Salt and pepper to taste

Sauté garlic in oil until cooked but not browned. Add other stuffing ingredients, and combine. Season to taste with salt and pepper.

Place the filets on a cutting board, skin side down. Spread each filet with a layer of the stuffing and roll toward the tail. Skewer several together, brush with a little olive oil and grill over a hot fire on both sides until filets are cooked through. Serve with lemon wedges.

Pickled Herring

For 5 pounds of herring

Preliminary curing:

2 quarts water

1 quart vinegar

10 ounces salt (coarse or Kosher salt is preferable)

Filet or pan-dress the fish. Place in a stainless steel or glass bowl. Combine the water, vinegar and salt and cover the fish, reserving any excess for the final pickling. Refrigerate for 48 hours, drain and cover with fresh water. Soak for several hours to remove excess salt, drain and proceed with the final pickling.

Sweet and Sour Pickle

1 small red onion, thinly sliced

1 carrot, thinly sliced

2 tablespoons commercial pickling spice mixture

Water and vinegar

Salt and sugar to taste

Arrange the cured fish in layers alternately with the onion, carrot and spices. Cover with a mixture of 2 parts vinegar to 1 part water, adding salt and sugar to taste. Refrigerate for another 24 hours or more before serving.

Sour Cream Pickle

Cover with half sour cream and half vinegar-water mixture (2 parts vinegar, 1 part water) and omit the sugar. Add a little Dijon mustard, if desired.

Herring Roe Sautéed with Bacon

Try this variation on the theme of "bacon and eggs" as an appetizer in a meal featuring grilled or baked herring.

Serves 8 as an appetizer

1 pound herring roe
2 slices bacon, diced
Lemon wedges for garnish

Herring roe is available during herring season at many fish markets.

Discard any roe sacs that are badly damaged, as they will disintegrate in cooking. Soak the intact roe sacs in salted water for at least 30 minutes and drain.

Sauté the bacon in a large skillet until crisp. Remove bacon, pour off all but 2 tablespoons of fat, and sauté the roe over moderate heat until it just turns opaque. Squeeze some lemon juice over the roe in the pan, and serve with the bacon and additional lemon wedges.

JACK MACKEREL

(Trachurus symmetricus)

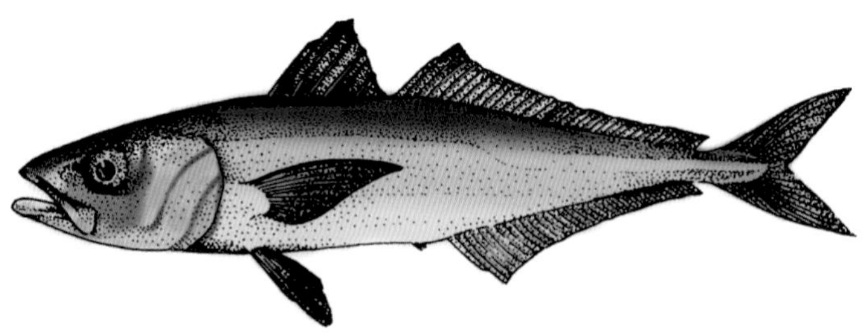

Other Names: *Spanish mackerel, Pacific jack.*

Description: *Metallic blue to olive green above. Silver below.*

Size: *To 1 pound.*

Range: *Pacific coast. Mainly central Mexico to southern California.*

Season: *All year. Less common in summer.*

Fat Content: *High.*

Yield: *50% filet.*

Available Forms: *Round.*

In taxonomic terms, this is a jack and not a mackerel, but in culinary terms it is interchangeable with the mackerels and bonito.

JACKSMELT

(Atherinopsis californiensis)

Description: *Greenish blue fading to silver. Prominent light blue lateral line.*	**Range:** *California coast.*
	Fat Content: *Moderate.*
Size: *½–1½ pounds.*	**Yield:** *80% pan-dressed.*
Season: *Winter and spring.*	**Available Forms:** *Round.*

Jacksmelt is an underrated and underutilized fish. It has mild, fairly firm flesh which pulls away easily from its large bones. Jacksmelt can be marinated in olive oil and herbs and then grilled, baked in sauce, braised as in Braised Mackerel with Tomatoes, Rosemary and Garlic (page 145) or breaded and pan-fried.

JOHN DORY

(Zenopsis spp.)

Other Names: *St. Pierre.*

Description: *Pale silver. Black dot surrounded by a yellow halo.*

Size: *3–6 pounds common.*

Range: *Northern Atlantic. Mediterranean. Western Pacific continental slopes.*

Fat Content: *Moderate.*

Yield: *25% filet.*

Available Forms: *Filet.*

This vertically compressed fish is occasionally available on the West Coast in filet form, and has excellent cooking qualities. Its fine flavor and texture make it suitable for sole recipes.

LINGCOD

(Ophiodon elongatus)

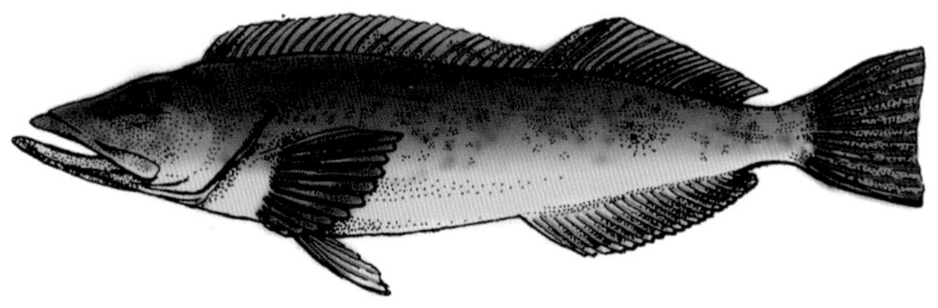

Description: *Variable. Brownish green to vivid blue-green. Dark spots or mottling.*

Size: *3 pounds and up.*

Range: *Baja California to Alaska.*

Season: *All year. Primarily winter.*

Fat Content: *Low.*

Yield: *40% filet.*

Available Forms: *Round, filet, steak, smoked.*

While not a true cod, lingcod is one of the more important food fishes on the West Coast. Several species of the unrelated but similar greenlings (*Hexagrammos* spp.) are also marketed as lingcod, and are interchangeable in cooking characteristics. The lings vary in more than skin color; the flesh of some individuals, especially juveniles, is a bright blue-green although this color disappears with cooking.

The relatively dense flesh of lingcod takes a surprisingly long time to cook. Thinner tail filets are easily grilled or broiled, but thicker pieces are better suited to slower, moist-heat methods. Smaller filets may be used interchangeably with rockfish or cabezon.

Alternatives: *Cod (A,P).*

Baked Lingcod with Tapenade

Tapenade is a pungent Provençal-style spread well suited to mild-flavored fish.

Alternatives: *Angler (A), firmer rockfish* *Serves 4*

1–1½ pounds lingcod filets

Lemon wedges for garnish

Tapenade

4 canned anchovy filets, rinsed and chopped

3 or 4 cloves garlic, peeled

½ cup Niçoise or other black olives, pitted and roughly chopped

1 tablespoon capers

1 teaspoon lemon zest

Black pepper to taste

Preheat oven to 500°.

In a mortar and pestle or blender, mix the anchovies and garlic to a paste, add the olives, capers and lemon zest; blend until smooth, adding a bit of olive oil if necessary. Add black pepper to taste.

Place the lingcod filets skin side down on a piece of aluminum foil large enough to completely enclose them. Spread the top with the *tapenade* and fold over the foil, sealing around the edge. Bake on a sheet pan for 8–12 minutes, or until a skewer poked through the foil easily penetrates the thickest part of the filets. Place the package on a warm platter and slit open the side opposite the seal; the filets can then be slid out of the package complete with the cooking juices. Serve with lemon wedges.

Individual Serving Method

Cut the filet into individual slices or scallops. Place each on a rectangle of parchment or baking paper (available in cookware shops), spread with the *tapenade* and seal the packages. Bake 6–8 minutes. Serve the fish in its packages, allowing each diner to open his own to release its wonderful aroma.

Indonesian Curried Lingcod

This recipe comes from a delightful book, *Indonesian Food and Cookery* by Sri Owen (Prospect Books, London). Indonesian fish curries often combine coconut milk with aromatic spices such as turmeric and coriander, producing more delicate flavors than Indian curries.

Alternatives: *Sculpin, rockfish, sablefish, catfish*

Serves 4 as a main course

2 tablespoons oil

1 tablespoon chopped garlic

4 shallots or *1 large yellow onion, chopped*

1 tablespoon chopped ginger

½ tablespoon dried or *1 blade fresh lemongrass, chopped*

1 teaspoon chile powder

1–2 teaspoons ground coriander

1 teaspoon turmeric

1 tablespoon tamarind paste (page 43) dissolved in 3 tablespoons cold water

1 cup coconut milk (page 39)

1 pound lingcod filets, cut into 1-inch cubes

Mint or cilantro for garnish

Sauté the garlic, shallots and ginger in oil, in a wok or large skillet, until the shallots are translucent. Add lemongrass, chile powder, coriander and turmeric, and sauté the mixture for 2 minutes. Add the tamarind water and coconut milk. Simmer slowly for 2–3 minutes. Add the fish filets. Cook until the fish is done. Garnish with mint or cilantro. Serve over rice.

This dish may be accompanied by Fresh Cilantro Chutney (page 265).

LOBSTER

American Lobster

(Homarus americanus)

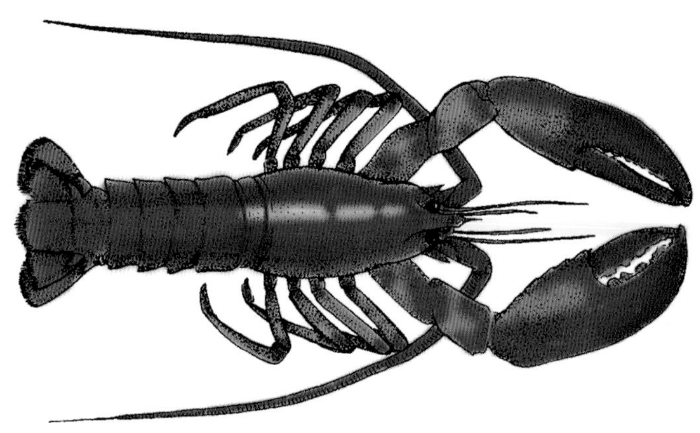

Other Names: *Maine lobster.*

Description: *Orange-red to blue-green with dark mottling. Bright red when cooked.*

Size: *1–5 pounds.*

Range: *New England to southern Canada.*

Season: *All year.*

Fat Content: *Low.*

Yield: *25% meat.*

Available Forms: *Live, picked meat.*

Lobster is the most prized American seafood and one of the most expensive. Due to overfishing, populations have diminished noticeably. Unless current trends are altered (which seems unlikely) or there is a breakthrough in lobster aquaculture, supplies will continue to decrease and prices continue to rise.

The roe of female lobsters, called "coral," is prized as an ingredient in sauces. "Tomalley," the liver and surrounding fat, is found in both sexes and is also delicious.

Traditionally, lobster is boiled, steamed or grilled and served with a range of sauces, often quite rich. It can be made into a deliciously rich soup or bisque such as Crayfish Bisque (page 117) or served cold with various mayonnaises (pages 257–59).

The Chinese stir-fry pieces of lobster tail in black bean sauce, as in Stir-Fried Crab (page 114).

Spiny Lobster

(Panulirus spp.*)*

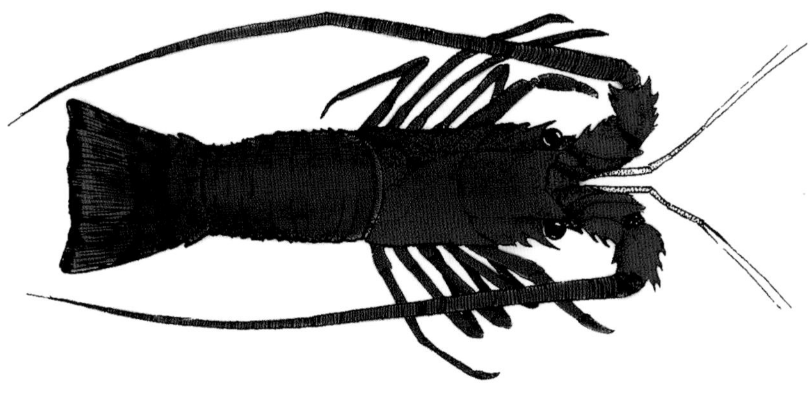

Other Names: *Rock lobster, crayfish, langouste.*

Description: *Similar to the American lobster but with brighter mottling and no claws. Bright red when cooked.*

Size: *1–4 pounds.*

Range: *Warm coastal waters of the world.*

Season: *All year.*

Fat Content: *Low (in meat).*

Yield: *25% meat.*

Available Forms: *Live.*

Spiny lobster makes up the bulk of the frozen lobster market. Many are imported from South Africa and the far Pacific. Lobster tails are usually split and grilled or broiled. They can be boiled in a flavored stock such as Crayfish Boil (page 116). Use in recipes for crayfish or lobster.

PACIFIC MACKEREL

(Scomber japonicus)

Other Names: *Boston mackerel, American mackerel, chub mackerel.*

Description: *Dark blue with wavy black lines above. Silvery green with yellow highlights below.*

Size: *To 2 pounds.*

Range: *Throughout the Pacific.*

Season: *All year. Less abundant in summer.*

Fat Content: *High.*

Yield: *50% filet.*

Available Forms: *Round.*

The ubiquitous mackerels are perhaps our most undervalued family of fish. They have had more bad press down through the years than any other variety, primarily from people who don't like garlic, anchovies, olive oil or other Mediterranean flavors. When truly fresh and prepared with other robust-flavored ingredients, mackerel can be delicious. Of all fish, however, it demands freshness; everything that has been said about old mackerel is true.

Grilling and braising are appropriate cooking methods. Mackerel may also be poached and used in salads, or used in Sashimi (page 245), or Ceviche (page 70). Boned mackerel may be baked in foil with a bread crumb stuffing as in Grilled Stuffed Herring Brochettes (page 133) or Sicilian-Style Stuffing (page 57).

Alternatives: *Any species of Atlantic or Pacific mackerel, jack mackerel, bonito.*

Braised Mackerel with Tomatoes, Rosemary and Garlic

Alternatives: *Jacksmelt, tuna, bonito* *Serves 4*

4 whole mackerel, approximately ½ pound each

2 tablespoons olive oil

½ pound tomatoes, peeled, seeded and chopped

2 teaspoons chopped garlic

1 teaspoon fresh rosemary or *½ teaspoon dried*

¼ cup white wine

Dress the mackerel, leaving the heads on or discarding them as desired. In a skillet with a tight-fitting lid, heat the oil over moderate heat. Add the fish and cook briefly on each side, just until the flesh begins to stiffen. Add the remaining ingredients, cover, and cook until the fish is thoroughly cooked, about 7–10 minutes. Remove the fish, season the sauce to taste, reduce if necessary, and serve over the fish.

Steamed Mackerel with Daikon *and* Wasabi

Alternatives: *Bonito, tuna, any moderate-to-rich fish* *Serves 4*

2 cups grated and peeled daikon *(Japanese white radish, available at Asian groceries)*

1–1½ pounds mackerel filet, skin on

Soy sauce

1 teaspoon wasabi *powder (page 44)*

Squeeze the excess moisture from the *daikon* and drain in a sieve or colander. Cut the fish into serving pieces and marinate in the soy sauce.

Sprinkle the *wasabi* over the *daikon* and combine. Spread this mixture on a plate. Arrange the fish pieces on top of the mixture and steam until the fish is done by the skewer test.

Serve the fish on a bed of *daikon*. If a sauce is desired, make a dipping sauce of a little more *wasabi* dissolved in soy sauce.

Grilled Mackerel with Egg Glaze

Alternatives: *Yellowtail, mahi-mahi, wahoo* *Serves 4*

2 egg yolks

1 teaspoon sherry

1 teaspoon soy sauce

½ teaspoon sugar

1–1½ pounds mackerel filets, skin on

Combine the egg yolks, sherry, soy sauce and sugar. Dip the filets in the egg mixture and grill 2–3 minutes on a side, or until done, basting with the egg mixture. Serve as is or with a dipping sauce made from soy sauce and lemon juice.

MAHI-MAHI

(Coryphaena hippurus)

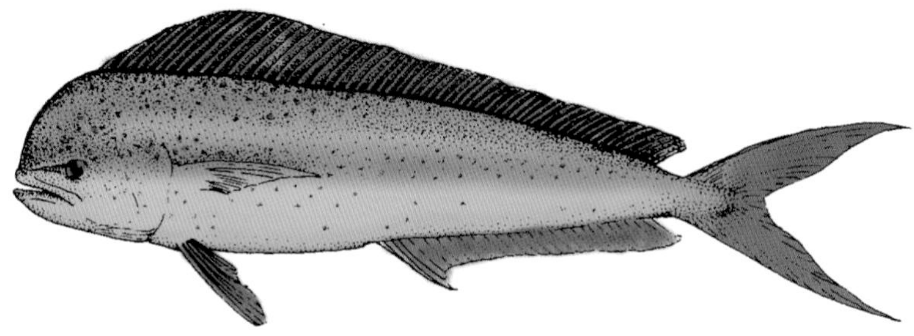

Other Names: *Dolphin, dolphinfish, dorado.*

Description: *Bright blue and green above. Yellow with blue spots below. Yellow tail.*

Size: *13-35 pounds.*

Range: *Warm oceans of the world.*

Season: *Spring-summer, sporadically all year.*

Fat Content: *Moderate.*

Yield: *25% filet.*

Available Forms: *Filet, steak.*

While this fish is properly called a dolphin, in order to avoid confusion with the mammal of the same name the Hawaiian name of mahi-mahi is becoming more widespread. A popular and beautiful game species, it is also available commercially, primarily from the waters of the far Pacific. However, the annual catch is quite small, and considerably more fish are sold than are actually caught; yellowtail and other jacks often make up the difference.

This firm, flavorful fish is best simply grilled or broiled. It really needs no sauce, just a squeeze of lemon or lime.

Alternatives: *Wahoo (A,P).*

MUSSEL

(Mytilus edulis and *M. californianus)*

Other Names: *Blue or bay mussel.*

Description: *Bivalve. Dark blue to black. Smooth shell.*

Size: *12 per pound average.*

Range: *Atlantic coast from central United States to southern Canada. Pacific coast bays.*

Season: *All year in the East. November-April in the West.*

Fat Content: *Low.*

Yield: *40–50% edible portion.*

Available Forms: *Live, shucked in the East, smoked.*

Highly regarded in Europe and generally neglected in this country, mussels are abundant and delicious. They are widely and successfully aquacultured in Europe, and are beginning to be produced in quantity in New England. Mussel culture on both coasts will probably become much more extensive in the near future.

Neither *M. edulis* nor the indigenous California mussel, *M. californianus*, has been widely harvested commercially on the Pacific coast, but they can be easily gathered from rocks at low tide. The California variety grows quite large; only mussels under 3 inches are tender. Both species are quarantined on the Pacific coast during the summer (page 281).

Mussels are generally steamed open when recipes call for shucked mussels; they may also be cooked in the shell. Substitute mussels in recipes for cooked clams or oysters.

To Clean and Debeard Mussels

To clean mussels, first grasp the "beard" (the bundle of fibers protruding from between the shells) and remove it with a quick tug. Check to see that the mussel is alive by twisting the shells against each other along the seam; shells of a live mussel will not slide easily. Discard any open mussels which do not close when handled. Scrub the shells well with a brush or a synthetic scrub pad, and rinse with fresh water. (Note: Mussels will not live as long after cleaning as they will unmolested, so avoid cleaning them before the day when they will be cooked.)

Fried Mussels with Tarator Sauce

Alternatives: *½ pound shucked oysters*

Serves 4 as an appetizer

1½ pounds mussels, cleaned and debearded

All-purpose flour

1 egg, beaten

½ cup fine bread crumbs

Oil for frying

1 recipe Tarator Sauce (page 262)

Steam open and shuck mussels (or shuck them raw); drain well. Dip mussels first in flour, then egg, then roll in bread crumbs. (Mussels may be prepared up to this point several hours in advance and refrigerated.) Fry at 375°. Drain on paper towels. Serve with Tarator Sauce.

Spinach Salad with Mussels and Cream

When mussels are in season, chef and teacher Jeremiah Tower serves them in many imaginative ways at the Santa Fe Bar & Grill in Berkeley and the Balboa Café in San Francisco. This is one of them.

Serves 2

½ pound mussels, cleaned and debearded

¼ cup white wine

¼ cup cream or Crème Fraîche (page 39)

½ pound fresh spinach leaves, washed, with stems removed

Juice of ½ lemon

Salt and pepper to taste

Steam the mussels open. Shuck them, reserving about 1 tablespoon of the juices, and chill. When cold, add the cream to the mussels and soak for several hours or overnight, refrigerated.

Dry the spinach well, taking care not to bruise the leaves. Toss them in a salad bowl with the lemon juice, salt and pepper until evenly moistened. Add the mussels and cream and toss until all the leaves are well coated.

Arrange on chilled plates, largest leaves on the bottom, with mussels in a circle on top.

Warm Spinach Salad with Mussels, Ginger and Garlic

Serves 2

½ pound fresh spinach leaves, washed, with stems removed

1 tablespoon lemon juice

Salt and pepper to taste

¾ pound mussels, cleaned and debearded

3 tablespoons olive oil

1 teaspoon chopped ginger

1 teaspoon chopped garlic

Dry the spinach leaves and toss them in a salad bowl with the lemon juice, salt and pepper until evenly moistened.

Steam and shuck the mussels. Heat the oil in a skillet; add the mussels, ginger and garlic and sauté gently, but do not brown. Pour the oil over the spinach and toss immediately, until the leaves are wilted but not cooked. Serve on warm plates.

Broiled Stuffed Mussels

Serves 4 as an appetizer

1 pound mussels, cleaned and debearded

¼ cup dry white wine

¼ cup bread crumbs

¼ cup grated Parmesan cheese

1 tablespoon chopped garlic

1 tablespoon melted butter

1 tablespoon chopped parsley

½ teaspoon black pepper

Lemon wedges for garnish

Preheat the broiler. Steam the mussels open in white wine in a heavy saucepan. Shuck the mussels and return them to half-shells. Combine the remaining ingredients and pack this mixture loosely into the shells on top of the mussels. Broil until the stuffing begins to brown, about 3–5 minutes. Serve with lemon wedges and pass Tabasco or another hot pepper sauce if desired.

Steamed Mussels with White Wine and Shallots

Moules Marinière

Serves 4 as an appetizer *Serves 2 as a main course*

2 pounds mussels, cleaned and debearded

1 tablespoon chopped shallots

1 tablespoon chopped parsley

¼ cup dry white wine

Black pepper to taste

Combine all the ingredients in a heavy saucepan with a tight lid and bring to a boil. Steam the mussels until open, about 3–5 minutes. Serve in soup bowls with the liquid along with plenty of French bread to soak up the broth.

Steamed Mussels with Tomato, Garlic and White Wine

Serves 4 as an appetizer *Serves 2 as a main course*

1 tablespoon olive oil

1 tablespoon chopped garlic

1 tablespoon chopped shallots

½ pound tomatoes, peeled, seeded and chopped or *½ small can tomatoes, chopped*

2 pounds mussels, cleaned and debearded

1 tablespoon fresh herbs—parsley, thyme, basil

¼ cup dry white wine

Black pepper

Rouille (page 261)

In a heavy saucepan large enough to hold the mussels, sauté garlic, shallots and tomatoes in oil until soft. Add mussels, herbs, wine and pepper. Steam until mussels open, 3–5 minutes.

Serve as a soup with French bread and a garlicky mayonnaise such as *rouille*.

Rice Pilaf with Mussels

Serves 3–4

1 tablespoon oil

1 tablespoon chopped garlic

1 tablespoon chopped shallots

1 teaspoon paprika

1 cup white rice

2 cups chicken stock or mild fish stock, lightly salted

Salt to taste

Zest of 1 lemon (optional)

2 pounds mussels, cleaned and debearded

Chopped parsley for garnish

Sauté the garlic, shallots and paprika in oil in a large shallow casserole with a tight-fitting lid; do not brown. Add the rice and sauté until it begins to color. Add the stock, salt and lemon zest; cover, bring to a boil and reduce heat. Cook until the liquid is almost absorbed, about 15 minutes. Add the mussels, replace cover and cook another 5 minutes or so until mussels open. Garnish with chopped parsley.

OCTOPUS

(Octopus spp.*)*

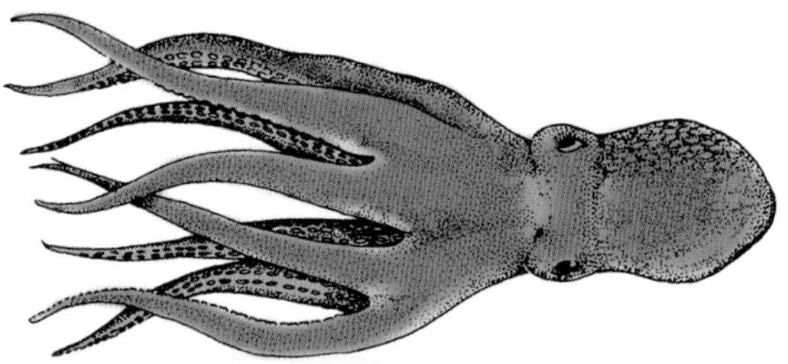

Other Names: *Devilfish, pulpo.*

Description: *Variegated orange to purple skin.*

Size: O. punctatus—*15-50 pounds,* O. binoculatus—*to 5 pounds. Smaller sizes more desirable.*

Range: *Temperate and tropical oceans of the world.*

Season: *All year.*

Fat Content: *Low.*

Yield: *80% meat from smaller species.*

Available Forms: *Whole or piece, fresh or cooked.*

Like squid, octopus is a cephalopod. Unlike squid, it requires tenderizing or long, slow cooking.

Octopus is delicious in tomato-based stews, and should be simmered for 20-25 minutes before it is added to the pot. It can be grilled after tenderizing and served with Lemon-Garlic Butter (page 255) or just a squeeze of lemon, or basted with Teriyaki Sauce (page 264) and grilled.

Stewed Octopus with Fennel

Serves 4

1–1½ pounds octopus, tentacles and body

1 tablespoon olive oil

1 large yellow onion, julienned

2 tablespoons chopped garlic

1 cup fennel bulb, sliced ½ inch thick crosswise

½ cup white wine

2 tablespoons chopped parsley

2 canned anchovy filets, roughly chopped

Cut octopus tentacles and body into ½-inch slices or strips. Blanch in salted water for 5 minutes and allow to cool in liquid, then drain.

Sauté onion, garlic and fennel in oil in a casserole or large saucepan until soft; do not brown. Add octopus, wine, parsley and anchovy; cover and simmer for 30 minutes or longer. Serve in soup bowls with French bread.

OYSTER

Pacific Oyster

(Crassostrea gigas)

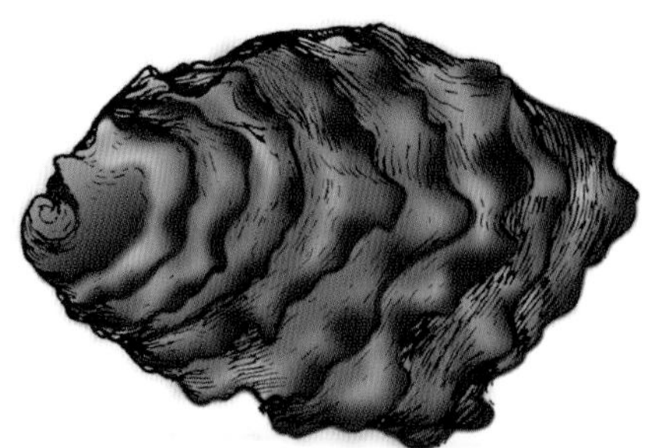

Other Names: *Japanese oyster.*

Description: *Bivalve. Elongated, thin shell.*

Size: *2½ inches and up.*

Range: *Pacific coast.*

Season: *All year.*

Fat Content: *Low.*

Available Forms: *Live, shucked, smoked.*

Eastern Oyster

(Crassostrea virginica)

Other Names: *Blue point, Cape Cod, Apalachicola, Chesapeake.*

Description: *Bivalve. Thick and slightly elongated shell with a deep cup.*

Size: *About 3 inches, ideal for the half-shell.*

Range: *Atlantic coast and the Gulf of Mexico.*

Season: *All year.*

Fat Content: *Low.*

Available Forms: *Live, shucked.*

Belon

(Ostrea edulis)

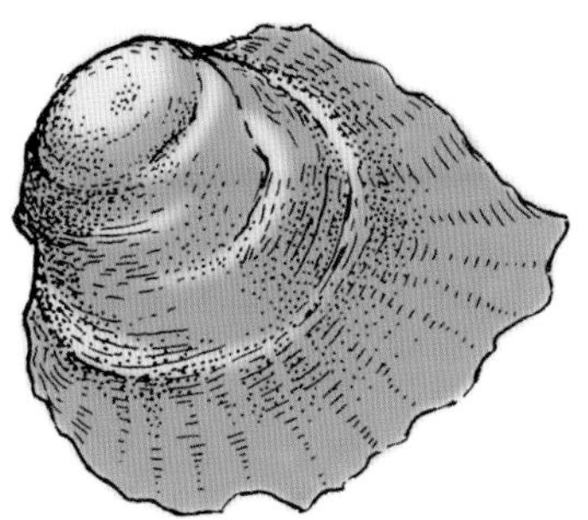

Other Names: *Plate oyster.*

Description: *Bivalve. Flat. Often almost perfectly circular, thin shell.*

Size: *1½–3½ inches.*

Range: *Aquacultured in Moss Landing and Tomales Bay in California, Washington and Maine. Indigenous to France.*

Season: *All year.*

Fat Content: *Low.*

Available Forms: *Live.*

This oyster has a slightly metallic taste. It is delicate and tender, ideal for the half-shell.

Olympia

(Ostrea lurida)

This indigenous western oyster has been over-harvested; whole oysters are available only in Washington state. Shucked Olympia oysters can occasionally be found in West Coast markets.

Oysters vary considerably in taste and appearance according to where they are grown. Blue Point, Cape Cod, Apalachicola and Chesapeake are, in fact, all *Crassostrea virginica*; they vary from bland and tender to salty and firm, according to water temperature, water composition and growing techniques. (For a detailed account of oyster aquaculture in California, see "The California Oyster Story," page 278.)

Oysters spawn in the summer months (the months without an "r") when they tend to be fatty and less desirable for the half-shell. Summer oysters do have more protein, however.

Store oysters cup side down, covered with a damp towel and refrigerated. Never cover oysters with water.

For most oyster lovers, the best way to enjoy them is raw, on the half-shell. We agree for all but the large Pacific oysters, which we prefer cooked. When selecting oysters, the size of the cup is the best indication of the size of the meat.

Oysters can be prepared by a number of methods. Oysters in the shell can be steamed, baked or grilled. Shucked oysters can be stewed, battered and fried, sautéed or skewered and grilled. Several classic preparations such as oysters Rockefeller involve baking them on the half-shell.

The liquid in which oysters have been cooked is called "liquor" and is often used to enrich sauces.

To Shuck an Oyster

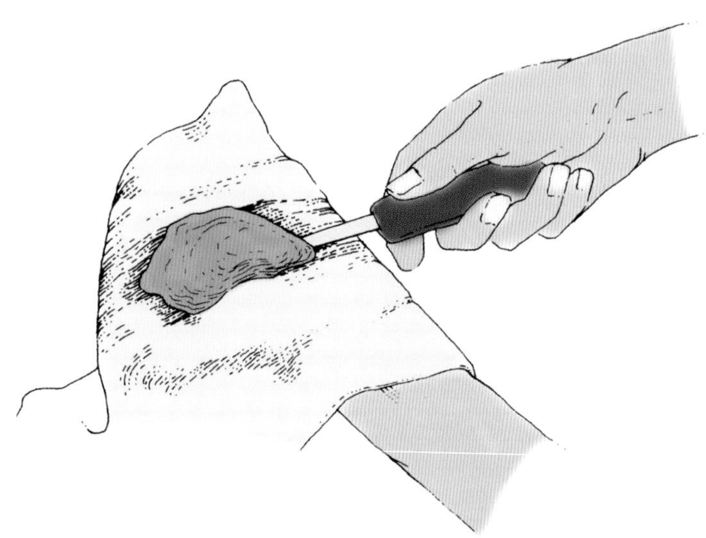

1 Hold the oyster cup side down, using several thicknesses of folded toweling or a potholder to protect your hand. Place the tip of an *oyster knife* (page 18) between the heels of the shells near the hinge, and pry upward. The shell will release with a pop.

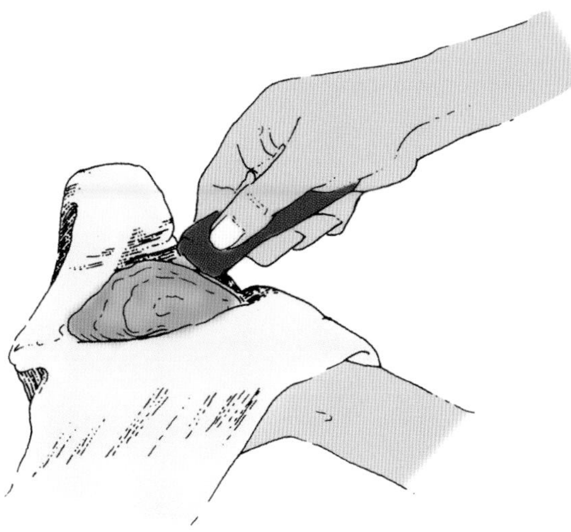

2 Slide the knife in along the top shell, being careful not to puncture the oyster. Sever the connector muscle, which is generally about two-thirds of the way from the hinge to the end, and remove the top shell.

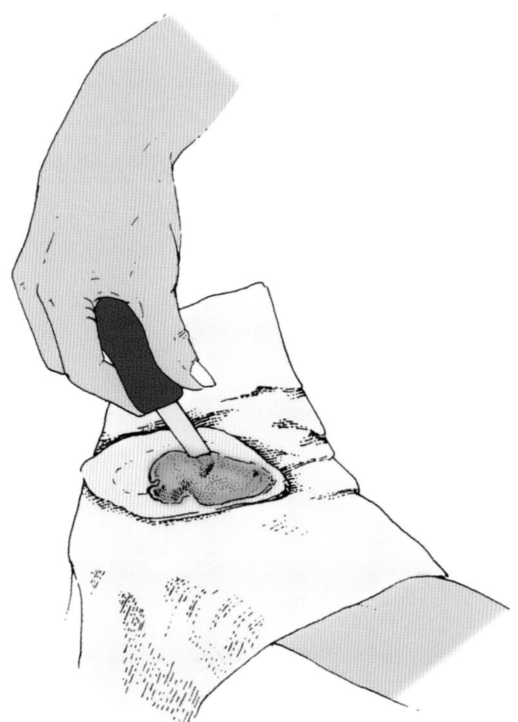

3 Slide the knife under the oyster and sever the bottom muscle. The oyster should now slide around freely in the shell.

4 For certain oysters (especially the Japanese or Pacific variety grown by the cultchless method) that have fragile shells and tend to break at the heel when the above shucking method is used: Find the seam between the shells along the right-hand side; gently slide the tip of the knife between the shells; with a back-and-forth rocking action, work the knife in toward the muscle; proceed as above once the muscle has been reached.

Oysters on the Half-Shell

Shuck oysters, allowing 6 per person for an appetizer. Serve the oysters on the half-shell with a little lemon juice or with Sauce Mignonette (page 263) or Green Chile Sauce (page 264) made with shallots instead of garlic.

Barbecued Oysters

Oysters do not need elaborate preparation. They can be barbecued in their shells with a delicious result. Grill the oysters, cup side down, so they cook in their own juice. Don't turn them during cooking. They are done when the shells pop open, about 8 minutes. Serve the oysters on the half-shell with any of the following sauces: Beurre Blanc (page 253); Green Chile Sauce (page 264); Fresh Tomato Salsa (page 262); Lemon-Garlic Butter (page 255); Fresh Cilantro Chutney (page 265).

Oysters Bienville

William Marinelli

William Marinelli, a marine biologist and oyster enthusiast, provided the following three recipes as well as most of the information on oyster culture.

Serves 4

24 oysters in the shell	*2 teaspoons curry powder*
1½ cups Fumet (page 252)	*Juice of 1 lemon*
¼ cup olive oil	*Salt to taste*
¼ cup all-purpose flour	*Cayenne to taste*

Preheat the broiler. Scrub the oysters to remove sand and grit.

Steam oysters in a little *fumet* until the shells open. Remove the top shells. Reserve the steaming liquid.

Heat the oil in a heavy saucepan. Add the flour a tablespoon at a time, whisking to combine the oil. When all the flour is added, you should have a thin paste. Add the curry powder and cook over low heat for 3–4 minutes. Do not brown the *roux*. Add the *fumet* and steaming liquid, whisking to form a smooth sauce. Simmer slowly for 5 minutes, add the lemon juice and remove from the heat. Season to taste with salt and cayenne.

Spoon 1 tablespoon of sauce over each oyster. Broil the oysters until heated through, 3–5 minutes. Serve immediately.

Oysters with Pasta

William Marinelli

Serves 4

24 oysters in the shell
Dry white wine
1 tablespoon chopped garlic
4 tablespoons butter
Juice of 1 lemon
1 pound fresh or dry pasta, such as fettucine or linguine
Chopped parsley
Grated Parmesan cheese

Scrub oysters to remove sand and grit. Place them in a steamer or heavy pot. Steam the oysters in about ½ inch of white wine until they open, approximately 10 minutes. Set them aside.

Strain the remaining liquid through cheesecloth or a coffee filter. Return the liquid to the pot, add the garlic, butter and lemon juice, and reduce by two thirds.

Cook and drain the pasta. Reheat oysters in the sauce, arrange oysters on the noodles and pour the sauce over the noodles. Sprinkle with parsley and cheese.

Stewed Oysters with Vegetables

William Marinelli

Serves 4

1 pint shucked oysters, with liquor

½ cup milk

1 teaspoon lemon juice

¼ teaspoon cayenne

¼ cup olive oil

½ cup onions

1 tablespoon chopped garlic

¼ cup finely diced carrots

½ cup finely diced celery

½ cup finely diced mushrooms

¼ cup grated Parmesan cheese

2 tablespoons chopped parsley

Marinate the oysters in the milk, lemon juice and cayenne for 30 minutes.

In a skillet large enough to hold all the ingredients, sauté the onions and garlic in the olive oil until the onions are soft. Add the carrots and celery. When the carrots are nearly cooked, add the mushrooms. Cook briefly, then add the oysters and their marinade. Cook over medium heat for 3–5 minutes, depending on the size of the oysters.

Serve over pasta or rice, garnished with Parmesan cheese and parsley.

Oyster Loaf

This recipe is a popular entrée at the Gulf coast Oyster Bar in Oakland, which features seafood flown in from the Gulf and prepared in the cooking styles of New Orleans. In Louisiana this sandwich is also called an Oyster Po' Boy.

Serves 4

24 small oysters, shucked

Milk to cover (about 1 cup)

2 teaspoons Pernod or *other anise liquor*

Oil for frying

Zatarain's Fish Fry (available in many gourmet shops) or *fine cornmeal*

1 loaf French bread, cut in half lengthwise and hollowed out so that little more than crust remains

2 cups shredded romaine

½ cup Creole Mayonnaise (page 258)

Marinate the oysters in milk and Pernod for at least 30 minutes. Drain the oysters and pat dry.

Heat the oil to 375° in a wok or large pot. Coat the oysters with Fish Fry or cornmeal. Fry them in oil until they are golden brown. Drain on paper towels. While the oysters are cooking, toast the French bread. To make a sandwich, moisten both halves of the bread with mayonnaise. Cover one half with shredded romaine and the other half with the oysters. Cut the sandwich into quarters and serve while the oysters are still hot.

Broiled Eggplant Stuffed with Oysters

This dish is rich and satisfying, though not as caloric as it tastes. It can be served hot or warm.

Serves 8 as an appetizer *Serves 4 as a main course*

2 large eggplants

4 tablespoons oil

2 medium yellow onions, chopped

2–3 tablespoons chopped garlic

1 cup bread crumbs

¼ cup chopped parsley

1 teaspoon fresh thyme or *other herbs*

1 pound shucked oysters

½ cup grated Parmesan cheese

Cayenne to taste

Juice of 1 lemon

Slice the eggplants in half lengthwise. Broil them until soft, 8–10 minutes. Remove the pulp with a spoon without cutting through the skin. Cut the pulp into 1-inch dice.

In a large skillet, sauté the onions and garlic in oil until soft. Add the eggplant pulp, bread crumbs, parsley, thyme and oysters. Stir and cook for 1 minute. Remove from heat and add cheese, cayenne and lemon juice.

Preheat the broiler. Fill each eggplant half with a generous amount of the stuffing. Broil until the bread crumbs brown, about 5 minutes.

Oyster Stuffing for Fish

Use this stuffing for large, boneless pieces of firm fish, such as grouper, boned sections of large fish, or small whole fish such as pan-sized salmon.

Yield: About 1½ cups

1 tablespoon butter or oil
1 teaspoon chopped garlic
1 scallion, finely chopped
½ pint shucked oysters, with liquor
¼ cup bread crumbs
2 teaspoons chopped parsley

Sauté garlic and scallion in butter until cooked. If using small oysters such as Olympias, add them whole; otherwise, chop the oysters into ½-inch or smaller pieces and add them with their liquor. Add the bread crumbs and parsley and cook gently until the liquid is absorbed. Season to taste. Allow to cool before stuffing fish.

PERIWINKLE

(Family *Littorinidae)*

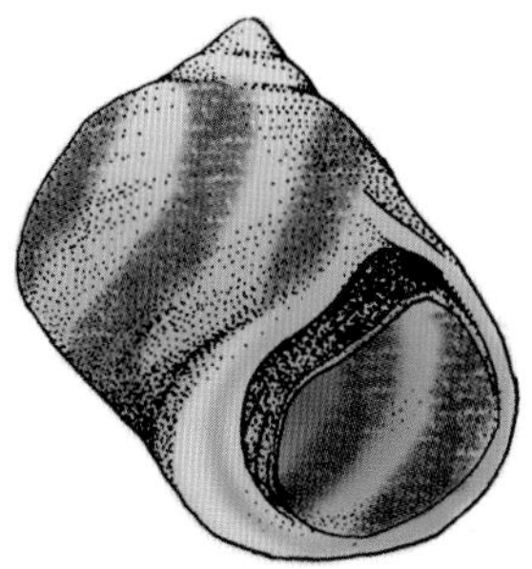

Description: *Univalve. Small, grey. Usually found in large colonies.*

Size: *½ inch and up.*

Range: *Some species exist along all the coast of the United States.*

Season: *All year. Abundant in summer months.*

Fat Content: *Low.*

Available Forms: *Live.*

Periwinkles are popular here primarily among Italian and Asian communities. They will probably become better known as beachcombers seeking mussels and clams discover the culinary possibilities of these abundant shellfish.

Scrub the shells to remove sand and grit. Boil in salted water for 10 minutes or until the operculum (plastic-like shield covering the open end) opens. The meat can be removed with a toothpick or, better still, an unfolded paper clip. Dip periwinkles in Lemon-Garlic Butter (page 255) or Aioli (page 260). Or, substitute boiled periwinkles for steamed clams in Clams in Black Bean Sauce (page 92).

REDFISH

(Sciaenops ocellata)

Other Names: *Red drum, channel bass, red bass.*

Description: *Metallic rosy gold fading to silver. Large scales. Red pectoral fins. One or more black spots on tail.*

Size: *3–10 pounds. Smaller fish more desirable.*

Range: *Southern Atlantic and Gulf coasts.*

Season: *All year. Most common warmer months.*

Fat Content: *Low.*

Yield: *33% filet.*

Available Forms: *Round, filet.*

This mainstay of New Orleans fish cookery is a member of the croaker family which also includes the white seabass and corbina. As Louisiana-style restaurants become more popular in other parts of the country, including California, redfish and other Gulf specialties are being more widely distributed.

Use redfish interchangeably with striped bass, white seabass, corbina and sea trout. Broiled or grilled redfish filets are delicious with Red Hollandaise Sauce (page 256) or oyster sauce (see Seabass with Oyster Sauce, page 198).

RED SNAPPER

(Lutjanus campechanus)

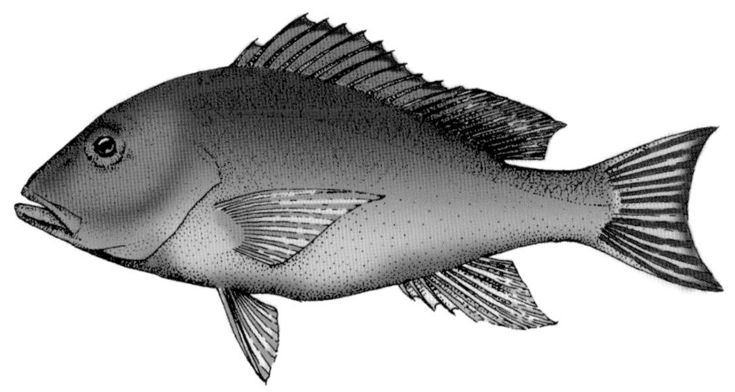

Description: *Vivid rose-pink fading to pink. Bright red eyes.*	**Season:** *All year. Especially summer.*
Size: *2–30 pounds.*	**Fat Content:** *Low.*
Range: *Mid-Atlantic to Gulf of Mexico and Caribbean. Also, the western Pacific.*	**Yield:** *33% filet.*
	Available Forms: *Round, filet.*

The fact that a wide range of Pacific rockfishes have been marketed as "red snapper" is a testament to the quality of this fish. Several other species of *Lutjanus,* including the grey and blackfin snappers, are caught commercially, but red snapper is the most valuable and desirable. Eastern snapper is occasionally available on the West Coast at a premium price; to distinguish it from the local pretenders, it is likely to be labeled "true red snapper." California regulations will probably continue to allow certain rockfish species to be sold as "Pacific snapper," but "red snapper" should refer only to the real thing.

This versatile and delicious fish is suitable to any cooking method. Most classic recipes from the Gulf and Caribbean regions calling for a firm white fish were originally developed for this species.

Alternatives: *Grouper (A,G,P), black sea bass (A), striped bass (A,P), fancy rockfish.*

ROCKFISH

(Sebastes spp.*)*

Other Names: *Rock cod, Pacific snapper, "red snapper."*

Range: *Southern California to Alaska.*

Season: *All year.*

Fat Content: *Low.*

Yield: *30–40% filet, depending on size and body shape.*

Available Forms: *Round, filet.*

The rockfishes are the largest and the most common family of Pacific coast food fishes; they are also one of the most varied and confusing. In terms of cooking quality, they may be grouped into four categories as represented below, beginning with the choicest species.

Without carrying a technical field guide in the market, you can use a few guidelines in judging an unfamiliar rockfish. The best general indicator of quality is the overall shape: the deeper-bodied species tend to have firmer and better-flavored flesh than the more elongated species. This is not to say that bocaccio, for instance, is an undesirable fish, simply that its milder flavor and softer flesh is not appropriate to certain cooking methods.

There is also a strong correlation between quality and price. Chinese fish markets often display half a dozen species, the most expensive being three times the price of the cheapest. (Incidentally, the more choice species tend to be "loners" rather than school fish, which adds to their market price.)

Rockfish in the first two categories are excellent and suitable for virtually any cooking method. Their flesh is firm enough to approach real snapper in both flavor and texture. These varieties are definitely superior for Chinese recipes for steamed or fried whole fish. Where a recipe or alternative calls for "fancy rockfish," choose one from these two categories.

Yellowtails, blues and blacks are fairly common in the market. Their flesh is firm enough for fileting and grilling, but slightly less flavorful than the fancy varieties. Filets of bocaccio and its equivalents, however, are difficult to handle as they tend to fall apart easily. For these varieties, baking whole fish in a sauce and other moist-heat methods are preferable to grilling or sautéing; filets may also be broiled with a compound butter, as in Broiled Sablefish with Anchovy Butter (page 183).

Bolina

(S. auriculatus)

Other Names: *Brown rockfish, sand bass.*

Description: *Brown, mottled with orange-brown.*

Size: *To 5 pounds.*

Similar Species: *Gopher rockfish* (S. carnatus), *copper or barriga* (S. caurinus), *China* (S. nebulosus).

Goldeneye Rockfish

(S. ruberrimus)

Other Names: *Yelloweye, turkey red rockfish.*

Description: *Bright pink, black tips on fins. Yellow eye.*

Size: *To 10 pounds.*

Similar Species: *Flag or tree* (S. rubrivinctus), *canary or fantail rockfish* (S. pinniger).

Yellowtail Rockfish

(S. flavidus)

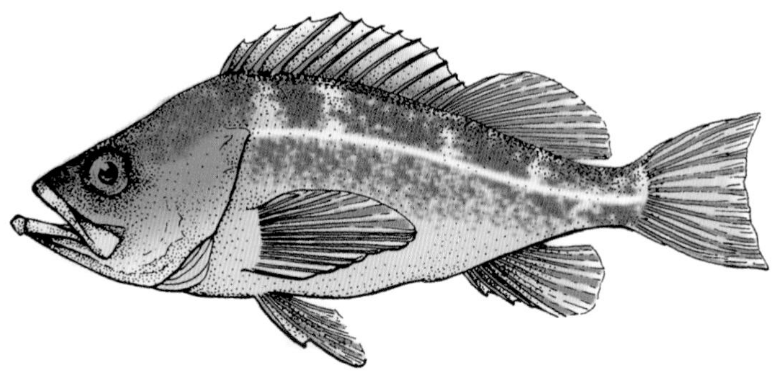

Description: *Olivaceous to brown. Bright yellow fins and tail.*

Size: *1–4 pounds.*

Similar Species: *Black* (S. melanops), *blue* (S. mystinus), *vermillion* (S miniatus).

Bocaccio

(S. paucispinis)

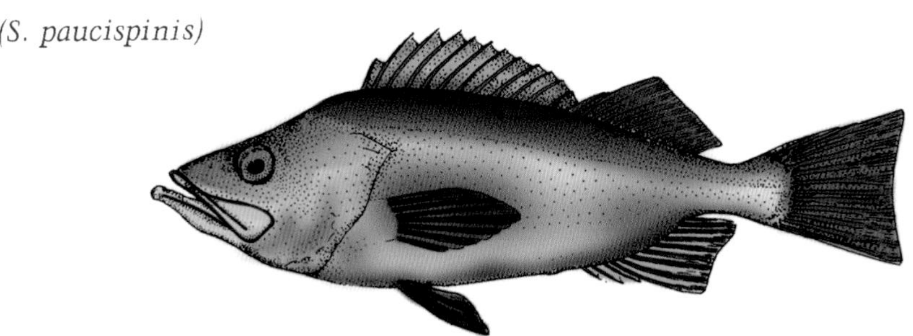

Description: *Dusky red fading to pinkish. Mouth opens above eye.*

Size: *1–20 pounds (mostly under 5 pounds).*

Similar Species: *Chilipepper* (S. goodei), *widow* (S. entomelas), *shortbelly* (S. jordani), *strawberry* (S. elongatus).

Baked Rockfish Veracruz Style

Huachinango á la Veracruzana is perhaps Mexico's most famous seafood dish. Around the Gulf of Mexico it is made with red snapper. On the West Coast, snapper is an expensive luxury, but the local rockfish makes a more than adequate substitute. In fact, any firm-fleshed white fish will do. Instructions are given below both for dressed fish and filets.

Serves 4

1 4–5-pound rockfish (yellowtail or better), dressed, or *2 smaller fish* or *1½-2 pounds filets*

Juice of 1 lemon or *lime*

Salt

2 tablespoons olive oil

1 medium onion, julienned

1 bell pepper, julienned

1 tablespoon chopped garlic

2 medium tomatoes, peeled, seeded and roughly chopped or *1 small can peeled tomatoes*

¼ cup sliced green olives

1 tablespoon capers

*1 or 2 pickled chile peppers (*jalapeños *or* serranos en escabeche, *available canned at Latin American groceries)*

Preheat oven to 450°.

Sprinkle fish with lemon or lime juice and salt, and set aside. Sauté onion, pepper, garlic and tomatoes in olive oil until just softened; do not brown. (If using canned tomatoes, add them after the onion and pepper are soft.) Simmer sauce until most of the liquid is evaporated.

For whole fish: place fish in an oiled deep baking pan. Pour the sauce over the fish and scatter the olives, capers and chiles on top. Cover the pan with a tight-fitting lid or foil and bake 10 minutes to the inch, or until flesh flakes easily from the tail. Serve with the accumulated sauce from the pan.

For filets: cut into individual portions, place on squares of foil or baking paper as for Baked Lingcod with Tapenade (page 140), top with sauce, olives, capers and chiles, seal edges and bake 8–10 minutes.

Grilled Rockfish Yúcatan Style

This is the traditional treatment for grilled fish in the Yúcatan. There, it is typically used for *cazón* (a small dogfish), but it is well suited to any type of shark as well as rockfish.

Alternatives: *Shark* *Serves 4*

1 tablespoon achiote *(page 36)*

¼ teaspoon black peppercorns

¼ teaspoon oregano

¼ teaspoon cumin, whole

2–3 cloves garlic, peeled

½ teaspoon paprika

Pinch cayenne

Juice of: 1 lemon, 1 lime, 1 orange and 1 small grapefruit

1½ pounds rockfish filet (yellowtail or better)

Grind the whole spices in a spice grinder. Transfer them to a blender jar, add the remaining ingredients and blend to a smooth paste. Spread the paste on the filets and set aside for several hours to season.

Grill the fish until just done. Serve with lemon or lime wedges and rice. Or, serve with warm tortillas, Black Bean Paste (next page) and Fresh Tomato Salsa (page 262), letting each person make tacos.

Black Bean Paste

This bean paste is appropriate for any seafood or other burrito.

½ pound black (turtle) beans

5 cups water

½ onion, peeled and stuck with a few cloves

A few ounces bacon or *ham trimmings, pork rind* or *a pork bone*

½ teaspoon dried summer savory, or *a large sprig of fresh*

2–3 small dried chiles or *1 large dried chile such as* ancho

Salt to taste

2–3 tablespoons chicken or *duck fat* or *lard*

Check the beans for pebbles or other foreign objects. In a large heavy saucepan or casserole, cover the beans by at least an inch with water. Add the remaining ingredients except the salt and fat. Bring to a boil, cover and reduce heat. Simmer until the beans are fully cooked, adding more water if necessary to prevent them from drying out. Season to taste. (Beans may be prepared to this point a day or two ahead and refrigerated.)

Purée the beans, together with their broth, through a food mill or in a blender or food processor. (Use care if blending hot beans.) Heat the fat in a large skillet and fry the bean mixture, stirring to prevent sticking, until a thick paste is formed.

Hot Pickled Rockfish

Pescado en Escabeche

Alternatives: *Any firm white-fleshed fish* *Serves 6–8 as an appetizer*

1 pound rockfish filet (yellowtail or better) at room temperature

Salt

Juice of 1 lemon or *lime*

1 teaspoon black peppercorns

½ teaspoon coriander seed

½ teaspoon cumin seed

2 cloves or *¼ teaspoon ground cloves*

2 allspice or *¼ teaspoon allspice powder*

12 cloves garlic, peeled

½ cup wine vinegar

½ cup water

¼ teaspoon cinnamon

½ teaspoon oregano

1 or 2 bay leaves

1-2 teaspoons salt

½ teaspoon sugar

1 red onion, sliced thin for garnish

Season the filets with salt and lemon or lime juice and set aside. Grind the whole spices in a blender or spice grinder. Press two of the cloves of garlic into a skillet; add the ground spices, water and vinegar and bring to a boil. Add the remaining ingredients and simmer for a few minutes.

Slice the fish into bite-size pieces. Arrange them in a serving dish, and pour over the vinegar mixture. The heat of the liquid should be enough to cook the fish.

Serve warm or cold, garnished with red onion slices.

Steamed Rockfish with Fresh Herbs

Bruce Cost

This is a variation on the classic Cantonese approach to whole fish. Use the best rockfish available.

Alternatives: *Small striped bass (A,P), snapper (A,G), black sea bass (A)*

Serves 3–4 as a main course

2½–3-pound fancy rockfish, cleaned, with head on

⅓ cup oil

⅓ cup finely shredded ginger

1 cup finely shredded scallions

⅓ cup finely shredded red or *green peppers* or *mild chile peppers such as Anaheim*

1 cup chicken stock

Salt to taste

½ teaspoon white pepper

1 tablespoon cornstarch dissolved in ¼ cup water

Cilantro for garnish

Rinse and dry the fish.

Steam it on a plate for 15–20 minutes (page 64) or until the thickest part is easily pierced with a skewer. Transfer the fish to a warm serving platter. Meanwhile, heat the oil in a saucepan to near smoking. Scatter the ginger, half the scallions and half the peppers over the fish. Start the stock boiling. When the oil is hot, pour it over the fish. Add salt and pepper to the stock and thicken it with the cornstarch mixture. Pour the sauce over the fish. Scatter the rest of the vegetables on top. Garnish with cilantro and serve.

Seafood Hot Pot with Fish Balls

This dish takes its name from its method of presentation. A large pot of seafood, noodles and vegetables is kept warm at the table as each diner helps himself to several servings in small rice bowls. In Chinese restaurants it is served in a vessel known as a fire pot or hot pot, but a large chafing dish or fondue pot will do.

Serves 10 or more as a side dish *Serves 6 as a main course*

3 quarts rich chicken stock (reduce regular chicken stock by half)

18 or so Fish Balls (below)

½ pound Chinese cabbage, chopped

¼ pound transparent Chinese vermicelli (available in Asian groceries)

½ pound medium or large shrimp, peeled

½ pound sea scallops

½ pound shucked oysters, with their liquor

¼ cup cilantro

Bring the chicken stock to a boil in a pot large enough to hold all the ingredients. Add the fish balls and cabbage and cook for about 5 minutes. Add the rest of the ingredients and cook until the shellfish are done, about 3 minutes longer.

Transfer the seafood and liquid to a preheated hot pot or fondue dish. Garnish with cilantro. Serve in bowls and pass soy sauce, white vinegar and a hot sauce such as Chinese hot chili oil or Tabasco sauce.

Fish Balls

Inexpensive varieties of rockfish are often used to make Chinese-style fish balls.

1 pound rockfish filet	*1 teaspoon grated ginger*
4–6 tablespoons ice water	

Grind the fish filets with a meat grinder or chop them by hand until you have a smooth, thick paste. Add the ice water a tablespoon at a time and then mix in the ginger.

Fill a small bowl with ice water. Form the paste into balls about 1½ inches in diameter, dipping your fingers into the water frequently. (The moisture keeps the fish from sticking to your fingers and the cool temperature helps the balls stick together.)

Refrigerate the fish balls for at least 1 hour so they will hold together during cooking.

California "Bouillabaisse"

Since rockfish is so plentiful, cheap and easy to filet (the bones and head are good for stock, too), it is the logical base for a California fisherman's stew. However, many other varieties of fish can be used (page 180).

Of all seafood dishes, none has as many "authentic" versions, each with its own loyal followers, as that Mediterranean standby, bouillabaisse. Rather than enter the debate, we have qualified our version both with quotation marks and the California appellation, so no enraged Marseillais can accuse us of putting forth a bastard version of his favorite dish. Besides, we think it's pretty good.

A variety of saltwater fish is one key to a good bouillabaisse. Bear in mind that this dish, like all fisherman's stews, began as a way of cooking the day's catch. Don't be afraid to improvise, or to throw in some of the stranger varieties in the fish market. A few guidelines, however, are in order:

A variety of textures is desirable. For example, combine a firm, coarse-fleshed fish such as rockfish with a finer-textured flounder or sole and a dense, meaty-textured angler or shark.

Strongly flavored fish such as mackerel will easily dominate the dish. Use them sparingly if at all. On the other hand, the robust tomato and garlic flavors of the broth will do nothing for more fine-flavored fish such as salmon or snapper.

Shellfish add flavor and texture variety as well as color. Mussels, clams and even shrimp and crab would be welcome additions.

Serves 6

2 tablespoons olive oil

½ cup diced leek tops or *scallion tops* or *yellow onion*

4–6 cloves garlic, chopped

¼ cup chopped fennel leaves or *¼ teaspoon fennel seeds*

2 pounds ripe tomatoes, chopped, or *1 large can tomatoes, drained*

2 quarts water

2–3 pounds fish heads and bones, well rinsed

2-inch strip of orange peel

Pinch of saffron

Bouquet garni *of celery, thyme, bay, parsley and marjoram* or *oregano*

1–1½ pounds boneless fish and shellfish (see above suggestions)

½ cup Rouille (page 261)

In a large kettle or stockpot, heat the oil and gently sauté the leek tops, garlic and fennel without browning. Add the tomatoes (juice, seeds and all), stir and cook a few minutes to evaporate some of the liquid. Add the fish heads and bones and water, bring to a boil, reduce heat and skim any scum from the surface. Add the orange peel, saffron and *bouquet garni* and simmer 45 minutes. Strain the liquid, discard the bones and vegetables and return the stock to the pot.

Add the fish and shellfish to the simmering stock in the order of their required cooking times: 8–10 minutes for clams in the shell or uncooked crab; 6 minutes or so for dense fish such as angler; 4–5 minutes for mussels, most other fish and cooked crab; and about 3 minutes for thin filets of flatfish.

Serve in shallow bowls with French bread, stirring in *rouille* to taste.

Baked Stuffed Rockfish

Alternatives: *Speckled trout, small snapper (A,G) or grouper (A,G,P)*

Serves 3–4 as a main course

4 tablespoons olive oil

1 green bell pepper, chopped

1 medium yellow onion, chopped

2 serrano *or other fresh hot chiles, chopped*

2 tablespoons chopped garlic

3 tomatoes, peeled, seeded and chopped or *1 cup canned tomatoes*

¼ cup cilantro

1–1½ cups cooked white or *brown rice*

Salt and pepper to taste

1 2½–3-pound rockfish (yellowtail or comparable species), dressed or boned

Lemon wedges for garnish

Preheat oven to 400°.

Sauté the bell pepper, onion, chiles and garlic in olive oil. When the onion is translucent, add the tomatoes and cilantro. Cook another minute, combine with rice and season to taste with salt and pepper. Transfer the stuffing to a bowl to cool.

Stuff the body and head of the fish. Wrap it in foil and seal carefully. Bake for 25–30 minutes, or until done by the skewer test. Remove the stuffing from the fish. Arrange on a tray with the fish in the center, surrounded by the stuffing and the lemon wedges.

SABLEFISH

(Anoplopoma fimbria)

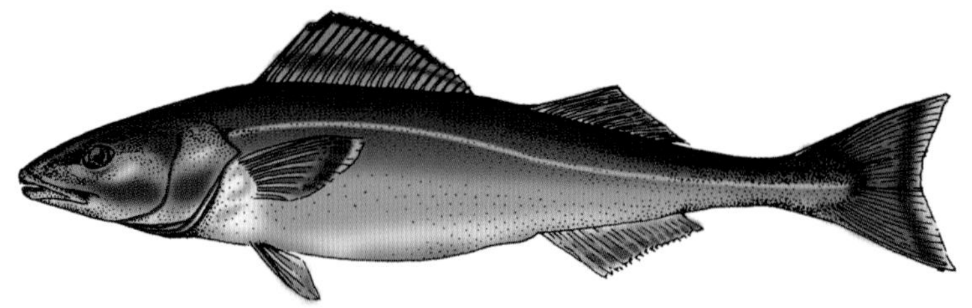

Other Names: *Black cod, butterfish (filets only).*

Description: *Black fading to grey.*

Size: *1–15 pounds.*

Range: *Northern Pacific (well offshore).*

Season: *All year.*

Yield: *40% filet.*

Fat Content: *High.*

Available Forms: *Filet, round, smoked, chunk.*

"Butterfish" filets are widely available in supermarkets as well as fish markets. While not suited to every method, it can be delicious if properly cooked. Broiling with a well-flavored compound butter is the best dry-heat method. With its mild flavor, sablefish is ideal for curries and other highly seasoned stews and braised dishes.

Grilled Salmon with Fennel

By midsummer, ocean salmon become firmer and fuller-flavored, and are more suitable for grilling than poaching.

Serves 4

1 large or *2 small fennel bulbs (about ½ pound)*

4 6–8-ounce salmon steaks

3 tablespoons olive oil

Coarse ground black pepper to taste

Beurre Blanc (page 253)

Trim the fennel bulbs, reserving the leaves and tender stems. Slice the bulbs lengthwise in half or into ½-inch slices. Blanch them in salted water for 30 seconds or until they soften slightly. Rinse them with cold water to stop the cooking. Marinate the fennel slices and salmon in olive oil and pepper for at least 1 hour.

Grill the fennel slices on one side. When they are lightly browned, turn them and add the salmon to the grill. A ¾-inch steak will be cooked rare in about 6 minutes over a hot charcoal fire and well done in 8 minutes. Baste the steaks with the marinade while grilling. When the fennel is tender, remove it to a warm platter or serving plates. Serve the fish and fennel with a Beurre Blanc to which have been added finely chopped fennel leaves and stems.

Grilled Salmon with Cilantro Cream Sauce

Carol Brendlinger

Serves 4

4 6–8-ounce salmon steaks
2 tablespoons olive oil
½ cup cilantro
2 quarts Fumet (page 252)
¼ cup chopped shallots
2 cups dry white wine
1 quart cream
2 tablespoons Crème Fraîche (page 39)
Salt and pepper to taste
Cilantro for garnish

Marinate the salmon in olive oil and half the cilantro for 1–4 hours.

Add the shallots to the *fumet* and reduce to 2 cups. Add the white wine and reduce slowly to ½ cup. In a separate saucepan reduce the cream by half. Strain the *fumet* into the cream. Add the *crème fraîche*. Simmer and whisk until the sauce thickens, about 2 minutes. Chop the remaining cilantro, add to the sauce and season to taste. Simmer for 1 minute. Keep the sauce warm over a double boiler or on the edge of the grill.

Grill the salmon. Serve it on a heated platter covered with the sauce. Garnish with cilantro.

Grilled Salmon and Scallop Brochettes

Salmon and scallops are nearly identical in density, and cook at the same rate. Grilling them together on skewers makes for a delightful combination of color and flavor. Use either bay or sea scallops, and cut salmon filet into pieces of similar size. Serve with Beurre Blanc (page 253) or a simple herb butter (page 255).

Gravlax

This is a classic Scandinavian recipe for curing salmon. It requires no special equipment or ingredient, only what you would usually have on hand in the kitchen. You can make it from two filets of a small salmon and use the quantities given here or cut the recipe in half and use two smaller filets.

Serves 40–50 as an appetizer

A 6–8-pound salmon or steelhead (or chunk from a larger fish)

½ cup coarse (kosher) salt

5 tablespoons sugar

1 teaspoon white pepper

2 tablespoons fresh chopped dill

Parsley, cucumber slices, red bell pepper slices for garnish

Filet the salmon, leaving the skin on. Combine salt, sugar and pepper and rub the filets with this mixture.

Lay one filet on top of the other, thick width to thin width. Wrap wax paper and then foil around the filets. Place the wrapped fish on a plate and place another plate on top. Rest a weight of about 2 pounds on the top plate to maintain firm contact between the filets. Refrigerate for 4–5 days.

To serve, cut the *gravlax* into thin strips and arrange in a circular pattern on a small serving tray. Decorate the center with parsley, cucumber slices and/or red bell pepper slices.

Smoked Salmon "Mousse"

Victoria Fahey

Victoria Fahey of Curds and Whey in Oakland provided this delicious creamy salmon recipe. It should be made with salmon that has been dry-smoked rather than a wet-cured lox. Serve chilled or at room temperature with crackers or rye bread.

Alternatives: *Smoked trout* *Serves 18 as an appetizer*

1 pound smoked salmon, skinned and well trimmed

1 pound sweet butter

2 tablespoons tomato paste

¼ cup lemon juice

¼ teaspoon ground mace

½ teaspoon fresh ground black pepper

¼ cup capers

½–1 cup sour cream or *Crème Fraîche (page 39)*

Additional capers or *thinly sliced lemon for garnish*

Cut the salmon into 1-inch cubes. Whip the butter until soft in an electric mixer. Slowly add the salmon, tomato paste, mace and black pepper. Mix on medium speed until the ingredients are fairly smooth but not completely homogenized. Spoon the mousse into a medium-sized serving bowl. Add the capers and toss the mixture gently with a spoon. Serve immediately or refrigerate.

Just before you serve, cover the mousse with a thin layer of sour cream. Garnish with capers or thin slices of lemon.

SAND DAB

(Citarichthys sordidus)

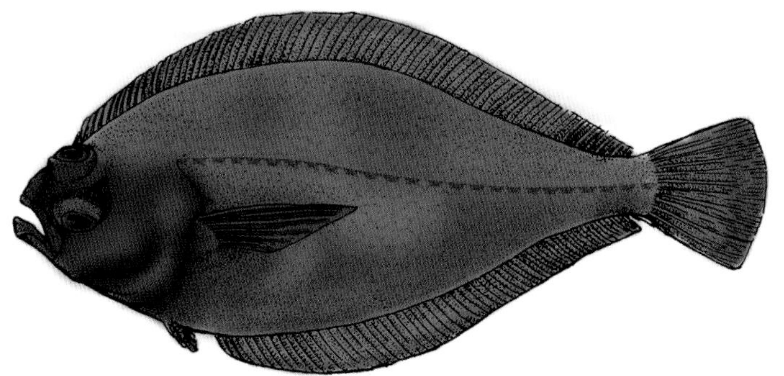

Description: *Brown with orange-black mottling.*	**Season:** *All year.*
	Fat Content: *Low.*
Size: *To 1 pound. 4–8 ounces typical.*	**Yield:** *50% pan-dressed.*
Range: *Southern California to Alaska.*	**Available Forms:** *Round, pan-dressed.*

This small flatfish is one of the most popular selections at San Francisco's old (and new) fish grills. The intense heat of the charcoal crisps the skin while the sweet flesh stays moist due to contact with the bones. Marinades are not really needed or desirable—just a little Beurre Blanc (page 253), a simple herb butter (page 255) or a squeeze of lemon juice.

Sand dabs are also frequently prepared *meuniere* (page 218) or in a bread crumb batter.

Sautéed Sand Dabs with Bread Crumb Batter

Alternatives: *Rex sole, other small soles, surfperch, butterfish, freshwater "pan fish"* — *Serves 2*

1½–2 pounds sand dabs, round

Salt and pepper to taste

Flour

1 egg, beaten

¼ cup milk

½ cup or more bread crumbs

1–2 tablespoons clarified butter (see below)

Juice of ½ lemon

Pan-dress the fish, season them lightly and set them aside. Combine the egg and milk in a shallow bowl. Dredge each fish in flour, then dip in the egg mixture and roll in the bread crumbs until thoroughly coated. (Try to work with just one hand in the egg mixture, keeping the other free to handle the finished product.)

Heat the butter in a large skillet. Sauté the fish, regulating the heat so that the batter does not get too brown. To test for doneness, try to slip a skewer between the filets and the bones from the head end. If it penetrates easily, the fish is done. Transfer the fish to a heated serving platter or plates, add the lemon juice to the remaining butter in the pan and pour over the fish.

To Clarify Butter:

In a small saucepan melt ¼ pound or more of butter over very low heat. Do not allow the butter to boil. The butter fat will separate from the whey and milk solids. Skim any floating solids from the surface and discard. Ladle the butter fat out of the pan, leaving the whey behind. Clarified butter may be stored in a tightly closed jar, refrigerated.

SCALLOP

Sea Scallop

(P. magellicanus)

Description: *Similar to bay scallop. Larger in size and slightly less symmetrical and flatter.*

Size: *5 inches across.*

Range: *Mid-Atlantic to New England.*

Season: *All year. More abundant in the summer.*

Fat Content: *Low.*

Yield: *15–40 per pound, shucked.*

Available Forms: *Shucked, occasionally live.*

Bay Scallop

(Pecten irradians)

Description: *Symmetrical bivalve. Cream with light brown, pink or light yellow mottling.*

Size: *2 inches across.*

Range: *Shallow bay waters and salt ponds of the Atlantic and Gulf coasts.*

Season: *Locally regulated. Generally available fall and winter.*

Fat Content: *Low.*

Yield: *Approximately 90–100 per pound, shucked.*

Available Forms: *Shucked, live (infrequently).*

The scallop is the only free-swimming mollusc. It cannot hold its shell together tightly and dies quickly out of water. It is shucked as a matter of course.

In America we eat only the abductor muscle, the large muscle which connects the shells; in Europe the muscle and roe or the entire scallop is eaten.

The bay scallop is a delight and rare on the Pacific coast. Most of what are sold here as bay scallops are small deep-sea scallops from Florida known as calico scallops *(Argopecten gibbus)*.

The larger sea scallop is the most widely available scallop and the basis of the commercial fishery. When fresh, sea scallops are excellent in flavor and texture and are suitable to a wider variety of cooking methods and ingredients than the more delicate bay scallop. Sea scallops make delicious Ceviche (page 70). They are frequently used in fish stuffings and mousse mixtures. Bay scallops are best simply sautéed or poached with a cream-based sauce.

Grilled Scallops with Bacon

Alternatives: *Large oysters* *Serves 4*

4 slices of bacon

1 pound sea scallops (if larger than 1 ounce each, cut in half across the grain)

Juice of 1 lemon

Blanch the bacon in boiling water for 3 minutes to remove some of the fat and to partially cook it.

Using small wooden or metal skewers, pierce one end of the bacon then skewer a scallop. Weave in the bacon and add another scallop. Fill the skewers, alternating bacon and scallops.

Grill 3–4 minutes over hot charcoal, or a little longer under a broiler, turning the scallops once. Serve on the skewers with a squeeze of lemon juice.

Sichuan Scallops

The spicy hot flavor of this sauce enhances rather than overwhelms the sweet taste of the scallops.

Alternatives: *Shrimp or prawns*

Serves 4 or more as a side dish
Serves 2 as a main course

1 egg white

½ pound sea scallops cut in half across the grain

2 tablespoons chicken stock

1 tablespoon Sichuan bean paste (page 43)

1 tablespoon dry sherry or *rice wine*

1 teaspoon soy sauce

2 tablespoons oil

1–2 tablespoons chopped garlic

2 teaspoons chopped ginger

1 stalk celery cut into ¼-inch slices

Beat the egg white until frothy. Toss the scallops in the egg white and refrigerate them.

In a small bowl, combine the stock, bean paste, sherry and soy sauce.

Drain the excess egg white from the scallops with paper towels. Heat the oil in a large skillet or wok. Sauté the garlic and ginger for 10 seconds over high heat. Add the celery and scallops and stir-fry for 30 seconds. Add the sauce mixture and continue cooking until the scallops are heated through, about 1 minute. Serve with rice.

Fried Sea Scallops

Alternatives: *Oysters, mussels* *Serves 2*

1 egg
1 tablespoon milk
Pinch of salt and pepper
¼ cup all-purpose flour
½ cup fine bread crumbs
½ pound sea scallops (if larger than 1 ounce, slice in half across the grain)
2 cups or more oil for frying

Beat the egg, milk, salt and pepper together. Dip each scallop into flour, shaking off the excess. Dip in egg mixture and coat thoroughly with bread crumbs.

In a heavy pot or wok, heat the oil to 350°. Add the scallops and cook until nicely browned, 3–4 minutes. Drain on paper towels.

Fried scallops are delicious served simply with lemon wedges. If a sauce is desired, try Fines Herbes Mayonnaise (page 258), Tartar Sauce (page 259) or Skordalia (page 260).

WHITE SEABASS

(Cynoscion nobilis)

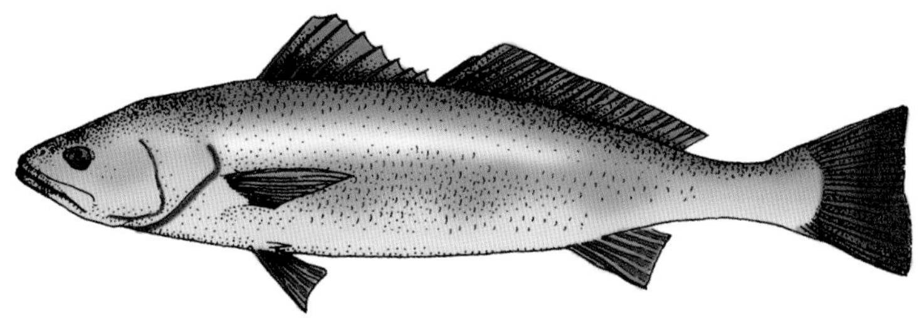

Description: *Blue-grey fading to silver. Large, heavy scales.*

Size: *To 80 pounds. 10–15 pounds more typical.*

Range: *Baja to central California.*

Season: *Spring-summer.*

Fat Content: *Moderate.*

Yield: *40% filet, 65% steak.*

Available Forms: *Pan-dressed, steak, filet, block.*

White seabass is the species traditionally sold as "sea bass" in California. It is now relatively scarce and expensive, but worth seeking out for its fine flavor and texture. Like the other croakers and striped bass, which it resembles in flavor, white seabass is ideal for grilling and broiling, but tends to dry out if overcooked. Seabass bones make a particularly rich stock.

Several other distinct species are likely to be marketed under this name and are treated separately (see grouper and striped bass). They are relatively close in cooking characteristics, and are generally interchangeable in recipes.

Seabass with Oyster Sauce

This is an adaptation of a New Orleans recipe for redfish.

Alternatives: *Striped bass, corbina, Pacific halibut, grouper (A,G,P), snapper (A,G), redfish (A,G)*

Serves 4

2 teaspoons chopped garlic

4 scallions, white and pale green parts, chopped

½ stalk celery, thinly sliced

4 tablespoons butter

¼ cup dry white wine

½ pint oysters with their liquor

½ cup cream or *Crème Fraiche (page 39)*

1½–2 pounds seabass filet

1 tablespoon chopped parsley

Salt and pepper to taste

Preheat the broiler.

In a skillet or heavy saucepan, sauté the garlic, scallions and celery in butter until softened but not browned. Add the wine, turn up the heat and reduce liquid by half. Add the cream and oyster liquor, reduce a little more and set aside while the fish is cooking.

Broil the fish on a buttered heatproof platter or roasting pan. Drain any liquid from the platter into the sauce. Add the oysters and parsley to the saucepan, and heat quickly until the oysters begin to curl. Pour the sauce over the fish and serve.

This sauce is suitable for grilled fish as well. Cut the filet into individual serving pieces, grill and serve in the same manner.

Shark Pie

This attractive dish makes a wonderful appetizer or main course.

Alternatives: *Swordfish, halibut*

Yield: 9-inch pie (6–10 servings)

Crust

6 tablespoons cold butter
2 tablespoons olive oil
2 cups unbleached flour
6 tablespoons ice water
1 teaspoon grated lemon zest

Filling

1 pound boneless shark, cut into 1-inch cubes
1 pound fresh tomatoes, peeled, seeded and chopped or *2 cups canned tomatoes, drained and chopped*
2–4 tablespoons chopped garlic
¼ cup green olives, pitted and sliced
2 tablespoons chopped parsley
2 teaspoons chopped capers
1 teaspoon fresh thyme or *oregano*, or *¼ teaspoon dried*
Pepper to taste

Cut the butter and oil into the flour in a food processor or by hand. Add the ice water a little at a time, along with the lemon zest. Form the dough into a ball and refrigerate for at least 30 minutes and preferably 1 hour.

Preheat the oven to 400°.

Cut the dough in half. Flour a cutting board and a rolling pin. Roll out the dough from the center until it is about 3 inches larger than the diameter of the pie tin. Carefully place the pie crust into the tin and press it firmly in place. Cut off the excess.

Bake for 5 minutes or until the crust just begins to color. Remove from the oven and allow to cool slightly.

Roll out the other piece of dough to a slightly smaller diameter. Fill the pie with alternating layers of shark and tomatoes mixed with the capers, olives, parsley and garlic. Cover the pie with the top crust, pinching the two layers together at the outer edge. Lower the oven heat to 350°. Bake for 45 minutes or until the top crust turns golden brown. Serve hot or warm.

SHRIMP AND PRAWN

Spot Shrimp

(Pandalus platyceros)

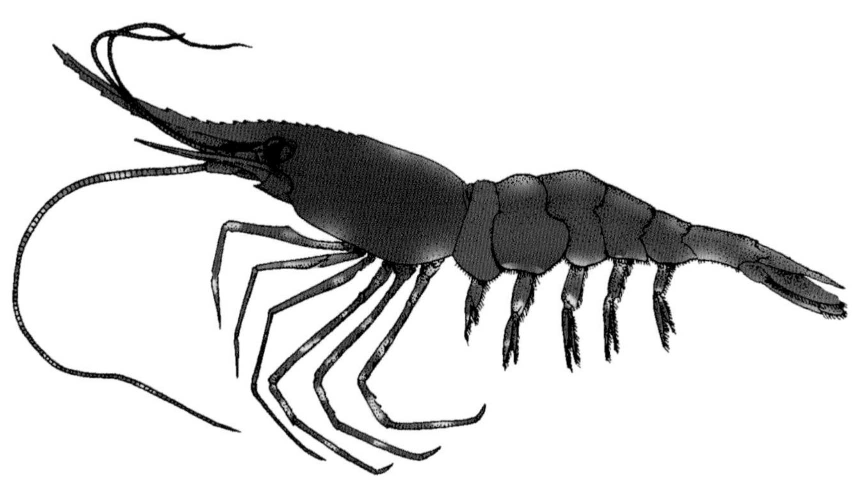

Other Names: *Monterey prawn, spot prawn.*

Description: *Pinkish red. Often with bright red roe attached.*

Size: *5–20 per pound.*

Range: *California coast, especially Monterey Bay.*

Season: *Spring–fall.*

Fat Content: *Low.*

Available Forms: *Whole or with heads removed.*

Grass Shrimp

(Hippolyte californiensis)

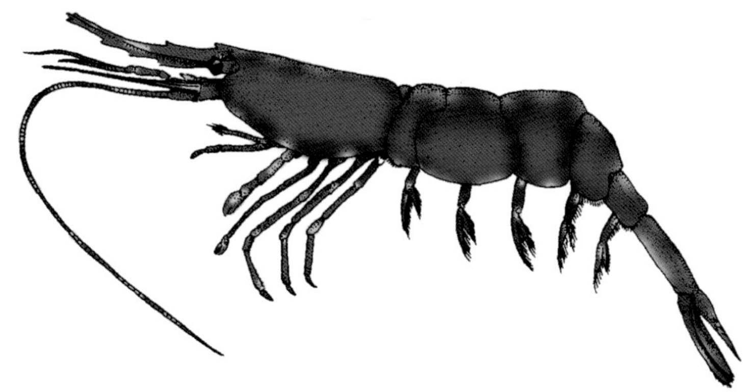

Description: *Translucent greyish-green.*	**Season:** *All year.*
Size: *150 per pound.*	**Fat Content:** *Low.*
Range: *Pacific coast.*	**Available Forms:** *Live, whole.*

The terms "shrimp" and "prawns" are used more or less interchangeably in the West, with prawns generally referring to the larger sizes. We have followed this usage although, strictly speaking, prawns are a distinct and unrelated group of freshwater crustaceans, including the aquacultured Malaysian prawn *(Macabrachium rosenbergii)*. Most of the shrimp available around the country are from the Gulf of Mexico and the waters of Baja California, and include several species of the family *Penaeidae*. The differences are of more interest to taxonomists than cooks, however.

Many cookbooks insist that shrimp should be deveined (the "vein" is in fact part of the digestive system extending through the tail). Others ridicule this practice as unnecessarily fastidious and a lot of trouble. Except where noted, we leave the choice up to the reader. The tiny grass shrimp can be cooked and eaten whole, although you may wish to remove the heads of the largest ones.

Shrimp tails are classified by size, according to the number of shrimp per pound. The largest sizes are preferred by most restaurants, and are likely to be more expensive than the smaller ones. Fresh shrimp are not as often classified by size as packaged tails, and may contain a wide range of sizes.

Shrimp are versatile; most varieties may be cooked by almost any method. All types are delicious grilled in the shell or peeled and sautéed.

Grilled Prawns

Grilling prawns in the shell always brings up the question of how to eat them. Shrimp and the smaller prawns can be eaten whole, shell and all, but the larger varieties must be peeled. Because they have to be eaten with the fingers, grilled prawns are most suited to backyard barbecues or other informal get-togethers.

Skewer the prawns through the tails with or without heads. After skewering, they can be marinated in olive oil mixed with fresh or dried herbs such as oregano, marjoram, thyme or rosemary, chopped garlic, salt and pepper.

Grill prawns over a hot fire, basting with the marinade. Large prawns will take 6–8 minutes to cook; they are done when the thick end of the tail is just turning opaque. Serve with Lemon-Garlic Butter (page 255), Fresh Tomato Salsa (page 262) or left-over *salsa* heated in butter.

Monterey Prawns with Green Tagliarini

The beautiful Monterey spot shrimp with their bright red roe are perfect for this dish. If these extra-large shellfish are not available, any other large shrimp or even crayfish tails will do.

Serves 4

1½–2 pounds whole prawns, including roe

¼ pound butter or *Shrimp Butter (see below)*

1 teaspoon chopped garlic

½ teaspoon fresh herbs, such as thyme, chervil or chives

1 cup cream or *Crème Fraîche (page 39) at room temperature*

1 pound fresh or dried spinach tagliarini or *linguine*

Salt and pepper to taste

Peel the prawns, reserving the heads and shells for Shrimp Butter. Set aside the roe, if any.

Heat the butter in a skillet; add the prawns, garlic and herbs. Sauté slowly, without browning the butter or garlic, until the prawns are nearly cooked. Meanwhile, cook the pasta. When the pasta is nearly ready, add the cream and roe to the skillet, turn the heat to high and reduce by one-third. Season to taste with salt and pepper, drain the pasta and toss it in the skillet until it is well coated with the sauce. Serve immediately on warmed plates, arranging the prawns and the roe on top of the pasta. (Note: If using dried pasta, reduce the sauce further, as the pasta will not absorb as much sauce.)

Shrimp Butter

Yield: ¼ cup

Heads and shells from 1½–2 pounds shrimp

¼ cup butter

Roughly chop the heads and shells with a knife or in a food processor. Place them in the top of a double boiler with the butter. Cook for at least 30 minutes, regulating the heat so that the butter does not boil. Strain the butter and discard the heads and shells. Refrigerate until ready to use, discarding any liquid which separates from the butter.

Shrimp butter freezes well, so it can be made any time you have shells; or, you can freeze shells until you accumulate enough to make a large batch. Crab, crayfish or lobster shells can be used in the same manner.

Kung Pao Shrimp

Bruce Cost

Alternatives: *Squid rings*

Serves 6 or more as a side dish
Serves 4 as a main course

1 pound shrimp (20–24 per pound) shelled and deveined or *grass shrimp*

1 tablespoon cornstarch

¼ cup red wine vinegar

Salt to taste

2 tablespoons light soy sauce

5 teaspoons sugar

1 cup oil

6–12 dried hot red peppers

1½ tablespoons peeled and chopped fresh ginger root

4–6 cloves garlic, chopped

2–3 tablespoons chopped scallions

Rinse and dry the shrimp. Dust them with cornstarch and set aside. Combine the vinegar, salt, soy sauce and sugar. Set aside.

In a wok or large skillet, heat the oil until hot. Add the shrimp and stir-fry until done, about 1½ minutes. Drain in a sieve or colander, pouring off all but 1½ tablespoons of oil. Fry the dried peppers until black in remaining oil. Add the ginger, garlic and scallions, then the vinegar mixture. Bring to a boil and add the shrimp, stirring until they are well coated and hot. Serve with rice.

Shrimp Tempura

Bruce Cost

Serves 3–4 as a main course

1 pound shrimp (20–24 per pound or larger), shelled and deveined

2 teaspoons salt

2 teaspoons baking soda

Oil for frying

Slice the shrimp almost all the way through the back and flatten. Mix the shrimp with salt and baking soda. Let stand for 30 minutes or so.

Dipping Sauce

1 tablespoon oil

1 tablespoon minced ginger

1 tablespoon tomato paste

2 tablespoons sugar

3 tablespoons white vinegar

1 tablespoon light soy sauce

½ teaspoon salt

1 cup water

1½ tablespoons cornstarch dissolved in ¼ cup water

2 teaspoons chili oil (available in Asian groceries)

In a saucepan, cook the ginger and tomato paste in oil until the oil is well colored. Stir in the sugar, vinegar, soy sauce, salt and water and bring to a boil. Add the cornstarch mixture and simmer until thickened and clear. Stir in the chili oil.

Batter

1 cup flour

½ teaspoon salt

2 teaspoons baking powder

1 cup water

Combine the flour, salt and baking soda. Stir in the water,

but don't overmix. The batter may be slightly lumpy. Rinse off the salt and soda from the shrimp under cold water and drain well.

Heat the oil to almost smoking (375 °). Dip the shrimp in the batter and fry until golden brown. Drain on paper towels and serve with the sauce.

Tempura is traditionally made with vegetables as well as shrimp. Most commonly used are thin-sliced sweet potato, carrot, green beans and zucchini or other summer squash.

Sautéed Shrimp

This recipe is adaptable to any kind of prawn or shrimp.

Serves 2

1 pound whole shrimp or *prawns*

3 tablespoons oil

1 teaspoon chopped garlic

¼ cup dry white wine

1 teaspoon chopped herbs such as parsley or thyme

1 tablespoon softened butter (optional)

1 pound tomatoes, peeled, seeded and roughly chopped

Salt and pepper to taste

Remove heads and shells from the shrimp, reserving them for Shrimp Butter (page 207). Devein if desired. Heat the oil in a skillet. Add the shrimp and cook until the meat is opaque. Remove the shrimp to a warm plate. Pour out all but 1 tablespoon of the oil. Add the garlic, white wine and fresh herbs. Reduce the liquid by half. Add the butter. Toss the tomatoes in the sauce until they are warmed. Return the shrimp to the pan momentarily to heat through.

Arrange the shrimp, tails pointed out, in a circle on individual plates. Place the tomatoes in the center. Pour the sauce over the shrimp.

SKATE

(Raja inornata)

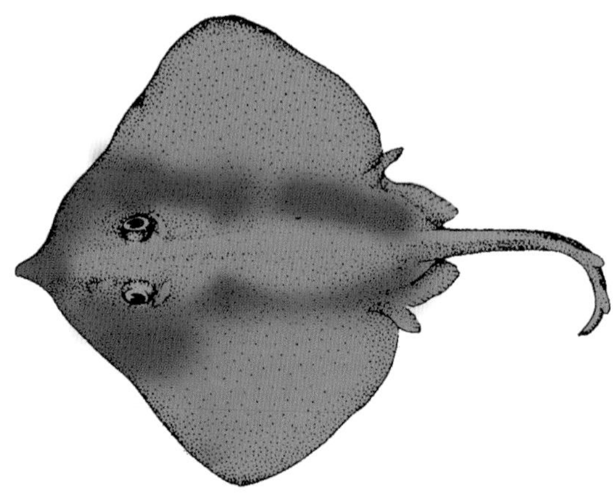

Other Names: *Ray, raja.*

Description: *Olive above, tan below.*

Size: *1-5 pounds (wings).*

Range: *California to Alaska.*

Season: *All year.*

Fat Content: *Low.*

Yield: *50% filet from whole wings, 65% from skinless.*

Available Forms: *Wings, skinned wings.*

Like shark, skate wings should be soaked in acidulated water or cooked in an acid liquid such as Court-Bouillon (page 251). It is possible to grill them, but they are more commonly poached, sautéed or served cold as in Angler Salad (page 59). Poached skate is typically served with Brown Butter (page 255). Kimberly Mowers of Monterey Fish in Berkeley suggests rolling skate wing filets around a bread crumb and vegetable stuffing and baking them sealed in foil. The cooking juices can then be enriched with butter to form a sauce.

SMELT

(Allosmerus elongatus)

Other Names: *Whitebait.*

Description: *Greenish gold dorsally. Silver sides.*

Size: *3–7 inches.*

Range: *California to Washington.*

Season: *Spring–fall.*

Fat Content: *Moderate.*

Available Forms: *Round.*

Similar Species: *Surf smelt* (Hypomesus pretiosus).

These tiny fish are frequently eaten whole; they may, however, be pan-dressed if desired. They are best lightly floured and pan-fried or deep-fried, and served with a lemon wedge. Larger fish may be used in recipes for herring or fresh anchovies.

Smelt Baked in Grape Leaves

Alternatives: *Anchovies* *Serves 6 as an appetizer*

6 cloves garlic, pressed
2 tablespoons olive oil
1 pound small smelt, boned
12 grape leaves
¼ cup white wine

Preheat the oven to 350°.

Combine the garlic and olive oil. Place 2 or 3 smelt at the bottom of a leaf and spread with a little of the oil-garlic mixture. Roll the leaf around the fish, forming an envelope. Place rolls seam side down in a small oiled baking dish. Moisten with the wine. Bake for 35–40 minutes. Serve hot or warm.

SOLE

Petrale

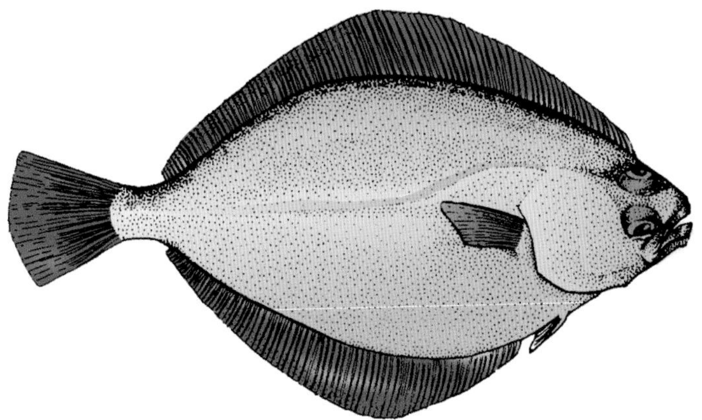

Other Names: *Petrale sole, brill.*

Description: *Uniform olive green to dark brown above.*

Size: *1–5 pounds.*

Range: *Central California to Alaska.*

Season: *All year. Most common in winter.*

Fat Content: *Low.*

Yield: *35% filet.*

Available Forms: *Round, filet.*

Rex Sole

(Glyptocephalus zachirus)

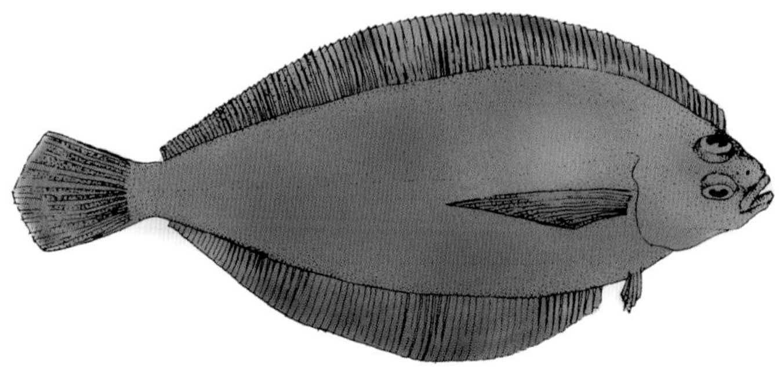

Description: *Medium brown above, variable color below.*

Size: *To 1 pound.*

Range: *Central California to Alaska.*

Season: *All year.*

Fat Content: *Low.*

Yield: *35% filet.*

Available Forms: *Round, pan-dressed.*

English Sole

(Parophrys vetulus)

Description: *Olive green to light brown above.*

Size: *½–2 pounds.*

Range: *Pacific coast. Mainly Monterey to British Columbia.*

Season: *All year.*

Fat Content: *Low.*

Yield: *20–30% filet.*

Available Forms: *Filet, only occasionally round.*

As European food writers are quick to point out, the many species of North American flatfish known as "sole" are not true soles, but flounders. Semantic quibbles aside, the name encompasses some of our most delicious and valuable species as well as some of our most undistinguished.

Petrale is the favorite among Pacific soles, and the finest in flavor and texture. It is mostly marketed in filet form, but is worth seeking out round as well. Rex sole is a close second, and is actually preferred by some. It is almost never available in filet form. While these two species are generally found under their own names, any fish labeled "filet of sole" without any further information is most likely English sole, a plentiful species of average to good quality.

The color of the skin on the underside of soles, especially rex and petrale, varies according to the bottom surface of the ocean where they are caught. Generally, the whiter the skin the better the texture and flavor of the flesh.

Classic French cuisine has built up a whole repertoire of fish preparations, from *à l'américaine* to Walewska, around the delicate flavor and texture of sole filets. Most of these involve poaching or sautéing; however, with practice and careful timing, they may be grilled with excellent results. Pan-dressed rex sole (and smaller petrale) are more easily grilled, or may be baked in batter.

Alternatives: *Filets of any species of flounder or John Dory may be substituted for sole.*

Filet of Sole Meunière

Serves 4

1½ pounds sole filets

Salt and pepper to taste

All-purpose flour

4 tablespoons butter

1 cup assorted vegetables, julienned and blanched, such as carrots, zucchini, leeks, celery root, summer squash

Juice of 1 lemon

1 tablespoon chopped parsley for garnish

Season the filets with salt and pepper and dredge them in flour. Sauté the fish over medium heat in 2 tablespoons of the butter until golden brown on both sides. (Thinner filets require higher heat to brown the coating without overcooking the flesh, while thicker filets must cook somewhat slower.) While the filets cook, sauté the vegetables in the remaining butter. Transfer the fish to warmed plates; deglaze the pan with lemon juice and pour over the fish. Garnish with the vegetables and top with chopped parsley.

Filet of Sole Florentine

In classic French cooking, "Florentine" denotes dishes prepared with spinach. Ours is a simple version of this dish. Shrimp Butter is a nice touch, but not essential.

Serves 4

¾ pound spinach, washed, with stems removed

2 tablespoons butter or Shrimp Butter (page 207)

1 tablespoon chopped shallots

½ teaspoon paprika

3–4 cups Fumet (page 252)

¼ pound cooked shrimp or *¼ pound mushrooms, sliced and sautéed (optional)*

½ cup cream

1½ pounds sole filets

In a covered saucepan, cook the spinach in just the water clinging to the leaves. Toss with a little butter if desired, and keep warm. Sauté the shallots and paprika in butter or Shrimp Butter. When they are nearly cooked, add ½ cup of *fumet*, the shrimp or mushrooms and the cream. Reduce by half and correct the seasoning. Meanwhile, poach the filets in *fumet*. Arrange them on a bed of spinach and cover with the sauce.

Filet of Sole Stuffed with Shrimp

Almost any kind of shellfish, including crab, scallops or even lobster, can be substituted for the shrimp. Handling the stuffed filets is not as tricky as it seems. Any excess stuffing or bits of stuffing that fall out of the rolled filets can be incorporated into the sauce.

Serves 4

2 tablespoons butter

2 cloves garlic, chopped

½ cup finely diced yellow onion

6–8 ounces cooked small shrimp

¼ cup chopped parsley

2–3 cups Fumet (page 252), heated

8 small sole filets (2–3 ounces each)

½ cup cream

Sauté the garlic and onion in 1 tablespoon of butter until soft; allow to cool. Combine all but 1 tablespoon of the shrimp with the parsley and the cooled onion and garlic. Divide the stuffing in eighths and roll each of the filets around the stuffing, allowing at least an inch of overlap.

Place the filets, seam side down, in a buttered or oiled pan just large enough to hold them and at least 3 inches deep. Pour the hot *fumet* into the pan, being careful not to wash the stuffing out of the rolled filets. Poach at a simmer until filets are just done.

Carefully remove filets to a warm serving dish or individual plates. Pour out all but ¼ cup of the *fumet*. Add the cream and the reserved shrimp and reduce. Correct the seasoning and pour the sauce over the filets.

Filet of Sole Stuffed with Mushrooms

This is prepared exactly as the previous recipe, but with a *duxelles* mixture replacing the shrimp stuffing.

Serves 4

2–3 cups Fumet (page 252), heated

8 small sole filets (2–3 ounces each)

½ cup cream

Duxelles

(Mushroom and Bread Crumb Stuffing)

2 tablespoons butter

½ cup chopped mushrooms

3–4 cloves garlic, chopped

½ cup finely diced yellow onion

¼ cup bread crumbs

2 tablespoons chopped parsley

Juice of ½ lemon

Salt and pepper to taste

Sauté the mushrooms, garlic and onion in butter until most of the liquid released by the mushrooms is evaporated. Add the bread crumbs and parsley, lemon juice and salt and pepper. Allow to cool before stuffing filets as described in previous recipe.

SPOTTED SEA TROUT

(Cynoscion nebulosus)

Other Names: *Speckled trout, sea trout, weakfish.*

Description: *Dark grey fading to silver. Black spots on upper body and fins.*

Size: *1–5 pounds.*

Range: *Atlantic and Gulf coasts.*

Season: *All year. Especially spring and fall.*

Fat Content: *Moderate.*

Yield: *33% filet.*

Available Forms: *Round, dressed, pan-dressed.*

Like redfish, this Atlantic croaker is becoming increasingly available on the West Coast. See seabass and corbina for recipes.

SQUID

(Loligo opalescens)

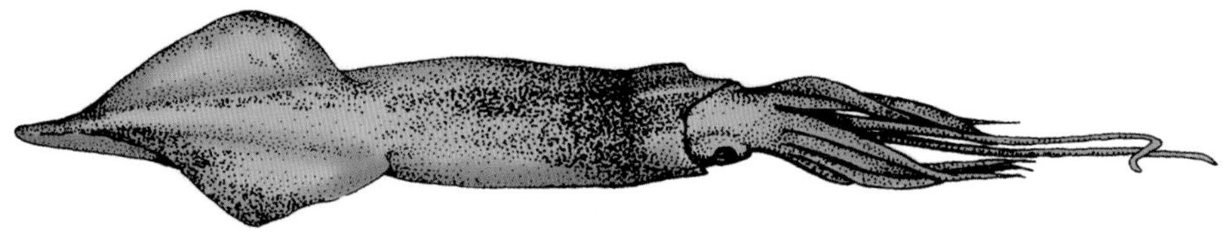

Other Names: *Market squid, common squid, calamari.*

Description: *Ivory skin with tiny purple to brown dots.*

Size: *4–10 per pound.*

Range: *Pacific coast from Southern California to Washington.*

Season: *April–October in northern California. December–April in southern California.*

Fat Content: *Low.*

Yield: *67% meat, including tentacles.*

Available Forms: *Fresh, fresh cleaned, frozen whole, frozen cleaned.*

This abundant and delicious mollusc has until recently been relegated to the bait box because of its odd appearance or because it is often overcooked and tough. It is becoming extremely popular because it is inexpensive and versatile.

Squid can be poached and used in salads, sautéed, fried, stuffed and baked, braised or grilled. Japanese species are eaten raw. For more information on squid, see *The International Squid Cookbook* by Isaac Cronin (Aris Books, 1981).

Cleaning Squid

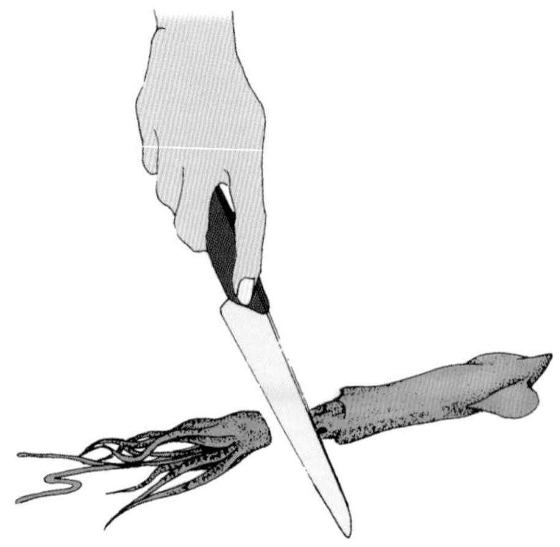

1 Cut off the tentacles just above the eye. Save them.

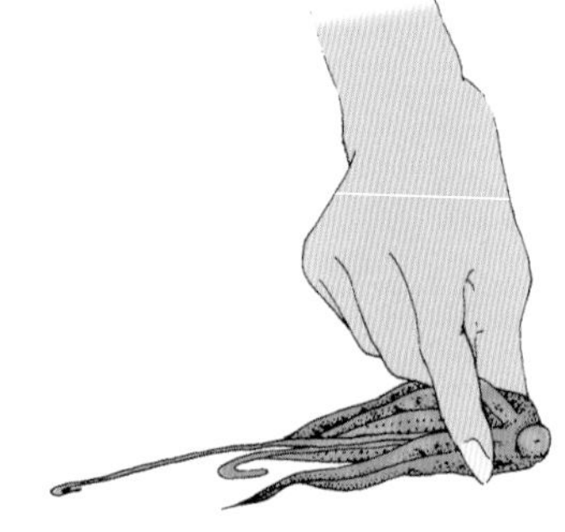

2 Squeeze out the beak, the squid's mouth, which looks like a garbanzo bean. Discard it.

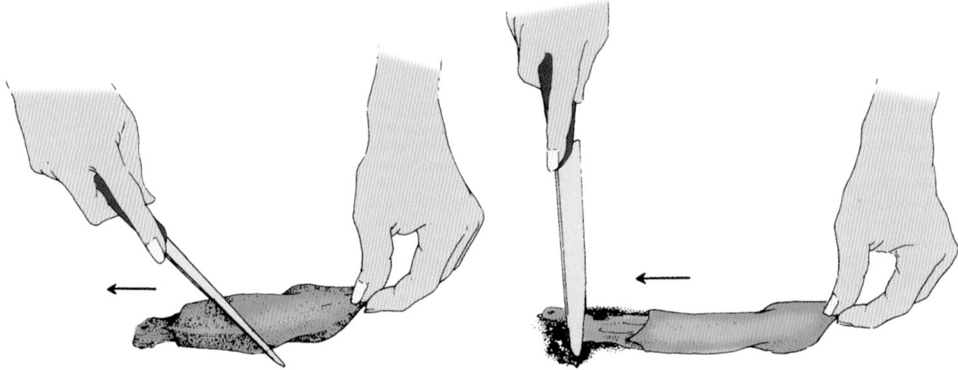

3 Holding the blade of a chef's knife almost flat, scrape along the body from the tail to the opening. Press down hard to squeeze out the entrails, but be careful not to break the skin. Don't worry about removing the skin, which is edible.

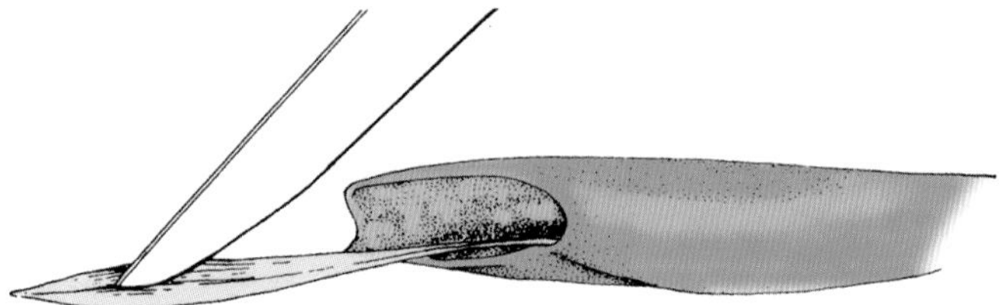

4 With the point of the knife, stab the transparent quill which protrudes from the body and hold it fast. Pull the

body away. The quill should remain under the knife. Discard the quill. The squid is now ready for stuffing. If you want to cook smaller pieces, cut rings crosswise ½–1 inch wide.

Squid Stuffed with Spinach

Serves 4

2 pounds large squid, cleaned for stuffing

2 tablespoons olive oil

1 medium yellow onion, chopped

½ pound spinach, washed, drained, stems removed and leaves chopped

¼ cup bread crumbs

1½ ounces Pernod or *other anise liqueur*

Salt and pepper to taste

2 tablespoons olive oil

1 cup cream

Chop the tentacles and set aside.

Sauté the onions in olive oil until soft. Add the spinach and cook until wilted. Add the tentacles and bread crumbs. Sauté for 2 minutes. Add half the Pernod and remove from the heat. (It is best to let the stuffing cool to room temperature before adding it to the squid. If this is impossible, make the stuffing and stuff the squid immediately before cooking.) Stuff the squid loosely with the spinach mixture, using a pastry bag, small spoon or your fingers. Seal each with a toothpick.

Heat 2 tablespoons of olive oil in a skillet large enough to hold all the squid in one layer. Add the squid and sauté until the bodies are opaque, about 4 minutes. Remove to a heated serving dish. Deglaze the pan with the remaining Pernod. Add the cream, turn up the heat, and reduce by two-thirds. Return the squid to the skillet to reheat.

Arrange the squid on a warm platter, removing the toothpicks in the kitchen if desired. Pour the sauce over and serve.

Squid with Black Rice

Serves 4

2 pounds squid, cleaned, bodies cut into rings, with tentacles and ink sacs reserved

2 tablespoons olive oil

¼ cup chopped yellow onion

1 tablespoon chopped garlic

1 cup white rice

1 teaspoon fresh thyme or *oregano,* or *¼ teaspoon dried*

1 bay leaf

Salt to taste

1 cup chicken stock and 1 cup water (if using canned chicken broth, decrease salt)

In a sieve placed over a bowl, crush the ink sacs with the back of a spoon. Pour the stock and water through the sieve to extract the rest of the ink.

In a medium-sized casserole, sauté the onion and garlic in the olive oil over medium heat; do not brown. Add the rice, stir and sauté a few minutes longer until the rice just begins to color. Add the seasonings and the stock. Cover, bring to a boil, reduce heat and simmer for 15 minutes or until most of the liquid has been absorbed. Taste for seasoning. Add the squid and cook 5 minutes more or until squid is opaque and rice has absorbed the remaining liquid.

Serve from the casserole or transfer to a serving dish, arranging the squid on top. Serve with an assortment of colorful vegetables.

Mexican Squid Salad

Calamares en Escabeche

Serves 4 as an appetizer

1 pound squid, cleaned, bodies cut into rings, with tentacles

1 tablespoon lemon or *lime juice*

1 teaspoon red wine vinegar

4 tablespoons olive oil

2 or more serrano or *other fresh chiles, seeded and chopped*

¼ cup chopped cilantro

1 medium tomato, seeded and cut into ¼-inch dice

2 tablespoons sliced scallion tops or *diced red onion*

Salt to taste

In a large saucepan or pasta pot with removable strainer, boil the squid in abundant salted water just until opaque, a minute or less. Drain and rinse immediately with cold water to prevent overcooking.

Combine the remaining ingredients in a bowl. Toss the squid in the dressing and marinate, refrigerated, for 1–4 hours. Correct seasoning. Serve on a bed of lettuce.

Squid with Salted Mustard Greens

Salted mustard greens are a common accompaniment for seafood and pork dishes in southern China. When the greens are boiled, they produce a rich broth which is the basis for soups and sauces.

Serves 4 or more as a side dish *Serves 2 as a main course*

¼ pound salted mustard greens (available in Asian groceries)

2 tablespoons oil

1 tablespoon chopped fresh ginger

1 tablespoon chopped garlic

1 pound squid, cleaned and cut into rings

1 teaspoon soy sauce

1 teaspoon cornstarch dissolved in 1 tablespoon water

Cover the mustard greens with water and simmer slowly for 45–60 minutes. Strain, reserving ½ cup of the liquid. Cut the mustard greens into ¼-inch slices. In a heavy skillet or wok, sauté the ginger and garlic in oil until almost cooked. Add the squid and sauté 30 seconds. Add the mustard greens, broth and soy sauce. Cook 2 minutes over highest heat. Add the cornstarch mixture. When the sauce thickens, remove from the heat and serve immediately.

Squid Stuffing for Pasta

Squid, after it is briefly blanched, can be made into a paste not that different from a meatball mixture. It can be formed into balls and sautéed or used as a stuffing for ravioli, tortellini or other stuffed pasta. Squid balls may also be braised in olive oil and chicken stock.

Yield: Enough filling for about 24 ravioli or 12 squid balls

1 pound squid, including tentacles, cleaned and cut into pieces

2 tablespoons grated Parmesan cheese

2 cloves garlic, chopped

1 tablespoon chopped parsley

1 egg yolk

¼ cup bread crumbs

Blanch the squid in boiling water for 10 seconds. Stop the cooking by rinsing the squid in cold water. Combine the squid and the rest of the ingredients in a blender or food processor. The mixture should form a very thick paste. Add more bread crumbs if necessary. Use immediately or refrigerate for up to 4 hours.

STRIPED BASS

(Morone saxatilis)

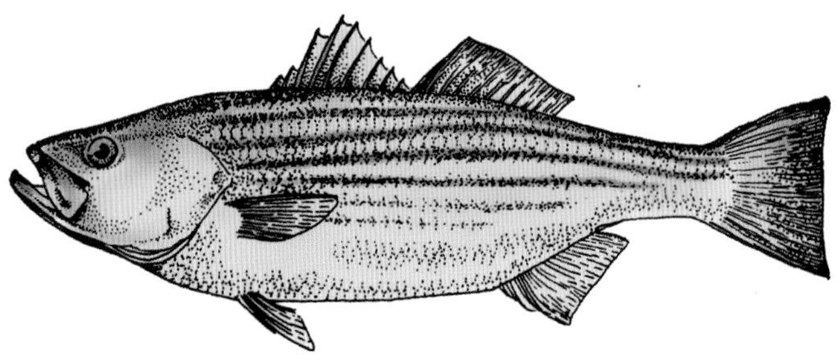

Other Names: *Striper, rockfish (Chesapeake Bay).*

Description: *Olive green fading to silver. 6–8 black longitudinal stripes. Large, heavy scales.*

Size: *To 50 pounds. 2–15 pounds typical.*

Range: *Atlantic coast from Chesapeake Bay to southern New England. Also introduced on Pacific coast from Monterey north.*

Season: *Fall–winter in the East. Early winter–spring in the West.*

Fat Content: *Moderate.*

Yield: *40% filet, 65% steak.*

On the West Coast, only anglers and their families and friends get to taste this delicious fish, as it is an introduced game species. Its flesh is firm and moderately sweet. Like other anadromous (freshwater-breeding) saltwater fish, it is susceptible to parasites and should not be eaten raw. Grilling, broiling, poaching and steaming are all appropriate cooking methods. For recipes, see corbina and seabass.

STEELHEAD

(Salmo gairdneri)

This is the common name for the migratory form of rainbow trout. The flesh of fish caught on their return to fresh water resembles salmon in color and flavor due to their oceanic diet. Although steelhead is a game fish in California, it is brought into our markets from the Columbia River. It may be cooked in any way appropriate to salmon. (See trout for a description of this fish.)

WHITE STURGEON

(Acipenser transmontanus)

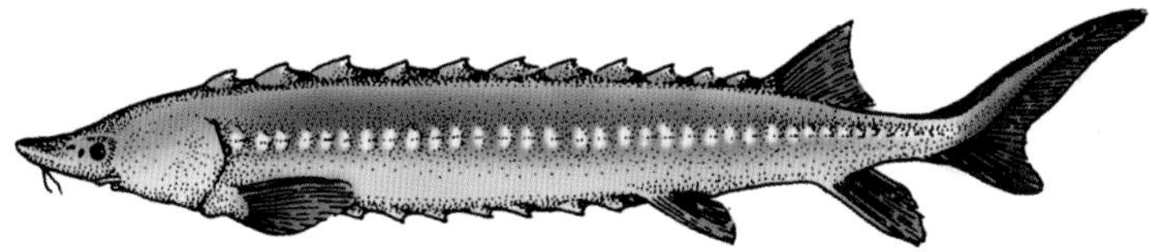

Description: *Uniform pale grey. Bony plates along back and sides.*

Size: *10–1000 pounds and up.*

Range: *Ocean, bays, major rivers from Monterey north to southern Alaska.*

Season: *Winter–spring.*

Fat Content: *High.*

Yield: *50% steaks.*

Available Forms: *Block, steak, filet.*

Similar Species: *Green sturgeon* (A. medirostris) *is a smaller, fattier species which is generally smoked; it is less desirable fresh.*

A sportfish in California, sturgeon is harvested commercially in the Columbia River, and is available here both fresh and smoked. The protected population in the Sacramento River system is slowly recovering from being overfished almost to the point of extinction. (Early in this century, California's caviar production was second only to the Russian and Iranian enterprises in the Caspian and Black seas.) With careful management, the California population may again support a commercial fishery.

Sturgeon's dense rich flesh varies somewhat in flavor. At best it is clean and sweet, but it may at times have a pronounced freshwater flavor. Check the aroma of any piece in question, and avoid those with a muddy smell. Like shark, sturgeon should be skinned, or the shrinking skin will produce misshapen steaks. Perhaps the best form for grilling or sautéing is thin diagonal slices or scallops, up to ½ inch thick. Marinate in olive oil and strong herbs and serve with an herb or brown butter.

Caviar

Tom Worthington, a young Bay Area chef, provided this recipe.

In the strictest sense, caviar is the salted roe of sturgeon. In Europe, only sturgeon roe may be sold as caviar, while in the United States similarly treated salmon roe is sold as "red caviar." Several other species produce roe which is commercially processed into "caviar," including Icelandic lumpfish and Great Lakes whitefish; these must, however, carry the name of the fish on the label.

Making caviar is a relatively simple process. Its success depends upon the condition of the roe as well as upon thorough cleaning and careful handling. The following recipe may be used for any edible roe if sturgeon or salmon roe are unavailable. (Caution: Do not use roes of cabezon or alligator gar, which are toxic.)

Choosing the Roe

Test the tenderness of the roe by crushing one egg between your fingers. The roe is good to use for caviar if the egg offers no resistance as you pop it. Roe which is too firm makes tough caviar.

Test the roe for flavor by breaking one raw egg with your tongue against the roof of your mouth. Here too, the egg should offer no resistance. It should taste fresh, not fishy, and should leave no aftertaste.

Separating the Roe

Cut the egg sac in half. Make a cut along the length of each of the two pieces. Cut just deep enough to pierce the outer membrane. Open the egg sac flat on a board and, with a knife, scrape the eggs away from the membrane into a glass or stainless steel bowl.

Cleaning the Roe

Place the loose eggs in a fine-meshed sieve. Gently pour several batches of cold water over the roe until the water that drains through is perfectly clear.

Curing the Roe

Carefully cover the roe with a lukewarm 7% brine solution (2.24 ounces salt per quart of water). Let the roe sit in the brine solution for 15 minutes, or until the eggs have reached the desired saltiness (test by tasting a few eggs).

Aging the Caviar

Pack the caviar in jars. Store, refrigerated, for at least a week before serving. (This aging improves the flavor; the caviar is, however, perfectly edible right after salting.) Keep refrigerated until ready to serve, and use within a month after packing.

SWORDFISH

(Xiphias gladius)

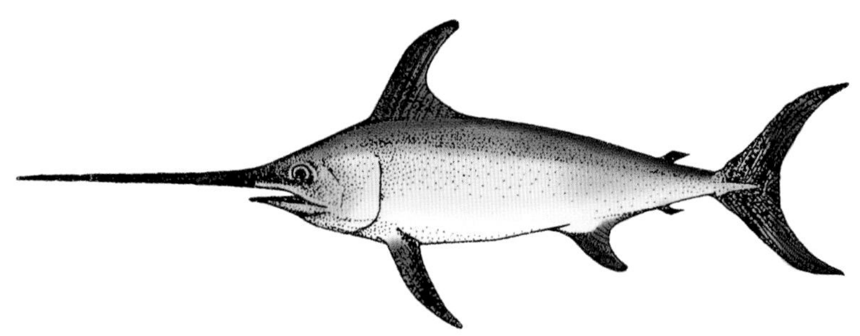

Description: *Dark grey above. Yellowish below.*

Size: *100–200 pounds typical.*

Range: *Worldwide in temperate and tropical oceans.*

Season: *All year.*

Fat Content: *Moderate.*

Yield: *80% meat from block.*

Available Forms: *Block, steak.*

Among sportfishermen, swordfish is one of the most popular of the billed fishes, and has the best eating qualities. It gets its name from its long, flattened bill with which it slashes and impales its prey. It has been known to attack boats and other floating objects.

Until recently, swordfish were taken mainly by harpoon as they sunned themselves near the surface. Recent developments in fishing methods, including long-line angling and gill netting, and the discovery of the wintering grounds, have resulted in swordfish being available all year.

The firm, dense, fine flesh of swordfish is the most meatlike in texture of all fish, and one of the most popular. It is a universal favorite for grilling and broiling, and takes well to sauces with such pronounced flavors as anchovy, rosemary, garlic and mustard. However, this fish is much in demand and tends to be expensive.

For an inexpensive alternative, ask the fish dealer for a chunk from the base of the tail which should be available at a lower price. With a bit of carving, you can separate pieces of tender flesh from the whiter, sinewy portion. Cut these into ½–1-inch pieces for brochettes, or use in place of shark in Shark Pie (page 203).

Grilled Swordfish with Gin-Vermouth Beurre Blanc

Carol Brendlinger

Alternatives: *Salmon or steelhead steaks or filets* *Serves 4*

⅓ cup mixed white wine vinegar and lemon juice

⅔ cup white vermouth

2 shallots, chopped

1 tablespoon gin

1½ teaspoons crushed juniper berries, roasted and coarsely ground

¼ cup butter

1–1½ pounds swordfish steaks

Combine the vinegar, lemon juice, vermouth and shallots in a saucepan and slowly reduce the liquid to a thick paste. Add the gin and ½ teaspoon of the juniper berries and combine. Whisk in the butter, an ounce at a time, over gentle heat.

Strain the sauce through a fine sieve, and keep it warm in a double boiler or water bath.

Dust one side of the swordfish with ½ teaspoon of the ground juniper. Place that side face down on the grill. When the fish is half cooked, dust the top side with juniper and turn. Serve the swordfish covered with sauce.

TILEFISH

(Lopholatilus chamaeleonticeps)

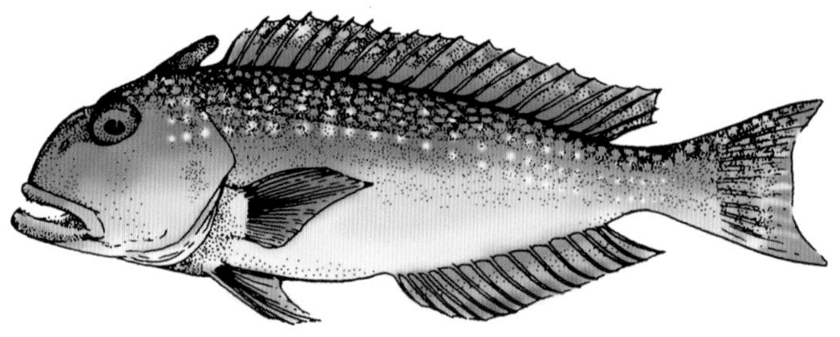

Other Names: *Tile bass.*

Description: *Sea green with yellow spots fading to cream.*

Size: *2–30 pounds.*

Range: *Atlantic and Gulf of Mexico.*

Season: *All year. Least common in summer.*

Fat Content: *Low.*

Yield: *40% filet.*

Available Forms: *Dressed, filet, steak, chunk.*

A common East Coast variety, tilefish serves the same need there as rockfish does on the West Coast: a plentiful, mild fish suitable to a variety of cooking methods. It is occasionally available here, and may be used in any rockfish recipe.

Tilefish Steamed in Spinach Leaves

In Southeast Asia, fish is often cooked in banana leaves. The result is moist and delicate. Spinach leaves are a good substitute as they impart a little water, and the entire package is delicious to eat.

Alternatives: *Rockfish, sablefish*

Serves 4 or more as a side dish
Serves 2 as a main course

½ pound tilefish filet, cut into 1-ounce scallops or slices

2 stalks fresh lemongrass, cut in thirds, or *2 teaspoons dried lemongrass soaked in water for 30 minutes*

4 thin slices of ginger

¼ cup oil

6–8 large spinach leaves, stems removed

¼ cup chicken stock

1 tablespoon fish sauce (page 40)

Marinate the filets in the lemongrass, ginger and oil for 1–2 hours. Blanch or steam the spinach until wilted and set aside to cool.

Wrap each piece of fish with a spinach leaf. If you are using fresh lemongrass, put a piece in each package; if using dried lemongrass, discard it. Pour the chicken stock and fish sauce onto a plate in the top of a steamer. Bring the water to a boil. Add the spinach packages and steam until done, about 5 minutes. Remove the lemongrass stems and reseal the packages. Pour the sauce from the plate over the fish and serve.

RAINBOW TROUT

(Salmo gairdneri)

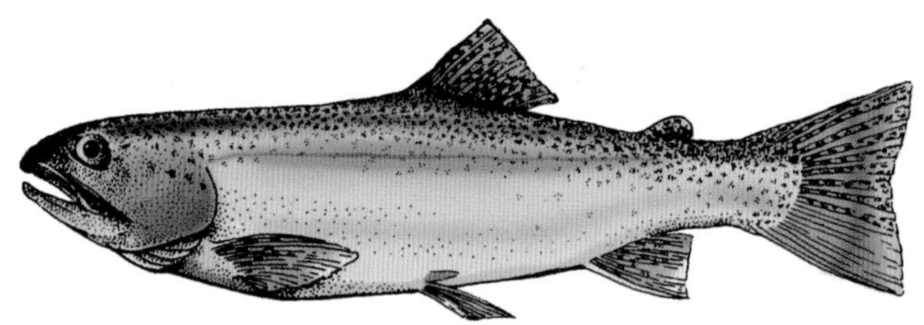

Other Names: *Steelhead (in ocean-run form).*

Description: *Olive green fading through rainbow hue along lateral line to silver. Irregular black spots.*

Size: *Typically 1–2 pounds in the wild, but up to 50 pounds. 8 ounces–1 pound when aquacultured.*

Range: *Western North American streams. Widely aquacultured throughout the United States, especially in the West.*

Season: *All year.*

Fat Content: *High.*

Yield: *67% from aquacultured fish.*

Available Forms: *Dressed, boned, smoked.*

Similar Species: *Other game species such as golden, brown, brook, Dolly Varden and cut-throat trouts are also prized as food fish.*

Probably the most familiar aquacultured fish in the United States, rainbow trout is widely available fresh. Its flesh is whiter and milder in flavor than that of wild trout. Most fish are marketed at exactly 8 ounces dressed weight, a concession no doubt to the needs of restaurants and hotels for portion control.

Dressed fish may be grilled, sautéed or poached in a Court-Bouillon (page 251). Boned fish may be stuffed with Oyster

Stuffing for Fish (page 166) or Bread Crumb Stuffing (page 133) and baked or flattened and sautéed *meunière* style. With its mild freshwater flavor, trout needs a sauce with assertive ingredients. Capers are a classic companion, and like all the salmonids, trout shows a particular affinity for dill.

Alternatives: *Pan-sized coho or king salmon.*

Smoked Fish Salad

Bruce Aidells of Poulet in Berkeley created this hearty fish and potato salad.

Alternatives: *Smoked whitefish*

Serves 6 as a first course

12 small new potatoes, peeled, boiled, sliced (or cubed) and chilled

1 small red onion, thinly sliced

1 pound boneless smoked trout, cut into small pieces

¼ cup oil and vinegar dressing

¼ cup Mayonnaise (page 257)

1 tablespoon chopped parsley

Fresh dill to taste

Lettuce

In a large bowl, toss all the ingredients until the potatoes and fish are well moistened. Serve each portion on a bed of lettuce.

TUNA

Albacore

(Thunnus alalunga)

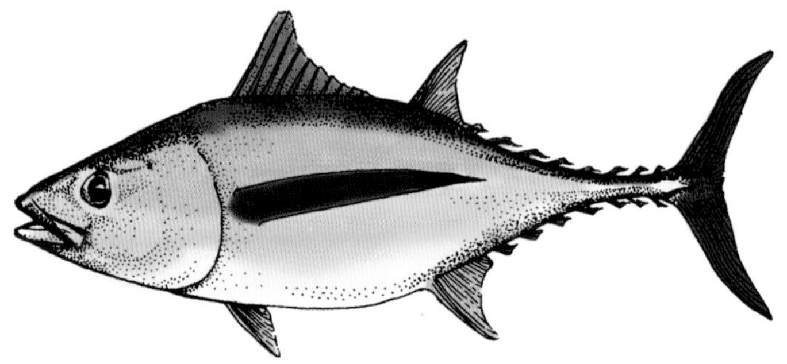

Description: *Steel grey or blue fading to lighter blue. Extremely long pectoral fin.*

Size: *To 40 pounds.*

Range: *Tropical and temperate oceans of the world.*

Season: *Summer and early fall.*

Fat Content: *High.*

Yield: *60% filet or steak.*

Available Forms: *Dressed, filet, steak.*

Yellowfin Tuna

(T. albacares)

Description: *Similar to albacore but darker. Bright yellow in most fins.*

Size: *To 300 pounds.*

Season: *All year. Most plentiful in summer.*

Similar Species: *Bluefin tuna* (T. thynnus), *bigeye tuna* (T. obesus).

While albacore commands the highest price among canned tunas, it can be the least expensive fresh tuna during its short season. The other tuna species, with darker flesh and full flavor, are the types marketed in cans as "light" tuna. They are also the choice varieties for Sashimi (see below) and *sushi*.

All the tunas have fairly firm, distinctively rich-flavored flesh suitable to dry-heat cooking. To those who have only tasted tuna from a can, a fresh tuna steak grilled over charcoal and served with a Maître d'Hotel Butter (page 254) will be a pleasant surprise. The canned version will also pale in comparison to a salad made with freshly poached tuna (page 35). Tuna also makes a nice topping for pizza (page 269).

Alternatives: *Bonito, wahoo, spearfish.*

Sashimi

Christopher Lally

Sashimi is a Japanese style of eating raw fish and shellfish. It requires two things above all—fresh seafood and smooth, quick cutting with a sharp knife.

Sashimi cutting is traditionally done with a thin-bladed knife, although a chef's knife will do. To preserve the texture of the fish, the blade should be pulled rapidly through the flesh in an even motion. Sawing will tear the fish. All the *sashimi* cutting techniques we have included were demonstrated by Christopher Lally, Bay Area chef and cooking teacher.

Serve *sashimi* with a mixture of soy sauce and *wasabi* (page 44) to taste or with soy sauce and lemon juice.

Tuna Sashimi

The following cutting instructions are for a section of filet from the back (dorsal) side of a fairly small tuna. Step 1 shows the filet placed skin side down on the cutting board.

1 Pieces A,B and the two triangles of C are generally used for sashimi. The large portion of C is cooked and served with a sauce (see below). The small end piece of C is discarded.

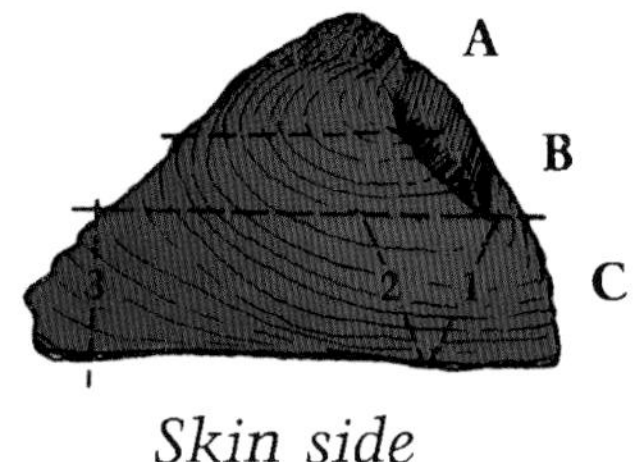

Skin side

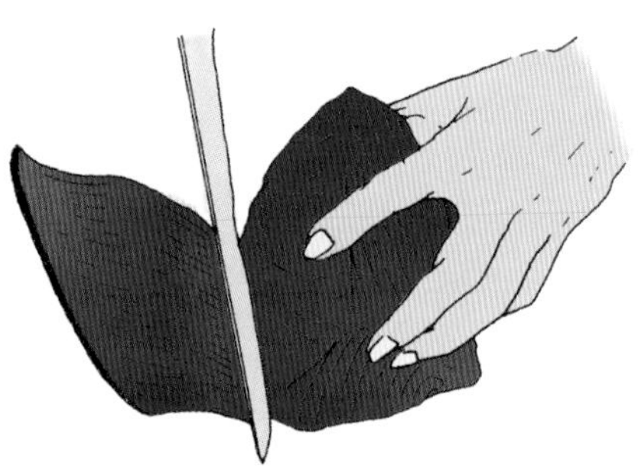

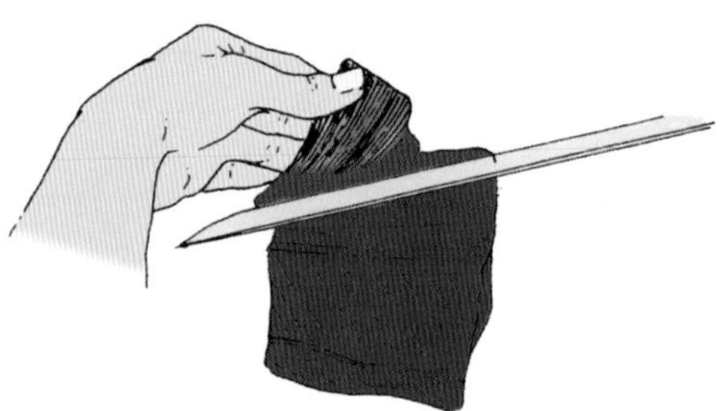

2 Skin the filet.

3 Cut off the dark material and discard it.

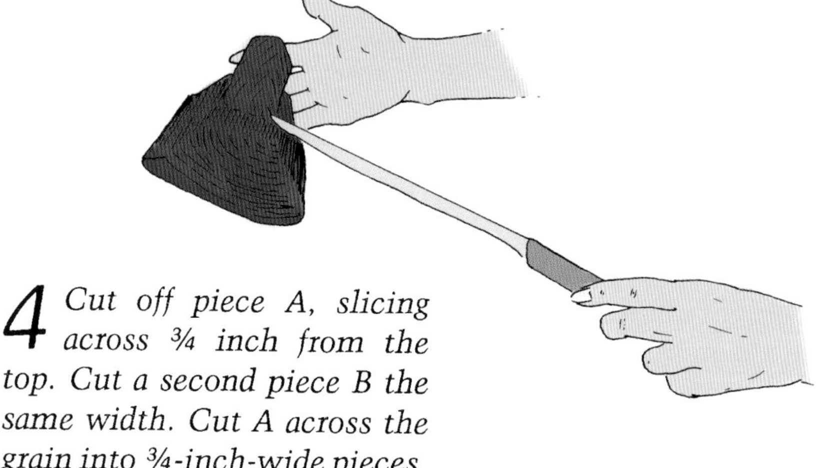

4 Cut off piece A, slicing across ¾ inch from the top. Cut a second piece B the same width. Cut A across the grain into ¾-inch-wide pieces.

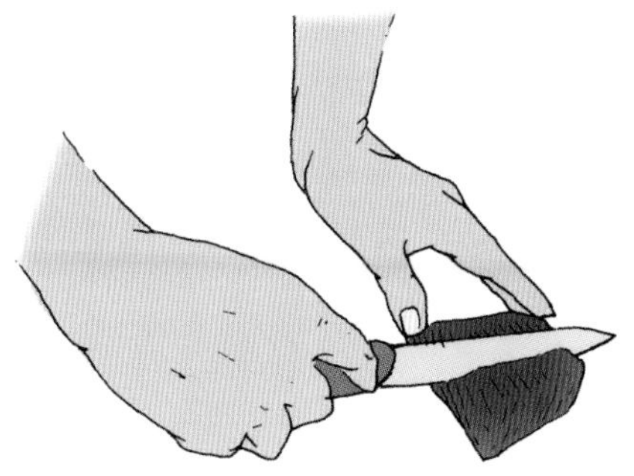

5 Cut B in half with the grain. Cut both B pieces into ¾-inch-wide pieces.

6 Make two triangular-shaped pieces by cutting lengthwise along lines 1 and 2 on C (not illustrated).

Section C, which is not typically used for *sashimi,* can be trimmed and poached in a green tea-soy sauce mixture as follows:

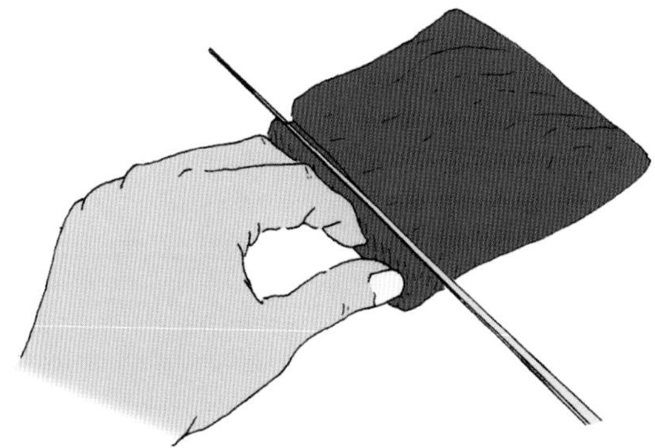

7 Trim and discard the tough fibrous end of section C by cutting along line 3.

8 Cut, with the grain, into ¾-inch slices. There should be 5 or 6 pieces. These pieces can be prepared in the following manner:

Poaching Liquid for Tuna

¼ cup green tea liquid
1½ ounces soy sauce
½ tablespoon crushed ginger
1 tablespoon chopped scallion

Combine all the ingredients and poach tuna in the mixture for 3 minutes. Remove the tuna from the liquid and let it cool. Serve the fish with the poaching liquid as a sauce.

Squid Sashimi

One exception to the rule of fresh seafood for *sashimi* is squid. The Japanese make *sashimi* from their own large variety known as *mongo ika*. This species is usually available in this country in frozen chunks.

After thawing the squid, pull off the transparent membrane which covers the body.

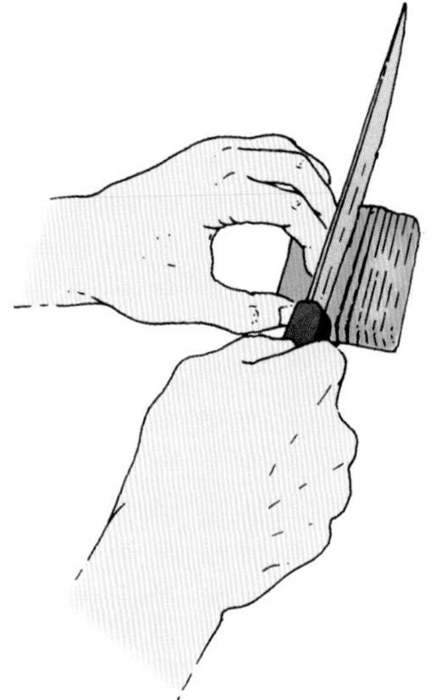

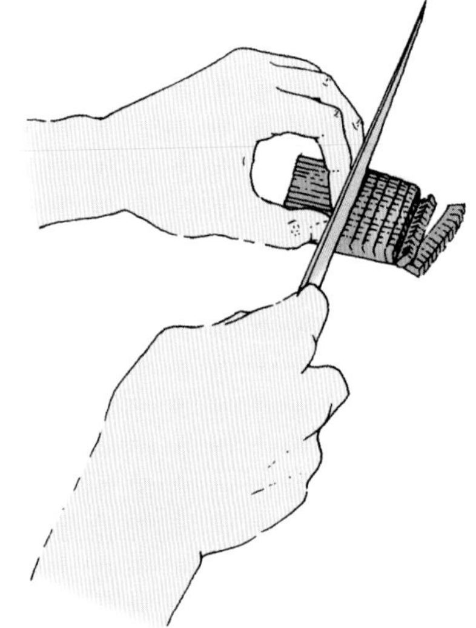

1 *Make parallel lengthwise cuts ⅛ inch apart, slicing to within ⅛ inch of the other side.*

2 *Cut 3/16-inch slices perpendicular to the first cuts.*

3 *Open up each slice into a half circle. Arrange the slices on a serving tray.*

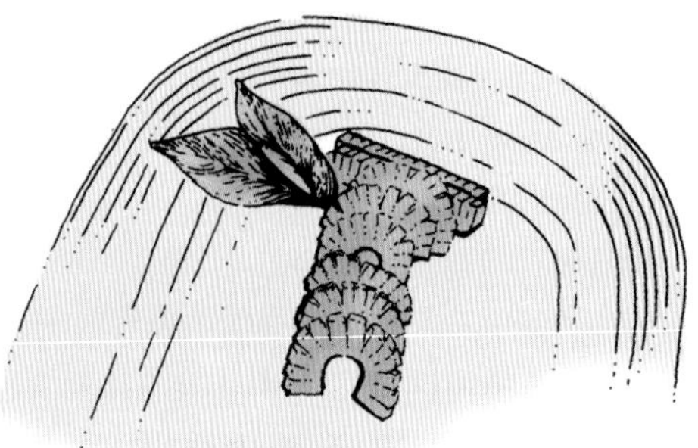

Mackerel Sashimi

Dress and filet a small mackerel, reserving the skeleton and head (pages 23–28).

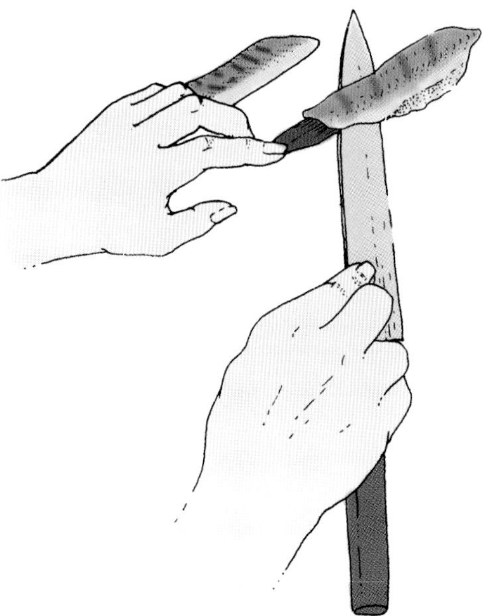

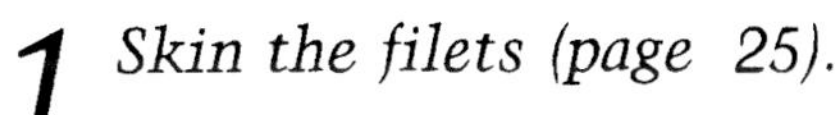

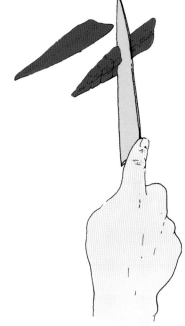

1 *Skin the filets (page 25).*

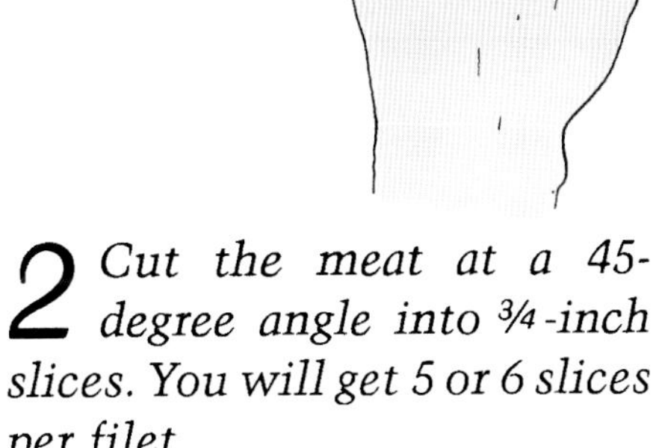

2 *Cut the meat at a 45-degree angle into ¾-inch slices. You will get 5 or 6 slices per filet.*

3 *Prop the head and tail up with pieces of* daikon *(page 146), carrot or other vegetable. Arrange both filets on top of the bones, overlapped like fish scales.*

Fresh Tuna Salad

Alternatives: *Halibut, shark, bonito*

Serves 4 as an appetizer

2 red or green bell peppers, seeded and cut in half

½ pound tuna filet, poached in wine or Fumet (page 252), marinated with olive oil and chilled

1–2 teaspoons chopped garlic

3 tablespoons or more olive oil

1–2 tablespoons lemon juice

Salt and pepper to taste

1 head butter or red leaf lettuce, washed and thoroughly dried

Preheat the broiler.

Char the outsides of the peppers. Remove the skins by rubbing each piece with a paper towel. Cut the peppers into thin slices. Combine the peppers, tuna, garlic, olive oil, lemon juice and salt and pepper in a small bowl. Toss until the tuna and vegetables are well coated with the dressing. Marinate at room temperature or in the refrigerator for 30 minutes to 2 hours. Serve the salad on a bed of lettuce.

This salad may also be dressed with a flavored mayonnaise (pages 257–59), thinned with oil and lemon juice.

WAHOO

(Acanthocybium solandri)

Other Names: *Ono.*

Description: *Grey-blue fading to silver. Random silver lateral stripes.*

Size: *20–40 pounds and up.*

Range: *Worldwide in warm oceans.*

Season: *Winter–spring.*

Fat Content: *Moderate–high.*

Yield: *60% filet.*

Available Forms: *Steak, filet.*

Frequently called the gourmet's mackerel, this delicious fish is also a sportfisherman's favorite. It occasionally comes into our markets from Hawaii, often under its local name, *ono*, which means "sweet." Its flavor is milder than that of the mackerels, to which it is related, and more like that of albacore. Use wahoo steaks or filets in place of tuna or bonito.

WHELK

(Buccinum undatum)

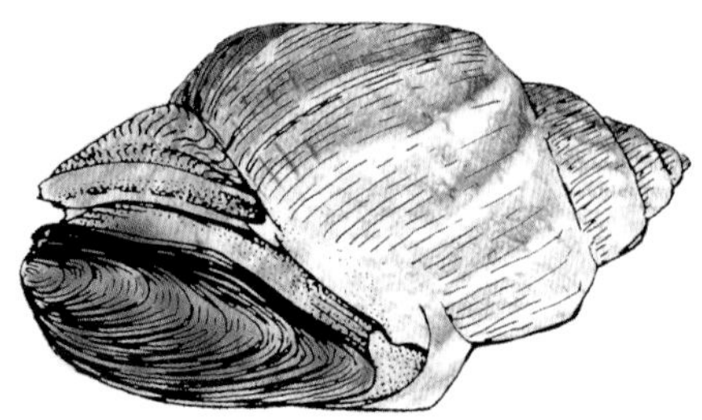

Other Names: *Conch, scungilli, sea snail.*	**Range:** *Different species are found from the mid-Atlantic states to Canada.*
Description: *Grey to brown snail.*	**Season:** *Spring-fall.* **Fat Content:** *Low.*
Size: *Up to 8 inches. Commonly 2 per pound.*	**Available Forms:** *Live, shucked.*

Whelk is popular in the Italian community. A Pacific Coast species can occasionally be found in Chinese markets.

Whelk is delicious when properly prepared. It has a rather tough texture, but becomes pleasantly chewy after slow cooking. Cook as for abalone after pounding, or use in Ceviche (page 70).

Whelk Vinaigrette

Serves 4 as a first course

4 whelk, in the shell
4 tablespoons olive oil
2 tablespoons lemon juice
1 teaspoon prepared mustard
2 teaspoons chopped parsley or other mild fresh herb
Salt and pepper to taste

Boil the whelk in lightly salted water for 3 minutes. Remove the meat from the shell. Cut the lighter-colored meat away from the soft entrails, which are not edible. Simmer for 30 minutes. Cut the meat into thin slices. Combine the remaining ingredients in a bowl large enough to hold the whelk. Add the meat to the vinaigrette, and toss thoroughly. Marinate for at least 4 hours, and preferably overnight.

Serve on a bed of lettuce or spinach, garnished with diced tomato and red onion if you like.

YELLOWTAIL

(Seriola dorsalis)

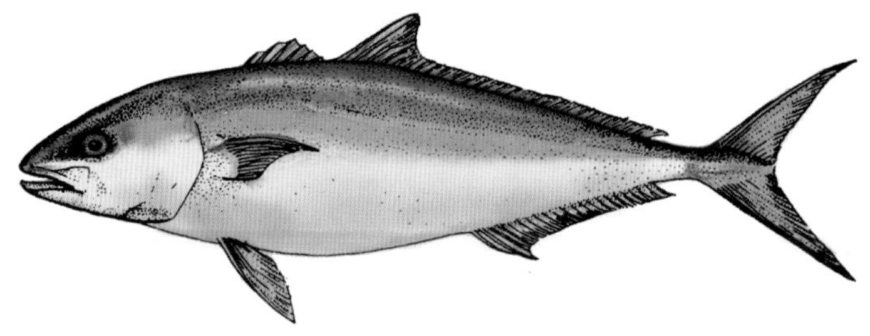

Other Names: *Yellowtail jack.*

Description: *Grey-green above. Broad yellow lateral line. Silver below.*

Size: *4–20 pounds.*

Range: *Southern California coast. Also northern Chile.*

Season: *Spring–summer.*

Fat Content: *Moderate.*

Yield: *60% filet.*

Available Forms: *Round, filet, steak.*

Yellowtail is primarily a game fish, but is occasionally available commercially. It is a member of the jack family, which includes the Florida pompano and several other popular game and food species. While less rich, it approaches tuna and wahoo in flavor and texture, and is suitable for the same cooking methods. Yellowtail is also popular for *sushi* and Sashimi (page 242), and is aquacultured in Japan.

Court-Bouillon

Poaching Liquid

Court-Bouillon is a seasoned liquid used for poaching fish, meats or vegetables. Its composition varies according to its use; the following is a fairly typical one for fish. After being used to poach fish, the liquid makes a good base for a *fumet* made with the remaining bones or trimmings.

Yield: 2 quarts

To 2 quarts water, add several sprigs of parsley or a handful of parsley stems, a few celery leaves, a bay leaf or two, 1 teaspoon cracked peppercorns, a few fennel or anise seeds or chopped fennel stalks, and a small onion, peeled and quartered, or a handful of green onion or leek tops. Adding some form of acid, either a cup of dry white wine or ¼ cup white vinegar or lemon juice, will help the fish keep its color and will absorb any ammonia flavors from shark or skate.

Bring all ingredients to a boil, simmer 20 minutes and strain.

Fumet

Fish Stock

Any part of the fish except the entrails and gills may be used to make *fumet*. Crab and shrimp shells add flavor, as do shrimp heads. Fish stocks do not need to cook nearly as long as meat stocks because the bones render their flavor quickly. Thirty minutes of cooking will produce a fairly rich stock which may then be strained and reduced.

Yield: About 3 quarts

2–3 pounds fish and shellfish heads, bones and trimmings

½ cup diced celery

2 medium yellow onions, peeled and diced

2 bay leaves

¼ cup parsley stems

Thyme, oregano or other dried herbs

Water and white wine to cover or *Court-Bouillon* *(page 251)*

Wash fish parts well. Split heads and crack large bones. Simmer all the ingredients for 30 minutes to 1 hour, skimming any foam from the surface. Strain and reserve the stock.

To freeze, pour cooled stock into a container or ice cube tray. If using a container, seal it well. Fish stock will keep 3 months in the freezer.

Beurre Blanc

This delicious and versatile sauce can be used to accompany almost any grilled, broiled or poached fish, as well as many vegetables. The reduction may be made in advance and stored, refrigerated, for several weeks. Left-over *beurre blanc* may be used as a compound butter, or may be mixed into the next batch if added very gradually.

Yield: 1 cup

¼ cup finely chopped shallots

¼ cup white wine or *vermouth*

¼ cup lemon juice or *white wine vinegar* or *a mixture of the two*

½ pound sweet butter, cut into cubes of 1 ounce or less

In a non-aluminum saucepan, combine the shallots and the liquids and reduce until nearly dry but not too dark. Watch carefully, as the reduction will scorch easily at this point. Remove the pan from the heat and add one or two pieces of butter. Stir steadily with a whisk or wooden spoon until the butter is melted. Return the pan to the heat and incorporate the rest of the butter, one or two pieces at a time. If the butter separates, the heat is too high; remove from the heat and stir rapidly to re-emulsify.

Serve the sauce immediately or hold it in a double boiler over barely simmering water.

Beurre Rouge

Follow the same procedure as above, using red wine and red vinegar to produce a pale rose-colored sauce which is very attractive on white-fleshed fish.

Compound Butters

Compound butters—softened butter combined with herbs, spices and other flavorings—make simple and delicious sauces for grilled, broiled or poached fish. Rolled into a cylinder in wax paper, wrapped tightly and frozen, they may be kept on hand and sliced off as needed for an instant sauce.

Maître d'Hôtel Butter

Yield: ½ cup (enough for 8 servings)

2 ounces butter, softened

1 tablespoon chopped parsley or chervil

1 teaspoon chopped shallots

¼ teaspoon lemon juice

Salt, pepper, lemon juice to taste

Beat the butter by hand or in an electric mixer until quite soft and light. Wrap the chopped herbs in a towel and squeeze out as much liquid as possible. Combine the herbs, shallots, lemon zest and butter and season to taste. Use immediately or freeze for future use; if left overnight unfrozen, the shallots will become unpleasantly strong.

Variations

Use the same procedure as above, adding salt and pepper to taste. In each case the amounts given are for 2 ounces of butter.

Anchovy Butter *(excellent on grilled shark, angler, halibut or swordfish): 1–2 anchovy filets, rinsed and chopped; zest of ½ lemon, grated and finely chopped; pinch black pepper; 1 clove garlic, blanched, peeled and pounded (optional); 1 teaspoon chopped capers (optional).*

Cilantro-Lime Butter *(goes well with strong-flavored fish such as tuna or salmon): 2 tablespoons chopped cilantro; 1 teaspoon soy sauce; 2 teaspoons lime juice.*

Wasabi Butter *(best suited to members of the tuna family and other rich fish): 1–3 teaspoons* wasabi *(page 44); 1 teaspoon soy sauce.*

Ginger-Lime Butter *(for delicate-flavored fish): 1 teaspoon chopped or grated young ginger root; 1 teaspoon lime juice.*

Hot Butter Sauces

The simplest type of sauce for grilled or broiled fish is melted butter with herbs and other seasonings added. The basic procedure is the same for all the hot butters: Melt the butter in a skillet; add the garlic or shallots and cook until they lose their raw flavor. Avoid browning the butter or overcooking the sauce, which will produce bitter or harsh flavors.

Most of the compound butters, especially those involving anchovies, may be served as hot butters as well.

The following quantities are for 2 ounces of butter, enough for 4 servings.

Basil-Garlic Butter *(use on full-flavored fish): 1 small clove garlic, chopped or pressed; 1–2 teaspoons chopped or shredded fresh basil* or *parsley* or *thyme.*

Lemon-Garlic Butter: *same as above, but substitute juice of half a lemon for basil.*

Chervil Butter *(use on delicately flavored fish): ½ teaspoon chopped shallots; 2 teaspoons fresh chervil leaves.*

Grenobloise Butter *(a classic French treatment for trout, but also delicious on grilled squid): 1 tablespoon capers; juice of half a lemon.*

Brown Butter *(good with poached skate or other poached white fish; actually a variation on Grenobloise Butter): cook Grenobloise Butter or butter and lemon juice until the butter browns.*

Red Hollandaise Sauce

This procedure, which can be used for Béarnaise or any other Hollandaise variation, does not involve clarified butter; the liquid from the melted butter is incorporated into the sauce in place of the water normally used to thin the sauce.

Yield: ⅔ cup

⅓ cup butter
½ teaspoon paprika
Pinch cayenne (or to taste)
2 egg yolks
1 tablespoon lemon juice or vinegar
Salt to taste

Melt the butter with the paprika and cayenne over low heat, without boiling. Set it aside to cool a little. When fully separated, skim off any floating solids.

In a non-aluminum double boiler or mixing bowl over hot water, beat the yolks over low heat until pale yellow and foamy. Add the lemon or vinegar and a pinch of salt, and continue beating over the heat until the mixture thickens. (Regulate the heat so the yolks do not cook too quickly. If the mixture begins to look like scrambled eggs, it is overcooked.) Remove from heat, ladle about a tablespoon of melted butter into the egg mixture, and beat until all the butter is absorbed. Add the remaining butter gradually, pouring or ladling the butterfat off the milky liquid on the bottom and beating constantly to incorporate all the butter into the sauce. If the sauce is too thick, thin it with some of the remaining liquid from the butter. Correct the seasoning.

Hollandaise may be served immediately or kept warm in a warm water bath for an hour or more.

Béarnaise Sauce

Yield: 1 cup

¼ cup white wine vinegar

¼ cup dry white wine or *vermouth*

2 teaspoons chopped shallots

2 teaspoons chopped fresh, or *vinegar-packed, tarragon*

⅓ cup butter

2 egg yolks

Salt and white pepper to taste

In a non-aluminum saucepan, bring the vinegar, wine, shallots and tarragon to a boil and reduce until almost all the liquid is gone. Let the mixture cool, add it to the egg yolks and proceed as for Red Hollandaise. Add more chopped tarragon to the finished sauce, if desired.

Mayonnaise

Yield: About 1½ cups

2 egg yolks

¼ teaspoon prepared mustard

¼ teaspoon salt

Pinch white pepper

1¼ cups oil (half olive and half peanut is a good blend)

3 tablespoons lemon juice or *white vinegar*

Have all ingredients at room temperature. If the mixing bowl is cold to the touch, warm it with hot water and dry it.

Place the egg yolks in a stainless or glass mixing bowl with the mustard, salt and pepper. Beat the mixture until pale yellow and foamy. Add a spoonful of oil and beat until it is absorbed. Continue adding oil in small quantities, beating constantly, until the mixture thickens. Once a smooth emulsion is formed, the oil may be slowly poured into the bowl; however, if the sauce does not readily absorb the oil, stop adding oil and beat until smooth.

After about half of the oil has been added, alternate oil and lemon juice or vinegar. Continue until all the oil is incorporated. Correct seasoning.

Mayonnaise can also be made in a blender, food processor or tabletop mixer. Follow the same basic procedure, substituting 1 whole egg for the egg yolks if using a blender, and being careful not to add the oil too quickly.

Homemade mayonnaise will keep for several days, refrigerated and covered tightly.

Mayonnaise Variations

The following amounts are all for 1 cup of mayonnaise. The ingredients should be mixed in *after* the mayonnaise has emulsified.

Creole Mayonnaise: *Add ½ teaspoon dry mustard, ¼ teaspoon* each *ground white pepper, cayenne and coriander.*

Green Mayonnaise: *Add ¼ cup chopped parsley and 4 or 5 scallions blanched, cooled and finely chopped.*

Basil Mayonnaise: *Pound a handful of basil leaves in a mortar with a pinch of salt and add. (Optional: Add a clove of garlic to the basil.)*

Curry Mayonnaise: *Add ½ teaspoon or more of curry powder which has been sautéed in a small amount of oil and cooled. (This preliminary cooking prevents a bitter flavor.)*

Fines Herbes Mayonnaise: *Add 1 tablespoon or more of chopped fresh herbs—parsley, chervil, tarragon, thyme, etc.*

Jay's Tartar Sauce

1 cup Mayonnaise (page 257)
2 tablespoons chopped capers
1 tablespoon finely chopped cornichons or gherkins
2 tablespoons finely chopped red onion
Juice of 1 lemon

Combine and serve immediately. If the sauce is stored overnight, the onion becomes strong in flavor and makes the sauce pink.

Isaac's Tartar Sauce

1 cup Mayonnaise (page 257)
2 teaspoons chopped garlic
1 anchovy filet, rinsed and chopped
1 dill pickle, finely chopped
1 tablespoon chopped capers
1 tablespoon lemon juice
1 teaspoon prepared mustard
Pepper to taste

Combine all the ingredients and mix thoroughly. Serve cold or at room temperature.

Aioli

Garlic Mayonnaise

Serve with cold poached fish, grilled fish or boiled crayfish.

Yield: About 1½ cups

3 or 4 large cloves garlic, peeled

2 egg yolks

¼ teaspoon prepared mustard

¼ teaspoon salt

Pinch white pepper

1¼ cups oil (half olive and half peanut is a good blend)

3 tablespoons lemon juice or *white vinegar*

Pound the garlic in a mortar to a smooth paste. Add the egg yolks and combine. Scrape this mixture into a mixing bowl and continue with the mayonnaise procedure (page 257).

Skordalia

This all-purpose almond mayonnaise is traditionally served with firm-fleshed fish such as swordfish or shark.

Yield: About 2 cups

1 cup Aioli (see above)

½ cup ground almonds

½ cup bread crumbs

2 tablespoons lemon juice

Combine and thoroughly mix all the ingredients. Serve cold or at room temperature.

Rouille

This hot garlic sauce is traditionally served with *bouillabaisse* and other fish soups. The recipe is from *The Book of Garlic* by Lloyd J. Harris.

Yield: About 1 cup

½ cup fresh bread crumbs (firmly packed)
¼ cup cold water
10 cloves garlic, finely chopped
2 teaspoons dried red pepper flakes
½ teaspoon salt
6 tablespoons olive oil

Soak the bread crumbs in water for several minutes, then squeeze dry. Pound the garlic, pepper flakes and salt to a fine paste. Add the bread crumbs and pound slowly; when they are well incorporated, stir in the oil, a tablespoon at a time. Use as much oil as is needed to make a smooth paste. The sauce should almost hold its shape in a spoon.

Parsley Sauce

For grilled mild fish.

Yield: About ¾ cup

2 teaspoons chopped garlic
¼ cup finely chopped parsley
¼ cup bread crumbs
1 hard-boiled egg
6 black olives, pitted
¼ cup or more olive oil
Salt and pepper to taste

Purée all the ingredients in a blender or food processor until smooth. Serve immediately or refrigerate and serve chilled. This sauce will keep 3–4 days.

Tarator Sauce

This is not related to tartar sauce, despite the similar name. Serve with fried shellfish or grilled fish.

Yield: About 1 cup

¼ cup bread crumbs
¼ cup walnuts
1 tablespoon minced garlic
2 tablespoons lemon juice
2 tablespoons white vinegar
⅜ cup olive oil
Salt and pepper to taste

Blend all the ingredients until smooth in a food processor or blender. If making the sauce by hand, chop the nuts finely, and combine all the ingredients in a bowl; beat until smooth.

Fresh Tomato Salsa

Yield: 1 cup

1 large tomato, peeled, seeded and diced
¼ cup chopped scallions or *mild onion*
1 or 2 serrano *or other small hot chiles, seeded and finely chopped*
2 tablespoons chopped cilantro
Salt to taste

Combine all ingredients at least an hour before serving to allow flavors to marry. If more chile flavor is desired, add more seeded and chopped chiles. For a hotter sauce, the seeds and veins of the chiles may be included.

Leftover *salsa* will not have the crisp texture of the fresh sauce, but may be used in hot dishes or heated in butter for grilled crab or other shellfish.

Sauce Mignonette

Yield: Enough for 24 oysters served on the half-shell

1 shallot, finely chopped
2 teaspoons dry white wine
Red wine vinegar and black pepper to taste

Combine all the ingredients. Serve at room temperature.

Soy-Sesame Dipping Sauce

This is a dipping sauce for boiled or steamed crab, or grilled mild fish.

Yield: About ½ cup

¼ cup red wine vinegar
2 tablespoons soy sauce
2 teaspoons chopped ginger
1 teaspoon sesame oil
1 teaspoon sugar

Combine all the ingredients and mix thoroughly. Serve at room temperature.

Teriyaki Sauce

This recipe first appeared in Isaac's *International Squid Cookbook.*

Yield: 1½ cups

½ cup medium soy sauce

½ cup mirin or *½ cup dry sherry*

½ cup water

2 tablespoons lemon juice

1 teaspoon cornstarch dissolved in 1 tablespoon water

To use as a marinade, combine all the ingredients except for the cornstarch.

To make a basting sauce, heat the marinade until it boils and then add the cornstarch mixture. When the sauce thickens, remove it from the heat and let it cool slightly.

Green Chile Sauce

Somchai Aksomboon

This spicy mixture from Thailand is delicious with any grilled fish or shellfish.

Yield: About ½ cup

2 ounces jalapeño or *other medium-hot chiles, chopped*

¼ cup plain distilled vinegar

2 tablespoons chopped cilantro root

1 tablespoon chopped garlic

Salt to taste

Pureé all the ingredients in a blender or food processor. Serve at room temperature or chilled. This sauce does not keep well.

Fresh Cilantro Chutney

This easy-to-prepare chutney is a fine condiment for grilled or broiled fish. It is best eaten fresh, but will keep refrigerated for a day or so.

Yield: About ½ cup

1 cup cilantro

4 scallions, roughly chopped

1 tablespoon lemon juice

2 small hot green chiles

1 teaspoon garam masala *(page 40)*, or *¼ teaspoon each ground turmeric, cinnamon, cloves and cumin*

Blend all the ingredients in a blender or food processor until smooth, adding a tiny amount of water if necessary to make a smooth paste.

Red Curry Paste

This spicy paste is the basis for a number of Thai curries, usually in conjunction with coconut milk (page 39) and fish sauce (page 40). It will keep for 3–4 days in the refrigerator.

Yield: ¼ cup

5 dried red chiles, seeded, soaked in water and then drained

Salt and pepper to taste

2 teaspoons ground caraway seeds

2 teaspoons ground coriander seeds

1 teaspoon coriander root

2 teaspoons finely chopped fresh lemongrass or *1 teaspoon chopped dried lemongrass*

1 teaspoon finely chopped Laos root (page 41)

1 tablespoon chopped shallots

½ teaspoon shrimp paste (optional) (page 43)

Pound all the ingredients together in a mortar, or blend them in a food processor. The paste should be as smooth as possible.

SEAFOOD PIZZA

Wood-burning pizza ovens are turning out to be to the early eighties what charcoal grilling was to the late seventies—the latest rediscovered cooking technique. While home ovens cannot match the heat of such specialized equipment, baking pizza on an unglazed earthenware surface can produce nearly the same result. Some cookware shops are carrying special round "pizza tiles," but a cheaper solution is available in the form of terra cotta quarry tiles, about 12 inches square, available at building supply yards.

The following recipe gives the general procedure for seafood pizza and a few suggestions for topping combinations. Note that none of these calls for cooked tomato sauce, which can easily overwhelm the other ingredients.

Pizza Dough

Yield: Four 11-inch pizzas or 4 calzones

1 package (1 tablespoon) baker's yeast

1½ cups warm (100°) water

4 cups unbleached bread or *all-purpose flour*

1 tablespoon olive oil

Rice flour, unbleached bread or *all-purpose flour* or *cornmeal*

Olive oil

Dissolve the yeast and 1 tablespoon of flour in ¼ cup of the water. Make sure the yeast bubbles, indicating it is active. Set the yeast aside for 10–15 minutes. Pour the rest of the flour into a bowl. Add the yeast liquid and a little of the water. Stir with a large spoon. Add the rest of the liquid and the olive oil and mix thoroughly, using your hands. This whole procedure can be accomplished quickly in a food processor, using the plastic dough blade. Knead the dough by hand or by machine until it is smooth and resilient. Form into a ball. Oil the bottom of a bowl, and place the dough in it. Cover with a damp towel. Let it rise until it doubles in size, about 2 hours. Punch the dough down and divide into 4 pieces.

Making the Pizza Crust

Form each piece of dough into a ball. Roll each ball on the pastry board with one hand until the top surface is smooth. Place them on a tray at least 2 inches apart, cover with a damp towel and let them rest at least 30 minutes and up to 3–4 hours. (Dough may be prepared to this point and refrigerated overnight; allow at least 1 hour for the dough to warm up to room temperature before forming the pizzas.)

To form pizzas by hand: Dust the board lightly with rice flour, unbleached bread, all purpose flour or cornmeal. With the fingertips, press the dough into a circle of equal thickness, about 6 inches in diameter. Pick up the circle between the palms and fingers of both hands and gently stretch the edge of the circle. Work around the edge, letting the dough hang. As the dough stretches to about 8 or 9 inches in diameter, drape it over the back of one hand and wrist and stretch with the other hand. Continue working around the circle until the dough is about 11 inches across.

With a rolling pin: If the above procedure is too difficult to follow, the dough may be rolled out into an 11-inch circle with a rolling pin. The crust will, however, have a heavier texture than a hand-formed pizza.

Place the dough on a baking sheet sprinkled with cornmeal or, if baking directly on a tile surface, on the *underside* of a baking sheet sprinkled with cornmeal. If there are any holes or very thin spots in the dough, stretch enough from a thicker spot to close them. Compress or roll the edge of the dough slightly, forming a raised rim. Brush the dough lightly with a little olive oil, the best possible quality. Sprinkle with chopped garlic and the remaining toppings, such as those suggested below. If baking on tiles, gently slide the pizza onto the tiles, taking care not to dislodge the toppings or tear the dough. Bake until the edge of the dough is golden brown. With a wide spatula or two, transfer the pizza to a serving platter or a cutting board which can go to the table. Sprinkle with a bit more olive oil and fresh herbs, if desired.

Pizza Toppings

The following are some suggested combinations, each listed in recommended order of assembly. Most contain at least one salty ingredient, so additional salt will not be needed, but black pepper should be added to taste.

Yield: Enough for 11-inch pizza

Shrimp and Feta: *½ cup peeled, seeded and sliced tomato, ¼ cup crumbled feta cheese, fresh oregano or marjoram, 4–6 ounces peeled small shrimp.*

Clam and Mussel: *½ cup grated Parmesan or Romano cheese, ¼–½ pound steamed and shucked clams or mussels, extra garlic, chopped parsley.*

Tuna with Fresh Herbs: *½ cup tomato, 4–6 ounces fresh tuna, bonito or squid in ¾-inch cubes, 2–4 anchovy filets (rinsed and coarsely chopped), fresh thyme, marjoram or oregano.*

Mixed Shellfish Calzone

Calzone, a sort of pizza turnover originally from Florence, is becoming very popular in many of the newer upscale pizzerias. The classic version contains only cheeses, herbs and *prosciutto* or *pancetta;* the addition of tomatoes is considered heresy in Florence, but is fairly common here. Our version uses a typical cheese mixture, an atypical assortment of seafood, and no tomato.

Serves 2

⅓ cup grated mozzarella cheese

⅓ cup ricotta cheese

¼ cup grated Parmesan cheese

½ teaspoon chopped garlic

1 tablespoon chopped parsley

Salt and pepper to taste

½ cup assorted shellfish: steamed and shucked mussels or clams; shucked and drained oysters; peeled shrimp, roughly chopped if large; and squid, cut into rings and blanched

¼ recipe Pizza Dough (see above)

Combine the cheeses, garlic and parsley and season to taste. Add the shellfish and set aside. Preheat oven to 500°.

Lightly dust the pastry board with rice flour or all-purpose flour. Roll the dough out to a 12-inch circle. Place the cheese mixture on one side of the dough, leaving at least a 2-inch margin. Brush the edge of the dough with a little water and fold the other half of the dough over the filling, matching the edges. Fold the sealed edge inward in a decorative pattern. Bake on tiles or a baking sheet until crust is golden brown and sounds hollow when tapped. Brush the top with olive oil and sprinkle with Parmesan, if desired. Serve with knives and forks.

(Note: Smaller, individual calzones may be made, but will require proportionately more dough.)

A Cook's Seafood Miscellany

PART III

A FISHMONGER'S DAY

(Editor's Note: The following is an account of a typical day for Paul Johnson and those who work with him. Paul is a wholesale and retail fish dealer in daily contact with all facets of the seafood business. As is true for many of his colleagues, his concern for quality and freshness is evidenced by the rigors and challenges of his day. For all his success, Paul is very modest and resisted the inclusion of this portrait. The editor, however, prevailed.)

PAUL wakes up at 3:15 am. As he drives from the East Bay and through San Francisco, he passes newspapermen, garbage collectors and a few transients sleeping in doorways. Otherwise, the streets are empty.

At 4, give or take ten minutes, Paul arrives at the wharf in San Francisco. On any given day, where he stops first depends on which wholesalers have boats out fishing and on what kind of fish they are likely to catch. Today, the first call is on Standard Fish. He buys 400 pounds of rockfish, including fantails, boccacios, yellowtail and blacks. There is no time to check the quality of each fish, but Paul knows how they were caught and when the boats arrived, and makes his selections based on that information. He will return to this dealer later in the morning, so he reports his weights and leaves without signing the bill.

By 4:30, the wharf is bustling with activity. The distributors and their crews are hard at work unloading and moving fish, shoveling ice and filling orders. Paul comes to the wharf five days a week; one of his assistants does the buying on a sixth. He knows the buyers and sellers and they all know him. Their business dealings follow a strict but unwritten code which it has taken Paul awhile to learn. His experience and his reputation as a consistent, steady customer for large quantities of fresh seafood enable him to obtain quality seafood every day.

Paul knows that two boats fishing for two different companies are due to arrive at 4:30. He makes an educated guess as to which one will have the fish he needs—in this case the rather scarce halibut—and drives along the Embarcadero to the docks. Today, he has guessed right. Hayes Street Grill will be pleased with the 150 pounds of large halibut.

Fifteen minutes later he drives back to the wharf and stops at another wholesaler. He buys another 400 pounds of rockfish, which he will filet a few hours later in his shop in Berkeley. Paul exchanges wharf gossip and information as he waits in line for a bill. As he leaves, Paul is approached by another wholesaler who has arrived a few minutes late, missed all his connections and ended up empty-handed. Paul sells him some of the halibut which he hustled to find, knowing the favor will be returned.

As he hands over the fish, Paul learns that a drag boat has just docked with a good catch. Losing no time, he walks over to the end of the wharf. A crowd of wholesalers has already gathered. This is winter and fish are somewhat scarce. Paul quickly sizes things up and places his order. He buys 500 pounds of the prized petrale sole, 150 pounds of rex sole, and 250 pounds of lingcod.

A few minutes before 7:00, Paul picks up a 250-pound crate of crabs which had been delivered after Paul left the wharf the day before. (Having learned yesterday that there would be no fresh crabs today, he phoned ahead to have some set aside. They are waiting for him in a covered box, stored in the ocean.) The van is nearly full now with more than a ton of fish.

Earlier, Paul had looked for the California Seafood Express, a daily express truck delivery from San Pedro. He has 470 pounds of Hawaiian tuna on order but today he will have to do without. The driver, seeing the name "Monterey Fish" on the box, thought Paul's tuna belonged in Monterey, which is where he left them. Paul has to make substitutions; there is no time to fret over mistakes. Fortunately, another wholesaler hears of his plight and offers him some wahoo which have not yet been claimed.

Just before 8:00, Paul leaves San Francisco, crossing the Bay Bridge against the rush-hour traffic. When he arrives at the shop, he and his staff, who opened up an hour earlier, unload the fish and begin fileting and sorting. While Peter and Jed cut,

Paul is on the phone to his suppliers. He calls San Pedro to enquire about his tuna and to request mackerel, squid (fresh from Southern California during the winter months) and bonito for tomorrow. Another call, this time to Washington state for steelhead and geoduck clams. Then he phones a San Francisco broker who will arrange for the shipment of scallops, mussels and angler from the East Coast. Finally, Paul speaks to an Hawaiian broker who will send him more tuna, mahi-mahi and spearfish.

Around 9:00, the restaurants begin to call in. Each of Paul's restaurant accounts orders daily, selecting from a list patiently recited for each customer. Some have called in requests the night before on his answering machine. Paul has dealt with most of his customers for years and knows their likes and dislikes, so he has bought accordingly. Most of them serve a variety of fresh seafood, listing their daily selection on a chalkboard or a clip-on list attached to their menus. The orders are quickly assembled by Joan and Robert, as much of the fish is needed for lunch.

By 10:30, Peter leaves with the San Francisco deliveries, and Jed heads for the East Bay restaurants with the other truck. After delivering fish to the Hayes Street Grill, Balboa Cafe, Zuni Cafe and Squid's, Peter heads for San Francisco Airport to pick up 400 pounds of steelhead which have just arrived by air from Washington. Jed makes the rounds to Chez Panisse, the Fourth Street Grill, Santa Fe Bar and Grill, Augusta's and Bay Wolf, then returns to the shop to assemble other orders for dinner.

Paul, Jed and Peter spend the early afternoon filling dinner orders and making additional pick-ups at the airport and other deliveries wherever they are needed. Paul tries to finish his day by 3:00, but sometimes he works much later. With luck, he will get to bed by 8:00 so he can rise at 3:15 to begin his day again.

WINE AND SEAFOOD

Along with the dramatic increases in the quality and worldwide reputation of California wines has come a steady increase in the sophistication of the American wine drinker. Many are learning to trust their own tastes more than the oversimplifications of traditional wine and food affinity charts. It no longer seems heretical to suggest, for example, that some red wines be served with fish.

Of course, the traditional combination of dry white wines and seafood is still valid. But many of the attributes of the classic seafood wines apply equally to certain red wines: good acidity, little or no tannin, light to medium body and not-too-pronounced varietal character. Conversely, a big, powerful oak-aged white wine (including many of California's most celebrated wines) may be too much for simple seafood dishes.

Rather than suggesting specific wines to go with each recipe in this book, we offer the following guidelines. Limitations of space prevent us from mentioning many other suitable wines.

One classic combination with which we cannot argue is *oysters and Champagne.* Chablis (the real thing from Chablis, not the ubiquitous domestic version) and Côteaux Champenois (basically Champagne without the bubbles) are also excellent choices, and Muscadet is a more than adequate alternative. All are bone dry with good acidity and a characteristic soil flavor which goes nicely with the rich texture and fresh seawater flavor of the oysters.

For most simple preparations of *grilled, poached or broiled fish,* choose a dry white of light to medium body. If there is an all-purpose seafood wine, it may be Sancerre, which has a definite Sauvignon Blanc character in delightful harmony with the local soil. Other choices would be lighter California Chardonnay or Sauvignon Blanc, dry Chenin Blanc or French Colombard; Mâcon or other light white Burgundy, Pouilly-Fumé, white Bordeaux, Muscadet or Alsatian Riesling; or various Italian whites such as the Pinot Bianco or Pinot Grigio of the Northeast or Gavi from Piedmont.

For richer fish and shellfish, especially when prepared with cream, some of the bigger whites, California Chardonnays and whites from the Côte de Beaune in particular, should be added to the above list in place of some of the lighter wines.

Fish with a pronounced flavor, such as tuna, and preparations with such Mediterranean flavors as anchovy, garlic and olives, are better served by a fuller-bodied white, blanc de noirs, rosé or a light red. With these dishes, try some of the following: whites and rosés from the Rhône and Provence or from southern Italy; slightly chilled Beaujolais, red Côtes du Rhône, Chianti, Valpolicella or California Gamay; or "white" wines made from red grapes, especially Pinot Noir, which are labeled under a variety of names such as Pinot Noir Blanc and Vin Gris.

Latin American, Southeast Asian, Chinese and Creole cuisines are harder to match with wines. For milder dishes, follow the above guidelines. A white wine with a very pronounced aroma and flavor, such as Gewürztraminer, is frequently suggested with such flavors as pepper, ginger and garlic; some experts suggest Sancerre or another Sauvignon instead. (Another expert, wine importer and writer Gerald Asher, has suggested a different approach to wine and Chinese food. The array of flavors and textures in a Chinese meal, he says, is only confused by the addition of an assertive wine. He recommends instead a mild, off-dry wine such as a Chenin Blanc, to serve as a "silk curtain" behind the food.) Where fresh or dried chiles are a major ingredient in a dish, no wine will be complemented by the food, and the wine is mainly a refreshment. A little sweetness goes a long way in softening the effect of hot pepper on the palate, so an off-dry to slightly sweet wine might be in order. For really hot dishes, however, the best beverage is beer.

Riesling seems especially well suited to *freshwater fish.* Several German producers are once again shipping dry or nearly-dry wines in addition to the better-known sweet wines. Look for the word "Trocken" or "Halbtroken" on the main label or neck label. Try these with trout, steelhead or salmon.

If wine is used in any quantity in a dish, serve the same or the same type of wine.

THE CALIFORNIA OYSTER STORY

THE oyster has an exotic reputation in almost every culture where it is a food. Its reputation as an aphrodisiac is legendary and often overshadows the oyster's culinary virtues. For now we will leave aside its effects on human sexual behavior to consider the no less interesting story of the oyster's own reproductive life.

California oyster aquaculture began in the first days of the Gold Rush. Oysters were a delicacy much in demand in the strike-it-rich atmosphere of the mining camps. Local supplies of the indigenous Pacific oyster were quickly exhausted by the huge demand. The cry for oysters was so loud that Eastern oysters were dispatched by boat around South America, and small Pacific oysters were sent from Oregon and Washington to be transplanted in the San Francisco Bay to mature.

Completion of the transcontinental railroad encouraged the shipment of small Eastern oysters to the West Coast and they, too, were grown to full size in the Bay. However, they never reproduced here and eventually that part of the industry died out.

As the water quality of the Bay deteriorated, all "grow-out" activity declined, and by 1939 the San Francisco Bay oyster industry disappeared.

In the early 1930s, Japanese oyster seed was brought to the Pacific coast. The Japanese oyster was ideally suited to the region and has flourished despite a period of decline during the 1940s and early 1950s. Today, the Japanese oyster is the single most important species in California. It is grown primarily in Humboldt, Drake's, Tomales and Morro bays. The French Belon oyster was introduced to California seven years ago and it does quite well here too; in fact, Belon seed is now exported back to France.

Oyster Aquaculture

There are two methods for growing oysters, known in the trade as *cultch* and *cultchless*.

Cultch Method

In the *cultch* method there are two different techniques. In one, more common in Pacific bays, the fertilized eggs are spread on strings of oyster shells suspended in the water; the strings are hauled out of the water for harvest and re-seeded. The other, termed the broadcast technique, is more common in Eastern and Gulf coast oyster beds. The fertilized eggs are spread (broadcast) over the beds of shells; the oysters are harvested by dredging, after which the beds are rebuilt and re-seeded. Since string culture uses more of the water's depth than broadcasting, it allows more yield per acre.

Cultchless Method

In the cultchless method, each fertilized egg attaches itself to a tiny piece of ground shell. The process begins in the laboratory under carefully controlled conditions. Separate tanks of male and female oysters are induced by warm water to spawn; the eggs are then fertilized by hand. The fertilized eggs are poured into tanks containing warm filtered seawater and fed a diet of cultured microscopic algae.

After a few weeks of steady growth they are poured through screens. The biggest oysters are caught and the smaller (and slower growing) ones fall through to be discarded. This sizing process, which is repeated every few days, produces a uniformly sturdy stock with a high survival rate. Growth and screening continue for two weeks. Finely chopped shell is then introduced and the oysters grow a foot which attaches to the small pieces in the same way that cultch oysters attach to strings or beds of shells. At this stage, oysters are known as "spat." Selective screening continues until the spat reach a size of 2–3 mm. Oyster spat can be packed into small boxes—a tiny crate will hold thousands—and shipped any place in the world where water conditions are suitable for grow-out. The survival rate of properly handled spat is well above 50%.

In the "nursery stage," the spat are floated in salt bays in boxes covered with fine mesh, washed and sometimes screened. The oysters are transferred to various containers to mature: nets suspended from rafts; bags suspended on racks extending above the bottom of the bay; or bags resting on the bottom. The oysters mature in 9–10 months, then are removed, washed and packed for immediate shipping, or held for later use in tanks containing purified seawater.

This approach, which was perfected in the 1960s, allows for quicker and more uniform growth and a higher survival rate than the cultch. The oysters also tend to be leaner and more flavorful.

AN OUNCE OF PREVENTION

WHILE seafood is widely and rightly viewed as healthful food, there are a few health risks associated with fish and shellfish. These include toxins inherent in the fish, toxins produced by other organsms, and parasites. Fortunately these dangers are relatively rare, and high-risk situations are easily identifiable.

Two fish that have *poisonous roe* are commonly eaten by Americans: cabezon (a Pacific coast sculpin) and alligator gar (a large Gulf coast species). The flesh is perfectly safe; only the eggs should be avoided.

Certain freshwater or anadramous species such as salmon are occasionally infested with a *tapeworm* (*Diphllobothrium* sp.) which is contracted during their freshwater cycle. These worms, which parasitize humans as well as animals, are easy to avoid. Either eat only anadramous fish caught in the open sea, or follow the precautions suggested by the National Center for Disease Control:

> Fish tapeworm infection. . . can be prevented by cooking until all parts of the fish reach a temperature of at least 113° for five minutes. Freezing to 0° farenheit for 24 hours can also prevent infection. Preparation by placing the fish in a brine solution may be effective if appropriate salt concentration, filet size and contact time are observed. Commercially prepared lox is usually brined before smoking and should not constitute a source of infection.

Tapeworms can cause extremely unpleasant symptoms and precautionary measures should be taken. Freshwater and anadramous fish which have not first been frozen are not recommended for *sashimi, ceviche* or any other uncooked preparation.

Certain fish species, notably mahi-mahi and tuna, contain large quantities of an amino acid called histadine which converts to histamines after the fish is caught. If the fish is not properly iced, as is sometimes the case in tropical fishing grounds, histamine production is accelerated. Individual sensitivity to histimine varies, and in some people these fish may produce *histamine poisoning.* Symptoms commonly include flushing, headache, dizziness, thick tongue and heaviness in the chest. The symptoms come on quickly, much like an MSG reaction, although they are more severe and last longer. Histamine poisoning is routinely treated with antihistamines; after proper care the ill effects disappear quickly.

The most serious threat to health is also the best known—*shellfish poisoning.* Shellfish poisoning is the result of a one-celled organism, a *dynoflagellate* called *Gonyaulax catenella,* which "blooms" only in temperate waters during the summer months. There is an official quarantine on all wild bivalves in California from May 1 to October 31. During that period it is unsafe to eat mussels, oysters or clams; these bivalves are filter-feeders which ingest *dynoflagellates* in large quantities and concentrate the toxin in the dark portions of their meat. Harvesting of commercial oyster beds is carefully monitored by the Federal Trade Commission for *dynoflagellate* levels during summer months. Harvesting is halted whenever there is a significant risk. Fresh aquacultured oysters are therefore available through most of the summer. Shellfish poisoning can be fatal. The toxin is not destroyed by freezing, cooking or aging, and there is no simple way to determine whether a particular bivalve is toxic before you eat it.

Sustainability Resources

Choosing sustainable seafood is not a simple process. The following is a list of websites that compile the latest catch information and recommendations from government and private agencies such as the Monterey Bay Aquarium Seafood Watch and the Seafood Choices Alliance. As a consumer, you can ask these questions to help you make informed decisions: How was the seafood caught or raised? Where was it caught? Does it have a long reproductive cycle? Is the fishery well managed?

Monterey Bay Aquarium Seafood Watch
www.montereybayaquarium.org/cr/seafoodwatch.aspx

Environmental Defense Fund Seafood Selector
www.edf.org/page.cfm?tagID=1521

World Wildlife Fund Sustainable Seafood Consumer Guides
http://wwf.panda.org/what_we_do/how_we_work/conservation/marine/sustainable_fishing/sustainable_seafood/seafood_guides

Blue Ocean Institute Seafood Guide
www.blueocean.org/seafood/seafood-guide

Marine Stewardship Council
www.msc.org/where-to-buy/msc-labelled-seafood-in-shops-and-restaurants

Charting Nature Sustainable Seafood Guides
www.chartingnature.com/seafood-guides.cfm

Seafood Choices Alliance
www.seafoodchoices.com/home.php

National Resources Defense Council Sustainable Seafood Guide
www.nrdc.org/oceans/seafoodguide/page4.asp

Food and Water Watch Smart Seafood Guide
www.foodandwaterwatch.org/fish/seafood/guide

SeaChoice
www.seachoice.org

Greenpeace Seafood
www.greenpeace.org/usa/en/campaigns/oceans/seafood

BIBLIOGRAPHY

Davidson, Alan, *Mediterranean Seafood*, Louisiana State University Press, Baton Rouge, Louisiana, 1972.

Davidson, Alan, *North Atlantic Seafood*, Viking Press, N.Y., 1979.

Gates, Doyle and Frey, Herbert, "Designated Common Names of Certain Marine Organisms of California," California Department of Fish and Game, Sacramento, California, 1972.

Johnson, Myrtle and Snook, Harry, *Seashore Animals of the Pacific Coast*, Dover Publications, N.Y., 1927.

Miller, Daniel and Lea, Robert, *Guide to the Coastal Marine Fishes of California*, California Department of Fish and Game, Sacramento, California, 1972.

McClane, A.J., *The Encyclopedia of Fish Cookery*, Holt, Rinehart and Winston, N.Y., 1977.

McClane, A.J. (Ed.), *Field Guide to Freshwater Fishes of North America*, Holt, Rinehart and Winston, N.Y., 1965.

McClane, A.J. (Ed.) *Field Guide to Saltwater Fishes of North America*, Holt, Rinehart and Winston, N.Y., 1965.

Index

Italic page numbers refer to the encyclopedic entries for each species. Other references to a given species (as an alternative or in passing) follow in Roman type. Recipes are listed in boldface.

Contents

Introduction

"... the catfish is a plenty good enough fish for anybody ..."

Mark Twain wrote that in 1883 when catfish were at the peak of their popularity. In fact, prior to the 1960s largemouth-bass fishing boom, Americans always looked upon catfish as highly desirable sport and food fish.

That changed when bass tournaments became the rage, and anglers began focusing more attention on trout, walleyes, and other fish. Catfish anglers became nonentities. Most tackle manufacturers ignored them. The outdoor media snubbed them. Some even tried to shame them.

All the while, however, Americans continued catfishing. Throughout the 1960s, 1970s, and 1980s, catfish maintained their position as the country's third most popular fish. Only black bass and panfish were more in demand. Such is still the case today.

In recent years, anglers, manufacturers, and media realized they no longer could ignore these whiskered pole-benders' many positive attributes. Catfish are widespread, abundant, grow large (130 pounds and heavier), eagerly take a variety of baits, fight hard, and are delicious. What's not to like?

Number and Distribution of Catfish Anglers

According to the US Fish and Wildlife Service's *2006 National Survey of Fishing, Hunting, and Wildlife-Associated Recreation*, approximately 6.95 million US anglers age sixteen and older fish for catfish, 27.3 percent of our 25.4 million adult freshwater anglers.

More than half of all US catfish anglers (3.99 million) reside in just ten states: Texas (1.035 million), Missouri (448,000), Georgia (395,000), Florida (389,000), Illinois (335,000), Tennessee (298,000), North Carolina (294,000), Ohio (288,000), Oklahoma (264,000), and Alabama (245,000). But catfish also are popular in states with fewer anglers. In Nebraska, for example, no other fish are more sought with 69,000 catfish anglers statewide. Catfish rank second in popularity behind black bass or panfish in Arkansas (235,000 anglers), Mississippi (218,000), Kansas (216,000), Iowa (214,000), and Louisiana (207,000).

Most catfish anglers reside in the South or Midwest where catfish are most plentiful. The fewest live in the Northeast and West, which are regions at the periphery of catfish range with fewer fish available. Ten states report few to no catfish anglers: Alaska, Connecticut, Hawaii, Maine, Montana, New Hampshire, North Dakota, Rhode Island, Vermont, and Wyoming. Catfish also rank low in popularity in Colorado, Delaware, Idaho, Maryland, Massachusetts, Michigan, Minnesota, New Jersey, New York, Nevada, Oregon, Pennsylvania, South Dakota, Utah, Washington, and Wisconsin.

Demographics

Few angler surveys have been conducted to ascertain the demographics of catfish anglers. One was conducted in 2010 in Texas, a

state where catfish exceed even black bass in popularity. No other state has as many catfish anglers (1,035,000) or a larger percentage of anglers who target catfish (56 percent).

About 51 percent of survey respondents preferred fishing for channel catfish, 35 percent preferred blues, and 12 percent preferred flatheads. Only 2 percent had no preference or preferred bullheads.

On average, respondents had been catfish anglers twenty-nine years and spent twenty days annually catfishing. Approximately 65 percent of trips were spent fishing from a boat and 35 percent from shore. One-third of trips included night fishing. Eighty-one percent used a rod and reel most often, 9 percent used trotlines, 7 percent jug lines, and 3 percent limb lines.

A 2001 Missouri survey provided demographics for the nation's number-two catfishing state (448,000 catfish anglers). Show-Me State catfish anglers are primarily male (79 percent), between ages thirty-six and fifty-five (52 percent), and live mostly (73 percent) in rural communities or small towns (73 percent). Seventy-five percent favored channel catfish, 14 percent flatheads, 9 percent blue catfish, and 2 percent bullheads. More than 80 percent preferred fishing with rod and reel. When asked to choose which scenario (i.e., one twenty-pound catfish, two 10-pound catfish, four 5-pound catfish, or ten 2-pound catfish) best described the number and size of catfish they preferred to catch and keep, most preferred four 5-pound catfish or ten 2-pound catfish. However, age influenced responses. Catfish anglers younger than thirty-five years old preferred catching fewer but larger catfish. Anglers older than fifty-five preferred catching more but smaller catfish.

A 2001 survey of catfish anglers throughout the Mississippi River basin found fishing for fun was the most important reason respondents fished, but catching bigger fish enhanced their trip. More than 70 percent took at least one trip annually to pursue trophy catfish. Trophy anglers preferred blue and flathead catfish, whereas non-trophy anglers preferred channel catfish.

Despite many similarities between catfish anglers and other anglers, a 1999 Mississippi survey found fundamental differences. Catfish anglers, as compared with those fishing for largemouth bass, crappie, and sunfish, placed more importance on harvest levels and catching large fish while showing the least support for harvest restrictions. This survey also discovered catfish anglers had more diversity in age, gender, and ethnic backgrounds than other anglers.

Catfishing Today

Catfishing is extremely varied. Participants fish night and day, year-round, for big fish and small, from boats and shore, using natural and artificial baits on everything from ultralight combos to heavy-action bait-casting rigs, plus trotlines, jugs, and limblines. Nevertheless, today's catfish anglers fall within two basic categories: those targeting smaller catfish (usually channel cats) to eat or those targeting big catfish (blues and flatheads) primarily for sport.

"Folks who want to catch a few cats and take them home to a hot skillet are still the mainstay in catfishing," said Jeff Williams, owner of Team Catfish Tackle in Grove, Oklahoma. "They greatly outnumber trophy anglers, but availability of high-quality educational information through the Internet and other media has created a new breed of trophy-catfish angler. Info on catching big cats was guarded by old timers in the past but now streams across televisions and computer monitors like water through a faucet. The desire to tangle with a true giant, a catfish over fifty pounds, is what this new breed is laser-focused on."

T.J. Stallings, director of marketing for TTI Blakemore Fishing Group in Wetumpka, Alabama, concurs. "Unlike bass fishing, catfishing doesn't need that 'perfect cast,' so novices can jump into the sport with relative ease," he said. "The biggest attraction, however, is the battle. Nothing in freshwater fights like a large blue or flathead. Once an angler lands a big cat, he can't wait to do it again."

So how do you fit into this picture? I pose the question, but the answer really doesn't matter. No matter what type of catfish you hope to catch—channel cats, blues, flatheads, or bullheads, big cats or small, cats to keep and eat, or trophy catfish you battle and release. In the pages that follow, you'll learn top-notch cat-catching techniques developed by America's most innovative catfish guides and anglers. You'll read scientific information about catfish behavior and how it affects your fishing. You'll discover baits, rigs, and tactics used by the catfishermen of yesteryear that are still highly effective today. You'll master regional catfishing tactics that, until now, haven't been widely known. And through it all, if I've done my job well, you'll enjoy a chuckle now and then, an occasional surprise, and a good read all the way through.

I hope *Hardcore Catfishing* lives up to your expectations. It's been fun to write. Good fishing.

Keith "Catfish" Sutton

About the Author

Keith Sutton didn't earn the nickname "Catfish" for nothing. This is his fifth book about catfishing. His passion for the sport has taken him to blue-ribbon catfishing waters throughout the United States and in Mexico, Canada, Venezuela, and Brazil. His special insights about catching these whiskered warriors were garnered through fifty years of on-the-water research and countless hours of discussions with biologists, researchers, and expert anglers.

Sutton is a prolific freelance writer, photographer, editor, and lecturer with more than 3,500 feature articles published in *Outdoor Life, Field & Stream, Sports Afield, Cabela's Outfitter Journal, North American Fisherman, In-Fisherman,* and many other state, regional, and national periodicals. His works as an award-winning photographer have been featured in a broad spectrum of books, magazines, newspapers, and calendars. In 2011, he was inducted into the National Freshwater Fishing Hall of Fame as a Legendary Communicator.

Sutton lives in Alexander, Arkansas, with his wife Theresa. They have six sons. Visit his Web site at www.catfishsutton.com.

Section I

Zeroing in on Channel Cats

Facts About Channel Catfish

The channel cat is the pin up of the catfish world—sleek, muscular, and one of the best reasons to be a kid with school out and a good fishing hole nearby.

If you like catfishing, chances are good you love the channel catfish (*Ictalurus punctatus*). This freckle-flanked, mid-sized cat is targeted by more anglers than any other species thanks largely to its abundance and extensive range. Most anglers who pursue the species do so because channel cats are incredibly delicious, and they want some fish to take home and eat. But everyone who targets this whiskered warrior also enjoys its truculent nature, savoring to the utmost the water-churning skirmishes that always ensue when a channel cat is on the line.

Description

Channel cats aren't colorful fish. The back and sides are silvery-gray to coppery-brown, speckled with a few too many small black spots. The belly is white. The tail has a deep fork. Breeding

Channel catfish as big as this pair from Manitoba's Red River are uncommon except in a few extraordinary waters.

Channel catfish

males take on a deep blue-black hue, and their head becomes greatly enlarged with thickened jowls and lips.

Blue cats are very similar in appearance but rarely exhibit the black speckling seen on all but the oldest channel cats. The best way to distinguish the two species is to examine the anal fin. On channel cats, this fin has twenty-four to twenty-nine rays and a rounded outer edge. Blue cats have a straight-edged anal fin with thirty or more rays.

Size

In July 1964, an angler fishing in South Carolina's Lake Moultrie caught a forty-seven-inch-long channel cat that weighed fifty-eight pounds. That world record still stands, and many experts believe it will never be broken. Only four states—South Carolina, Arkansas, Mississippi, and California—have produced channel cats exceeding fifty pounds, and in no place are channel cats that size regularly caught.

In waters with healthy channel cat populations, one- to five-pounders tend to be abundant and six- to ten-pounders only slightly less common. To catch a channel cat that exceeds fifteen pounds, however, is quite extraordinary except in a few very productive waters. In the Red River below Lockport Dam near Selkirk, Manitoba, for example, twenty- to twenty-five-pound channel cats comprise a large percentage of the catch. Elsewhere, you can consider yourself quite lucky if you land a twenty-pounder. Thirty-pounders are as rare as twelve-pound largemouths.

Food Habits

Until they reach about twelve inches long, channel cats feed extensively on large aquatic insects, small fish, and a variety of invertebrates, such as terrestrial insects, crayfish, and mussels. Fish such as minnows, chubs, and other catfish comprise a larger part of the diet when channel cats exceed a foot in length, but as they grow, the catfish continue chowing down on invertebrates and other available foods. The bigger a channel cat becomes, however, the more fish it is apt to eat. By the time it reaches several pounds in weight, a channel cat subsists almost entirely on other fish.

Small black spots on the sides identify the channel catfish regardless of where it is caught. Some older specimen may lack these spots, however.

Range

The original range of channel catfish stretched between the Rocky and Appalachian mountains, from the Hudson Bay drainage to the Gulf of Mexico, and north and east of the Appalachian Mountains. Transplants to new waters have expanded the species' range to include every state but Alaska, plus six of the ten Canadian provinces and many lakes and rivers in Mexico as well. Channel cats are considered important sport species in at least thirty-two US states.

Habitat

Channel cats are amazingly adaptable, inhabiting nearly any body of water that's not too cold, too polluted, or too salty. Anglers catch them in everything from clear creeks, fertile farm ponds, and turbid sloughs to huge man-made reservoirs, natural lakes, and slow-moving bottomland rivers. Channel catfish thrive best in clean, warm, well-oxygenated water with slow to moderate current and abundant cover, such as logs, boulders, cavities, and debris.

Basic Fishing Tactics

A small spinning or spincast outfit spooled with six- to fifteen-pound-test monofilament line is ideal for catching channel cats you'd like to keep and eat. Upgrade to heavier tackle only if you're targeting trophy fish specifically. The other tackle you'll need can be carried in a small tackle box: a few hooks, sinkers, and bobbers, some extra line, a stringer, and some pliers for removing hooks from the catfish's tough mouth.

Any catfishing rig can be used, but the simplest usually work best. One such rig, the slip-sinker, is easily made by placing a small egg sinker on your main line above a barrel swivel tied at the line's end. Add an eighteen-inch leader to the swivel's other eye, and tie a hook (1/0 to 3/0 bait-holder, octopus or Kahle) to the end of that.

Another easy rig that works well is just a bobber above a medium-sized hook with a split shot pinched on the line between the two to sink the bait.

The list of good baits you can use is extensive. Some of the best include fresh chicken liver, night crawlers, minnows, crayfish, stinkbaits (commercial

Channel cats have a rounded anal fin with twenty-four to twenty-nine rays.

Despite popular misconceptions, channel cats feed actively year-round, even in the coldest part of winter.

and homemade), catalpa worms, shrimp, hot dogs, and frogs.

Despite what many anglers think, fishing for channel cats is not just a summer sport. You can fish year-round and expect to do well even during the coldest part of winter. Night fishing often produces more cats because they tend to be in the shallows more at night, and shallow shoreline waters are where most anglers fish. Channel cats feed actively during all hours, however, and are easily caught even during daylight hours if you fish prime hotspots, such as outside river bends, dam tailwaters, river wing dikes, and holes, tributary mouths, bottom channels, riprap, log piles, stump fields, and deep holes in ponds.

Although rod-and-reel fishing is most popular, all species of catfish are also targeted by anglers using other types of tackle, including trotlines, jugs, limb-lines, and yo-yos.

Crashin' & Thrashin'

Getting cats out of trees can be a tough job unless you know the proper technique.

The best way to learn new catfishing tricks is to pick the brains of your catfishing friends. Every hardcore cat man has special tricks and tactics no one else seems to know. One catter whose brain I've picked is Denny Halgren, a Dixon, Illinois, angler who uses unconventional tactics to get cats out of trees—channel cats, that is.

If you came upon Halgren on Illinois' Rock River, where he's guided catfishermen for more than forty years, you might wonder if he were in trouble. Chances are his boat would be smack-dab on top of a big tree laid over in the water. He might be in the boat, but more likely, he'd be standing on the tree with a rod and reel. Some who have come upon Halgren in this situation believed he'd crashed his craft into the timber. In a way, they were right.

You see, Halgren has perfected an advanced catfishing tactic he calls crashin' and thrashin'. In a nutshell, it works like this. First, you "crash" your boat into big timber to reach those hard-to-get-at catfish hotspots other anglers wouldn't dare fish from. Next, you drop a bait into the swirling water at just the right spot. Then, if a catfish is there, you experience the thrashin' part of the name. The fish nabs the bait, you set the hook, and you try to hoss a thrashin' log kitty from its hidey-hole. Sometimes you win. Sometimes you lose. But

Dixon, Illinois, catfishing guide Denny Halgren shows a nice channel cat taken using his unique crashin' and thrashin' technique.

when you learn Halgren's technique, you'll be battling far more jumbo catfish than your still-fishing buddies.

A Tree and a Boil

The key, Halgren says, is pinpointing the exact spot where a big cat will be. Each spot has two primary components: a big tree and a big boil.

"The ideal place," he says, "is where current has undercut a tree and toppled it into the water. At least part of the tree must be in shallow water—two to three feet deep—and there must be at least moderate current coming across the tree. With the right amount of current, the biggest most territorial catfish centralize. In other words, the current causes them to hold in specific spots where they can easily grab food carried within. Without proper current, the fish could be anywhere and are difficult to pinpoint. When the current is right, you can find them every time."

When scouting a river, look for a single fallen tree perpendicular to the bank with the root end close to shore in shallow water. A big drift pile with numerous trees would seem better. But Halgren says a thick tree that "looks like a fence post"—with few branches—may draw bigger fish.

"In the best spots, current washes beneath the tree's trunk in shallow water and creates a channel," he says. "As water goes through that channel, it's funneled through to the downstream side of the tree and creates a big boil. Right in that boil is where you want to fish. You may catch smaller catfish in other spots around the tree's perimeter. But the biggest cat on that piece of cover will almost always be in the biggest boil."

Catfishermen scouting a river for crashin' and thrashin' hot spots should watch for a single fallen tree perpendicular to the bank with the root end close to shore in shallow water.

Crashin'

The crashin' part of this technique isn't as dangerous as it sounds. Ideally, after spotting a good tree/boil location, the boat operator slows the boat and slides it gently onto the tree trunk or into the tree's branches. Done properly, the boat will catch and hold. The fisherman then can drop his bait into the boil.

"You must be positioned so you can drop your bait straight down into the largest boil on the downstream side of the trunk," says Halgren. "What's surprising to most anglers is that riding your boat up on that tree rarely spooks the fish. Big cats just don't spook, so you can move right in on top of them."

The Right Bait and Rig

When fishing woody cover, Halgren says, it's important to use bait that triggers quick hits from feeding fish. His favorite is a commercial cheese-flavored dip bait, JoJo's Pole Snatcher made by Cat Tracker Bait Company.

"There's no flour in this bait," he says, "so the bait doesn't slough off. If that happens, the catfish will eat the bait, but he won't get your hook. You can't catch him that way. The Cat Tracker bait stays on the worm where it's needed."

The "worm" Halgren refers to is a Cat Tracker Tubie 2000 or Cat Tracker Egg Worm. These special-made, soft-plastic baits are ribbed so the dip bait clings when the worm is pushed into it. The Egg Worm comes prerigged with a two-foot section of twenty-pound-test mono run through the worm and tied to a small treble hook that fits snuggly against the tail end. The Tubie 2000 is made to be rigged by the angler.

Halgren uses single 2/0 or 3/0 Tru-Turn hooks on both rigs—catfish hooks with the Tubie 2000 and worm hooks with the Egg Worm. The rig is tied to his main line—twenty-pound Stren mono—with a 1/4-ounce split shot or bullet sinker on the line above the worm. When a bullet sinker is used, a split shot is placed below it to peg it on the line.

"If I'm dropping baits into a spot with a lot of branches, I slide the weight down so it almost touches the top of the worm," Halgren says. "If the boil is behind the trunk and pretty free of

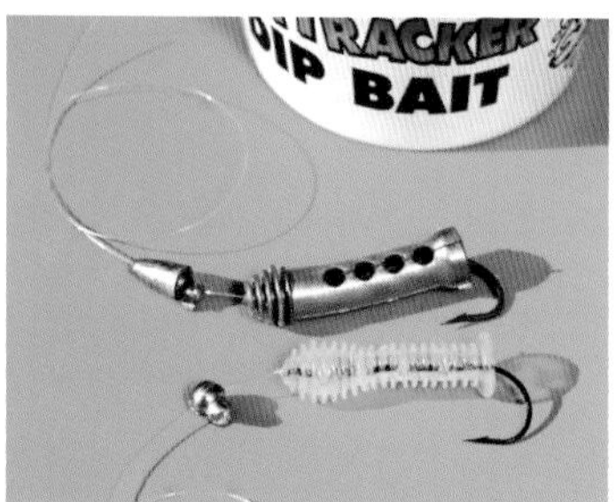

Variations of Denny Halgren's crashin' and thrashin' rig.

obstruction, I slide the weight up above the worm about six inches." This type of rig is simple and ideal for fishing in these situations. In four to five miles per hour current, the bait will stay on about forty-five minutes.

"I drop the rig in the boil then leave it," he says. "You can't move the bait, even if you think it's hung. You'll probably get a hit right away. If not, wait up to ten minutes. If you don't have a catfish by then, move and try another spot."

Thrashin'

This tactic often produces channel cats from four to twelve pounds, Halgren says. "Even though they're hefty cats, you can set the hook, keep a tight line, and get them out. Get them up, and let them thrash at the top of the water. That way they won't get wrapped up, and you can get them out."

Getting a cat out of a tree is never easy, whether it has fur or fins. You may get scratched. You could fall. You have to be brave—some say crazy—to try.

But if, like Denny Halgren, you're brave enough or crazy enough to fish where other anglers won't, big channel cats will be your prize. Crashin' and thrashin' is proven to catch cats when other tactics fail.

Fiddlers for the Table

Targeting eating-sized catfish differs considerably from trophy fishing.

When I advise people wanting to catch trophy-class catfish, I start by telling them they must be patient and persistent. Catching trophy cats doesn't happen every day, even for those thoroughly familiar with their habits. You may spend hundreds of fishless hours trying to pinpoint a single trophy fish. Sometimes you must travel long distances to reach the best waters, which are usually big rivers and reservoirs. You need high-quality tackle (often expensive), and your chances are much better if you have a boat equipped with sonar. The baits you use must be fresh and sometimes are hard to get.

When you finally do hook a trophy-class cat, that's no guarantee you'll land it. You'll probably lose as many as you catch, and the disappointments may seem overwhelming. If you do land one, it's best that you release it. After all, today's releases are tomorrow's trophies.

Some enthusiasts listen intently then pack up their tackle and head straight for a big river or lake. They love a fishing challenge, and giant cats certainly provide that.

Many folks have a different reaction, however. "I'm not interested in catching a huge fish," is

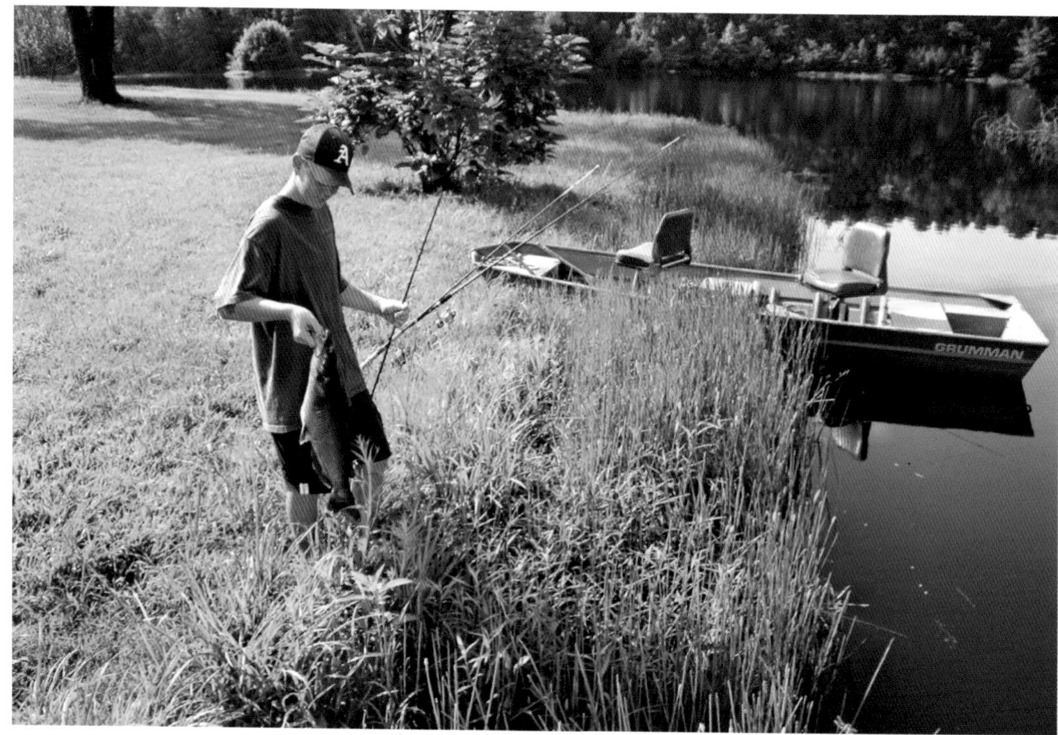

Catfish anglers usually have one goal in mind when they go fishing: catching a fish for dinner.

their typical response. "I just want to have fun and maybe catch a few fish to eat."

When you zero in on eating-sized cats, those ten pounds or fewer, the experience is vastly different than trophy fishing. Patience and persistence are rarely required because eating-sized cats are abundant in many waters, including ponds, small streams, and urban lakes. The baits you need can be bought in a grocery or discount store, and expensive gear is hardly a prerequisite. A cane pole or discount fishing combo works great.

When the cats are active (they usually are), you might catch a score or more during a few hours of leisurely bank fishing. And because smaller cats are common, you need not feel guilty keeping some to eat. In fact, keeping is encouraged. Populations do best when folks keep the little ones thinned out.

Targeting smaller catfish is also great when you're fishing with kids. Eating-sized cats are not especially wary, so your child will probably catch some even if he's got ants in his pants. A five-pound cat is on the small side in reality, but to a youngster, one that size is gigantic. Even little cats fight like blue blazes, so it's always fun. Take a kid catfishing, and you'll make memories together that will last forever.

Where to Go

Begin with a call to the freshwater fisheries department of your state wildlife agency. Ask for the names of some waters in your area that receive regular stockings of eating-sized cats. State and federal agencies stock millions of one- to two-pound catfish every year, and most will gladly send you a stocking list that shows where the fish were released. Most also

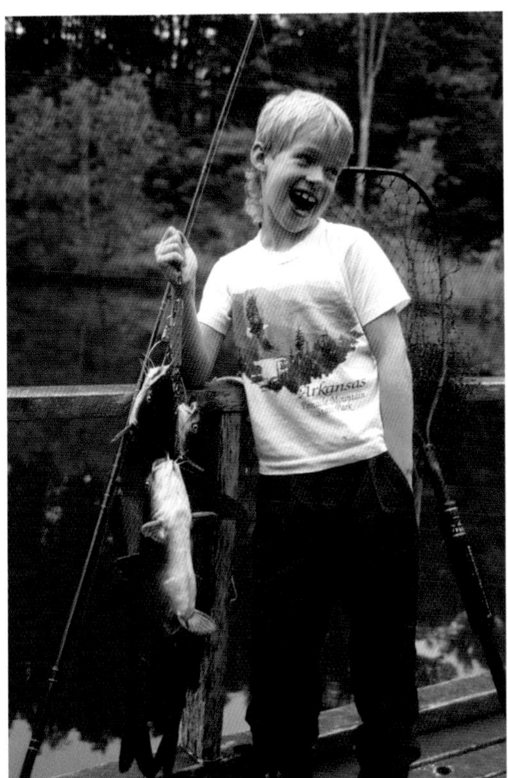

Catching a stringer full of hard-fighting, good-eating catfish will put a smile on any kid's face.

list good catfishing waters on their Web sites. Either way, you'll probably turn up several potential honey holes, including perhaps some small lakes with good bank fishing areas, fishing piers, or a little stream where you can sit in a lawn chair on shore and wait for a bite.

Tackle Tips

A small spinning or spincast outfit is ideal for this type of fishing. I keep mine spooled with six- to ten-pound-test monofilament.

The other tackle you'll need can be carried in a small tackle box: a few hooks, sinkers, and bobbers, some extra line, a stringer, and some pliers for removing hooks from the catfish's tough mouth.

Any catfishing rig can be used, but the simplest usually work best. A slip-sinker rig, my favorite, is easily made by placing a small egg sinker on your main line above a barrel swivel tied at the line's end. Add an eighteen-inch leader to the swivel's other eye, and tie a hook (1/0 to 3/0 baitholder, octopus or Kahle) to the end of that.

Another easy rig that works well is just a bobber above a small hook with a split shot pinched on the line between the two to sink the bait.

If you need to, you can get along quite well with just a box of hooks and some bait. In catfishing circles, this is called fishing naked. The hook is tied on, baited, and cast out. The bait then sinks enticingly in the water, attracting hungry cats without any extra terminal tackle that might spook the occasional wary fish.

Bait Choices

Unlike heavyweight cats, which rarely eat anything but fish, eating-sized whiskers aren't the least bit finicky when it comes to food. Buy some worms or minnows at the bait shop or pick up some fresh chicken liver, hot dogs,

Small catfish aren't finicky eaters, so bait choices are legion. Night crawlers and other good baits can be purchased at most bait shops.

bacon, cheese, or shrimp at the supermarket. Small pieces of the latter five work extremely well on bullheads, channel cats, and small blues and flatheads.

Commercial dip baits and doughbaits also work great and usually can be found in the sporting goods department of discount stores. When using these, you might want to pick up a few of the specialty items often used to fish these soft baits, including some catfish "worms" (ribbed, soft-plastic lures used for fishing dip bait, or some spring-wound doughbait treble hooks.

Exposed Hooks Work Better

You probably won't have trouble finding eating-sized cats, but beginners often are frustrated when they can't hook those that bite. It's a common complaint, but fortunately, there's a simple though often overlooked solution.

The secret is fishing with an exposed hook. Many catters think hiding the point of the hook means more cats when actually the opposite is true. Catfish don't know or care what a hook is. If you continually bury your hook in your bait, you'll miss fish more than half the time.

If you're fishing minnows, don't push the hook's barb back into the fish. Slip it once through the lips, back, or the narrow part of the tail, and leave the point exposed. If you're using worms or night crawlers, thread the hook through two or three times, but don't hide the point. Do likewise when fishing with bacon, hot dogs, or other grocery baits.

When fishing with chicken liver, here's another rigging tip. Liver has a tendency to fly off the hook, but you can overcome this problem by wrapping the liver in a small square of nylon stocking, pulling the four corners together, then threading your hook through the corners, leaving the point exposed. A treble hook attached to your line with a swivel also works. Unsnap the swivel, remove the hook, push the eye of the hook through the liver so the liver is impaled on the three barbs, then reattach the hook to the swivel.

Night or Day?

The biggest catfish often prowl more at night, but eating-sized cats are active day or night, so go fishing whenever you can. My favorite fishing period is around daybreak, five a.m. to eight a.m. There's nothing magical about this time, but on many waters, peak feeding activity occurs just as the sun is rising. Fish then, and you're almost guaranteed to increase your catch.

Seasons

Despite what many anglers think, catfishing is not just a summertime sport. In fact, you can fish year-round and expect to do well.

My favorite months for catching eating-sized cats are January and February. Many ponds in my area are stocked with channel cats and bullheads, and when the water, temperature is between forty and fifty-five degrees, these fish move to the deepest water, where they gather in huge schools. I drop a rig baited with chicken liver into the hole, let it reach the bottom, then crank the reel handle a few times so the bait is a foot or so above the substrate. The cats usually strike quickly, and in a couple hours, it's not unusual to catch fifteen to twenty weighing one to seven pounds. It's a great way to liven up a dreary winter day, and catfish never taste better than when fresh-caught from icy cold water.

Have Fun

Targeting trophy catfish is an exciting challenge no doubt. But if you're like me, there are times when you're happy just sitting under a shade tree on a lake and catching a few small cats for

Young, old, boys, girls—channel catfish are an exciting catch for anglers of all ages and sexes.

dinner. For many of us, catfishing is a way to relax or enjoy a few hours fishing with the kids. If a big cat is caught now and then, so much the better. But catching big fish is secondary to just being there, enjoying the outdoors, and tussling with a decent fish now and then.

Zero in on some eating-sized cats this season. Take your children or some kids from the neighborhood along. It's fun. It's relaxing. It's enjoyable. And as soon as you smell the aroma of those catfish fillets frying up golden and delicious, you'll be ready to do it again.

Section II:

How to get the Blues

Facts About Blue Catfish

Once ignored by all but a small cadre of hardcore cat men, in recent decades the blue cat has become the target of choice for many anglers hoping to land the biggest fish of a lifetime.

Size is the attribute most responsible for the increasing popularity of the blue catfish (*Ictalurus furcatus*). The only North American freshwater fishes that grow larger are the alligator gar, lake sturgeon, and white sturgeon. However, these species have much more restricted ranges than blue cats and rarely are abundant. Anglers hoping to catch a freshwater fish weighing fifty to one-hundred pounds or more are fishing for America's widespread, abundant blue cats in greater numbers than ever before. As a result, dozens of new state and world records have been established in recent decades.

Description

The blue catfish closely resembles its channel cat cousin. The slate-blue to grayish-brown back and sides fade to a whitish belly. The tail is deeply forked. On blue cats, however, the anal fin contains more rays—usually thirty

In recent years, more and more anglers have begun pursuing the blue catfish, one of North America's most abundant, widespread heavyweight sportfish.

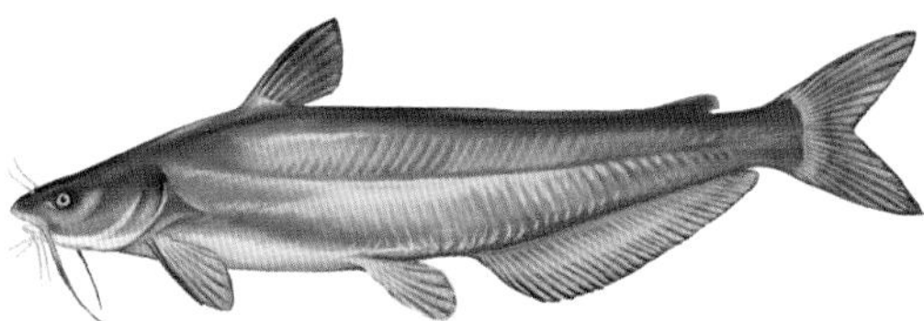
Blue catfish

to thirty-five as compared to the channel cat's twenty-four to twenty-nine—and has a straight, not rounded, outer margin. In muddy environments, some blue cats appear albino, the pale skin evoking the common nickname

A straight-edge anal fin, shaped much like an old-fashioned barber's comb, helps identify this as a blue catfish.

This blue cat weighed 72 pounds. The species has the potential to grow more than twice this size.

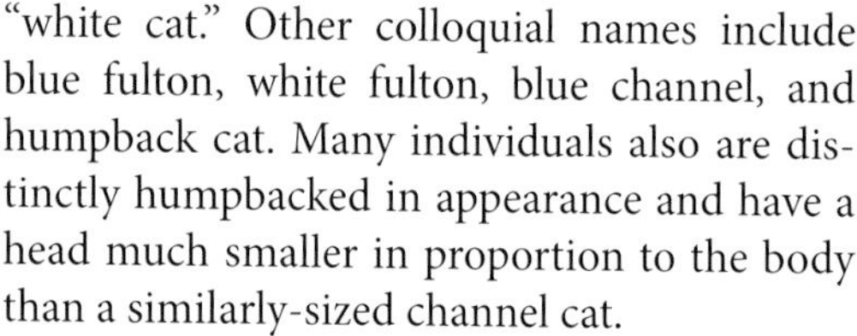
"white cat." Other colloquial names include blue fulton, white fulton, blue channel, and humpback cat. Many individuals also are distinctly humpbacked in appearance and have a head much smaller in proportion to the body than a similarly-sized channel cat.

Size

Healthy populations of blue cats usually contain numerous individuals up to twenty-eight inches or about ten pounds. Larger older fish are less common, but in some prime waters, catching several twenty- to forty-pound blues during a few hours of fishing is not considered unusual during peak fishing times. The largest specimens, those weighing fifty pounds or more, are much scarcer and often difficult to find and catch, but more and more anglers enjoy the challenge of targeting these big hard-hitting trophies. Nothing can prepare an angler for their astonishing power. These Goliaths fry drags, bust rods, and snap line like sewing thread. A really big one can pummel an angler till his arms and legs tremble.

In recent decades, blues exceeding one hundred pounds have been caught from waters in several states, including Alabama, Arkansas, California, Illinois, Indiana, Kansas, Kentucky, Louisiana, Missouri, Oklahoma, South Carolina, Tennessee, Texas, and Virginia. Fishing in Virginia's Kerr Reservoir on June 18, 2011, Nick Anderson of Greenville, North Carolina, landed

the current all-tackle world record, a massive 55-inch-long blue that weighed 143 pounds.

Food Habits

Blue catfish are opportunistic feeders, consuming a variety of animals that include fishes, insects, crayfish, and freshwater mussels. Larger individuals eat mostly fish and larger invertebrates. They are particularly fond of shad, herring, and other schooling baitfish and often are found associated with schools of these baitfish. Blue cats frequently suspend in deep water beneath shad being eaten by striped bass, picking off the wounded and dead baitfish left by the stripers. They also feed on wounded baitfish that pass through the turbines of dams and baitfish killed by cold winter temperatures.

Blues seem intermediate between the other two species of big cats in feeding habits, not insisting on live baits as flatheads do but generally ignoring many specialty offerings, such as stinkbaits and blood baits, often used to catch channel cats. Blue cats feed year-round except during spawning activities. Feeding diminishes, however, when the water temperature falls below forty degrees Fahrenheit.

Range

Blue cats occur in twenty-nine states from South Dakota to Texas and Washington to Florida. Their native range encompasses major rivers in the Mississippi, Ohio, and Missouri basins. Blues have been introduced in Washington, Oregon, California, Arizona, Colorado, Maryland, Virginia, South Carolina, and Florida.

Blue cats are scarce at the fringes of their range. In many rivers and reservoirs in the South and Midwest, however, ten- to fifty-pounders are as common as two- to five-pound largemouths, and blues to 100 pounds surface with astounding regularity.

Habitat

Blue catfish were originally fish of our big rivers, spending their lives in deep, swift channels and flowing pools. Today, large specimens frequently inhabit the fast-moving tailwaters below dams, where they feed on abundant baitfish like shad and herring. Many also thrive in the open waters of large man-made reservoirs. Although sometimes stocked in ponds and small lakes, blue cats seldom thrive in these environments unless schools of shad or other baitfish are plentiful.

Basic Fishing Tactics

When targeting blue cats, remember they are active year-round. Most catfish fans fish during warm months, but many are learning the blue cat's proclivity for gathering in large winter feeding schools. Each school may contain several trophy-class fish holding near deep, well-oxygenated bottom structures. A quality sonar unit is essential for finding them.

You also should understand that blue cat behavior differs considerably from that of channel and flathead catfish. In fact, in many respects, blue cats behave more like striped bass than other catfish. Shad, herring, and other schooling baitfish comprise most of their diet, and like stripers, blue cats are migratory, following baitfish from area to area. To catch them, you, too, must follow the schools.

Dam tailwaters are among the best river fishing areas. Position yourself a short but safe distance below the dam, and cast your rig into the rushing discharge. Let it sink, then gently pick the weight up, letting the current wash it downstream a few feet. Let the weight down again, and repeat the process. Doing this, you can cover most of the bottom, and cats have a chance to detect the bait and take it.

When fishing outside tailwaters, look for river blues holding near deep, open-water structures.

Anglers targeting trophy blue cats must use sturdy tackle to subdue these hard-fighting heavyweights.

The edges of river channel drop-offs produce many trophy fish, as do deep holes at the confluence of two streams, deep edges of gravel bars, undercut banks near outside bends, and fast deep-water chutes around islands. Blues in lakes usually follow shad schools or can be found near bottom channels, humps, and deep holes.

Stout tackle is a must for subduing trophy-class blues. Rods should be eight- to twelve-foot heavy-action models. Reels, whether level-winding or spinning, should have drags in good working order. Hooks should be no smaller than 5/0 to 9/0, and you'll need plenty of sinkers to hold your bait on the bottom. Use top-quality line, thirty- to one-hundred-pound-test.

Small blues will eat any of the baits used for channel catfish, but shad and herring are the baits of choice for trophy-class fish. You can use them live or dead, whole, or cut into fillets or chunks.

An egg-sinker rig works fine in most situations. Run the sinker up your main line, and tie a sturdy barrel swivel below it. To the other eye of the swivel tie a twenty-four-inch leader to which you've tied a hook. Impale a baitfish or piece of baitfish on the hook, leaving the point of the hook exposed.

If your hook strikes home, prepare for action. A sizeable blue cat can strip a hundred yards of line before you ever turn its head, but if you can keep the fish away from cover and play it properly, you may with any luck eventually subdue it.

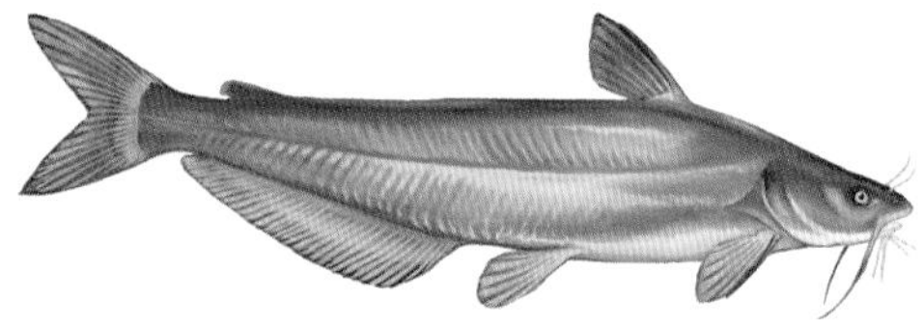

Drift-Fishing

Drift-fishing is the ideal technique for catching hot-weather blue cats on the move.

Blue catfish tend to be nomadic in the summer, moving here and there as they follow schools of baitfish and seek comfort zones in their home waters. They're scattered and difficult to pinpoint, a fact that frustrates many anglers.

In many respects, the behavior of these fish parallels that of striped bass. Like stripers, blues feed almost exclusively on shad, herring, and other schooling baitfish. Consequently they tend to be more migratory than other cats and are more frequently found in open-water

habitats. You can sit on the bank and try to catch a mess, but it's not likely to happen. If you try drift-fishing, on the other hand, you may catch dozens of blue cats in a few hours. This is an active approach to catfishing that can make your catch rate soar.

Drift-fishing is just what the name implies. You drift in your boat using the wind, current, or a trolling motor for propulsion. With one or more baited lines out, you keep on the move so you cover more water and increase your odds of crossing paths with a blue cat. Here's some information on this underused catfishing tactic from two experts in the field.

Santee-Cooper Tactics

Joe Drose, a catfishing guide from Cross, South Carolina, often uses drift-fishing to find the big blues inhabiting Marion and Moultrie, the Santee-Cooper lakes.

"Drift-fishing is the only reliable method for catching summer blue cats here," says Drose. "In fact, it's the best way to catch blues throughout most of the year. In spring, we anchor and fish certain spots in the shallows. The blues come shallow then and are more schooled up. The rest of the year, blues roam around and are scattered. Drift-fishing allows you to cover more water so you can find them. If you want to catch blues, you've got to take your bait to them. You can't wait for them to come to your bait."

Santee-Cooper catfish guide Joe Drose displays a nice blue cat taken while drift-fishing on Lake Marion. Note the drift-fishing rigs in the background.

Some fishermen drift blind. In other words, they have no idea what type of structures or cover is beneath the water. They simply start drifting and hope their hit-and-miss tactics produce more hits than misses. Drose prefers to watch a sonar fish-finder as he drifts with the wind or moves with a trolling motor guiding his boat over and along structures where blue cats are likely to be. Blues may be roaming around, he says, but they'll still do most of their roaming around bottom channels, humps, and other bottom features.

"Most of the time, we're moving back and forth over underwater hills or ridges, moving the bait from twenty to forty feet of water and back," he says. "You never know for sure where the cats will be. Some days you catch most fish in shallower water. Some days most are in deeper water. Some days you'll catch them shallow and deep. That's the thing with summer blues. They're moving all the time. You never know what to expect. That's why drift-fishing works best."

Drose uses one rig—a float rig—when drifting.

"The main line is run through the eye of a 1-1/4- to 1-3/4-ounce pencil weight," he says, "and a barrel swivel is tied below it to keep the weight from sliding down. A four-foot leader is then tied to the lower eye of the swivel. A 2-1/2-inch crappie float is added in the middle of the leader, and a 3/0 or 4/0 wide-bend Eagle Claw hook is tied at the end.

"The float suspends the baited hook above the bottom to help prevent snags," he continues. "By sliding the float up or down the leader, you can adjust the depth at which the bait floats depending on what the catfish are doing. The bait we use is four- to five-inch whole blueback herring."

Drose has caught blue cats up to seventy pounds when drifting and says it's common to catch trophy-class fish—thirty pounds and heavier—using this method. He drifts with one-hundred yards of twenty-five-pound-test line out to keep his rig moving smoothly across the bottom. With lesser lengths of line running behind the boat, the weight has a tendency to drag or snag causing the bait to jump and move wildly about. Four seven- to eight-foot Shakespeare Tiger rods held in rail-mounted rod holders are used for each drift. Each is outfitted with a Shakespeare Tidewater reel that holds up to three hundred yards of twenty-five-pound-test line.

"A high-capacity reel is a must," Drose notes. "If you have one-hundred yards of line out and a big blue hits, you better have plenty of line still on the reel, or you could get spooled."

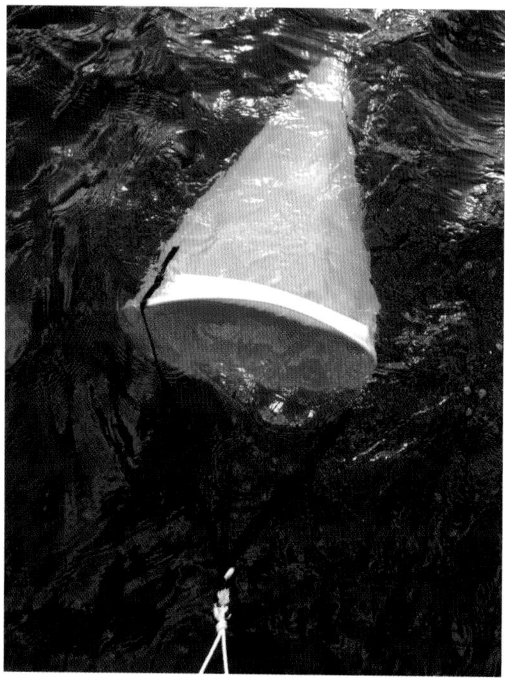

A sea anchor helps maintain proper boat speed when drifting big waters under prime weather conditions.

Drose fishes from a large party barge. To slow his drift, he employs one or two custom-made sea anchors (drift socks), each six feet in diameter and attached to the boat with short lengths of nylon rope. The wind pushes the craft along, while the sea anchors govern the drift to a proper speed.

"The best time for drift-fishing is when the water's white-capping some," he says. "You've got to have the sea anchors to control your speed, or you'll go too fast. The anchors also help hold your boat straight so you have a controlled drift and not just a bouncy boat ride."

Jim Moyer's Advice

Jim Moyer of Clarksville, Tennessee, was a long-time catfish guide on Tennessee's Cumberland River and fishes for blue cats on prime waters throughout the country. He agrees with Drose that drift-fishing is one of the best ways for catching scattered summer fish.

"Drift-fishing allows you to cover a lot of water in a short time," says Moyer. "You can cover great distances and cover any depth under controlled conditions. It allows you to present a bait at a specific target or a specific depth. It permits you to target fish from the surface to the bottom. It's very effective in lakes using wind current as your propulsion or in rivers where you're propelled by current."

On the snag-infested waters of Santee-Cooper, Joe Drose must confine his drift-fishing to daylight hours. Moyer, on the other hand, does much of his catfishing on big rivers or open lakes where night fishing often is preferable.

"A lot of times drift-fishing on lakes is at its peak at night because catfish are more active

then," he says. "In a river, you can target the fish either in daylight or darkness, but again, the dark hours are best most of the time."

Moyer's technique is very similar to Drose's. On lakes, he drifts with the wind using a trolling motor for direction control and a drift sock to control his speed. In rivers, current carries him along, and a trolling motor keeps him on the right path. A drift sock may be used here again to slow and control the drift.

"Using a trolling motor and a depth-finder," he says, "you can drift along the contours of a river drop-off or other structures where blue cats are likely to be. If you're drifting on a river and the water is high, shallow flats and rocky banks should be your major targets."

Moyer notes, too, that drift-fishing is not limited to a boat. "Baits can be drifted from the bank just as effectively," he says. "Just cast upwind and let the wind or current move your bait into the strike zone. The beauty of this is that a bait can be put in the water a distance away from the target and floated into the strike zone very quietly."

When in a boat, Moyer carries buoys with him to mark locations where fish are hooked. This allows him to drift back through an area again to determine if more cats are present.

"If you catch another fish after your buoy is out, then it's a good idea to anchor and fish the area thoroughly," he says. "When the fish quit biting, retrieve your anchor and buoy and continue to drift."

Moyer offers these tips on proper gear.

Boat: "The type of boat is very important. Boats with high sides are normally harder to drift than boats with low sides."

High-capacity reels, long sturdy rods, and quality rod holders firmly mounted on the rails improve the angler's odds of hooking and landing a trophy cat while drift-fishing.

Rods: "Your rod should be seven to seven-and-a-half feet long with a fairly heavy action."

Reels: "A bait-casting reel with a bait runner function is preferable over a spinning reel. The reel should have a fairly large line capacity and an extremely good drag system."

Rod holders: "Rod holders are a must. A twenty-five- or ninety-degree rod holder works best. The rod holder should be designed so the butt of the rod sits deep in the holder but can be easily removed."

Line: "Line should be fairly heavy because of snags and other obstacles encountered while fishing."

Floats: "Floats should be large enough to support the bait and sinker but shaped to create very little resistance in the water when a fish pulls one down. Adjustable floats work better than floats designed to be fixed to the line."

Sinkers: "Sinkers vary as to the type of drifting you are doing. The sinker should be just heavy enough to hold your bait at the depth that you desire."

Hooks: "Hook size is a preference of the fisherman based on the size and type of bait being used. I prefer a minimum of an 8/0 hook. I also find that treble hooks don't work well in drifting situations because they hang more easily."

Three basic rigs comprise Moyer's drift-fishing arsenal.

The drift rig—used for floating live, cut, or dead baits at controlled depths—has a hook, barrel swivel, and sinker configuration from the line's end up. This rig can be tight lined, or a float can be added above the sinker and adjusted on the line so the bait drifts at a preferred depth. In most cases, this rig does not work well in fast drifting situations.

The bottom-bouncing rig—used for a vertical presentation—allows the angler to maintain his "feel" of the bottom when drifting along drop-offs or other structures. A bank sinker is tied to the line's end. A leader to which the hook is tied is positioned on the line above the sinker to hold the bait up off the bottom. When using this rig, the rod should be hand held.

Drifting with multiple poles set at different depths can help anglers determine at what depth catfish in a river are feeding.

When fast drifting baits across the bottom of a river or lake, Moyer considers the bait-walker rig to be the most dependable. Used with cutbait or dead bait, this rig consists of a one- to three-ounce bait-walker sinker tied to the line with a two- to six-foot hooked leader tied to the sinker's top eye.

"Before you start drift-fishing," says Moyer, "study the area of the lake or river you're planning to fish. Know something about the water depth, structure, water clarity, wind speed, and water speed. Set your rigs at various depths, and let the fish tell you where and how they want the bait.

"Remember what your rig was doing when you caught the fish," he adds. "The first fish could be an accident. The second one could be luck. The third one tells me that the fish are there and are wanting the bait in the same manner.

"Remember, too, that catfish are opportunists, and feed from the surface to the bottom. Use your electronics to help you find the fish, but don't depend totally on this gear because when you're drift-fishing, you're targeting active fish. Just because you don't pick up fish on your initial drift doesn't mean they're not there.

"And finally, because you're targeting active fish, you can expect to catch great numbers when drifting. Twenty or more fish a day are not uncommon."

The key word when drift-fishing, as with any form of catfishing, is experiment. Try to figure out how catfish are likely to react in the type of water you're fishing, then adapt your tactics to conform with those expectations. But if your game plan doesn't produce within a short time, try something different. Sooner or later the innovative cat man discovers a pattern that allows him to capitalize on the situation.

Drift-Fishing Tips

Drift-fishing isn't all luck. Here are tips to improve your success.

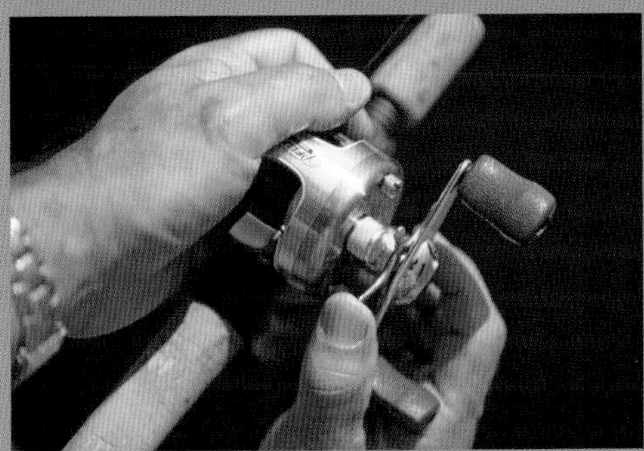

A properly set drag reduces the chance of a trophy cat breaking the drifting angler's line.

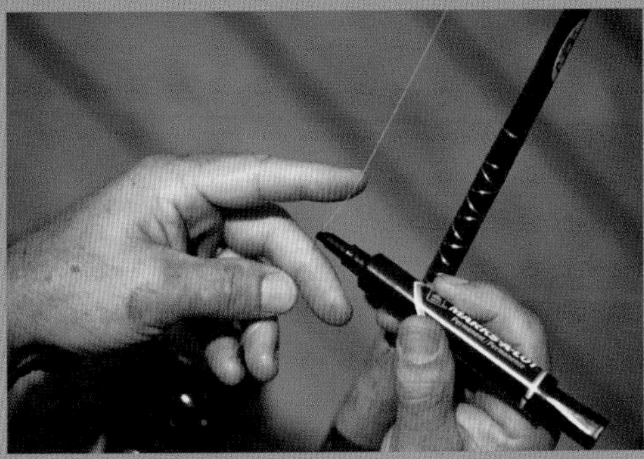

If you can do so without losing the fish, mark your line when you set the hook in a cat before you reel it in. This allows you to drift again at the same depth where the first fish was caught, improving your chance of catching another. Release line until you see your mark, and you're back in the strike zone.

- It's important to know how much line you have out when a catfish hits. After you set the hook, mark the line just in front of your reel using a waterproof felt marker. When you release line to that mark and drift through the area again, you know your bait will be at the same depth as before.
- Be sure to properly set your drag.
- Clamp-on rod holders fitted around the transom work OK in some situations, but it's better to use permanently mounted models that won't be torn off when a big cat hits.
- The number of lines you can drift with effectively depends in some degree on the experience of the angler. Experts can sometimes handle four or five rods, but most beginners should start with no more than two. Check local regulations for restrictions.
- How much line should you have out when trolling? The ideal distance varies with water clarity, speed, bait type, and other factors. Experiment to see what works best.
- Let the fish and the motion of the boat do the hooksetting. Wait until the rod has a definite bend in it, then remove it from the holder and boat the fish. Don't stop the trolling motor. Before you get the first fish off, another may be on.
- Watch the birds. Gulls, terns, and other birds will often feed on schools of shad and other baitfish being driven to the surface by white bass, largemouths, stripers, etc. Blue cats will often be under this type of action feeding on crippled bait drifting to the bottom.

Winterkill Patterns

When cold-stressed shad start dying, blue cats begin their annual feeding frenzy.

The big blue cat cruised the lake bottom beneath an enormous school of shad. The water was cold, nearly forty-five degrees, but the catfish was anything but lethargic. He moved rapidly, gorging on scores of baitfish that had become stressed by the low water temperature.

Most of the shad still swam together in a tightly packed school that offered some individual protection from the heavyweight predator and others of his kin. But now and then, a shad succumbed to the icy temperature and swam erratically away from the cluster. Before it swam far, it was wolfed down by the ravenous catfish.

Savvy anglers know that winterkill periods are among the best times for targeting trophy-class blues.

Sitting in a boat above, a man studied a sonar unit and watched as this catfish and others like it cruised the lake bottom. The cats showed up as little animated pixel fish moving across the unit's screen. The shad school appeared as a broad band of black nearly three feet thick. The school was suspended at twenty feet in thirty-five feet of water, too deep to be seen with the naked eye. But now and then, a cold-crippled shad would make its way to the surface, and the fisherman would glimpse its silvery form as it did its death dance in the waning January light.

The man had thrown a cast net across another school of shad thirty minutes earlier near the boat ramp. A dozen live threadfins thus captured had been placed in a round aerated bait tank, and two dozen more were thrown atop the ice in his cooler. With a dip net, the fisherman snatched up a live one, hooked it behind the dorsal fin, and free-spooled his rig to the bottom. He turned the reel handle two revolutions to bring the baitfish up just above the lake bed then placed the rod in a holder affixed to the transom.

As the man was baiting a second rig, the first rod went down. The angler lifted the rod, then without setting the hook, he turned the handle. The circle hook he used required no setting. It caught cleanly in the corner of the big cat's mouth.

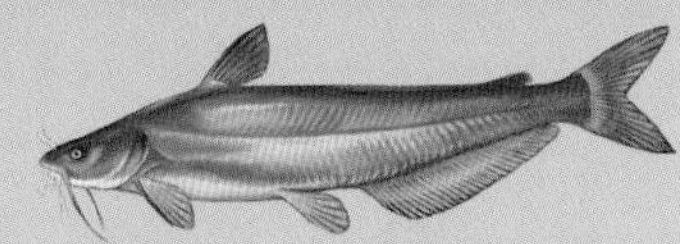

During the fifteen-minute battle that ensued, the man forgot all about the cold. The catfish surged straight away at first then began spinning, wrapping itself in the line. Pulling the catfish sideways through the water made it feel like a behemoth, and though it was actually small on a blue cat scale—twenty-one pounds—the man was proud when he finally brought it aboard.

Another shad was rigged and free-spooled to the bottom. Once again, a catfish hit before a second rig could be baited. It, too, was landed, and during the next hour and a half, another and another and another joined it. None were fifty-pounders as the man had hoped, but all were larger than the biggest largemouth bass a man could dream of catching. He caught five cats in ninety minutes, each weighing between eighteen and twenty-six pounds.

The man was not surprised. Catfishing is like that when winterkill begins.

The scene just described may sound like fantasy, but it's not. I was that angler, and I caught those fish using the tactics described.

I learned about the winterkill phenomenon from Joe Drose, a veteran catfishing guide on South Carolina's Santee-Cooper lakes, Marion and Moultrie. You might think the water in this famous Southeastern catfishing hotspot never gets cold enough to produce a shad kill, but such is not the case.

"We usually see some winterkill in December or January," Joe told me. "As the shad start dying and filtering out of the schools, catfish move in by the hundreds and get under baitfish. They gorge on the crippled shad as they drift down out of the schools, a pattern that may last three to four weeks at a time.

"When the temperature is right and this is happening," he continued, "a catfisherman should ride around in his boat and watch his sonar until he finds a big school of baitfish. He then takes a cast net and throws it over the school to collect his bait. The smaller shad seem to work best—those about an inch or two long. Hook two or three at a time on a single hook, running the hook through the eyes and leaving the barb exposed. Then lower your rig all the way to the bottom, reel it up from the bottom about a foot, and get ready for the action that's likely to follow.

"When the catfish are really gorging on shad, you can't use more than one rod per man because they're biting so fast. You drop a bait down and reel it up a little, and before you set the rod in the holder, you'll have a big one on. The action really heats up, and all of a sudden you remember why you're out there fishing on such a cold day. There's nothing more fun and exciting."

On the January day when Joe described this to me, the weather was unseasonably mild, and winterkill had not yet begun. I listened attentively, however, and was eager to learn more when I returned home. Before applying Joe's lesson, I studied the phenomenon. This is what I learned in books and later on the water.

The Reason for Winterkill

Gizzard and threadfin shad are among the most common and widely distributed baitfish in North America. They are mainstays in the diet of blue cats wherever blues and shad are found together. Like striped bass, blues follow shad schools year-round, moving from one spot to another, usually in open-water environments, as they dog their prey.

Both gizzard shad and threadfins are intolerant of severe cold. If the temperature dips below forty-five degrees Fahrenheit in waters where they live, they become cold-stressed. If the cold persists and the water temperature continues

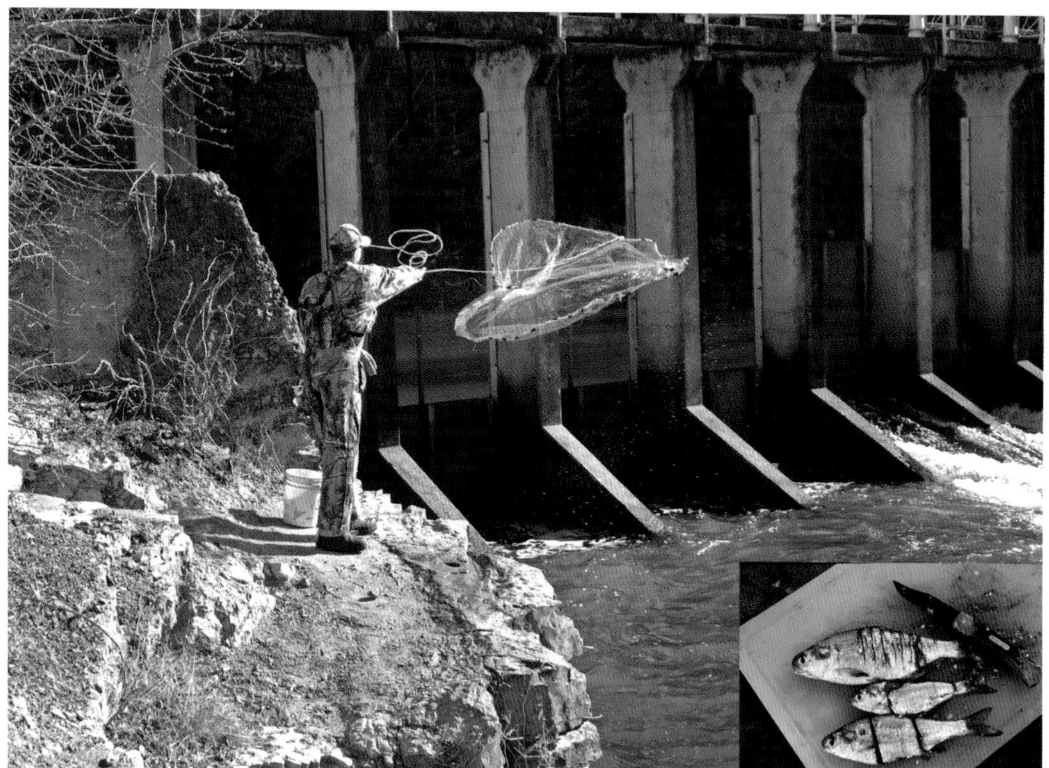

Above: A cast net provides the best means for gathering fresh shad baits to use during winterkill periods. **Inset:** Shad baits can be scored, filleted, or cut in chunks. If one preparation doesn't work, try another, and be sure to use only freshly killed baitfish.

dropping, thousands of shad soon die. This phenomenon, a yearly event on many first-rate blue cat waters, is known in many areas as "winterkill." Some call it "coldkill."

Blue cats feed continuously throughout winter, and when winterkill starts, they flock around shad schools like buzzards around roadkill. Dying baitfish that flutter down through the water column are quickly inhaled by waiting cats one after another after another until the die-off has passed and the catfish are gorged. The pattern may last a day or a month depending on the weather. But while it lasts, fishing for big blues is at its best. Savvy catfishermen capitalize on this cold-weather pattern.

Obtaining and Preparing Shad Baits

The first order of business for winterkill anglers is obtaining shad for bait. At times this is simple; just use a dip net to scoop dead and dying shad from the water, then use them whole or as cutbait. The baitfish should be fresh and will attract more cats if you keep them on ice until you need them.

A cast net is the most effective way to catch live shad, but be sure to check local regulations for restrictions. You can pinpoint the baitfish using sonar, then throw your net over the school, or you can throw a cast net "blind" near shore in areas of well-oxygenated water where shad tend to gather. At times, shad can be seen

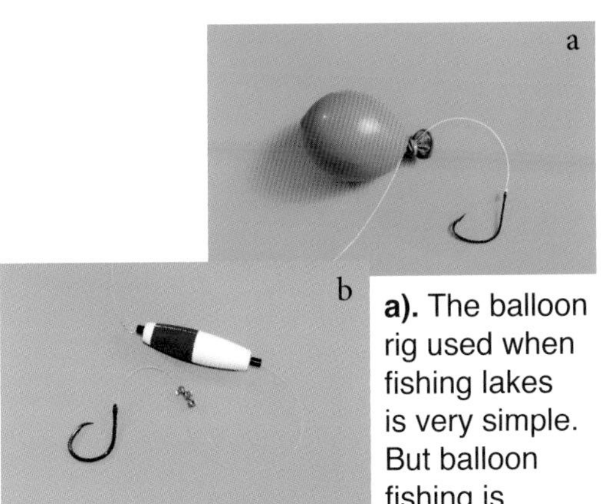

a). The balloon rig used when fishing lakes is very simple. But balloon fishing is most productive if the angler uses sonar to pinpoint schools of shad with larger fish beneath them. Sometimes the big fish prove to be striped bass, but often as not, they're blue cats looking for easy meals. **b).** The author's float rig used when fishing a tailwater.

breaking the water's surface, and the fisherman can move in close and throw a net over the school that has thus been sighted.

If you have a round aerated bait tank that holds at least twenty to thirty gallons of water, you might want to try keeping the shad alive during the entire time you are fishing. A live wiggling baitfish will sometimes outperform cutbait, especially in clear waters, where catfish use sight to locate food. In most situations, however, whole dead shad or shad sliced for cutbait are just as effective as live ones as long as you use baits that were freshly killed. Some anglers prefer to fillet the baits and use strips of the side meat. Others prefer cutting each fish crosswise into sections—head and tail or head, middle, and tail—and use the resulting chunks. Still others use only the guts, "shad gizzards" as they're often called.

I prefer using small shad (those up to three or four inches long) whole, but I score the sides of each bait to release cat-attracting juices into the water. If only a few larger shad are caught, I cut each into three pieces—head, middle, and tail—and I always start by using the middle or "gut" section. Shad guts definitely attract more blue cats than the flesh alone. When I am able to catch dozens of large shad, I use the guts alone, reserving the other parts for use when my bait supply runs low.

Tailwater Tactics

Dam tailwaters serve up some of the best big-river fishing during winterkill periods. Shad that die above a dam drift through the turbines or open gates, and many are sliced and diced in the process. Big blue cats are attracted by the resulting "chum" and often stack up like cordwood in the tailwater, gorging on the easily gotten pieces of shad that float to them.

In this situation, I prefer a float-rig presentation, so the shad bait drifts through catfish holding areas in much the same way as it would if drifting naturally in the current. The simplest such rig consists of nothing more than a fixed bobber above a hook and perhaps a split shot or two. A more versatile version employs a large sliding bobber. I prefer a three-inch foam egg-shaped model that is brightly colored on top. A bobber stop and plastic bead are placed on the line so the sliding bobber just beneath them will suspend the bait at the desired depth. I usually start by fishing the bait only two feet beneath the surface then move progressively deeper after every five casts until catfish are found. Beneath the bobber, tie an 8/0 to 12/0 circle hook or octopus hook, then if necessary, add several split shot to sink the bait.

Cast this rig as close as possible to the face of the dam, and allow it to drift with the current. I prefer using a twelve-foot surf rod/spinning reel combo, which allows longer casts and permits me to maneuver the rig so it drifts through different areas where blue cats might

be holding. I find it particularly effective to bring the rig into the slower-moving water in the "grooves" between the dam gates. The bait will often stop momentarily in these spots, and if the winterkill bite is peaking, a blue cat is sure to strike when it does. Other tailwater fishing hotspots include eddy holes (whirlpools) at the end of rock wing dikes, areas of reduced current beside and behind boulders, and along the upstream edge of scour holes created by the churning water releases.

Balloon Fishing in Lakes

I first experienced balloon fishing while fishing for winter striped bass in a large reservoir. My guide used sonar to pinpoint schools of shad with striped bass holding beneath them. He then positioned the boat over the school of baitfish and used a balloon rig to present the bait to the stripers waiting below.

A live shad was placed on a single wide-gap hook with the hook point piercing it through the eyes. Above the shad, the guide tied a balloon. This was nothing more than a regular round party balloon that was cinched to the line with a tight overhand knot after being inflated to the size of a baseball. The balloon was pushed up so its position on the fishing line was the same as the depth the big fish were holding. The guide then slid the entire rig into the water and let the breeze blow the balloon out over the school of fish.

"We use a balloon on the line because when a fish hits, you can reel it right in," the guide explained. "The balloon will slip off the line when it hits your rod tip without causing any problems."

The tactic worked on stripers, and it works just as well on blue cats. Identify a school of shad on sonar, then look for bigger fish holding below it. These could be striped bass if they are present in the lake you're fishing, but blue cats follow shad schools, too. They often suspend beneath the school, waiting for cold-shocked bait to drift down in the water column. Two or three small shad (live or dead) impaled through the eyes on an 8/0 Kahle hook have proven most effective for me in this situation. When shad were unavailable, I've also used three- to four-inch shiner minnows with success. It's best to use no sinker. This allows the bait to flutter down naturally just like a dead or crippled shad. Blues waiting below can't resist.

Cast Net Info

The cast nets used to collect shad are sized in feet. For example, a six-foot cast net has a radius of approximately six feet. When thrown, it opens into a circle twelve feet in diameter. The thing to remember is that larger cast nets are more difficult to throw. They will, however, catch more shad with each throw. A five- or six-footer with three-eighths-inch mesh usually works well for the weekend angler.

Throwing a cast net properly requires lots of practice. First, tie the retrieving line to your wrist, and with the same hand, grasp the net where it is attached to the line. Hold the weighted line with the other hand and your teeth. Then, twisting like a discus thrower, hoist the net into the water. The net should open into a big circle so the weights pull it down to surround the fish. Then pull the line to draw the net shut and retrieve the baitfish.

Section III

Chasing Flatheads

Facts About Flathead Catfish

These fast-growing, cover-loving catfish can be persnickety and hard to catch, but many anglers target them because they're among the most delectable of all freshwater fishes and often grow to huge sizes.

The flathead catfish's scientific name, *Pylodictis olivaris*, comes from Greek and Latin words meaning olive-colored mud fish. That's not a very flattering moniker, but it's a truthful one, for the usually olive-colored flathead often lays on the muddy bottom of a river or lake as it waits to ambush its prey, and that is where it usually is caught by anglers who tempt it with lively fish baits. North America's other big catfish, the channel cat and blue cat, belong to the genus *Ictalurus*. But flatheads differ so much in their physical characteristics that they have been placed in the genus *Pylodictis*, to which no other fish belongs.

Description

The flathead is aptly named, as it has a wide, flattened head unlike other North American catfish. Individual fish may differ in color from others in the same population, ranging from mustard yellow to dark brown or black. In most

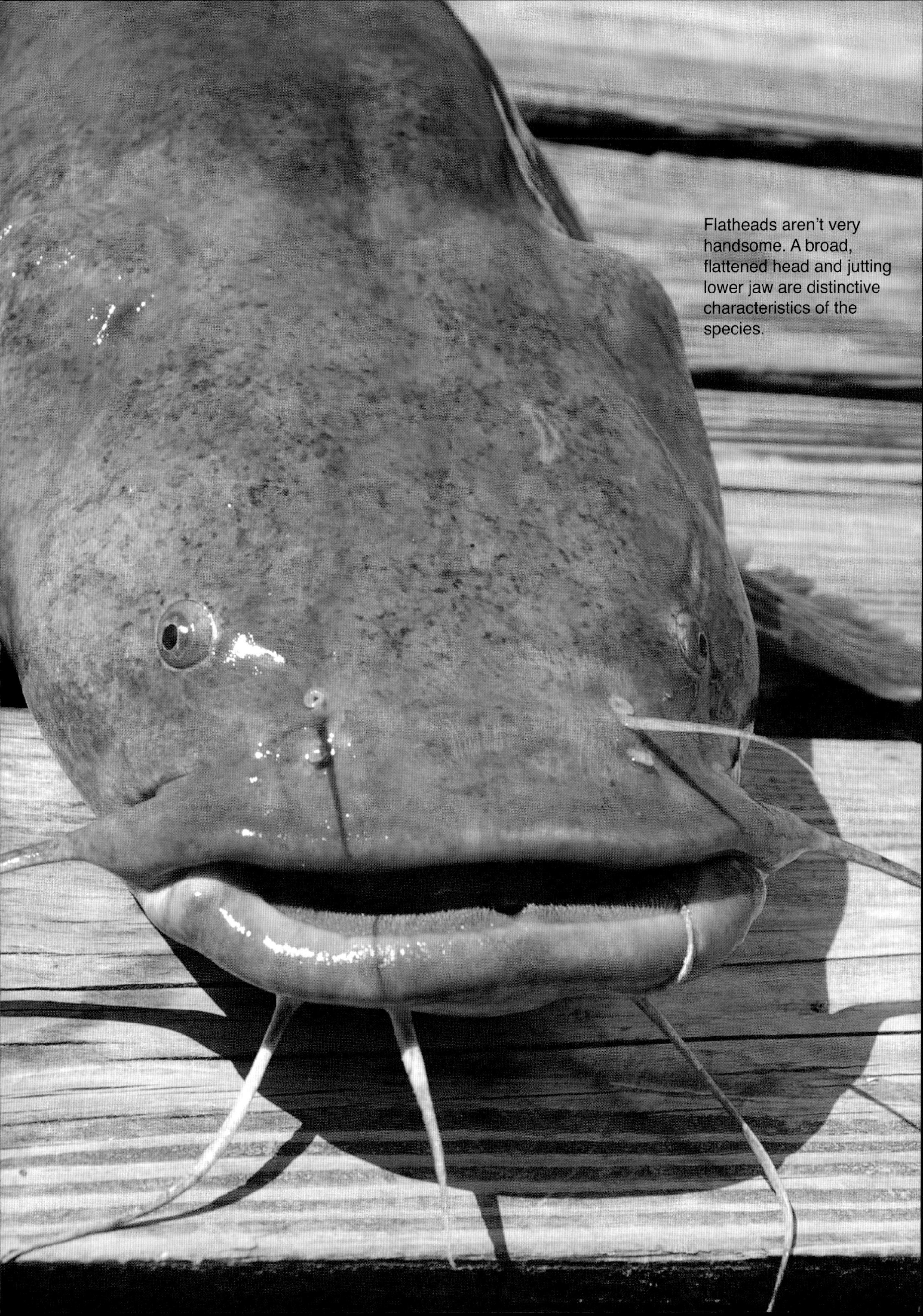

Flatheads aren't very handsome. A broad, flattened head and jutting lower jaw are distinctive characteristics of the species.

Flathead catfish

waters, however, the typical flathead is olive-green to yellowish-brown, often with darker mottling. The belly is pale yellow to cream-white. The tail does not have a deep fork like the tails of channel and blue catfish but is only slightly notched. The flathead also has a distinct underbite—its lower jaw sticks out farther than the upper jaw—which helps distinguish it from other catfish. Small flatheads often resemble bullheads, but the two are easily separated by examining the tooth pad on the upper jaw. On flatheads, this pad has a crescent-shaped backward extension on each side. Bullheads lack these extensions. Their tooth pads are rounded.

Individual flatheads may vary greatly in coloration.

Size

On prime waters during prime times, it's not unusual to catch a dozen or more one- to five-pound flatheads in a few hours of fishing. But flatheads don't stay that small very long. When they reach three years of age, they begin a major growth spurt, commonly adding two to five pounds per year through age eight. After that, they continue packing on the pounds but at an even greater rate. Tag returns indicate older fish may add up to ten pounds annually in some Southern waters.

In lakes and rivers with plentiful forage and good habitat, flatheads exceeding fifty pounds are commonly caught. Of the thirty-three states that list state-record flatheads, 23 have records exceeding 70 pounds. The all-tackle world record is a 123-pounder caught in Kansas' Elk City Reservoir, but flatheads weighing almost seventeen pounds more have been caught using commercial fishing tackle, indicating the possibility that a new world-record flathead might someday be caught on rod and reel.

Food Habits

Studies show that flatheads up to two feet long subsist primarily on a diet of invertebrates, mostly crayfish when they are available. Flatheads greater than two feet long eat mostly fish, including shad, sunfish, suckers, and other catfish.

Unlike channel cats and blues, flatheads rarely scavenge, preferring live foods over dead. Baits such as chicken liver, commercial stinkbaits, or cutbaits that frequently are used for tempting channel cats and small blues sometimes entice small flatheads. But for consistent success, savvy flathead anglers use live fish for bait and nothing else.

Adult flatheads feed primarily on live fish, and, thus, live fish baits are most likely to catch them.

In temperate climes, flatheads feed year-round, but feeding ceases when they are spawning, and they feed little or none when the water temperature falls below about forty-five degrees Fahrenheit. They are rarely caught in winter unlike blue and channel catfish.

Range

The flathead's original range encompassed much of the Mississippi, Mobile, and Rio Grande river drainages and the Great Lakes region in mid-America from North Dakota to Texas in the West and from Pennsylvania to Alabama in the East. Introductions have expanded the species' range to parts of Arizona, California, Colorado, Florida, Georgia, Idaho, Oregon, Pennsylvania, North Carolina, South Carolina, Virginia, Washington, and Wyoming, as well.

Habitat

Flathead catfish seldom exist in large numbers in small bodies of water, like ponds and creeks. However, they are well adapted to life in rivers, larger man-made reservoirs, and many natural lakes where thriving populations often produce excellent fishing opportunities. In rivers, they generally avoid heavy current but sometimes feed in swift water at the ends of dikes and in tailraces below dams.

When looking for flatheads during daylight hours, focus your attention on areas with dense woody cover. These predators often hide around or within submerged logs, piles of driftwood, toppled trees, snags, and cavities in mid-depths, waiting to ambush passing prey. At night, they leave these sanctuaries and move into more open, shallow waters to feed. Adults tend to be solitary and often are aggressive toward others of their kind. Thus, a single spot of cover usually yields only one or at most two or three adult flatheads.

Basic Fishing Tactics

In rivers, look for flatheads in areas with a steady water flow and hardened mud or gravel bottom. The outside bends of rivers are among the most productive hotspots, especially where

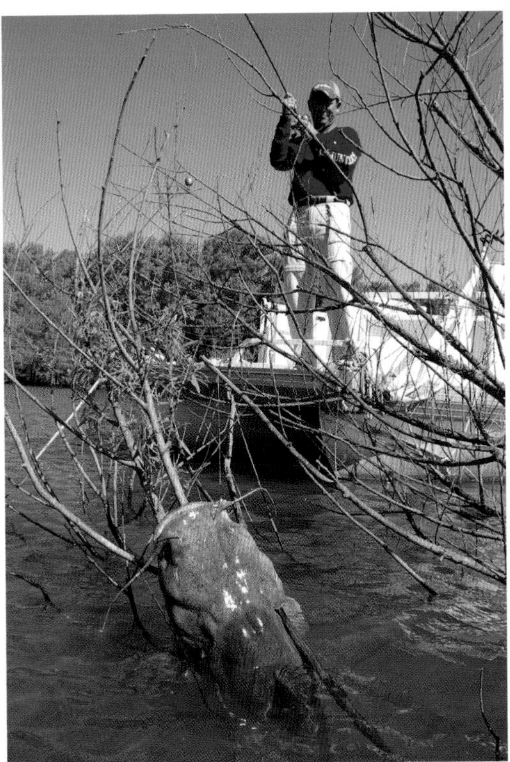

Big flatheads are cover lovers, often found buried in treetops, log jams, and other woody cover from which they ambush their prey.

trees have toppled into the water and the river has gouged deeply into the bank, forming undercuts. Potholes or slight depressions in the river bottom also tend to concentrate flatheads, as do the upstream sides of underwater humps, shallow flats and drops near tributary mouths, and the whitewater tailraces below big dams.

Reservoir flatheads usually seek cover near areas of fast-breaking structure. A sonar unit can help locate flatheads holding on or near stream channels meandering across the bottom. Inundated ponds are honeyholes because they offer flatheads easy access to both deep-water holding areas and shallow feeding spots. Other areas to investigate include current-breaking cover where streams feed the lake, sloping points near the junctions of inundated channels, and steep rocky ledges with adjacent timber. Prime hotspots provide well-oxygenated water, plenty of cover and food, and some current.

When trophy fish are targeted, heavy tackle is a must. Most ardent flatheaders favor heavy-action rods eight to twelve feet long, big level-wind reels, and thirty- to fifty-pound line. The baitfish is hooked through the eyes, nose, or back using a 5/0 to 8/0 hook tied below an egg sinker heavy enough to hold the rig on the bottom. More complicated rigs can be used, but this simple version works fine for most situations.

When fishing from a boat, lower the rig straight down into the spot you've selected and leave your reel in free-spool while you wait for a cat to take the bait. Bank fishermen can hold their rod or place it in a firmly anchored rod holder. Leave the reel in free-spool until you detect a strike, and always be sure your reel's drag is properly set.

High-Rise Flatheads

Flood-stage rivers and lakes can be fished if you employ the right tackle and techniques.

Flathead catfish differ from other cats in many ways. For example, flatheads aren't very mobile. During a year, they usually roam no more than a mile from the single unit of cover they call home. Blue and channel catfish often travel many miles.

Flatheads also are solitary fish and aggressive to others of their own kind unlike blues and channels, which frequently live in small groups or loose schools. A prime piece of flathead real estate—usually a log pile or other protected site where woody debris has accumulated—rarely contains more than one adult fish.

I mention these two characteristics in particular because they affect the catch rates of many catfishermen, especially those of us who enjoy fishing from shore. If you fish primarily from the bank and not a boat, you must depend on the enticing movement, taste, and smell of a live baitfish—the best flathead attractor—to draw your quarry in. The problem is that flatheads don't move much, and when they do, they roam alone. An angler working a pool from the bank is lucky to catch one decent flathead during several nights of fishing.

Spring Spree

There is a time, however, when flatheads abandon these typical patterns. In spring, when heavy rains cause rivers and lakes to rise and become muddy, flatheads go on a run-and-gun feeding spree. Some anglers believe they are hungry after a winter on lean rations, and the sudden influx of food animals washed into the water by warm rain stimulates feeding activity. Others believe the spawning urge draws the fish together, and they feed ravenously to fatten up before the austerity of egg laying and nesting. Whatever the case, this is a boon time for flathead fans. No better situation exists for catching flatheads in numbers.

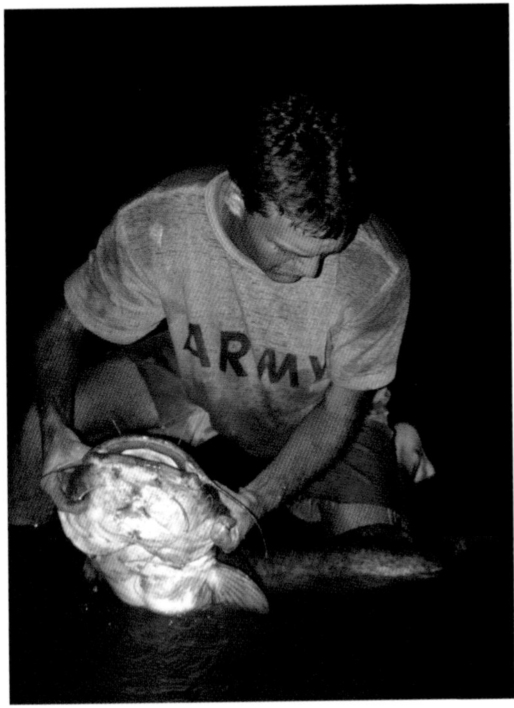

When fishing floodwaters for flatheads, the bank fisherman often finds himself battling a big cat in extremely shallow water.

Flatheads feed ravenously during high water periods in spring, making this one of the best times for multiple hookups with big fish.

My best night fishing for flatheads was on the lower Mississippi River in April under conditions such as those I just described. The river was well above flood stage and muddy enough to track a coon across. Fishing a steep, timbered bank of revetment, two friends and I boated more than 150 flatheads that weighed two to twenty-five pounds.

Nights such as that are unusual even in high water, but if you use proper techniques, high-rise flatheads will provide exciting action. Safety considerations must be foremost on your mind, of course. And for that reason, bank fishing is actually the best choice in this situation. I prefer fishing the points on both sides of a tributary mouth, where I can work a broad swath of water, but areas above and below log jams, wing dikes, and bridges also have proven productive.

Hands-on Fishing

Leave your rod holders home. This is active fishing with the rod in your hand. I work the bait one to two feet beneath an orange-sized

Few anglers target catfish during spring floods because fast-moving waters can be dangerous and make fishing difficult. Nevertheless, this is one of the best periods for finding flatheads on the move, as they gorge on the abundance of food brought into the water by rain.

float (high-rise flatheads seldom feed deep), casting it upstream as far as possible then allowing the rig to drift on a fairly tight line. When my rig nears the end of each drift, before it gets snagged near the bank downstream, I reel in, cast upstream again, and repeat the process. I work from far to near (in relation to the bank) on successive casts.

Because huge flatheads are possible, maybe even a one-hundred-pounder, I use large sturdy hooks, stout line, and a tough rod-and-reel combo. Favored tackle consists of a ten- to twelve-foot surf rod for increased casting distance and better rig control, a heavy spinning reel spooled with fifty- to eighty-pound-test braided line, and an 8/0 to 12/0 circle hook. I prefer a simple more snag-free rig with no weight other than the bait itself due to the large amount of floating debris in the water. And the bait is not always the live fish (sunfish, carp or bullhead) I prefer during other seasons. In flood waters, flatheads feed more indiscriminately, and I often catch them on crawfish, shad guts, and large balls of big night crawlers in addition to fish. Night fishing always is best.

Other game plans may work as well or better, and like I always say, experimenting is half the fun of catfishing. Try your own rigs and techniques, but be sure you don't miss out on this seasonal catfishing bonanza.

Autumn Angles

Autumn flathead fishing runs a dead heat with spring in terms of action.

There's no doubt that flathead feeding activity increases in October, November or December (depending on the latitude). My catch rate improves as summer's heat dissipates and days grow shorter. And I've spoken to dozens of flathead men who experience the same thing. Why the bite improves is a matter of speculation, but like many cat men, I believe flatheads feed more in autumn because they sense a season on low rations is about to begin.

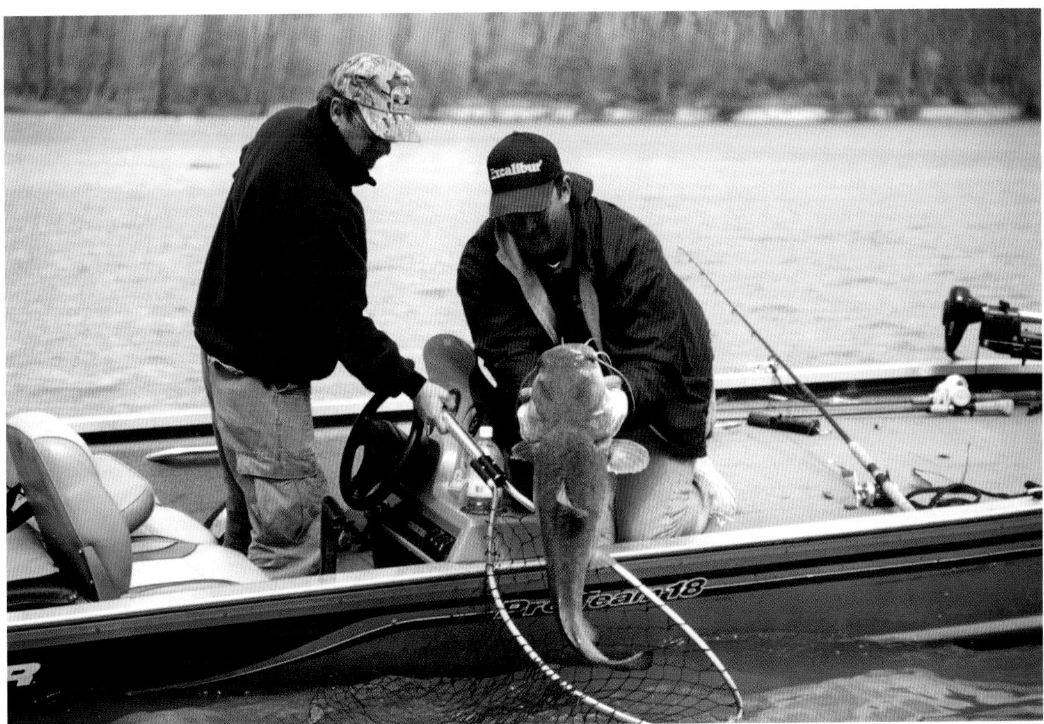

Autumn fishing often produces big flatheads like this.

"Flatheads are like bears," one old-timer told me. "They have to fatten up in fall because they're gonna hibernate till spring. That's why the fall bite is so good." Some dispute that claim, saying flatheads feed actively throughout winter. Maybe in some places, they do. They don't where I fish, however, and I don't know a single flathead man who actively pursues his quarry when the water temperature drops below the mid-forties. There's just not enough feeding activity to justify the effort.

Hardcore Evidence

Two hardcore divers I know provided additional evidence that flatheads become inactive in cold water. Both men noted they often see flatheads congregated in deep water during winter. Invariably, they say, the flatheads are lying on the bottom, sometimes covered with silt, and the fish are so lethargic the divers can actually touch them without spooking them, something that's impossible during other seasons. The flatheads, they report, appear to be in suspended animation.

All this evidence lends veracity to the old-timer's hibernating bear analogy. There's a distinct peak in flathead feeding in autumn because these fish follow instinctive urges to put on weight before the cold "starvation" period ahead.

The reasons why flatheads go on a feeding binge in fall are not as important as the fact they do. Autumn is prime flathead time, and if you want to waylay a trophy specimen, fish as often as possible until harsh winter cold sets in.

It looks almost impossible to fish—a huge rotating mat of floating logs and debris. But eddy-water log rafts like this are prime spots for targeting autumn flatheads.

Fishing Log Rafts

Eddy-water log rafts are my favorite structures to fish this season. These are mats of floating logs and debris that form in big-river backwaters, usually during high-water periods. As the river's current velocity increases, the moving river water presses against the seam of quieter backwater and causes it to circulate like a giant slow-moving vortex. Logs and other woody debris in the river are sucked into this big eddy and form rafts sometimes several hundred yards across. The rafts attract baitfish and other forage animals, which in turn attract flatheads.

To fish these rafts, secure your boat off to one side or find a bank-fishing spot that allows access to the outer edges of the raft. Flatheads often hold beneath central portions of the raft, but it's much easier to fish the edges where flatheads also feed. Live fish baits work best, as they almost always do for flatheads, and can be presented on a simple egg-sinker rig—a one-ounce egg sinker above a barrel swivel to which your leader and hook are tied. Don't use an overly large sinker. You want the eddy to grab your rig and pull it under the outer edge of the log raft. Use just enough weight to carry the bait slowly to the bottom in whatever current is present. Then, after casting, hold your rod tip high and strip line manually from your reel, guiding your rig beneath the rotating maze of logs. If a bite hasn't come by the time your line is caught by a piece of driftwood, move it and try again. If flatheads are present, they'll usually bite within a few minutes after your bait touches bottom.

Tributaries

Tributary mouths are good places to focus your efforts on lakes. If current flow is good in the inflowing creek or river, eddy water can be found here, too. And if some type of dense woody cover is present, as well—log rafts, blowdowns, drift piles, etc.—flatheads are likely to be lying in wait.

In this situation, I usually fish a sliding-bobber rig: a bobber stop and big slip bobber above a few split shot and a hook. By moving the bobber stop up or down your line, you can fish different depths easily, and this type of rig can be cast great distances using a long rod. Cast upstream as far as you can in the tributary, then use your rod tip to guide your rig past the woody cover. Make a drift through one area, then if a bite isn't forthcoming, cast and drift through again, moving your bait past different structures. If a fall flathead is in the neighborhood, you'll nail him on one drift or another.

Section IV

Bullhead Fishing

Facts About Bullhead Catfish

Bullheads don't get very big, but these pugnacious little catfish can provide hours of fun for the panfishing enthusiast.

Because bullheads rarely weigh more than two pounds, many people shun them and focus their fishing efforts on larger species of catfish. Nevertheless, lots of folks love these little cats, because bullheads often are plentiful and always fun to catch. Their scaleless bodies, big-lipped mouths, and long whiskers won't win them any piscatorial beauty contest. But when rolled in seasoned cornmeal and fried golden-brown, bullheads earn a blue-ribbon for scrumptiousness. Their abundance and ready catchability make them perfect targets for kids eager to catch some fish.

Description

Six species of bullheads inhabit North American waters. Three of these—the flat bullhead, snail bullhead, and spotted bullhead—average less than a foot in length and have restricted ranges in small portions of the Southeastern United States. Few people fish for them. We'll focus our attention on the other three

Some anglers frown when they catch a bullhead, detesting this little catfish for its bait-stealing habits and diminutive size. Many, however, prize this bantam brawler, which can provide hours of fun in waters where it is abundant.

species—black, brown, and yellow bullheads—which reach larger sizes, have extensive ranges, and are popular targets of catfish anglers throughout much of the country.

Black bullhead

The black bullhead (*Ameiurus melas*) is a dark, robust, small-eyed catfish with an almost square or slightly notched tail. Adults are a solid brownish yellow to black and have no mottling. The anal fin has seventeen to twenty-one rays. Gray or black chin barbels are present but never white. The pectoral fin spines have weakly developed teeth along the rear edge or no teeth at all.

Brown bullhead

The brown bullhead (*Ameiurus nebulosus*) has light-brown sides that are distinctively mottled with darker markings. The degree of mottling, however, is highly variable. This species is similar to the black bullhead but differs from it in having well-developed teeth on the rear edges of the pectoral spines (versus no teeth or weakly developed teeth) and in having twenty-one to twenty-four anal fin rays (versus seventeen to twenty-one). Unlike the yellow bullhead, its chin barbels are pigmented with gray or black.

Yellow bullhead

The yellow bullhead (*Ameiurus natalis*) closely resembles the brown and black bullheads, with a squat body and a round or square tail, but it differs from these species in having white chin barbels (versus gray or black barbels) and in having twenty-four to twenty-seven anal fin rays (versus having twenty-four or fewer). It differs from blue and channel catfishes in having a straight or rounded margin on its tail versus a forked tail. Adults have a solid yellowish to brownish or black body with no mottling.

Many colorful nicknames are used to describe bullheads. "Horned pout" seems universal, and the nicknames "greaser" and "slick" also are widely used. Other colloquial names include polliwog, polly, paperskin, mudcat, stinger, snapper, butterball, bullcat, and bullpout.

Size

A two-pound bullhead, regardless of species, is considered a big healthy specimen in most waters. Much larger ones are occasionally caught, however. Black bullheads reach the largest maximum size. The all-tackle record weighed eight pounds, fifteen ounces. The brown bullhead record is six pounds, five ounces, and the record yellow bullhead tipped the scales at four pounds, fifteen ounces.

Food Habits

Bullheads eat many types of foods from minnows and crayfish to carrion and insects. "They will take any kind of bait," wrote Henry David

Thoreau, "from angleworms to a piece of tomato can ..."

While using a piece of tomato can for bait might be stretching your luck, there's no denying these little cats are not temperamental. You can catch them on everything from bacon and hot dogs to minnows and crayfish. Among the best baits, however, are fresh chicken liver, worms, and stinkbaits.

Range

The black bullhead ranges from southern Canada, the Great Lakes, and the St. Lawrence River south to the Gulf of Mexico and from Montana and New Mexico east to the Appalachians.

The range of the brown bullhead encompasses most of the eastern half of the United States and Southeastern Canada. It also has been widely introduced outside its native range. In parts of New England, the brown bullhead is the only catfish available to anglers.

The yellow bullhead swims in waters throughout the Eastern and Central United States with many transplants elsewhere.

Habitat

Oxbow lakes, river backwaters, pools in small streams, and other areas with quiet, turbid water and a silty bottom are the preferred home waters of black bullheads.

The brown bullhead prefers moderately clear, heavily vegetated streams and lakes.

The yellow bullhead tends to inhabit smaller weedier bodies of water than its cousins and reaches its greatest abundance in areas of dense vegetation in shallow clear bays of lakes, ponds, and slow-moving streams.

Basic Fishing Tactics

You can catch bullheads using the same tactics employed for catching eating-sized channel cats, but you may want to downsize your fishing tackle for these small fish. Small hooks, light line, and ultralight rod-and-reel combos work great.

Bait choices are legion. Bullheads are the fish world's equivalent of barnyard hogs. There's hardly anything they won't eat. Live crayfish, minnows, nightcrawlers, shad, catalpa worms, salamanders, leeches, maggots, tadpoles, or toads will do just fine. Dead stuff such as chicken liver, mussels, shrimp, and fish guts are on the menu, as well. Weird things, too, like dog food, corn, soap, sour grain, hot dogs, marshmallows, bread, cheese, and even bubble gum are acceptable. Indeed, bullheads will engulf anything remotely resembling food, so you'll probably catch one sooner or later no matter what your bait choice.

Those big rubbery lips make bullheads somewhat hard to hook, so always use extra-sharp hooks.

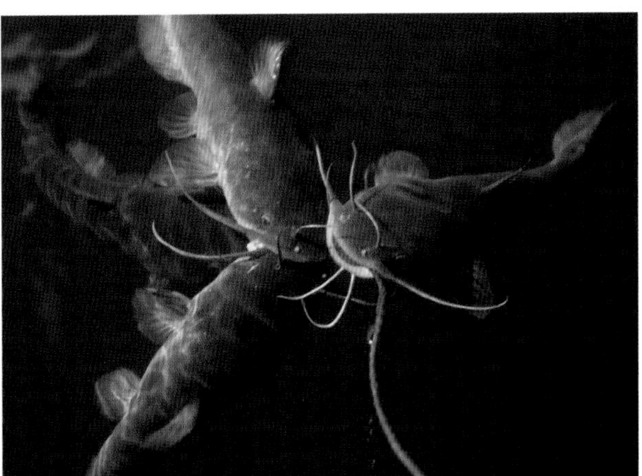

A stringer of fat bullheads provides the makings for a delicious fish dinner.

How to Catch Record-Class Bullheads

Massachusetts catfishing expert Roger Aziz has caught some of the biggest bullheads ever documented. The tips he shares can help you land some monster bulls, too.

Call him The Bullhead King or just plain bullheaded. Either way, Roger Aziz Jr. of Methuen, Massachusetts, will take it as a compliment. Hundreds of thousands of people in this country love bullhead fishing, but no one loves fishing for these pugnacious little catfish more than Roger.

No one knows more about bullhead fishing, either, a fact exemplified by the many record bullheads Roger has caught. Aziz has established International Game Fish Association line-class records for yellow bullheads four times and for brown bullheads twice. The National Fresh Water Fishing Hall of Fame has recognized ten brown bullheads he's caught as line-class and all-tackle records plus five yellow bullhead line-class records.

Roger's biggest bullhead to date was a six-pound, four-ounce yellow bullhead caught May 25, 2008, in the fifty-five-acre Forest Lake in Methuen. Twenty-three inches long with a thirteen-inch girth, that fish was a giant of its kind and is recognized as the current Massachusetts state record. The currently recognized IGFA all-tackle world record is just two ounces heavier. Aziz caught a previous Massachusetts record—a three-and-a-half pound brown bullhead—in 1985. To give you an idea of how hard it is to catch a bullhead even of that size, the record stood more than twenty years before being broken.

While bullhead fishing is one of Roger's specialties, let's not cubbyhole the man into that single niche. Roger is one of the few freshwater fishing guides in Massachusetts with more than

Roger Aziz Jr. shows off the six-pound, four-ounce yellow bullhead he caught, which was certified as Massachusetts state record. This is one of the lar bullheads ever documented.

twenty-five years experience fishing for a wide variety of sportfish—everything from trout, salmon, and American shad to bass, carp, and saltwater species. "If it has fins, I can catch it," he says. He's also a tournament champion, angling consultant, lecturer, and writer. Make no mistake about it, however, Roger Aziz knows as much about catfishing, and particularly bullhead fishing, as any angler in the world. His tips will prove useful to anyone desiring to catch the biggest bullheads swimming where they fish.

Developing a Game Plan

"I started fishing for bullheads at a very early age," says Aziz, who was born in 1961. "Like sunfish, they seem to show up on your line no matter where you're fishing. Most don't get very big—maybe a pound or two. A three-pound bullhead is quite unusual—equivalent to, let's say, a ten-pound largemouth bass. When I started catching some bullheads that size, I knew I was on to something good. So I began my own research projects to learn more about the way these monster bullheads function."

Although bullheads inhabit a variety of waters, Aziz determined that ponds stocked with trout tend to be home waters for the biggest bulls.

"In New England, trout are stocked in two basic types of ponds: those that are spring fed and those that are not," he says. "Most stocked ponds that are spring fed have a low fish kill rate. Trout thrive in these waters year-round. But ponds that aren't spring fed tend to be eutrophic (rich in nutrients) with little or no trout survival due to oxygen depletion and other factors.

"The eutrophic ponds are best for bigheads," he continues. "Dead trout lay on the bottom of the ponds, and something is going to eat them. Most likely, that something will be bullheads, which often consume carrion. And the more trout the bullheads consume—the more raw protein they eat—the bigger they get."

In spring-fed lakes, natural trout die-offs are rare, but many trout still perish due to angling pressure and mishandling.

"Big bulls become more predator-like in these spring-fed lakes," Aziz says. "But they still can be caught if you use the right tactics."

Tackle

Were you to accompany Aziz on one of his bullhead-fishing junkets, you might be rather amazed at the tackle he uses, much of which is unfamiliar to American anglers.

"I opt to use Euro tackle," he says, "the same stuff our fishing pals from across the pond use for carp fishing. My rods are thirteen feet long with a three-and-three-quarter-pound test curve. By American standards, this is a heavy-action rod with a fast tip, which provides enough loading power that I can catapult a bait rig great distances. My reels are bait-runner reels that allow the line to be pulled out by a fish without an open spool. These are loaded with fifteen-pound-test Berkeley Big Game Solar line tipped with a forty-pound-test fluorocarbon shock leader six feet long."

Aziz fishes with this European-style carp-fishing tackle.

Aziz sometimes fishes from a boat, but because most ponds he fishes at are relatively small, more likely than not you'll find him on shore when he's targeting big bullheads. He fishes with multiple rod/reel combos supported on a Gardner stainless-steel rod pod, a device developed by carp anglers that allows rods to lie horizontally and be tended hands-free. The pod is coupled with Delkim electronic strike alarms that detect the slightest line movement and rod vibrations. When a bullhead bites, these sound an alarm "loud enough to wake anyone from a deep sleep," says Aziz.

When night fishing, Aziz also carries at least three propane lanterns plus head lanterns and flashlights. All his equipment is carried in a Fox rucksack, which resembles a backpack with a four-legged frame to keep equipment stable and off the ground.

On the business end of each fishing line, Aziz ties a tandem bait rig.

"Each rig consists of a No. 2 wide-bend hook followed by a Kahle hook varying in size from 2/0 to 5/0. The hooks are connected to each other by snell knots, all following IGFA rules."

Unlike most catfish anglers, Aziz uses no lead sinkers on his rigs or very small sinkers. His baits—bacon, sunfish, or minnows—are sunk to the bottom with a bar of soap. Yes, soap.

Soaping

Using soap for catfish bait is nothing new (see Chapter 23). But Aziz has carried "soaping," as he calls it, to a whole new level.

"Soaping is a ground-bait technique I conjured myself," he says. "I take a bar of Dial soap, any exotic scent, and drive a homemade eye screw through the whole bar. The soap is part of my fishing rig and acts as both a weight and an

Bars of Dial soap rigged with homemade eye screws serve as weights and bullhead attractors on Aziz's fishing rigs.

attractor. The scent is limited to a radius of a couple of feet in lakes or ponds, but it's a real big bullhead attractant."

A long process of experimentation helped Aziz refine this tactic. He knew catfish rely heavily on scent to help them find food items. But experience showed that scent didn't have to be from something dead and rotten like a trout carcass.

"I figured if I could attract carp with ground bait, a concoction of bread crumbs and other household foods, why not bullheads?" he says. "The ground bait used for carp works OK but dissipates quickly in water. I wanted an attractor that would melt slowly and attract anything swimming by. Soap turned out to be that attractor. I tested a variety of scents to see which would work better, and it turns out they all work very well. I use Dial soap because it's very inexpensive and very heavy. I can cast it long distances, and it sinks quickly to the bottom. It comes in many sweet-smelling fragrances that attract monster bulls."

To prepare the soap for rigging, Aziz takes a six-inch piece of forty-gauge wire and grinds it flat on both ends. Then, using a wire-forming machine, he creates an eye on one end of wire with a long wrap. The wire can then be pushed and screwed into the middle of the soap on one end. The wire wrap below the eye works like a screw to keep the soap secure.

The wired soap is attached to the main line via a swivel on a sliding fish-finder sleeve. The main line runs through the sleeve with the sleeve held in place above the hooks using a small piece of plastic tubing crimped on the line. The hooks are then baited with pieces of bacon, small whole sunfish or minnows, or small pieces of cutbait prepared from the baitfish.

When fishing from shore, this whole rig is cast out, allowed to sink, and sits stationary on the bottom while Aziz waits for a bite. If he is fishing from a boat, however, Aziz's fishing method is a bit different.

"In a boat, I use a six-foot medium-heavy rod with a fast taper," he says. "I do not attach the soap to my line but instead chum bars of soap over the side of the boat. The area I chum is where I place my bait. I use a sinker that's as light as possible."

It's not a huge fish, but this four-pound, four-ounce brown bullhead caught by Roger Aziz is a giant of its kind. Only rarely do anglers catch bullheads this large.

Seasonal and Locational Information

Aziz doesn't ice-fish for bullheads but targets them whenever the New England ponds he fishes are ice free.

"Spring is when bulls are at their heaviest," he says. "They spawn from the latter part of May through early June and are filled with eggs.

"From the latter part of June through July, big bulls are more difficult to catch. This is the postspawn period when bulls are busy guarding their fry and not feeding heavily.

"From August until November, bullhead fishing can be great as long as the weed growth is light," he continues. "Big ones hold six to twenty feet deep then. I find that the monster bulls usually bolt when accepting the bait in the spring when weed growth is sparse. But in summer, when the weed growth is at its peak, monster bulls stay in their weed patches and don't move much at all. Finding the right weed patch is hard. It takes a lot of trial and error. Bullheads being omnivorous will feed on the weeds they lie in when other forage is not available. And in the weeds, the bite is not bolting and aggressive but subtle. I have to keep my eye on the line whether a bite indicator is used or not. The good thing is, competition from smaller bulls is not as much in weed patches. I usually catch big bulls when fishing these spots."

During the latter part of this period, from late October into November, fishing may be extremely difficult, Aziz notes.

The Electrical Sense in Bullheads

In 2011, Roger Aziz caught a five-pound, fifteen-ounce yellow bullhead from Stiles Pond in Boxford, Massachusetts. Instead of releasing the fish, he took it home and kept it alive in a three-foot by five-foot cooler so he could study it. Emma, as the fish was dubbed, taught him some amazing things about the unusual electrical sense in catfish.

"Catfish have ampullae organs like sharks," Aziz says. "These enable the cats to detect faint electrical fields from other living fish.

"I used an underwater camera and light to film Emma feeding in the dark, and I soon noticed that whenever the camera light was on—often opposite of where Emma was positioned—Emma would strike the camera lens, trying to engulf it. It did not matter where I put the camera. As long as the light was on, Emma was on the camera."

Observing this prompted Aziz to buy an underwater light to use when fishing.

"The light is hard to submerge, and its battery life is short," he says. "But it definitely attracts bullheads. I still don't know how far away the bullheads can feel the electrical fields from the light. But the light definitely attracts them, and the bigger the bulb, the better."

"This is when most weed growth is gone, and the ambient scent is less," he notes. "Big bulls now are more prone to forage on what is left over from the summer months. And as with all fish, their metabolism is very low and bites are less frequent. The fish never stop feeding, but they don't feed nearly as much as when temperatures are in their comfort range. Patience is a virtue during these months."

The Mad Monster Chase

Aziz's monster bulls have been caught in several New England ponds and lakes. Waters in other states have produced giant bullheads, as well, leading one to believe that an angler armed with the knowledge Aziz has shared here has a good chance of landing a new state, line-class, or world record somewhere within the range of these bantam brawlers.

"I've spent many years targeting bullheads," says Aziz, "and find these fish, especially the big ones, very fascinating. There's much more to catching the big ones than many people think. I hope that by sharing some of what I've learned, others will be able to experience the thrill of catching a real monster bull. That's an experience you never forget."

Twenty Can't-Miss Tips for Bullheads

You'll fill your stringer with plenty of good-eating polliwogs if you put these tips to the test.

Bullheads will pounce on any offering of edibles with wild abandon. They strike hard without any pretense of caution. They fight tenaciously. Rolled in cornmeal and fried golden-brown, they are delicious. It is not surprising, therefore, that millions of anglers love bullheads.

In Iowa, for example, bullheads lead in fish popularity polls with anglers catching 12.5 million annually. In the Bullhead Capital of the World—Waterville, Minnesota—residents gather each June to enjoy Bullhead Days, a celebration where deep-fried bullheads are served by street vendors. Bullheads are the only type of catfish available to many New England anglers, thus they are frequently targeted. Millions are stocked annually, particularly in small urban waters.

If you're among the many who enjoy catching and eating these bantam brawlers or a convert just learning the bullhead fishing craft, here are some tips to help you get the most out of your next polliwog junket.

Ponds and small lakes often provide the best bullhead action, and in most of the United States, fishing for these little cats is good spring, summer, fall, and winter.

Fish Light

Use ultralight spinning or spincast combos. Four- to eight-pound line is appropriate in all but the most snag-infested waters. Hooks for bullheads range in size from No. 4 to 1/0.

Fish Right at Night

Bullheads feed around the clock, but the night bite usually is best. Bullheads avoid current. Zero in on deep holes in creeks, backwater areas on rivers, weed bed edges in ponds and swamps, boat docks, long points, and underwater humps in lakes.

Keep it Simple

The simpler your fishing methods, the more you will enjoy bullhead fishing. Your strategy can be as unencumbered as using a cane pole and small hook to dunk a worm or piece of liver. Fish on bottom using a small sinker to carry your bait down. Or use a bobber to float the bait slightly above the bottom. You need not fish deep or far from shore.

Hooking What Bites

Bullheads have a propensity for holding the bait, letting the angler reel them in, then spitting the bait out at the last second. When tightlining, let the fish start moving off before you strike. Count to three, then set the hook with a quick upward snap. When bobber fishing, wait until the float disappears or starts moving slowly away. That's usually when the fish has the bait in its mouth.

Carry Plenty of Hooks

Bullheads are notorious hook swallowers, so carry plenty of hooks. You can remove hooks with a disgorger or long-nosed pliers, but it's quicker to cut the line and retrieve hooks when cleaning your catch. Better yet, use small circle hooks, which tend to hook the fish in the corner of the mouth and are easily removed.

Blow up a Worm

Night crawlers are irresistible to bullheads, especially when you use a hypodermic syringe to inflate them. Adding a shot of air in the body lifts the worms up, making them more visible to the fish. Your sinker sits on bottom; your crawlers ride high.

Really Red Worms

Soak worms in red pickled beet juice to make them more attractive to bullheads. This also toughens their "hides," making it harder for bullheads to steal them off the hook.

Soaking night crawlers in beet juice toughens them and makes them more attractive to bullheads.

Bait Options

A trip to the grocery will turn up many superb bullhead baits. Bacon works great, especially

hickory-smoked. Chunks of hot dog and cheese are relished, too, and fresh chicken livers can't be beat. Bread and even bubble gum work in a pinch.

Liver Rig

A small treble hook attached to your line with a snap swivel works great when fishing liver. Unsnap the swivel, remove the hook, push the eye of the hook through the liver so the liver is impaled on the three barbs, then reattach the hook to the swivel. The liver is now less likely to fly off when you cast.

Doughbait Recipe

Here's a popular formula for doughbait to entice bullheads. Run a pint of chicken livers through a blender until liquefied. Slowly add Wheaties cereal, and continue blending until the mixture turns into a ball. Roll into grape-sized pieces and place in a zip-seal bag. Cool to firm before using.

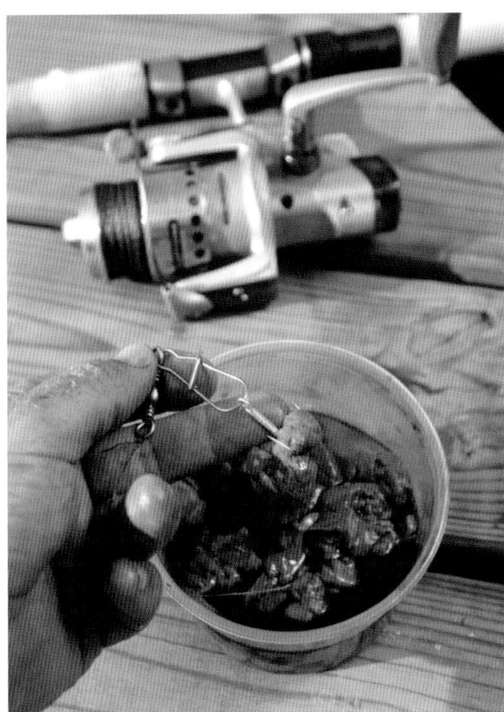

A great way to catch bullheads is with fresh chicken liver on a snap-swivel rig.

Bullhead Turnoffs

Bullheads can detect and will avoid even minute quantities of sunscreen, gas, oil, or insect repellent that come in contact with your bait. Avoid these if possible. If you can't, wear rubber gloves when handling bait.

Don't Get "Horned"

Avoid the bullhead's sharp pectoral and dorsal fin spines. If you get poked, old-timers recommend swiping the fish's belly across the wound to neutralize the stinging sensation. Household ammonia daubed on the wound has the same effect.

No Shadows

Bullheads scurry for cover when a shadow passes overhead. If you fish during daylight hours, you'll have more luck if you place yourself so the sun never casts your shadow on the spot where you are fishing.

Caution should be used when handling bullheads, which have extremely sharp spines.

Tie a Break Knot

Bullheads often dash for cover when hooked, causing hang-ups. An overhand knot tied above your hook will help you save your line should the hook become snagged in deep water. A quick jerk will break the line at the knot instead of the rod tip.

Winter Fishing

Some anglers say bullheads won't bite in winter. They're wrong. To enjoy light tackle fun during cold months, head for the nearest bullhead pond and drop a bait in the deepest water you can find. Bullheads often gather in huge concentrations in deep wintering holes, and if you can pinpoint such a place, you'll soon be enjoying fish-a-minute action.

Keep 'em Cold

If you catch bullheads in clean water and ice them down immediately, they're delicious. Fish taken in muddy or polluted water may have a disagreeable taste regardless of how you care for them.

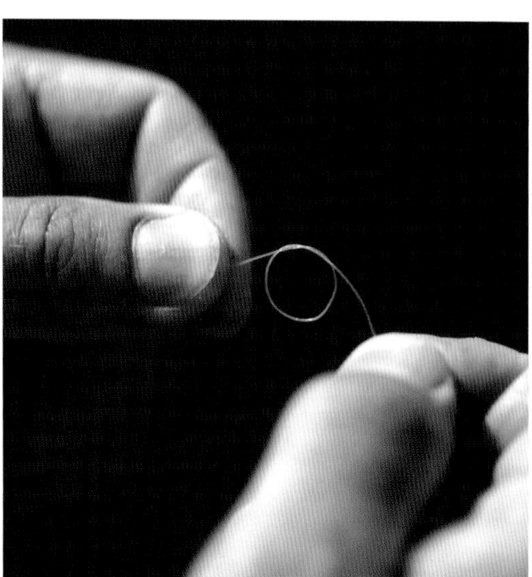

Bullheads often rush for cover when hooked. Tying a simple overhand knot in your line allows you to break it off easier if the fish gets too ensnarled for extraction.

Which Cat is That?

Want to know what kind of bullhead you caught? It's easy to separate the three common species by looking at the chin barbels (whiskers) and fins. Yellow bullheads have whitish or yellowish chin barbels. Brown bullheads have dark chin barbels like black bullheads, but on browns the pectoral fin spines on each side just behind the head have well-developed "teeth" along the rear edge; teeth are absent or weakly developed on the black bullhead's pectoral fin spines.

Cleaning Tips

Always skin bullheads and remove dark red meat along the lateral line. This rids the dressed fish of unsavory flesh. Avoid puncture wounds by snipping off the spines with wire cutters before cleaning your catch. Skinning is easier if you use an ice pick to secure the fish to a board or tree.

A Tasty Recipe

Here's a bullhead recipe that's hard to beat. Combine ¾ cup yellow cornmeal, ¼ cup flour, 2 teaspoons salt, ½ teaspoon cayenne pepper, and ½ teaspoon garlic powder in a large bag. Add fish and shake to coat. Fill a cooker half full of peanut oil and heat to 365 degrees Fahrenheit. Add fish and fry until the fish flakes easily with a fork, about five minutes. Serve piping hot.

Kids' Fish

Because they're abundant and rather easy to catch, bullheads are great kids' fish. Next time you fish for them, take a youngster along. It's a great way to spend a day.

Section V

Seasonal Savvy

Understanding the Spawn

There are good reasons your catch rate may fall when cats are spawning.

"The bluegills are bedding!" "The white bass are running!" "Crappie are spawning!" "Largemouths are moving up shallow!"

Spawning season is peak time to catch many gamefish, and when the rally cry is heard, folks flock to the water to enjoy some of the year's best action. The spawning habits of catfish, however, differ greatly from the spawning habits of other gamefish. Catfishing success may take a nosedive when blues, flatheads, and channel cats are on their nests, and unless you understand why this occurs, you're likely to return from a fishing trip frustrated and perplexed.

Spawning Behavior

Our major catfish species spawn during spring or summer when the water warms to an optimal temperature. Channel cats spawn at seventy to eighty-four degrees Fahrenheit, but eighty to eighty-one degrees is considered best. Flatheads spawn at sixty-six to seventy-five degrees. Blue catfish spawning requirements are believed to be similar to those of channel catfish.

The swollen head on this big channel cat indicates it is a male ready to guard a nest full of eggs. While protecting its eggs, it may not feed for days, making it tough to catch.

Spawning begins at different times in different latitudes progressing from south to north. With channel cats, for instance, spawning may begin in March or April in South Carolina or Texas, May in Kansas or Iowa, and mid-June to July in South Dakota or Wyoming. Blue catfish spawn April through June in Louisiana and early July in Iowa. Flatheads spawn in late June in Arkansas but not until weeks later in northern parts of their range.

All our cats are cavity nesters. Blue catfish deposit their eggs between rocks, in root wads, depressions, undercut banks, or other areas protected from current. Flatheads select sites such as hollow logs, excavated caves in clay banks, root masses from downed trees, or manmade structures, such as old tires, car bodies, and metal drums. Channel catfish have been observed to spawn directly on the bottom at sites with no nearby cover, but they usually select dark, secluded spots, such as crevices in piles of woody debris, burrows in banks, and spaces between and under rocks. If suitable spawning habitat is unavailable, catfish may migrate from a lake into a tributary stream, for example, to find it.

Catfish are cavity nesters, as the hatchery manager well knows. To provide spawning sites in hatchery ponds, old milk cans are often placed on the bottom where each female catfish can lay her mass of yellow eggs. Male cats then guard the eggs until they hatch.

A sexually mature male selects and cleans a nest site and spawns with a female he lures there. After the female lays her mound of sticky yellow eggs, the male fertilizes the mass, drives the female from the nest, and begins guard duty. He protects the nest from predators and fans the eggs with his fins to keep them aerated and free from sediment. The eggs hatch in six to ten days depending on water temperature, and the compact school of fry remains near the nest a few days before dispersing. The male guards the fry until they leave.

Cat fans fishing during the spawn may notice a sharp drop in catch rates because male catfish take little or no food while protecting the nest. Fortunately, the spawn is over in a few days. And because fish in a system don't all spawn at the same time, a section of river or lake may contain prespawn, spawn, and postspawn catfish. If water conditions are favorable, some active feeders will always be available to catch, so there may be no noticeable decline in fishing success. If poor fishing is noticed and can't be attributed to other causes, the angler can wait a few days until the spawning peak passes and male cats are feeding once again.

Spawning Season Tactics

Two rather unusual forms of catfishing were derived to take advantage of the catfish's cavity-nesting habits. Noodling, also called hogging and grabbling, is the practice of catching catfish with one's hands when they are in nest cavities (natural and manmade) and easily cornered. In a modification of this technique called bucket fishing, participants submerse weighted buckets or drums with a semicircular hole cut in the lid. Cats enter the containers to spawn and are captured by lifting the containers from the water using an attached line. This technique is highly effective. A ten-bucket line I helped run in a Louisiana lake produced ten channel catfish daily on three days in late May.

In waters where catfish are abundant, removing a few ready-to-spawn fish from the population is no more detrimental than removing a few egg-filled bluegills. However, we should all temper our catch-and-eat desires with some common sense catch and release. Keep a few smaller cats to eat, and release larger fish. Remember: today's releases are tomorrow's trophies.

Seasonal Movements in Rivers

As the seasons change, so do the home sites of catfish.

River catfish are like ducks. They can't fly, but just like waterfowl, many catfish—blues and channel cats, in particular—migrate with the seasons. In fall, schools of cats move downstream to wintering areas, just as flocks of ducks fly south to their wintering grounds. When spring rolls around, catfish return to upstream areas to spawn, much like ducks flying north to breeding grounds.

Catfishermen who study seasonal migration habits of catfish can enjoy better fishing success throughout the seasons.

The seasonal migrations of catfish don't cover thousands of miles as is the case with our feathered friends, but their movements are significant enough—from a few miles to several hundred miles—to be worthy of our attention. Duck hunters must know where the birds are gathered in order to be successful and so, too, must catfish anglers.

Platte River Study

A study conducted in Nebraska's lower Platte River, a tributary of the Missouri River, exemplifies the movement patterns existing in many small to mid-sized rivers. Thirty-eight adult channel cats implanted with radio transmitters were tracked in this river. Their movements showed distinct seasonal trends.

During spring, 54 percent moved upstream, and 46 percent made only local movements—short movements (short movements between resting and feeding areas). During summer, 7 percent of movement was upstream, 86 percent local, and 7 percent downstream. During autumn,

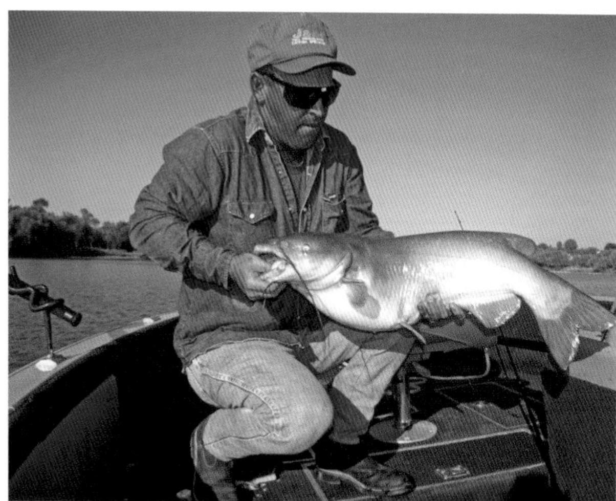

Anglers often think of channel catfish as sedentary creatures, but big ones like this sometimes migrate considerable distances. Knowing where these fish go and when allows the fisherman to find his quarry throughout the seasons.

33 percent of movement was local, and 67 percent was downstream. During winter, 100 percent of movement was downstream. Catfish traveled the longest distances in spring and autumn. Spring movements averaged 11.5 river miles with a range of 1.2 to 30.1 river miles. Average autumn movement was 26.1 river miles with a range of 2.5 to 74.5 river miles.

According to the researchers, these movement patterns suggest overwintering of channel catfish in deep scour pools in the Missouri River, followed by upstream spring movements to spawning and feeding areas, and a return downstream in autumn and winter to avoid ice cover in shallow streams. The movements correspond with changing temperature and discharge patterns in the river.

Additional Evidence

A study in the lower Wisconsin and upper Mississippi Rivers (Iowa and Wisconsin) found that many channel cats (44 to 84 percent, depending on the year) migrated from the smaller Wisconsin River into the Mississippi River to overwinter. In spring, most movement was in the opposite direction from the Mississippi into the Wisconsin.

We can't say channel cats always behave the same in other waters, but the movements described above are similar to those observed in many other small to mid-sized rivers.

Movements of Blue Cats and Flatheads

Blue catfish are even more mobile than channel cats with migrations often spanning several hundred miles. Again, however, movements follow general seasonal patterns—upstream in spring and downstream in fall with more local movements during other seasons. In the Mississippi River, for example, blue cats migrate downstream to wintering areas where water is warmest. By early summer, they have returned to upstream reaches.

Numerous studies involving river flatheads show these fish are very sedentary. They

Big blue cats like this may migrate hundreds of miles each year. They typically move upstream in spring to prime spawning sites and downstream in fall to wintering sites. During other seasons, movements are more restricted.

Flatheads are the least mobile of North America's big cats. Unlike blues and channel cats, which may move many miles as the seasons change, flatheads usually stay in the same areas year-round, rarely moving more than a mile from their homesite.

establish preferred use areas and seldom move far from those sites regardless of the season. To use one example, adult flatheads monitored from June through January in Mississippi's Big Black and Tallahatchie rivers moved less than one-half mile on average from their capture site during the entire six-month period.

Applying knowledge of these movements can help anglers determine where catfish are most likely to be throughout the seasons, thus increasing the chance of catching fish. Look for flatheads in the same locales season after season. Blues and channel cats concentrate near upstream spawning areas in small to mid-sized rivers in summer and near deep wintering holes in larger rivers during cold months. During spring and fall, they're on the move and may be caught almost anywhere. Adjust your tactics as necessary to pinpoint active fish.

Dog Days Cats

Learning this trio of feeding patterns will help you hook more summer catfish.

To catch catfish on a regular basis, the angler must acquire an understanding of the primary feeding patterns specific to these fish. What are catfish likely to be eating? When? Where? Armed with the answers to these questions and a considerable measure of patience and luck, the fisherman can expect to find and hook a beefy cat. Without these answers, luck alone determines the outcome.

Catfishermen must also realize that feeding patterns differ with the seasons. Different foods are available in different places during different seasons, and knowing which are available where and when is the key to finding and catching cats.

Herewith are three summer patterns you should know.

Skipjack Patterns

Skipjack herring are common in nearly all big rivers inhabited by blue cats. They comprise a major portion of the blue cat's diet in some

Anglers who understand how to pattern summer catfish find this a blue-ribbon season for hooking trophy fish.

areas, and many catfishermen use them for bait. They're easily captured in cast nets or on small jigs.

Like shad, skipjacks are active baitfish, moving about continuously in large schools. Unlike shad, however, which feed primarily on microscopic plants and animals, skipjacks are piscivorous. Minnows, shad, and other small fishes are their favored foods. This fact makes them doubly attractive to blue cats, especially in late summer. Here's why.

In many waters, skipjack herring are favored foods of catfish. Find schools of these baitfish, and cats are usually nearby.

In July and August, large schools of skipjacks often churn the surface of the water as they pursue young-of-the-year shad. This is a highly visible phenomenon, quite similar to the surface-feeding melees of stripers and white bass. You can see the fish swirling near the surface with little shad jumping all about as they try to elude the skipjacks. This activity usually occurs near dawn and dusk, frequently near creek mouths or at the junction of two big rivers.

When surfacing skipjacks are sighted, it's highly likely scores of blue cats are lurking below. They're attracted not only by the prospect of a skipjack entrée but also by the many dead and crippled shad left behind when skipjacks slash through a school. Sometimes striped or white bass join the feeding frenzy, too, working on skipjacks and shad alike. This increases the number of injured baitfish fluttering about, another drawing card for gluttonous blues.

For the dyed-in-the-wool blue cat angler, this is a setting like no other. A 1/64- to 1/32-ounce silver or white jig cast toward swirling fish will usually garner a strike from a skipjack that can be used for bait. Cut the skippy in small pieces, run a hook through one, then cast it toward the swirls and let it fall enticingly to hungry blues waiting below. Better yet, come prepared with a few small shad ready to rig.

Following the Schools

During summer's heat, catfish in reservoirs and rivers often move to deep pools and channel edges following schools of baitfish and searching for suitable temperature and oxygen levels. Baitfish are continually seeking comfort zones where plankton, young-of-the-year baitfish, and other foods are available. They may move several times and several miles during a twenty-four-hour period, or they may remain relatively stationary. Wherever they go, however, cats will follow with most holding in loose schools beneath the baitfish where they feed.

Find the baitfish, and you'll find the catfish; that's the key to capitalizing on this pattern. One way is using sonar to probe deep-water habitats for big fish holding beneath baitfish schools. Most will be on or near prominent bottom structure like channel breaks, humps, and holes—within the thermocline in stratified waters. When the angler sees "blips" indicating the possibility of a big cat beneath schooling baitfish at a specific depth, he anchors his craft, counts off the right amount of line, and places a piece of cutbait or a live baitfish in front of a fish. Some use a "stacked minnow" rig in this situation. Several large minnows are hooked through both lips on a single hook. These are then presented at the proper depth beneath a float. Catfish find the struggling school of crippled baitfish irresistible.

Drift-fishing with multiple poles is a good way to zero in on often-scattered schools of hot-weather catfish.

Drift-fishing is another method for finding scattered catfish in summer. Wind or a trolling motor moves the boat, while the angler watches a depth sounder and guides the craft along bottom channels and other structures where catfish are holding.

Many use a float rig for this type of fishing. The main line is run through the eye of a pencil weight, and a barrel swivel is tied below it to keep the weight from sliding down. A twelve- to eighteen-inch leader is then tied to the lower eye of the swivel. A bobber or float is affixed in the middle of the leader, and a Kahle hook is tied at the end. The float suspends the baited hook above the bottom to help prevent snags.

Drifting Bait in Small to Mid-Sized Streams

Small to mid-sized streams often serve up excellent summer catfishing. If water levels don't fall too low in the smaller streams, cats may migrate in from big lakes and rivers to take advantage of cooler water temperatures, higher oxygen levels, and plentiful food animals, such as crayfish, baitfish, and aquatic insects. The best fishing is usually at night, and most cats are caught by drifting natural bait beneath a bobber.

Bobbers can be clipped or pegged in place on the line, but this rigging is cumbersome to cast. A sliding-bobber rig works better because the bobber slides freely on the line, allowing you to reel terminal tackle close to the rod tip for easier casting. The bobber style is determined by current and bait size. In heavy current or when medium or large baits are used, use a larger, rounder, more buoyant bobber. In low or moderate flow or when small baits are used, a smaller cigar-shaped bobber is OK. The best baits are crayfish, creek minnows, or small sunfish, caught, when possible, in the water you're fishing.

Night fishing with a bobber/live-bait drift rig often produces big cats such as this when small to mid-sized rivers are targeted.

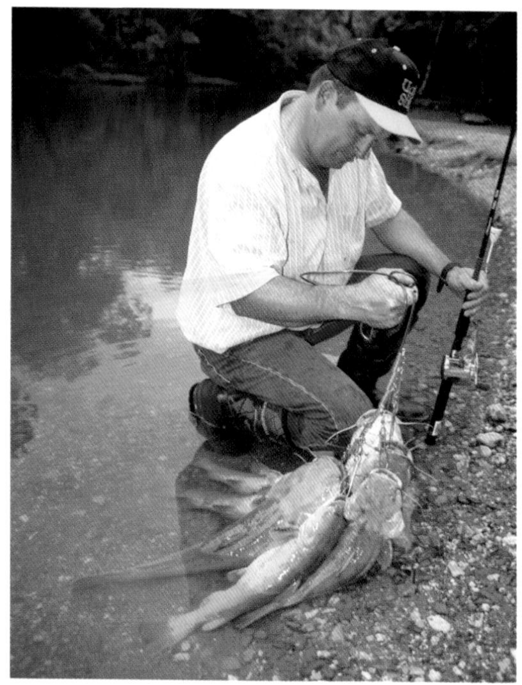

Drifting bait beneath a bobber in a cool stream is a good way to nab a mess of good-eating dog-days catfish.

Position the bobber stop so the bait hangs slightly above, not on, the stream bottom. Add enough weight to hold the bait down, then allow the rig to drift naturally, guiding it alongside catfish cover and structures. With practice and a long rod to keep your line off the water, you can become adept at steering the rig past holding areas with little worry about hang-ups.

Keep a tight line at all times. Slack line will bow downstream ahead of the bait. This leaves you in a bad position for setting the hook. Snatching slack line out of the water leaves no force in the rod's swing to drive the hook home.

Release line as the bait moves downstream. If the rig hangs up, your bobber will tip over or stop. Lift it a bit to get the bait moving again. Then tease the rig around boulders, ease it alongside fallen trees, and work it through holes below rapids. Drift through one side of a hole, then down the other, and finally right down the middle. If nothing happens after you've worked an area thoroughly, move your bobber stop up and drift through deeper. Or move downstream to another spot and try again.

These are just a few of the many summer feeding patterns exhibited by catfish. The fishing tips offered for each scenario may or may not work in the waters you fish. If they do, hallelujah. If they don't . . . well, learn to pattern catfish yourself. What are they eating? When? Where? Those are the questions you must answer. How? Examine the stomach contents of the next catfish you catch and the next and the next. You'll find the answers there.

Turnover Time

The fall turnover period doesn't have to be the nemesis many anglers perceive it to be.

Autumn is a golden season for catfishing fans. Summer's crowds have vanished. Lakes and streams shimmer beneath canopies of vermilion and amber leaves. Summer-fattened catfish are in prime condition, offering exciting possibilities for action-hungry anglers.

This season offers some of the year's best catfish action. But it is also a time of transition. The weather changes. Air and water temperatures cool. Catfish are on the move—shallow one week, deep the next. Where fish nailed most anything yesterday, they refuse everything today. As autumn approaches, many catfish anglers cringe with frustration because their favorite fish are so hard to figure out.

You'll often hear this referred to as the "fall turnover" season because the water is "turning over" as the cooling surface layer sinks and warmer bottom water is pushed upward. Some catfish anglers write this off as a terrible time to fish. But turnover needn't be the nemesis many perceive it to be. Catfish fans can actually benefit from this fall phenomenon if they understand it.

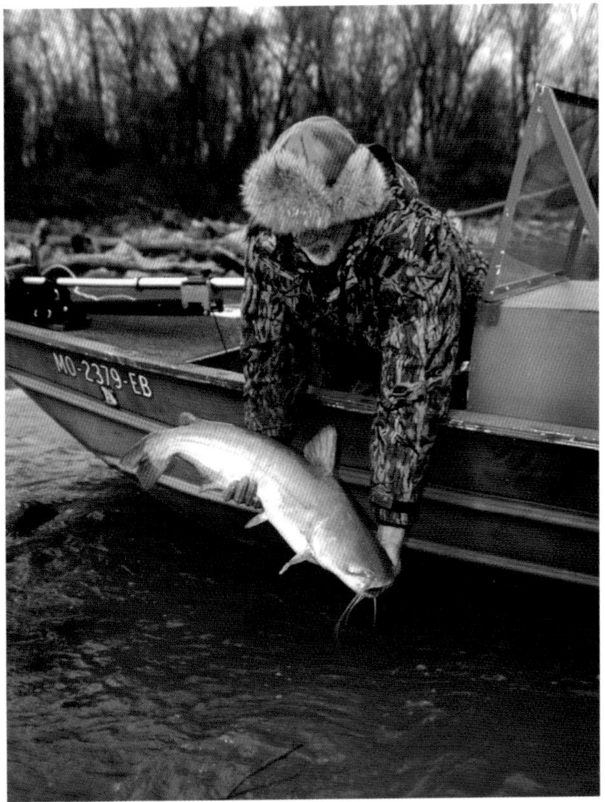

When air and water temperatures plummet in fall, catfishing may become uncomfortable for the angler, but catfish continue actively feeding and remain catchable for savvy anglers.

What is fall turnover?

During summer, many lakes stratify into three distinct layers. These lakes have a layer of cold, poorly oxygenated water on the bottom and a layer of warm, moderately oxygenated water on top. Since cold water is heavier than warm water (to a certain degree), the warmer water stays on top and colder water sinks to the bottom. In between lies a layer of cool, oxygen-rich water called the thermocline. Summer catfish usually stay in or near the thermocline in stratified lakes because that layer best satisfies their needs for proper oxygen levels and water temperature.

In late summer, fall, or early winter (the exact time depends largely on the latitude in which the lake lies), cool weather begins lowering the surface water temperature. As the upper layer cools, it becomes heavier and sinks. This action forces the warmer, lighter water below back to the surface. This water is subsequently cooled, just as the previous surface layer was, and descends as it cools. This mixing or "turnover" continues for several weeks until the thermocline disappears and all water in the lake is roughly the same temperature. This mixing effect also replenishes the oxygen in deep water.

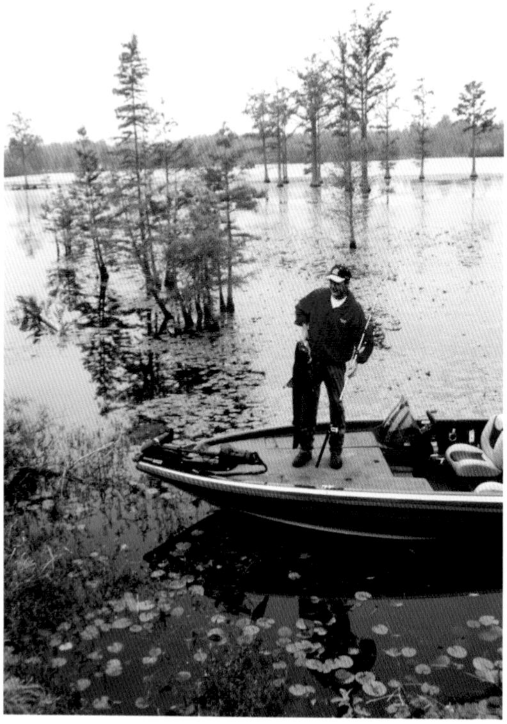

Moderate water temperatures in autumn allow river cats to reoccupy oxbows and backwaters that were too hot in the summer.

The end result is that fish formerly restricted to narrow bands of acceptable oxygen and temperature levels are no longer limited in their movements. Catfish that once were barred from dropping into the coolest depths because of low oxygen levels now may roam freely to much deeper water. Likewise, where once fish could not spend extended periods in extreme shallows due to high temperatures and low oxygen levels, after turnover even these areas are acceptable. Catfish now may be found in deep waters, shallow waters, or anywhere in between.

Technically, turnover continues until the surface water temperature drops below thirty-nine degrees Fahrenheit. Water is heaviest at this temperature and sinks to the bottom. Cooler water "floats" on top. This is why lakes freeze from the top down rather than from the bottom up. And this represents the annual end of the turnover process.

How do I know when a lake is "turning over"?

The time of year when turnover occurs varies by latitude. While catfishermen in cooler areas may begin turnover strategies in September, warmer regions may not have turnover until January.

On many lakes, the turnover is clearly visible. A change in water color is evident as circulating water brings up bottom debris. The water may take on a milky or brownish tint and smell like rotten eggs or decaying vegetation.

Turnover in some lakes is invisible and therefore confusing even to those familiar with the phenomenon. In these waters, the only indication turnover is occurring may be distinct

changes in catfish behavior after a few weeks of cool weather. For instance, catfish caught on deep humps one week may be ambushing baitfish near shorelines the next.

Some waters don't experience turnover because they don't stratify in summer. Most rivers are a case in point. So are many large, shallow, windswept lakes and some reservoirs with lock-and-dam facilities or hydroelectric generators. In extreme Southern areas, South Florida for example, temperatures may not drop low enough for turnover to occur.

What problems are associated with turnover fishing?

The biggest problem most anglers face is pinpointing fish. In summer, most catfish could be found in or near the thermocline. Shallow-water action might have been good during cool, low-light periods, but you could be certain no cats would be caught in the "dead zone" below the thermocline.

Fall turnover drastically changes all this. With acceptable levels of oxygen from top to bottom and no discernible temperature change from the shallowest shallows to the deepest depths, catfish can be almost anywhere.

Can I overcome this problem?

Yes. The secret to turnover success is realizing that catfish still concentrate in areas that provide the most comfortable living conditions and then learning to identify those areas. Theoretically, conditions are now such that catfish can live anywhere within the lake. In actuality, factors such as oxygen content, light penetration, and food availability still greatly influence a catfish's choice of living quarters.

Consider, for instance, that all the debris and poorly oxygenated water being pushed upward from the lake bed when turnover begins temporarily "trashes" the whole system. Catfish respond by seeking areas with better water quality. To find them, anglers should do likewise. An easy way to do this is to work tributaries bringing fresh water into the lake. Another way is to look for areas where turnover has not begun. On some large lakes, different arms of the lake turnover at different times, and anglers can concentrate their efforts in areas that aren't visibly affected.

When turnover causes excessive amounts of decaying debris to circulate in the water column, sudden significant drops in the oxygen level can result. When this happens, catfish must find oxygenated water immediately. They frequently solve the problem by going directly to the nearest source, which is surface aeration from wind and waves. Consequently, windswept shorelines in fairly shallow cover may be productive catfishing spots.

Are there other good turnover hotspots?

Brushy treetops and standing timber are classic catfish cover, and they don't get any more classic than during autumn when catfish concentrate in woody areas along channel breaks. When weed beds have begun to die and decay late in the fall, cats often migrate to open lake areas where inundated trees line long underwater creek and river channels. Here the fish can move shallow or deep as water and weather conditions dictate. On cloudy or windy days when light won't penetrate very far into the water, cats may actually be found within a few feet of the surface. Bright, sunny, post-frontal days may find them hugging the bottom. Again, you'll have to experiment to find the most productive depth, keeping on the move until you locate one of the few structures holding fish. But once a cat is landed, several can often be taken with just a few well-placed casts.

The places you can find fall catfish action are almost innumerable. Long sloping points are

If the water rises to cover it, this brush-covered hump in mid-lake will be a prime hotspot for turnover catfish.

always a good possibility, as are humps and inundated islands. Cats like old fencerows that run from shallow to deep water, and large trees that have toppled into fairly deep water near the shoreline should definitely be investigated. Other favorite areas include Christmas tree fish attractors, timbered areas edging underwater ditches and ponds, submerged rock piles, stump fields, and saddle areas between two islands.

Fishing vertical structures, such as this lock-wall edge, is a good way to zero in on cats during the final weeks of fall turnover.

I've heard that catfish often hold near ledges in fall. Is this true?

During the final few weeks of turnover as the water starts to clear, catfish often concentrate on vertical structures. This is some type of bottom feature that offers great depth variance with little or no horizontal movement necessary. Good examples are bluff banks, lock-wall edges, bridge pilings, and fast-dropping slopes along creek and river channels. In such places, catfish can alter their depth according to prevailing light penetration and other factors by merely moving up or down the structures as conditions dictate.

Because catfish orienting to vertical structures can be anywhere between the bottom to mid-depths, pinpointing them may require extra effort. Begin by thoroughly fishing different depths until fish are located. If the water is still discolored, light penetration will be restricted, and catfish may move shallower. Thus, the angler may want to begin by fishing shallow reaches. As the water clears, however, bright sunlight will drive most catfish into the depths or under heavy cover. In this situation, fish first around deeper hideouts.

The key is to efficiently check a variety of depths until a catfish is caught. Then work that depth thoroughly for additional fish. When you've established the level where fish are holding, move to other vertical structures and work the same depth. Chances are good you'll encounter more catfish at some point along the way.

Are there pointers on the best time of day to fish? The best baits?

Generally, most summer anglers enjoy their best fishing during low-light periods: morning, late afternoon, or night. During autumn, however, catfish are more prone to feed all day long instead of just during morning and evening. The sun is lower in the sky, and days are shorter. Thus, conditions are good for consistent action throughout the day.

Freshly caught baitfish, such as shad, are first-rate enticements for big autumn catfish. Fish them live when targeting flatheads, or prepare them as cutbait for big blues and channel cats.

As for the best baits to use during this time of year, it's strictly a matter of what you like best. Live fish catch more flatheads. Herring and shad cutbaits are hard to beat for blue cats. Channel cats feed on their usual smorgasbord of dinner items, everything from night crawlers to commercial stinkbait, but the bigger ones are likely to fall for live fish baits or cutbaits made from fresh fish.

Rivers don't "turn over" like many lakes, so anglers can fish these flowing waters and avoid the trauma of "turnover turmoil." Trophy cats are easier to find in this season because they're more likely to be roaming the shallows.

What about river fishing this time of year?

Because rivers are relatively unaffected by turnover, they provide an excellent alternative for anglers dealing with "turnover turmoil." In summer, high temperatures may drive river catfish to deep-water haunts, usually in or near the main river channel. Autumn offers more moderate water temperatures, allowing catfish to reinvade shallow, off-channel areas where they were found during the spring. During this season more than others, they're often found in backwaters, river-connected oxbows, and other areas where current is negligible. Because the water in these areas is shallower, these catfish are easier to find, too. And they're often more aggressive than they were during the hottest days of summer—hungry and eager to bite.

During the late weeks of summer and early weeks of fall, look for river cats near wing dikes, log jams, big snags, and other current-breaking structures in or near the main body of the river. As air and water temperature drop and autumn gets in full swing, you'll find a lot of them near

A prime site for river cats in fall, this brushy bend offers the kind of cover and structure almost sure to attract good numbers of hefty whiskerfish.

willows, cypress trees, and other woody cover off the main river in oxbows and backwaters. As autumn turns to winter, look for catfish moving back to deep-water haunts near the main river channel.

Is there anything else I should know?
Be patient and persistent. Turnover forces fish to roam, thus fishermen must also be willing to move frequently, forsaking likely looking spots or those that produced yesterday. If the tactics covered here don't produce catfish, improvise another strategy and keep trying.

The transition from summer to autumn is jolting for both fish and fishermen. Catfish find their once secure world literally turned over on them. Catfish anglers find their quarry more unpredictable than ever. Overcoming this seasonal nemesis will require all the skill, knowledge, and patience you can muster. But when you finally zero in on a big autumn cat, you're sure to agree that the rewards make the extra effort worthwhile.

Popsicle Pond Cats

When temperatures plummet, head for the nearest farm pond.

It was a polar afternoon. Alex Hinson and I were catfishing in a small farm pond.

I'd done it once before—fishing for pond catfish in the dead of winter, that is. Nearly thirty years have passed, but I remember vividly the enormous stringer of channel cats I caught that wintry day. I was twelve and hungry for some fishing, so I grabbed a rod and reel and a box of chicken livers from my grandmother's freezer. Soon, I was standing in snow on the bank of my uncle's fish pond, casting to the big cats that lurked therein but never really expecting to catch one.

To my surprise, the catfish were extraordinarily cooperative. I'd cast a bait into deep water by the dam, and before it hit bottom, a channel cat would take it. One after another, I hauled them in. I'd caught plenty of catfish before, including quite a few jumbos, but nothing like that afternoon. In less than two hours, I had twenty fat cats croaking atop the snow.

I shared the story with Alex one day, who suggested we plan another winter junket immediately. And so within the week we found ourselves sitting in a johnboat over a deep hole in the pond, dropping liver-baited hooks into the murky depths. Before each bait touched down, a sassy channel cat or bullhead would have it. Alex caught a five-pound channel cat then its twin. I caught several over three plus a two-pound yellow bullhead. Twenty-three cats fell prey to our tactics.

Active Winter Feeding
Many catfishermen still labor under the false impression that catfish don't bite in winter.

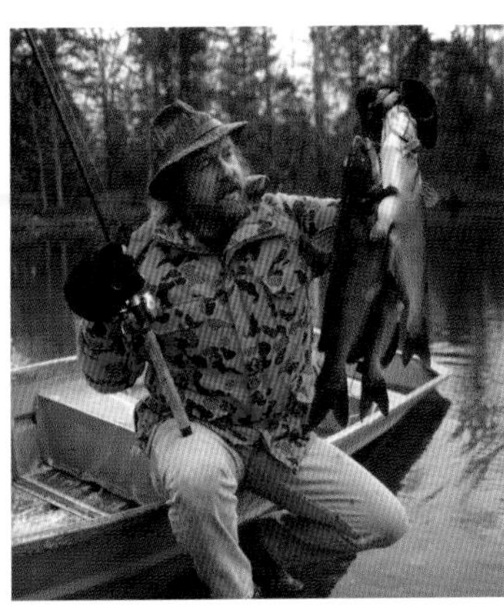

Fish a farm pond in winter? For catfish? Some might think it futile, but author Keith Sutton shows the result of a few hours fishing on a cold winter day.

That's not true. Take channel cats and bullheads, for instance. The experiences I outlined above show the exciting potential for catching these fighters during cold months. Even more amazing is the fact that both species are now common targets for ice fishermen in Northern states. Despite popular misconceptions, they don't lie in the mud and sulk when it's cold. They actively hunt food and bite readily even when lakes and rivers are frozen.

Pond Pointers

If it's eating-sized cats you're after, head straight for the nearest farm pond. Many are stocked with channel cats and/or bullheads, and despite what you may have thought, winter is the best season for catching them in these environ ments. You can expect good action December through February in the far North, in the deep South, and all points between. Expect the best pond catfishing, however, when the water temperature is between forty and fifty-five degrees.

Start by asking the pond owner to point out the deepest hole in the pond. During cold weather, that's where most cats will be. Fish from a boat if you can, lowering bait straight down into the hole. My typical rig consists of a 5/0 Daiichi octopus hook with a couple of split shot crimped on the line a foot above. When it reaches the bottom, I turn the reel handle a few cranks so the bait is a foot or so above the substrate where cats can better detect it. When bank fishing, I use a one-ounce Rubbercor sinker instead of split shoot and add a small cigar-shaped crappie cork on the line between the hook and sinker to float the bait just off the bottom.

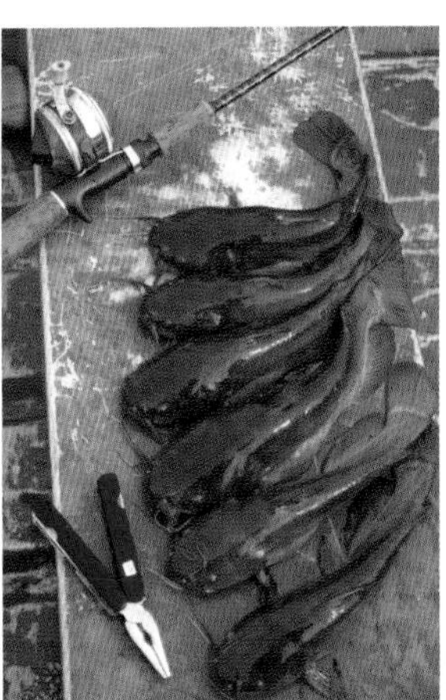

Bullheads, like channel cats, are often stocked in ponds and provide great winter action for the catfish fan.

Chicken liver is a top bait in this situation. Cats quickly zero in on the scent and taste of poultry blood dissolving from the tissue. Some catters prefer frozen livers because they stay on the hook better, but fresh liver has more cat-attracting qualities. Weave your hook through each piece several times, and you shouldn't have too much problem keeping it on.

Don't sit in one spot too long. If a cat is nearby, you'll have a bite before fifteen minutes passes. If you don't, move a short distance and try again. If catfish are biting, the action may end abruptly after you've caught a few fish. Once again, it's time to move and try another location.

When you're fishing for cats in winter, it pays to keep moving anyway just so you can keep warm. This is not a sport for anglers who detest the cold. You'll get chilly out there even when you're wearing the proper clothing. Your teeth will chatter, and your hands and feet will feel like popsicles.

The nice thing is when the cats start biting, that frigid feeling disappears. Nothing in the world warms you quicker than battling a rod-bending cat.

Section VI

Baits

Topwater Temptations

Catfish are bottom feeders, right? Not always, friend.

If you were to bump into one of your friends every time you visited a particular restaurant, you might start believing that's the only place your friend ever eats. That's not likely to be true, of course, but it might seem so nevertheless.

A similar situation exists between catfish and catfish anglers. Because we usually find catfish feeding on the bottom of our favorite lake, river, or pond, we have a tendency to think they always feed on bottom. This is a common misconception. In reality, catfish often feed at mid-depths, and if concentrations of nutritious foods can be found in surface strata, these whiskered warriors will actually feed right on top. Just ask any fish farmer who feeds his cats commercial chow.

Two natural foods that encourage a topwater bite are grasshoppers and cicadas. I've watched catfish slurping them from the surface on many calm summer mornings, evenings, and nights. Other insects are eaten, as well: mayflies, moths, caddis larvae, and hellgrammites, for example. But these miniscule offerings don't seem to appeal to larger cats the way a big buzzing cicada or fat grasshopper does.

Grasshoppers don't rate high on the list of the most popular catfish baits, but a big juicy hopper presented tantalizingly on the surface is a great enticement for jumbo cats.

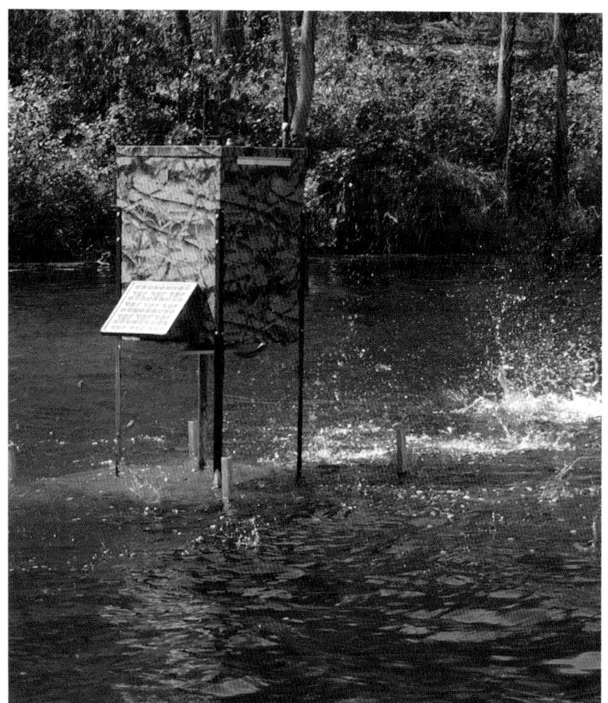

Topwater baits may seem preposterous to some anglers, but despite popular misconceptions, catfish readily take foods on the water's surface. For example, catfish churn the surface when given floating fish chow at aquaculture operations.

Grasshoppers

Because grasshoppers stay in grassy areas, not trees, they're much easier to catch than cicadas. And you don't have to wait until that special year to find an abundance. I've often pulled my boat up to a grassy margin on a river and caught several dozen. A good trick an uncle taught me is to spread an old flannel blanket across the grass and drive the hoppers to it. Their feet stick in the fabric. A fine mesh insect net, available at many pet stores, works well, too.

A friend likes to drift hoppers beneath a float on some of the Ozark streams he fishes. In my experience, they work equally on the surface, at mid-depths, or on the bottom. For real fun, though, fish them on top.

My catfishing uncle taught me another trick that never fails. Secure the hopper to a 1/0 or 2/0 gold Aberdeen crappie hook with a small rubber band, then flip it up beside a log or stump using a fly rod. You'll see every vicious strike and enjoy a rod-bending battle with each hungry cat. Catfishing was never more fun!

Cicadas

Cicadas, sometimes called locusts, spend most of their lives underground—up to seventeen years in some cases. When they emerge, they climb onto trees, shed their familiar shells, and start making the weird high-pitched noises we all associate with summer. It's tough to obtain them for bait, but on rare years when several year classes of cicadas emerge at once,

Cicadas are large insects, a fact that makes them a desirable food source for catfish, particularly in summer when these insects are abundant.

millions may cover the trees, making it much easier to find and catch them. All you need is a cricket cage to stuff them in and some youngsters who think bait catching is as much fun as fishing.

During one such year here in my native Mid-South, the buzzing of millions of cicadas filled the air with a steady hum, and the cicadas themselves filled the bellies of many catfish I caught. While fishing on a small lake, my father-in-law and I watched as dozens of cats—some of them quite large—rose to the surface to pick off cicadas that had taken a dip. A trip to the trees edging the bank provided plenty for bait. We hooked each through the hard shell on the back with a 3/0 octopus hook and cast on the water's surface with no weight, bobber, or other terminal tackle. Within seconds of each cast, we'd be playing a nice channel cat—and occasionally a blue cat—that rose to take the insect offering.

The next month, while fishing with a veteran catfisherman on Missouri's Osage River, I tried unsuccessfully to coax him into using cicadas for bait. He refused, thinking it nothing more than folly. When we pulled into the boat ramp eight hours later having caught no catfish, we were greeted by one of the man's friends who had been far more successful. "How'd you catch those?" the cat man asked, eyeballing the pile of five- to twenty-pound channels and blues in his friend's boat. "On cicadas," his friend answered. "I wasn't getting a bite on regular baits, but every time a cicada buzzed down and hit the water, a big cat would gobble it up. So I caught some and put 'em on a hook. Caught a cat on every cast. Never knew until today you could catch a cat on a topwater bait. And boy is it fun!"

Frogs for Trophy Channel Cats

Hook an amphibian to entice those giant whiskerfish.

Channel catfish aren't finicky eaters. They'll eat almost anything catfishermen offer. If you want to be consistently successful and catch lots of fish, however, be selective about the baits you use. Some are decidedly better than others.

Consider frogs, for example. If trophy channel cats are your quarry, these amphibians make hopping good lures. Small catfish relish them as well, but as a rule, the cats thus enticed are larger than average.

Master Angler Evidence

Records maintained by the Nebraska Game and Parks Commission exemplify this fact. During the ten-year period I studied, frog baits were used to catch eighty-six channel cats entered in the state's Master Angler Award program. These fish measured up to four feet long and thirty-six pounds and included many specimens in the sixteen- to twenty-seven-pound range—trophy channel cats in anybody's book. Qualifying fish were caught every month in a broad spectrum of waters—ponds, large and small reservoirs,

Frogs are among the most overlooked yet most effective live baits for jumbo channel cats.

large and small rivers, irrigation canals, and more—indicating the versatility of frog baits under widely varying conditions.

Check local fishing regulations for restrictions before using frogs as bait. Water-loving species work best, particularly the larger more common ones, such as bullfrogs, leopard frogs, green frogs, and pickerel frogs. Those with a body length of four to six inches are ideal.

Catching and Keeping Frogs

Sometimes you'll find them for sale in bait shops, but you also can catch frogs yourself. This is easily done by driving a rural road on a warm rainy spring night. Pick an area where traffic volume is low, and take a friend along. When the quarry is spotted, the passenger hops out, catches it, and places it in a lidded minnow bucket to which a little water has been added. Walking rain-dampened roads with a flashlight and a dampened pillow case for frog storage is also effective. It's possible to gather dozens of frogs this way on a single night.

You also can catch frogs by hand or with a small-mesh dip net along the shores of ponds, lakes, backwaters, bayous, and streams; in adjacent grass and weeds; or along the water's edge at night by shining a blinding light at them.

The leopard or grass frog, a common species throughout much of the United States, is among several species of aquatic frogs commonly used for catfish bait.

Live frog-bait rigs are simple—just a hook on the line and maybe a couple of split shot to carry the bait down. Hook the frog through a foreleg to keep it lively.

Store frogs in a cool place inside a dampened container to keep them lively.

Frog Rigs and Tactics

Most users hook frogs through both lips or in the thigh. I've learned, however, that hooking the amphibian through a foreleg maintains maximum swimming ability, making the frog a more enticing bait. I prefer using a 5/0 to 6/0 weedless hook that has a wire guard to prevent snagging in weeds or brush. In lieu of this, I use a similarly sized octopus or Kahle hook. Adding a couple of split shot on the line twelve inches above the hook completes the rig. No bobber is necessary.

This rig can be fished several ways. I like using a sturdy twelve- to sixteen-foot fiberglass or graphite crappie jigging pole to work the bait in beds of lily pads in ponds or shallow lakes. Position yourself along the pads, and reach out with the pole to ease the frog into small openings. Slack off to let it swim. You also can place the frog on a pad and let it jump off. Be ready, however, for the ensuing explosion. Lily pads are favored haunts for giant channel cats, and despite misconceptions, these fish will hit frogs on top, providing unparalleled thrills.

An equally effective tactic is casting the frog near catfish cover using a spinning or bait-casting outfit. The frog will immediately swim for the bottom, where it's easily spotted by foraging cats. If a bite is not forthcoming within a few minutes, raise your rod tip to stir the frog into action again. Most strikes come quickly when the bait is swimming. Lack of action should prompt you to relocate to another fishing area.

Strangely, few catfishermen use frog baits. I suggest you follow the Cornhuskers' lead. Live frogs will catch trophy channel cats no matter where you fish.

Mussel-Bound Blues

When mussels are on the menu, blue cats gather around the feeding trough.

If you've never used mussel meat for blue cat bait, you ought to give it try. Next to baitfish, freshwater mussels or "clams" are among the blue cat's favorite foods in waters where they are available. In fact, some ardent anglers claim blue cats like mussels better than baitfish. Channel and flathead cats eat them, too, but not with the same gusto of their larger relatives.

The Facts According to Joe Mathers

Joe C.K. Mathers was one of the first to write about the efficacy of mussels in his 1953 booklet *Catfishin'*. He rated them "excellent to superior" as cat bait and described how to use them.

"Remove from shells and use fresh or still better allow to sour for a day or two in an open container with plenty of 'clam juice' covering them,"

Catfish feed on many species of mussels from the tiny Asiatic clam to the mid-sized deertoe and even the very large yellow sandshell.

he wrote. "Steam over a fire to toughen before souring if you want a tougher bait. If soured 'just right' (sour, not rotten, determine by smelling), clams are one of the best catfish baits especially during mid-summer when few other baits are giving results. They make a tough, luring bait usable on all kinds of lines. Freshwater clams are found in ponds, lakes, and streams, certain kinds of flowing waters, and others in quiet waters. Collect in shoreline shallows or gather by dragging bottom areas with clamming hooks. Or, if there is a clamming industry along your river, just get a bucket of flesh after they have steamed off the shells."

The "clamming industry" Mathers refers to began in the late 1800s and continued through the early 1950s. During that period, most buttons on clothing were made from mussel shells. In fact, mussel harvesting and the button-making industry were big business throughout the Mississippi River Valley. Many river families made a living collecting mussels from the bottoms of our big rivers. Some dived to collect these mollusks. Others used clamming hooks, also known as crow's-foot dredges or brails. Each consisted of a long wooden or metal bar from which dangled numerous blunt four-pronged hooks attached with short lines. The entire unit was lowered into a river and slowly pulled downstream. The hooks raked the bottom and touched open mussels, which promptly closed on the hooks. Captured mussels were then hauled to the surface and removed from the brail.

Once collected, the mussels were "cooked out" along the river banks. Mussels were dumped in cauldrons of hot water so the fleshy insides could be easily separated from the valuable outer shell. The shells were then shipped to factories for processing into buttons.

The mussel-shell button industry died after the advent of plastics during World War II. But freshwater mussel shells are still important moneymakers for some people. Today, mussel shells are used primarily in the cultured pearl industry centered in Japan. The shells (usually collected by divers using scuba gear) are shipped overseas and processed into pearl nuclei by stripping the outer layer and punching appropriate-sized blanks into round pellets. These round mother-of-pearl nuclei are then inserted into pearl oysters suspended in cages in a suitable estuary or ocean bay.

The actual nucleus insertion procedure is a closely guarded secret of the Japanese cultured pearl industry. Oysters are allowed to secrete their own mother-of-pearl around the nucleus for six months to three years depending on the quality of pearl desired. Pearls are then harvested, graded, and sold for jewelry.

Luther's Lessons

Luther Gaither, a sheller on the White River at DeValls Bluff, Arkansas, was one of the first to pique my interest in using mussels for blue cat bait. I spent a day with him on the river, watching him go down for shells in a 175-pound diving helmet constructed from an old bomb

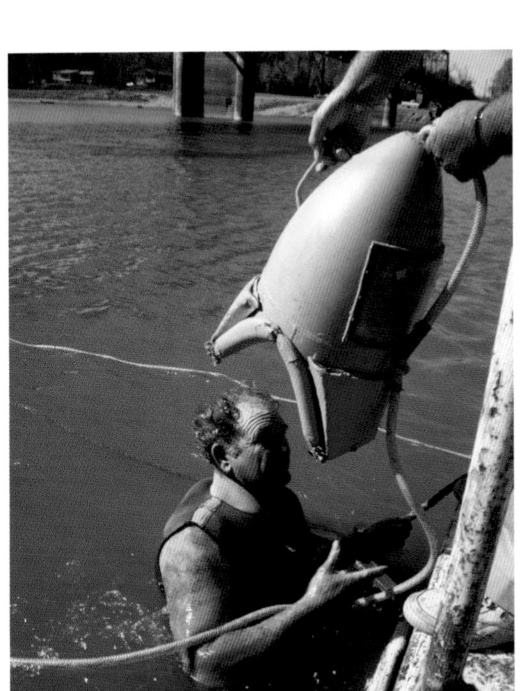
Luther Gaither prepares to dive for mussels in Arkansas's White River. His diving helmet is constructed from an old bomb casing.

casing. Air was supplied by a topside compressor, and a two-way radio allowed communication with his partner on the boat.

Later that day, Gaither showed me freshwater pearls collected from White River mussels, a collection of crow's-foot dredges, and a tubular tumbler used to sort shells by size and species. I also examined large metal vats, some fashioned from car hoods, where the mussels were steamed. When the shells opened, they were allowed to cool, and the meat was removed by hand and examined for pearls. I asked Gaither if the flesh of the mussels had any use.

"The meat's edible," he said, "but it's tough and rubbery as the soles of your boots. I guess we've tried every way in the world to fix it for eating—even grinding it up and trying to turn it into chowder meat or sausage. But nothing you can do makes it suitable for eating. A lot of it we give away for hog feed. But we always keep some for blue cat bait. I'll show you what we do to it."

Gaither took me aside and showed me several plastic five-gallon buckets full of mussel meat stewing in the hot sun.

"This is the best blue cat bait ever was made," he said, smiling. "You just toss the pieces in a bucket with some juice from the steaming process and let it sit a week or so till it sours a bit. We use it on trotlines mostly and catch everything from little eatin' size cats up to the big guys weighing seventy-five pounds and more. It's extremely tough, so it stays on the hooks well. And the blue cats swarm to it like kids to a candy shop. Some of the blues we catch, if you open their stomachs, you find they're stuffed with mussels of every sort. This is their favorite food year-round, so nothing works better for bait."

My own experiments over the next several years proved Gaither right. Mussel flesh took blue cats even when they turned their noses up at fresh shad and suckers. Mostly I used it on trotlines, but I also found it an excellent rod-and-reel bait, fresh or sour. I became a convert and often stopped at one of the local shellers' riverside shanties to bum enough mussel meat for a weekend's fishing.

Unfortunately, shellers like Luther Gaither have largely disappeared. River dredging, pollution, and commercial shelling have taken a toll on the mussels, and few commercially valuable shell beds remain in most of our rivers. Fewer still are the number of people willing to collect and prepare them for market. Nevertheless, if you look hard enough, you'll probably find a sheller here and there on most of the larger rivers in the Mississippi drainage. And if you're lucky, you can drum up an acquaintance with them and have a ready supply of mussel meat for your own blue cat forays.

Joe Drose on Mussels

In 1997, I met another blue cat angler familiar with the use of mussels for bait. Joe Drose of Cross, South Carolina, is one of the premier catfishing guides in the United States. He's been guiding full-time on lakes Marion and Moultrie—the Santee-Cooper lakes—for decades. Putting clients on giant catfish is his specialty.

"Personally, I think blue cats prefer mussels over anything they can eat," Drose told me on a February fishing trip. "In winter, most of the big cats here, the blues especially, are feeding on mussels. They move to sand edges in shallow water and stuff themselves in beds of small mussels. When the water in the lake is down, I watch for beds of shells and then come back and fish those areas because that's where the biggest fish—and the most fish—are likely to be. They'll eat on mussels in the shallows throughout the winter and up into May."

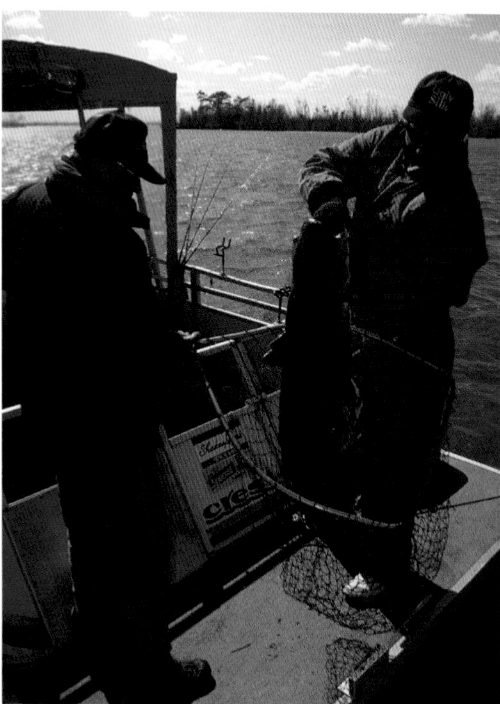

Guide Joe Drose helps a client land a nice Santee-Cooper blue cat caught while fishing one of the lakes' mussel beds.

When you think about it, Drose noted, it's easy to understand why cold-water catfish feed so heavily on mussels. First of all, mussels are slow. In fact, in winter, they don't move at all. That means they're easy to catch and eat. Second, mussels live in dense colonies called beds. There are lots of them piled together in very small areas. When the water is cold, catfish congregate around these beds where they can gorge day after day with little expenditure of energy.

These same factors make mussels an excellent food source regardless of the season.

"Catfish also feed on mussels in summer," said Drose. "In late June and July, the shallow water gets real warm, and a lot of the mussels die. Many float to the top and are carried around by the current in the lakes. Catfishing folks take a dip net and dip them right up. Then they open them up, get the meat out, and fish with it. That works extremely well on our catfish."

In his book *Masters' Secrets of Catfishing*, John Phillips describes a similar phenomenon on the Tennessee River in Tennessee and Alabama. "Every year, the Asiatic clams . . . experience a die-off," Phillips writes. "The dead clams open their shells, and the little animals inside float to the surface. When the clams start dying off, catfish in the area hear the dinner bell ringing and feed on these mollusks voraciously. Oftentimes, by observing the surface of the water, you can spot dead clams lying on top, scoop the clams up, bait them on your hooks, send them right back to the bottom, and catch cats . . . Many of today's topnotch catfishermen will

Zebra mussels, an exotic species, rarely grow larger than a man's fingernail, but catfish, particularly blue cats, gorge on them wherever they are present.

When water levels are low, it pays to scout for the location of mussel beds. Return when the water rises again, and you're likely to find catfish gorging on the bounty.

locate mussel beds on major waterways, swim down, collect the mussels in states where allowed, open the shells, and bait up for catfish."

The inch-long exotic Asiatic clam (*Corbicula*), now common in many North American lakes and rivers, is a special favorite for catfish, but native mussels, especially smaller varieties like lilliputs, wartybacks, and deertoes, are also relished. The bellies of some smaller cats I've examined were full of tiny zebra mussels, the noxious invader that has colonized many United States waters. Large cats sometimes contain yellow sandshells or other mussels that may be six to eight inches long and as big around as a man's wrist.

Shell and all is eaten regardless of the mussel species. Digestive juices kill the mussel, the shell opens, the flesh inside is digested, then the shell is passed by the fish.

To find mussel beds, search near shore in three to six feet of water. They can be pinpointed by sight during low-water periods, as Drose does, or you can find them by moving parallel to shore and probing the bottom with a cane pole. The shells produce a distinctive crunching sound when the pole hits them.

Catfish return to the same beds season after season, so once a bed is found, memorize its location or mark it on a map.

Joe Drose's techniques for fishing mussel beds are easily duplicated by any angler seeking trophy-class blues. He usually anchors his boat and still-fishes using sturdy tackle: 7-foot Shakespeare Ugly Stick Tiger Rods and Shakespeare bait-casting reels spooled with twenty-five- to eighty-pound-test monofilament line.

His primary fishing rig consists of an egg sinker on the main line above a barrel swivel with an eight- to twelve-inch leader connecting the swivel to a sturdy 3/0 to 5/0 Kahle hook. This bottom-fishing rig is baited, cast to a likely spot, and allowed to sit for up to fifteen minutes. If no bite is forthcoming, Drose moves to another spot and tries again. Several rigs may be presented at each location, and they may not be baited with mussels.

"I sometimes use commercial chunk baits or pieces of hot dogs for bait," Drose tells me. "These are about the same size as the small mussels the catfish are feeding on, and they seem to work real well.

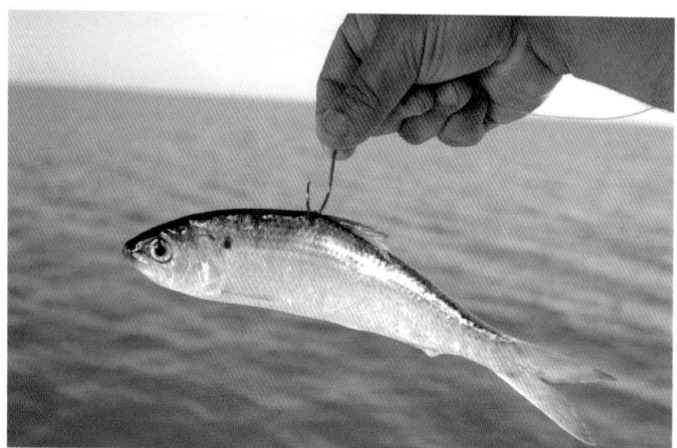

When catfish are feeding in mussel beds, they readily take other baits, as well, such as blueback herring.

"Most of the time we use small herring for bait," he continued. "Although the catfish are feeding on mussels primarily, they won't pass up a piece of herring that's properly presented."

If you use the actual mussels for bait, remove the flesh from the shell and use it fresh. Or better still, follow Joe Mathers' and Lester Gaither's advice: allow the meat to sour for a day or two in an open container with plenty of "clam juice" covering it. If there's a shelling industry along your river, visit a local sheller to get a bucket of flesh after he's steamed off the shells. Or gather your own mussels using a dip net or by feeling for them in mud or sand bottom in shoreline shallows.

Mussels and blue cats go together like minnows and crappie. So try shellfish for catfish this season. If trophy-class blues are what you're after, mussels can make it happen.

Endangered Species or Catfish Bait?

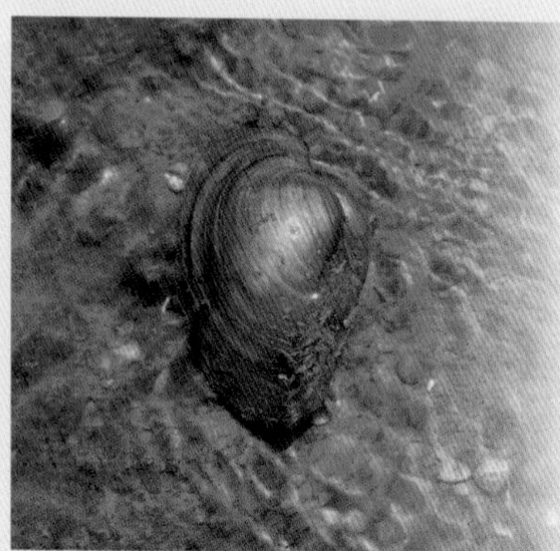

It's easy to find and collect mussels in shallow waters of many lakes and streams, but be careful you don't collect protected species.

Be cautious when collecting mussels for catfish bait. Many species, such as the Curtis pearlymussel, turgid blossom, pink mucket, speckled pocketbook, and fat pocketbook, are protected under the Endangered Species Act. You're not likely to find these species when looking for catfish bait simply because they are rare. But fines can be stiff for disturbing or harming these endangered animals. Check with your state wildlife agency to determine what's legal where you fish.

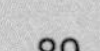

Catching Cats on Artificial Lures

You can catch catfish on a variety of artificial lures but only if you understand what makes these lures enticing.

Can catfish be caught using artificial lures? Yes, indeed.

Consider this evidence. In 2002, anglers submitted 415 qualifying catfish in Nebraska's Master Angler Program, including 309 channel cats, ninety-six flatheads, and ten blue cats. No qualifying blue cats were caught on artificial lures, but twenty-two of the channel cats were (7 percent) and a whopping twenty-six of ninety-six flatheads (27 percent).

Catfishermen rarely use artificial lures to entice their quarry, but if water conditions are right and the proper lure is used, cats will find the bait and strike.

Many types of lures enticed these Nebraska cats. Crankbaits produced the most channel catfish (seven), followed by spinners/spinnerbaits (five), jigs (four), plastic worms/lizards (three each), spoons (two), and topwater plugs (one). Flathead cats fell for crankbaits (ten), jigs (nine), spoons (five), and spinners (two).

Catfish use many senses to help pinpoint foods. For example, they have excellent eyesight that they use to see prey items in clear waters. When a fishing lure is seen, it, too, may be eaten.

Jigs tipped with minnows or night crawlers accounted for six of nine catches in the jig category.

How many of these cats were taken intentionally using artificials? I don't know. Program records don't include such information. I'd bet my next paycheck, however, it was few or none. Catfish fans rarely pursue their quarry with artificial lures. Most whiskerfish thus caught were probably incidental catches. While fishing for bass, walleyes, or other species, the angler nailed a dandy cat and submitted it for recognition.

Nevertheless, this information is intriguing enough to beg the question: is it possible to target catfish specifically with artificial lures? The answer is yes. If you use the right lures under the right conditions, it is likely you'll catch some catfish. Blue cats, flatheads, and channel cats all can be taken in this manner. Nebraska is at the edge of blue cat range, which accounts for the few entries in their Master Angler Program.

Understanding Catfish Senses

To increase your success using lures, it helps to understand factors influencing a catfish's food selection. To do this, we must first understand some basic facts about catfish senses.

Fact #1. Despite having tiny eyes, catfish have excellent sight. In muddy waters, good eyesight offers few benefits. But in clearer water, catfish use their acute vision to help pinpoint prey.

Fact #2. Catfish have good hearing, as well. The specialized construction of a catfish's internal auditory system allows it to detect sounds in a wide range of frequencies.

Fact #3. Low-frequency sounds undetectable to the catfish's inner ear are picked up by the lateral line. The catfish uses this system to pinpoint low-frequency vibrations emitted by food animals scurrying across the bottom, flopping at the surface, or swimming through the water.

Fact #4. The catfish's senses of taste and smell are unexcelled in the animal kingdom. The skin, whiskers, and surfaces of the mouth and gill rakers are covered with taste buds, and a highly evolved olfactory system allows catfish to smell some compounds at concentrations as minute as one part per ten billion parts of water.

Fact #5. A catfish uses as many senses as possible when searching for dinner. The sensory organs detect chemicals, sounds, vibrations, and visual stimuli from potential food items and send messages to the fish's brain telling it to find, chase, and eat the food.

What does this mean for a catfish angler fishing artificial lures? In a nutshell, it works like this. A lure that stimulates one of the catfish's senses may be attacked. A lure that stimulates two or more senses almost certainly will be attacked.

Let's say you're fishing a jig with a soft-plastic, shad body. This lure emits no sounds or scents. If you fish it in muddy water, it can't be seen, either, so it's useless as a catfish bait.

Let's say you fish that same jig in clear water. Now a catfish might take it because the lure can be seen. If you continued fishing the jig in muddy water and added a night crawler or minnow to the hook, again there's a chance of catching a cat because the fish can detect the scent or taste of the live bait added to the lure.

Now let's try a jig/minnow combo in clear water and change to a rattling jig head. Chances of catching a cat grow exponentially because now we're stimulating all the senses. Catfish can see

the lure, hear it, and feel the vibrations. They can taste and smell the added live bait. Starting to get the picture?

The Right Lures in the Right Places

The best lures resemble the catfish's natural prey items, such as baitfish, crayfish, frogs, or worms. And those that resemble injured or slow-moving prey items are probably best of all, a fact to consider when making your retrieve or working your lure.

It's also important to place the lure in the specific areas within a river or lake where catfish lurk, such as channel edges, riprap, and stream bends. Remember the high percentage of Nebraska flatheads caught on lures? I'm guessing most of those lures were used by bass anglers fishing near dense woody cover. Flatheads love this type of cover, and they're quick to attack live baitfish or lures resembling live baitfish, such as many crankbaits, jigs, spoons, and spinners. If those lures were tipped with live bait (as many were) or had rattles or components that vibrated or flashed (as many did), their effectiveness was further enhanced.

Why use lures when baits work better? For some catfishermen, it simply provides a welcome change of pace. And at times, using lures can be a highly effective method for catching cats.

So, should you target cats with artificial lures? That depends. If you prefer catching as many cats as possible, especially trophy cats, you'll probably do better sticking to "regular" cat baits. But if you enjoy more challenging endeavors, give lures a try. Catching cats on artificials adds another fun dimension to this multifaceted sport.

Home Brews for Catfish

Catfisherman are the alchemists of angling, hoping to turn unusual concoctions of smelly ingredients into golden formulas catfish can't resist.

Catfish love stinkbait, and almost every hardcore catfish angler has a top-secret stinkbait formula whiskerfish just can't resist.

One old-timer told me, "There are more stinkbait recipes than there are food recipes, and not all of them have been invented yet. The fun part is experimenting. When you come up with a brand-new formula, you're just as proud as you'd be if you made a delicious new barbecue sauce or a tasty marinade."

After I swore on a Bible I wouldn't reveal the ingredients, this aficionado allowed me to watch as he mixed up a batch of his secret-formula cat catcher. You'd have thought he was Emeril Lagasse preparing a sumptuous bisque. He whisked together a cup of this, a dollop of that and a spoonful of some top-secret ingredient. Then like a bon vivant sampling the bouquet of an expensive wine, he lifted a cupful to his nose and inhaled. Tears streamed down his reddened cheeks, his knees quaked, and it appeared he might throw up.

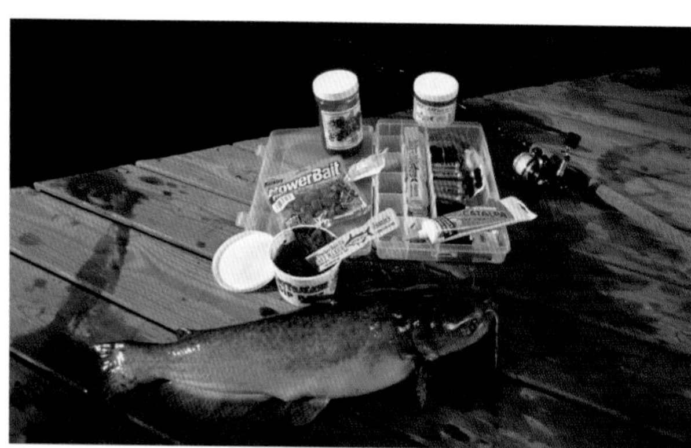

Many types of stinkbaits are available, along with a variety of paraphenalia made for fishing these specialty cat baits.

"Holy Moses!" he proclaimed, quivering like a headless chicken. "One whiff of that would kill a skunk. But it needs to be stronger."

Indeed, stinkbait chefs believe the worse it smells, the more catfish it will catch. To make it so, they add some rank ingredients to their brews.

Decomposing fish, for example. Heads and guts allowed to ferment several days reek like a week-old sardine sandwich, and nothing makes a catfish lick its whiskers quicker.

Limburger cheese, too. Normal humans can't eat it without holding their nose. Stinkbait manufacturers and catfish love it.

When making a batch of his locally famous Putrid Pudding—that's what he calls his rotten-fish stinkbait—one of my catfishing companions hides the container on top of his neighbor's barn. This serves three primary purposes:

1. It keeps the raccoons and neighborhood cats from getting into the bait (and possibly dying as a result);
2. It allows the brew to ferment properly in the hot sun.
3. It helps my chum avoid unnecessary exposure to the stinkbait's toxic fumes. The poor barn owner has searched unsuccessfully for years trying to pinpoint the source of the horrific stench.

To make Putrid Pudding, my friend puts two quarts of dead shad in a plastic bucket and allows them to decompose until only an oily residue remains. Then on a camp stove outside, he boils the residue and stirs in one quart of soured milk, two packets of dry yeast, and a half-pound of Limburger cheese. He heats this while adding flour and stirring until thick. The mixture then is carefully funneled into a plastic jug he plugs with cheesecloth. The jug sits on the neighbor's barn for a week or two at least, bubbling like a witch's cauldron. When my friend can detect the ghastly smell from home, he knows the stinkbait has properly aged and is ready to use.

Should the user get a drop of Putrid Pudding on his clothes, the garments must be burned. If it got on your skin, God knows what would happen. Great care must be taken to avoid contact.

My buddy handles the mix like it's radioactive waste. He fishes it by pushing a hooked square of sponge into the goo with a long stick. The sponge absorbs the mess and stays on the hook when cast.

Does he catch catfish with it? Yes, indeed. And when he goes catfishing, he has his favorite bank-fishing spot all to himself. No one can stand to fish near him.

How Stinkbaits Work

Despite popular misconceptions, stinkbaits don't work because they stink. I learned this while interviewing Dr. John Caprio of Louisiana State University, a neurophysiologist who has studied what fish taste and smell since 1971. His research has given him extraordinary insights into catfish feeding behavior.

"Catfish are swimming tongues," Caprio told me. "You can't touch any place on a catfish without touching thousands of taste buds. A six-inch catfish has more than 250,000—on the outside of its body, inside the mouth, and on the gill rakers. To use an analogy, it's as if the tip of your tongue grew out and covered your body. Consequently, the sense of taste is very keen.

"The sense of smell is equally keen," he continued. "Catfish can smell and taste some compounds at one part to ten billion parts of water. Catfish also use their lateral line to help sense

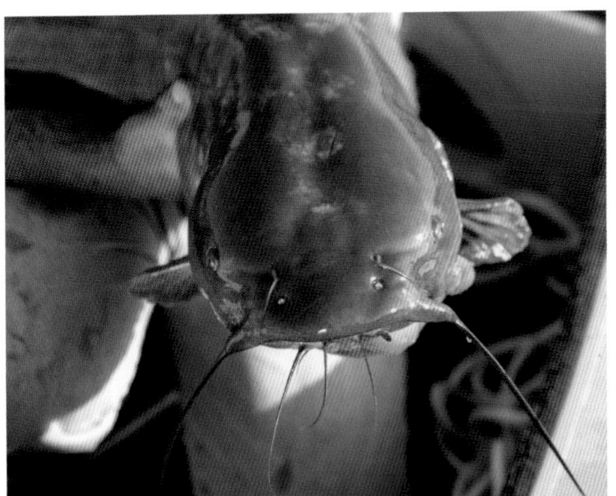

Thousands of taste buds cover the skin of a catfish with the largest concentrations of these sensory organs on the whiskers, mouth, and gill rakers. Catfish also have an extraordinary sense of smell, pumping water in and out of the paired nostrils so chemicals in the water can be detected.

prey, they can sense electrical charges in living cells, and they have an excellent sense of touch. Channel catfish have excellent sight. All these senses combined help catfish locate food."

Despite their extraordinary sensory abilities, however, catfish can't detect the odor of stinkbait that assaults a catfisherman's nose.

"What stinks to you and me doesn't stink to catfish," said Caprio. "People smell chemicals volatilized to the air, but animals living in water couldn't care less about volatiles because they can't detect them. They detect chemical compounds in the water. What you and I smell, fish can't smell."

So why do stinkbaits work? Water-soluble components of the stinkbait contact the taste buds covering a catfish's body, and when the taste buds detect these chemicals, they send a message to the fish's brain telling it to find the food. The catfish then approaches the food and picks it up. Taste buds in the mouth relay messages to another part of the brain and tell the fish to eat the food—or spit it out. In the case of good stinkbaits, they eat and consequently are caught.

Stinkbait anglers often include unusual ingredients in their home brews.

Species Specifics

Small channel cats and blue cats under ten pounds are most likely to be caught by anglers fishing stinkbaits. Young fish of these species scavenge more and eat a wider variety of foods than heavyweight adults. As channel and blue cats grow in size, their diet becomes less varied, consisting mostly of live baitfish, crayfish, and other abundant forage animals. Flatheads rarely scavenge, so stinkbaits rarely catch them.

Types of Stinkbaits and Ways to Fish Them

There are several types of stinkbaits, each with a particular consistency that requires a particular method of fishing.

Dip baits, like my friend's Putrid Pudding, have the consistency of . . . well, dip—the kind you

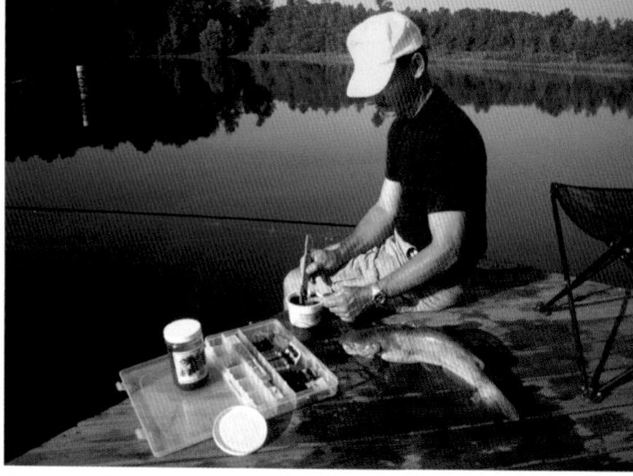
A pond fishermen prepares to fish a catfish worm covered with dip bait.

dunk potato chips in. (Be careful not to mistake one for the other!) They sometimes are called sponge baits because a sponged-covered treble hook is used to soak up the bait for fishing. Dip the sponge hook in the bait, squish it with a stick until it's saturated, then cast the weighted sponge rig to a spot that looks catfishy and wait for Mr. Whiskers to hone in on the scent.

Secret Recipes Revealed

Secret recipes for proven stinkbaits often are passed down from generation to generation with explicit instructions never to reveal the ingredients. I've discovered, however, that a little hooch shared by a campfire has a magical way of loosening tongues. Some recipes thus collected:

Blood & Oil Sponge Bait
Pour blood from a carton of fresh chicken livers into a jar or plastic container. Add the oil from a can of sardines or tuna. Stir. Sponge. Fish.

Knock-Out Cheese Bait
Combine equal measures of pork or beef brains or chicken liver and Limburger cheese in a plastic butter tub, mash together, cover, poke a few holes in the lid, then place in a hotspot—on the roof of your neighbor's barn, perhaps—for several days. Use as a dip bait.

Got-A-Bite Stinkbait
Mix two cups cottonseed meal, which can be purchased at farm supply stores, with two cups flour, then stir in one can condensed cheddar cheese soup, two tablespoons pancake syrup, and two tablespoons vegetable oil. Place in a zip-seal bag and refrigerate until ready to fish.

Mr. Whiskers Dough Balls
Mix in a large plastic tub one cup yellow cornmeal, one cup flour, one-quarter teaspoon anise oil, and one tin sardines packed in oil. Add small amounts of water to form a bread-like dough. Form dough into pieces the size of a ping-pong ball and drop into boiling water for three minutes. Remove, drain on paper towels, and allow to cool. Catch a cat with them.

Breakfast of Champions
Run a pint of chicken livers through a blender until liquefied. Slowly add Wheaties cereal, and continue blending until the mixture turns into a ball. Roll into golf ball size pieces and place in a zip-seal bag. Cool to firm before using.

Catfish Biscuits
Empty one can of tuna or mackerel into a mixing bowl, juice and all. Add the dough from two cans of biscuits. Mix by hand until biscuit dough and fish are well blended. Add some flour if needed to get the right consistency. Store in zip-seal plastic freezer bags. To use, pinch off a suitably sized chunk and place on a No. 4 treble hook.

Hot dogs marinated in strawberry Kool-Aid and garlic make great chunk baits.

Dip baits also can be fished on a "catfish worm," a ringed, soft-plastic lure that is dunked and covered in the smelly concoction. Dip baits melt quickly, so reapply frequently to keep it covered.

Doughbaits have pizza-dough consistency. Many won't stay hooked when casting, especially during hot weather. Cloth doughbait bags and spring-wound bait-holder treble hooks are helpful, but it's best to stick with thick doughbait mixtures that can be molded around a regular hook to form a firm ball that won't fly off when casting.

Make your own doughbait by mixing flour and water to form thick dough. Add a flavoring of your choosing—anise oil, blood, and rancid cheese are favorites—then roll the dough into balls and store in a plastic butter tub or similar container. Cool in an ice chest before fishing to firm it up.

To properly fish doughbaits, move the bait very little. Give careful thought to finding prime catfishing areas, then after you cast, allow the bait to sit a half hour or so. Doughbaits must melt to lay a scent trail. If there are no bites in the specified time, relocate.

Chunk baits are solid grape-sized baits. They melt slowly, so a cat must be close to find your offering unless you have time to wait. This fact, however, makes chunk baits highly desirable for baiting trotlines, limblines, and other set lines.

Make your own chunk baits by slicing inexpensive hot dogs into one-inch pieces and putting them in a plastic tub. Add a package of unsweetened strawberry Kool-Aid and two tablespoons minced garlic. Fill the tub with water, and allow the wieners to marinate overnight. Hook. Cast. Fish. Catch.

As you can imagine, creating and fishing with stinkbaits is a smelly situation. To be a true catfisherman, though, you must give it a whirl sooner or later. It's one sure route to catfishing success.

Stinkbait Precautions—Read Carefully!

A word of warning is in order here. You will notice I recommend the use of plastic containers when mixing and storing stinkbaits. This is because some stinkbait concoctions give off fermentation bubbles and gases that can cause a tightly sealed glass or metal container to explode with dangerous and gut-wrenching results. Always follow these rules when preparing stinkbaits:

- Use plastic containers, never glass or metal, for brewing and storing.
- Never tighten a lid on the mixture.
- Store all stinkbait mixtures outside at all times, preferably somewhere out of reach of animals.

Wild and Wacky Cat Catchers

Fish with whiskers eat stuff you couldn't imagine.

Catfish eat weird foods, no doubt. An 1847 edition of *Scientific American* reports, "A catfish was purchased in the Cincinnati market, lately, which, on being opened, was found to contain in its stomach a silver thimble, a gold ring, and a counterfeit dime, tied up in a rag."

The Manitoba Morning Free Press in Winnipeg (May 18, 1894) tells of a 140-pound Kansas catfish caught by one Douglass Smith. "In its stomach was found a small bottle, securely corked, containing this message: 'Whoever will find this will please send it back to me. H.E. Pipes.' Mr. Pipes had thrown the bottle in the Kaw River three years earlier, seventy-five miles from where the fish was caught."

The variety of baits that can be used to catch catfish is simply astounding.

Another weird tale of the catfish's gustatory habits comes to us via an 1867 edition of *Harper's Weekly*, which contained a story about soldiers rowing across a river who encountered a large fish floundering on the surface. "It proved to be a large cat-fish, which had swallowed a musk-rat. The animal's tail still hung out of its mouth."

In historical literature, we also find references to many unusual catfish baits. In *The Adventures of Huckleberry Finn*, for example, Huck and Jim "... bait one of the big hooks with a skinned rabbit and set it and catch a catfish that was as big as a man ..." Author Mark Twain may have seen such bait being used while plying the Mississippi as a steamboat pilot.

Another literary giant, Henry Thoreau, also wrote about the catfish's indiscriminate feeding habits. Bullheads, he noted, "... will take any kind of bait, from an angleworm to a piece of tomato can, without hesitation or coquetry."

Soap

While using a tomato can as bait might be stretching your luck, there are many old-fashioned baits seldom used by today's anglers that still work wonders for enticing catfish. One such allurement is Ivory soap. Proctor & Gamble probably didn't think their product would become a popular catfish bait when it was in-

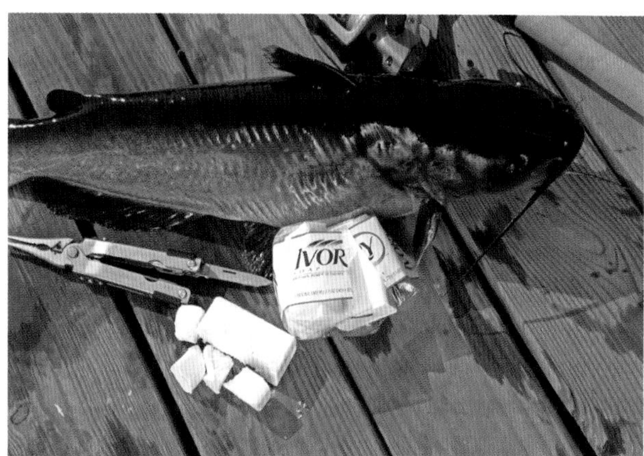

Some folks find it hard to believe, but soaps, such as Ivory, make superb catfish baits.

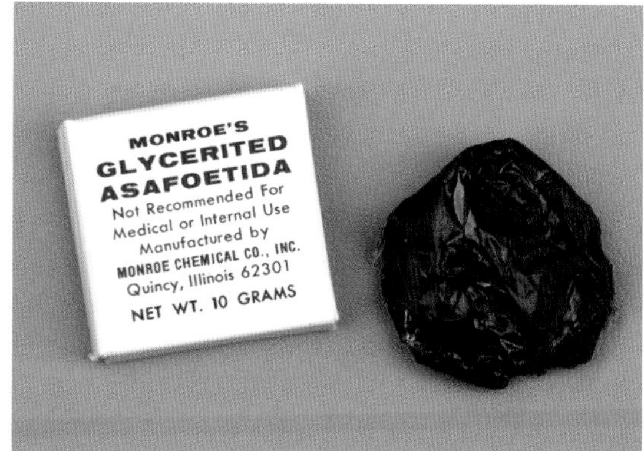

In decades past, catters often used asafetida as a cat attractant.

troduced in 1879. But it did. Hardcore catters have used it for decades with great success.

Old-timers on the rivers I fished as a youngster often baited trotlines with chunks cut from bars of Ivory soap. My uncle was one of these old-timers, and when we ran lines he'd baited in this fashion, it wasn't unusual to find a cat on every other hook. A small piece threaded on a hook works equally well for rod and reel anglers.

Although Ivory is the brand most often used, I've heard that Octagon and Zote soaps also work great. These are "pure" soaps without added scents or chemicals. Some catfishermen I know use old-fashioned lye soap made at home.

Asafetida and Other Scent Baits

Asafetida is another superb catfish enticement now largely forgotten. Also called stinking gum and Devil's dung, this product, made from plants native to Eurasia, comes in two primary forms—a resin and an oil—both of which are used to flavor foods and for medicinal purposes. In decades past, children often wore a pouch of asafetida around the neck to ward off winter colds—an embarrassing matter for the kids, for asafetida has a strong, repugnant smell.

Catfishermen used asafetida by mixing a bit of resin or oil in a bucket of water. A cotton trotline was then soaked in the mixture. When the line was set, catfish would come and rub against it, much like a feline playing with catnip. Many got foul-hooked, thus producing a catch without the angler having to obtain regular bait. Oil of rhodium, anise oil, and rotten eggs sometimes were used the same way.

Back in the 1960s, many men with whom I catfished carried a bottle of asefetida oil in their tackle box. We'd put a few drops in a can of water then soak a piece of cloth in the mixture and put it on our hook. We caught many catfish using this scent bait, all of which ate the bait just like they might eat a worm. You probably won't find asafetida in the local drugstore like we did back then, but it's available through several Internet sources.

Something Fruity

A few anglers still use another unusual catfish bait: fruit. The idea of a catfish eating fruit stretches the imagination, but cats are opportunistic feeders that will gorge on var-

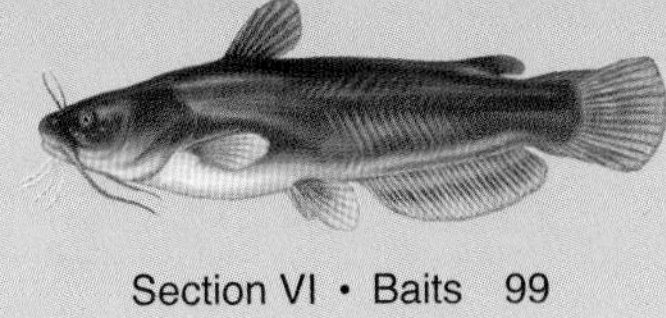

ious types of wild fruits when available. In South America, for example, the red-tailed catfish is considered especially delicious during high-water periods when it migrates into flooded jungles to feed on fruits falling into the water. Our own blue cats and channel cats are known to do likewise, gathering to feed on muscadines, mulberries, haw fruits, and even acorns and hickory nuts that drop from trees overhanging the water. When we fished flooded woodlands along the lower Mississippi when I was younger, the catfish we cleaned often had fruits and nuts in their bellies.

My father-in-law, Hansel Hill of Alpine, Arkansas, said anglers on Arkansas's Lake Greeson frequently use ripe persimmons for bait. "In fall when persimmons get ripe and start falling, it's not unusual to clean a catfish that has a belly full of them," he said. "Years ago, when folks discovered this, they started using persimmons for bait. And they learned real quick, when persimmons are available, they're one of the best catfish baits there is. I've seen folks load a boat with cats by baiting their hooks with nothing but persimmons."

On the Little Missouri River, a tributary of Lake Greeson, I've run into catfishermen using mulberries for bait. Unlike persimmons, which ripen in autumn, mulberries ripen in spring.

Persimmons are among many fruits catfish eat.

The banks along the Little Missouri have hundreds of mulberry trees overhanging the water, and when the ripe fruit starts falling, you can see schools of channel catfish fighting to grab each morsel that splashes down. The mulberry anglers gather the fruits and impale two or three on a baitholder hook. The fruit is lobbed out under a mulberry tree and rarely reaches bottom before a cat gobbles it up.

In his book *Masters' Secrets of Catfishing*, Alabama writer John Phillips reports on another top-notch fruit bait. "Golden raisins are good catfish bait if you're using set hooks, trotlines, or any method of fishing that allows the bait to be in the water for an extended time," he says. "The raisins are the most productive during the hot summer months—particularly when fishing at night ... The raisins swell up on the hooks and begin to ferment, giving off a very strong odor that calls catfish. Because of the raisins' bright-yellow color, the cats can find and eat them easily."

Catfish guide Phil King of Corinth, Mississippi, often uses raisins for bait. He reports that white grapes are another fruit anglers should try. "They're a good summer bait," he says.

Bullheads and Other Catfish

Bullhead catfish are the main prey of flatheads in many waters where both are common. They've been used as bait by flathead fans since at least the nineteenth century, but nowadays, relatively few anglers ever try them despite the fact that they may be the best bait available when you're targeting trophy-class flatheads.

In his 1953 book, *Catfishin'*, Joe Mathers called bullhead baits "excellent, especially for large catfish."

"Use small living forms, three to six inches long," he wrote. "Snip off the barbels, spines, and dorsal fin causing the fish to bleed and

Small bullheads have been used to entice big catfish for decades. They're tough and easy to keep alive.

flounder in the water. They are very tough, easy to keep alive and excellent for use on trot or other set lines. Small bullheads can usually be taken in great numbers with a seine or on hook and line from backwaters, bayous, ponds, and small lakes and streams . . ."

Georgia writer Jeff Samsel, an avid catfisherman, reports that channel cats sometimes are used for bait, as well. "For big flathead catfish, many long-time river fishermen contend there is no better bait than another catfish," he tells me. "Bullheads and channel cats are most commonly used, but whatever kind of catfish a flathead is accustomed to seeing in a waterway is probably the best cat to use as bait in that location. Any cat up to a couple pounds will do. Hook the bait in the back toward the tail, and suspend it just off the bottom."

Sometimes you can rig the bait just by catching it. When Dorothy Taylor of Fort Scott, Kansas, cleaned a fifty-three-pound flathead she caught, she found a one-and-a-half-pound channel cat in its belly. The channel cat, not the flathead, had her hook in its mouth.

Other Wacky Baits

John Phillips tells a story about a friend, out of bait, who resorted to using a roadkill possum on his hook. It worked. "I was very surprised," his friend said. "The catfish hit the possum bait better than they had the cut shad, live minnows, and worms I had been using."

"Some people say adding WD-40 or Preparation H to lures and bait brings added success," said Vince Travnichek in an article published in the *Missouri Conservationist*. The explanation is that both contain shark oil, which attracts fish. The manufacturer of WD-40 said that shark oil is not an ingredient in the product, but the manufacturer of Preparation H stated that their product contained 3 percent shark liver oil. Both said they had heard of these angling secrets but did not recommend using their products in such a manner."

Anglers in some areas say bubble gum can be a very effective cat-catcher.

James Patterson of Mississippi River Guide Service in Bartlett, Tennessee, says he has caught catfish using mulberries, bologna, and crickets and has cleaned cats that had such items as fried potatoes and pork chops in their bellies. "The most unusual thing I've found in a catfish was bubble gum," he notes. "I landed the fish, and it was squirting pink liquid everywhere. When I cut it open, it still had three full pieces of bubble gum inside."

Some anglers actually use bubble gum for bait. "We use Bazooka, Double Bubble, and Bubble Yum," a Georgia catfisherman told me. "They all catch cats so long as you chew the gum a little before baiting your hook. Don't chew all the flavor out, though, or they won't take it."

The wackiest cat bait? No bait at all. Jug fishermen on the White and Mississippi rivers in Arkansas catch channel and blue cats using only a gold crappie hook dangled beneath each jug. "Catfish see that flashy gold hook and grab it," one told me. "You don't need bait at all."

This just goes to prove what I've been saying all along: sooner or later you'll catch a catfish no matter what you dangle in the water. And that, my friend, is one of the things that makes catfishing so much fun.

"Grocery Store" Baits

As their name implies, grocery store baits can be purchased at your local supermarket. Among these are enticements such as shrimp, cheese, hot dogs, dog food, bread, bacon, and even squid.

Both fresh and frozen shrimp can be used to entice blue, channel, and flathead cats up to about ten pounds. Run your hook from the head of the shrimp out through the tail, and leave the hook point exposed.

Cheese is an ingredient in many stinkbait concoctions, especially smelly cheeses such as Limburger. In some areas, however, anglers simply use chunks of sharp cheddar or Velveeta, both of which are said to be effective cat catchers.

On South Carolina's Santee-Cooper lakes, hallowed water for catfish fans, hot dogs are used to entice cats—but not just any hot dogs. "They don't like all-beef hot dogs," one guide told me. "But they love the cheap kind made out of chicken or turkey." And you thought catfish weren't discriminating diners!

Will cats eat dog food? Indeed. Cat men in Mississippi, Tennessee, and Alabama swear Tender Chunks is head and shoulders above the rest. But an angler in Arkansas claims Kibbles and Bits is tops for small channel cats.

Bread doesn't seem like a great cat bait, but I once watched a tour guide mash an entire loaf into a big dough ball then drop it over the side of the boat into the clear waters of Silver Springs, Florida. One of the biggest cats I ever saw came up and swallowed the entire loaf of bread in a single gulp. Might be worth trying.

Massachusetts catter Roger Aziz has caught more line-class-record white cats than anyone. His favorite bait? Bacon. "Hickory-smoked bacon works best," he says. "Always."

In winter, when live baits are hard to come by, anglers must rely more on various types of grocery baits. Randle Hall, a Texas catfish guide told me, "I started experimenting and found that squid really works. I use noncleaned squid bought at a supermarket, half a squid per hook."

Section VII

Advanced Tactics

Cats in the Woods

In the eyes of many, flooded spring woods are the best catfishing spots bar none.

When I first saw the spring crawfish run, as my friend Jim Spencer calls it, the sight astounded me. I've witnessed this incredible natural phenomenon several times in the intervening years, but memories of my first run will always be most vivid.

Spring floodwaters were receding along Arkansas's lower White River, and when the river fell to the right level on the Clarendon gauge, Jim phoned.

"We need to go tomorrow," he said, "or they'll be gone. I'll pick you up at five a.m."

We met at the appointed time—Jim, me, and my son Josh—and drove to the river. After motoring a few miles downstream in a johnboat, we tied the craft to some old cypress steps on the river bank then made our way up and walked to a small oxbow off the beaten path. A bit of water still flowed through the run-outs connecting the river and oxbow lake, but in a day or so as the water continued falling, the connection between river and lake would be severed.

Only days before, the woods around the lake had been inundated beneath twelve to eighteen inches of water, the result of high water that

When floodplain woodlands are inundated by river overflows, catfish anglers may have to move into backwater areas off the river proper to find their quarry.

comes on average three years out of five. As the White River dropped, however, the water was pulled out, leaving behind muddy, leaf-strewn ground. But even now, with the water gone, the ground was hard to see, for thousands upon thousands of crayfish covered the damp earth. You couldn't step without mashing them beneath your feet, huge rusty-red crustaceans with pincers like Maine lobsters.

"Look, Dad!" Josh exclaimed. "They're everywhere! There must be a million of them!"

We had toted a one-hundred-quart cooler to the lake's edge, and each of us carried a wire fish basket in which to place our catch. Walking through the woods, we gathered crawfish—a dozen here, a dozen there—and when our baskets were full, we returned to the cooler and dumped the catch in. Little yelps emanated from the collection crew whenever a crawfish found its mark with those big pincers, but in less than an hour, the cooler was overflowing.

"This is the best of two worlds," Jim said. "We've got catfish bait and dinner, too, all in one cooler."

The catfish liked the crawfish almost as much as we did. That night, fishing with crawfish tails in the run-out between river and lake, each of us caught a dozen or more cats, and before the sun rose, the three of us had polished off more than ten pounds apiece of spicy, fresh-boiled crawfish apiece. I decided then and there that catfish, crawdads, and bottomland rivers form a minor trinity.

Woods Fishing

I had known for years that catfish migrate into flooded spring woods to eat crawfish. As a youngster, I often accompanied uncles on woods-fishing junkets, tying yo-yos and limblines to green branches along the edges of inundated forests and baiting them with the tails of crawfish caught in homemade dip nets. As we'd paddle through the woods making our sets, big cats would shoot this way and that, spooked by our approach. We'd see their wakes, sometimes the tip of a fin or tail, as they scurried away through the shallow water. By that sign, we knew our timing was right. Cats were in the woods gorging on the annual banquet nature provided, and by morning, we'd be weary from catching and cleaning catfish.

There was no doubt about the inspiration for this catfish celebration. The fish we caught—blues, channels, and flatheads—were literally stuffed to the gills with crawfish. Often, a fish would take our bait even though several crawfish could be seen protruding from its gullet. Their stomachs were distended like beer bellies with dozens and dozens of crawfish. Eating more was an impossibility but still they tried.

Woods fishing is one of the oldest yet most obscure forms of catfishing. Few cat fans are familiar with the tactic today, but earlier this century, it was widely practiced in the lower Mississippi River Valley. D.S. Jordan and B.W. Evermann were among the first to write about this unique sport in their 1923 book, *American Food and Game Fishes.*

"During the spring rise in the Mississippi, hundreds of square miles of the adjacent country become flooded, and then the catfish leave the rivers, lakes, and bayous, and 'take to the woods,'" they said. "Here the fishermen follow them, and 'woods' or 'swamp' fishing is resorted to. Short 'brush' lines with single hooks are tied to limbs of trees here and there through the forest, in such a way as to allow the hook to hang about six inches under water. The trees selected are usually those along the edges of the 'float' roads, and, that he may readily find his lines again, the fisherman ties a white rag to each tree to which he has attached a line.

"The lines are visited daily, or as often as practicable, and the fish are placed in a live-box, where they are kept until the tugboats from Morgan City (Louisiana) make their regular collecting trips. Then they are transferred to very large live-boxes or cars carried in tow by the tugs, and are taken to Morgan City, where the fish are dressed, put in barrels with ice, and shipped to the retailers in many States of the Union."

In *Catfishin'*, published in 1953, Joe Mathers also commented.

"Brush line fishing (also referred to as 'woods' or 'swamp' fishing) is employed by fisherman along the Mississippi and its large tributaries," he writes. "As the spring floods come, these rivers overflow their banks and flood the surrounding lowlands. The blue catfish especially characteristically leaves the rivers, lakes, and bayous and moves into these flooded areas. The fishermen follow them . . ."

Gorging on Crayfish

Because the ground in a river floodplain is low and flat, a rise in river level of only a few inches can flood literally thousands of acres of bottoms. As the water rises and the woodlands become flooded, a new food source—terrestrial crayfish—becomes available to catfish.

Catfish egg production in floodplain-river ecosystems is enhanced by the presence of numerous terrestrial crayfish during years of high water. Catfish caught during this time may be literally stuffed with these high-protein crustaceans.

Crayfish are extremely abundant in most bottomland hardwood forests, but during most of the year they live on land and are inaccessible to catfish. During overflow periods, however, the crayfish are forced to live in an aquatic environment, and catfish are drawn to them like kids to a candy store. Flatheads, blues, and channel cats all join the feeding frenzy, moving from rivers, lakes, bayous, and sloughs into the shallow water that now inundates many acres of bottoms. They will feed here as long as the water is high enough to swim in, sometimes for several months.

The Limbliner's Season

It would seem with so many actively feeding fish gathered in shallow water, it would be easy to catch them. But that is not the case. Fishing in flooded woods is difficult in the best of circumstances, and because the catfish are widely scattered and have an enormous supply of natural food, catching them on rod and reel is iffy.

Catching them with setlines is another story. This is the limbliners' season, and as soon as the bottoms are inundated, their fun begins. Setlines hung from low branches produce extraordinary numbers of catfish, particularly toward the end of flood season when the waters are warm.

Some limbliners make special sets with a piece of rubber inner tube tied in the middle of each line to act as a shock absorber that prevents catfish from pulling free. Others tie their sets on springy green limbs that function in a similar manner. Still others fish with yo-yos, the spring-wound Autofisher rigs popular in many parts of the South. Dozens of sets may

Limblines can be set individually at strategic fishing spots to catch catfish feeding in flooded woods.

be placed, and each is checked at regular intervals to remove the catch. This is an extraordinary time characterized by extraordinary fishing.

Run-outs and Run-off

If you're a die-hard rod-and-reel angler, you'll want to pay particular attention to the part of this phenomenon known as "the run-off." This occurs when a river "falls out of" a connected oxbow, usually in spring or early summer when overflow waters recede from the river bottoms. There comes a point when the water has fallen low enough that the only connections between an oxbow and its parent stream are small chutes or "run-outs" created by low points in the area topography. In some cases, only one run-out exists; in others, there are several. All run-outs, however, serve up extraordinary catfishing for savvy anglers.

A live crawfish or crawfish tail drifted through a run-out area is an irresistible enticement for cats in the woods.

The key to run-out fishing is timing. The best fishing will be during the few days before the river falls completely out of the lake. Water constricted in the run-out chutes increases in velocity. Crawfish and other forage animals are pulled by the current into the rushing stream of water and adjacent areas. When this happens, catfish gather in great numbers to gorge on the resulting feast. Some hold near cover at the head of the run-out in the lake. Others position themselves at the run-out's tail where the rushing water meets the river. All feed ravenously while the bounty is before them, and any bait—crawfish, night crawlers, cutbait, live fish—drifted through or along the run-out area is likely to be taken.

A float rig works great here with the bobber positioned so the bait floats just off the bottom. Cast above the run-out, and let the rig drift back through, or drift the rig through the current in the run-out tail. Live crawfish or crawfish tails are top baits in this situation, for rod-and-reel and setline fishing. But because these prespawn catfish are feeding ravenously, they'll accept almost any offering from night crawlers and chicken liver to live bluegills and cutbait.

Big blue cats such as this often feed in the run-out connecting an oxbow lake to its parent river.

For run-out fishing to be successful, you'll have to learn the river-gauge level at which the parent river will overflow into each oxbow. When gauge numbers are higher than this number, you know the river and oxbow are connected. When gauge numbers are lower than the "magic" number, the river level is so low it doesn't flow into the lake. Run-off conditions exist when the river level is just slightly higher than the magic number, and it is during the few days when this occurs that run-out catfishing is at its best.

The best way to obtain the "magic" gauge number is to inquire at local bait shops or ask area anglers. You then can read the current gauge number in local newspapers or by calling government hotlines to plan a trip during peak periods.

Although the popularity of woods fishing has declined in recent decades, this is still a top-notch tactic for catching lots of catfish, big and small. If you live in the lower Mississippi River Valley or anywhere else these floodplain-river ecosystems exist, give woods fishing a try this spring when the big rivers have overflowed their banks. When catfish are in the woods, it's a sure bet they'll be biting.

River gauges provide important water-level information needed by those who fish run-outs between oxbow lakes and rivers.

Scientific Evidence and Big River Conservation

Fishermen have known for decades that catfish feed heavily on crawfish in floodplain-river ecosystems, such as those found in the lower Mississippi Valley, but only in recent years have fisheries researchers studied this phenomenon. Don Jackson and Joe Flotemersch, researchers at Mississippi State University, studied the unique relationship between terrestrially burrowing crayfish and channel cats in channelized and non-channelized sections of Mississippi's Yockanookany River. Some of what they learned is old news to ardent woods anglers. For example, they found that "adult channel catfish aggregated in locations where the river channel and adjacent floodplain were coupled and subsequently foraged heavily on these crayfish." Sound familiar? It should. This is the typical run-out fishing scenario described in this chapter.

The most important information discovered during this study was not previously known. Jackson and Flotemersch learned that peak use of crayfish occurs prior to egg occurrence in channel catfish. And because the crayfish are excellent sources of essential amino acids and essential fatty acids, they are likely to be significant resources for egg development. In other words, if the rivers didn't overflow and the catfish couldn't reach the crayfish to feed on them, the catfish would not produce as many eggs. As a result, these floodplain-river ecosystems would not produce the astounding numbers of healthy cats now available for anglers to catch.

For this reason, all of us who enjoy catfishing in big bottomland river ecosystems should be concerned about flood-control and navigation projects that utilize channelization, dredging, and construction of levees and wing dikes. Such activities can "disconnect" floodplains and rivers and hurt catfish stock.

Woods Fishing Tips

- Big boats are practically useless when fishing flooded timber. Most woods fishermen opt for a lightweight narrow johnboat they can maneuver through the trees.
- Carry hip boots or waders because the best fishing spots may be unreachable except on foot.
- In the close confines around run-outs, use a five-and-a-half- to six-foot medium-heavy rod with a whippy tip and stout butt section. This will allow you to flip a bait in just the right spot with fewer hang-ups.
- If catfish seem persnickety, try peeling crawfish tails before putting them on a hook.
- Always practice selective harvest. Keep a few small cats to eat; release the big ones. Better yet, eat the bait. Crawfish are delicious!
- Know the fishing regulations where you fish before using setlines or other such tackle. On border rivers between two states, be sure you're properly licensed.

Tailwater Tactics

Zero in on the fast water below a big-river dam for blue-ribbon catfish action.

Catfish live in big reservoirs. You can find them in many smaller lakes. They swim in the long open stretches of our rivers and streams. But if you're fishing on your own and want to increase your odds for success, if you want to be catching fish instead of just fishing, drive to the nearest cat river and follow it upstream to the first dam. In that tumbling, foamy-white mass of fast-moving water right below the dam, you'll find them—cats as long as your leg, at least. You'll have to land one exceeding seventy-five pounds before you'll draw much notice in some tailwaters, but that's always a distinct possibility if you know your stuff.

Focus on the first mile or two of water below the dam. Study it. Fish it. Get to know it on intimate terms—every rock, every hole, every hump, every dike, every nuance of cover and current. And if you play the game right and Lady Luck is on your side, sooner or later you'll hook what will probably be the biggest fish you've ever battled in freshwater—a trophy-class cat.

The churning water below a dam creates conditions big catfish find much to their liking.

Why Tailwaters?

Catfish are drawn to tailwaters by an urge to procreate. As days grow longer and water warms, cats leave deep wintering holes and begin upstream runs toward spawning areas. Before dams were built, the only things interrupting this annual procession were natural barriers, such as shoals, log jams, and the like. Today, however, the runs usually are stopped short by dams.

This wouldn't concern catfishermen if spawning was all cats had on their minds. Upon encountering a dam, the fish would simply turn back to find spawning grounds. But that's not the case. With these fish, eating precedes breeding. And at every dam on every river, there's a banquet awaiting them.

Baitfish like shad and skipjack herring are especially plentiful. Some are washed from above and wind up crippled or dead after passing through turbines. Cats gather like kids around an ice-cream truck, gobbling every morsel that swims or drifts near.

Most catfish remain in the tailwater for days or weeks, gorging 'round-the-clock on the irresistible feast. But in the end, nature can't be ignored. Most catfish eventually move downriver to spawning areas. As some leave, though, others arrive. And if conditions remain good—if water flow is ample to maintain high oxygen levels and attract schools of baitfish—those that leave will return after spawning, staying as long as they're comfortable and well fed. Thus, fishing for cats remains excellent through several months from late spring through summer.

Tailwater Hotspots

To better understand the catfishing dynamics of a tailwater, it helps to divide the tailwater into three sections: 1) the whitewater reach, which is the uppermost portion of the tailwater near the dam and adjacent structures; 2) the middle reach, which begins where churning water from the dam starts smoothing out and slowing down; and 3) the downstream reach, which begins where man-made structures are replaced by natural habitat. Each section's length and breadth may vary considerably depending on the type of dam and the river's size, but all sections are easily identified, and each offers different types of structure and cover attractive to cats under differing conditions. Learn what to look for, and you'll improve your odds of hooking a big cat.

The Whitewater Reach

From late spring through summer, this section of the tailwater serves up the best action for trophy catfish. Current velocity, baitfish abundance, and oxygen content reach their highest levels here—conditions big catfish find much

When fishing the whitewater reach, look for catfish holding in the "grooves" of slower-moving water between openings in the dam.

to their liking. As upstream spawning migrations progress, catfish crowd into the food-rich water immediately below the dam in ever-increasing numbers with larger fish laying claim to most prime feeding locations.

Many jumbo catfish hold in the "grooves" or "current tunnels" of slower-moving water between openings in the dam. When water is released, the fastest flow is in the center of the discharge, and the slowest water is on the outer edges of the flow. All surface water appears to move at the same speed, but the area of water between two discharges—the groove or tunnel—is actually slower-moving water where cats usually hold. Fishing these grooves is more productive than fishing the main current.

Chunks of cutbait are the perfect enticement in this situation. Slice a shad, herring, or sucker into one-inch chunks. Larger pieces are difficult to present properly in the current. Push the hook once through the bait, leaving the point exposed to ensure a good hookset.

A basic three-way rig with a Kahle hook and bell sinker works great in this situation. The sinker should be heavy enough so the current drags your bait slowly across the bottom. Cast toward the dam and into the head of a groove, letting the rig sink. If you've hit the groove properly, your bait should stop—for a moment at least—as soon as it hits bottom. If you missed the groove, you'll feel the bait tumbling along at a fast clip. Practice enables you to know for sure what's happening.

When you hit the groove, allow your bait to remain in one spot as long as possible. Cats swim back and forth from one end of the cone-shaped groove to the other over and over again. The grooves are usually short—fifty feet or fewer—so it won't take long for a cat to find your bait. When one does, its strike will be hard and unmistakable. Drop your rod tip toward the cat when it hits, then set the hook.

If cats quit biting in one groove, reposition your boat in a similar location and try again. Water flow through a dam increases or decreases as power requirements or water levels demand. So even though water runs continuously, the flow may change several times daily. When the flow changes, cats often move and search out more slack water in which to feed.

The washout hole is another important catfishing area in the whitewater reach. This is a depression scoured in the river bottom by the forceful action of water released from the dam. In most cases, it starts at the dam face and extends downstream for a few to many yards. If safety factors permit, use sonar to pinpoint the downstream lip of the hole where most cats hold. This will appear as a sharp drop discernible as you move toward the dam. If the washout hole is within the danger zone off limits to boaters, you'll have to speculate on its position and fish it from a distance.

A jig/cutbait combo works great in this situation. Impale a chunk of cutbait on a heavy leadhead. Motor upstream as far as safety permits, then drop the bait to the bottom and crank it up a bit. As your boat drifts, use your motor to maintain a speed that keeps your line vertical below you. When you reach the downstream lip of the washout hole, the bait will start moving up the drop and dragging behind the boat. This is when most strikes occur. If you get one, great. If not, continue drifting until you're on the shelf below the hole, then reel up your rig, motor upstream, and drift through again.

It's important to remember that constant water flow through the dam is necessary to maintain good catfishing conditions in the whitewater reach. Should conditions exist that force dam operators to close all gates, catfishing success will take a nosedive until ample water flow is restored. The best catfishing generally coincides with periods of highest water flow when most or all gates are open.

Remember, too, the best catfishing locales in a tailwater are easily "fished out," especially toward either end of the prime late-spring/summer fishing period. You may catch dozens of catfish in the hotspots you identify one day then return to the same fishing areas on several consecutive days and not catch a single fish. If this happens, fish other sections of the tailwater while allowing a period of rejuvenation. Catfish from other reaches will eventually move in to repopulate prime feeding areas.

The Middle Reach

Moving downstream from the washout hole, you'll soon enter the middle reach, a stretch of calmer water where man-made structures, such as wing dikes and riprap, are still prevalent. A few cats, especially smaller fish, inhabit this section throughout the warm months, but trophy action peaks during short periods of reduced water flow through the dam. If one or several gates are closed, cats feeding in the whitewater reach often move to middle reach structures that attract schools of baitfish. They continue feeding here until water flow is restored to higher levels, drawing them away.

Trophy cats often hold near wing dikes, which are some of the most prevalent structures in the middle reach of a tailwater.

Wing dikes are the predominant cat structure in this part of the tailwater. These long narrow rock structures direct current into the main channel to lessen shoreline erosion.

Most actively feeding catfish hold near the river's bottom on a wing dike's upstream side. Reduced current exists in this area along the length of the dike, allowing cats to remain active without expending excess energy while feeding. Some active catfish feed along the crown and in the boil-line over and just downstream from the wing dike's crown. When resting, cats move to deeper scour holes, usually near the end of the dike. Occasionally these fish are enticed to bite but only when bait is presented right under their nose.

Bottom-fishing often is productive here, but a slip-bobber rig allows you to cover more water quickly. Position the bobber stop so the float suspends your bait just above the river bottom. Add enough weight to hold the bait down and stand the bobber up, then let the rig drift

into eddies and pockets of calm water along the dike. Tease the rig around the rocks, easing it alongside drift piles and other catfish-attracting cover. If nothing happens after you've worked an area thoroughly, move your bobber stop down the line and drift through shallower. Or move to another dike and try again.

Humps and boulders in the middle reach also merit attention. Those with shallow crowns may be visible or at least apparent due to the boil-line above them. Sonar may be needed to find those in deeper water.

Fish these structures as you would a wing dike. Most feeding cats are near bottom on the upstream edge with a few feeding near the crown and boil-line areas. Cats in slack water behind boulders and humps are usually inactive.

The Downstream Reach

You eventually reach a point below the dam where the river starts looking natural again. The channel begins meandering once more, trees have toppled in, cutbanks reappear, and the hand of man is less in evidence. This is the downstream reach of the tailwater.

The mouth of a tributary is a prime place to seek catfish in the downstream reach of a tailwater. Catfish will be more concentrated in this portion of the tailwater when water conditions in the whitewater and middle reach are poor.

When conditions in upper sections of the tailwater are ideal, the downstream reach may be almost devoid of large cats. But all catfish pass through this area at least twice each year during upstream and downstream migrations, and if conditions in the whitewater reach become unfavorable for extended periods in late spring and summer, catfish may frequent portions downstream for weeks on end.

Tributaries are important hotspots in this section. Cats ascend tributaries to spawn, and they congregate at tributary mouths during prespawn and postspawn periods. If the mouth of the feeder stream is deep at its confluence with the river or if the tributary channel joins the main river channel, the area also may have exceptional potential during winter when cats tend to gather in deep water near channel breaks. During summer, if a tributary brings a cool, well-oxygenated inflow to the river, catfish may move in if dam releases upstream are slight or nil.

Proper timing is the key to success when fishing here, but tributaries always merit a look when catfishing is unproductive in upstream reaches.

Other prime fishing areas in the downstream reach are the same you might find on any river: undercut banks and timbered holes in outside bends; deep-water chutes; bridge channels; rock, gravel, and sand bars; log jams; side channels connecting the main river with backwaters and oxbows; and so forth.

Study the tailwater each time you fish. Ask yourself where cats are most likely to be. If it's late spring or summer and there's lots of

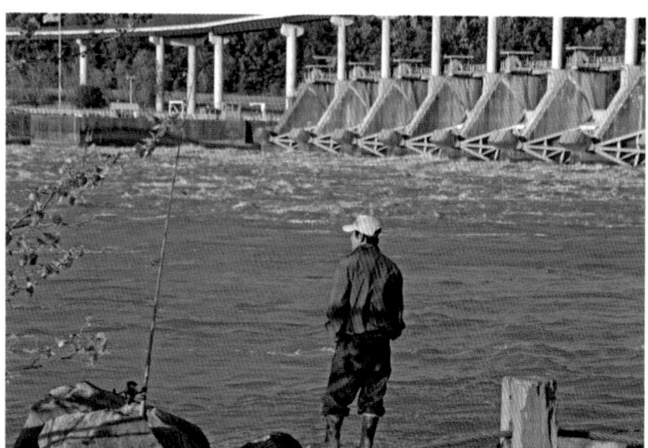
Dam tailwaters have produced some of the largest catfish ever taken in the United States, but to fish a tailwater effectively, the catfisherman must know where his quarry is likely to be based on water conditions and other factors.

water flowing from the dam, the whitewater reach likely will produce the most action. If water releases have been temporarily halted, the middle reach may be your best bet. You'll find some cats in upper reaches of the tailwater in autumn, winter, and early spring, but you'll probably do better around tributaries and other prime fishing locales in the downstream reach. Adjust your fishing tactics as necessary to capitalize on each situation.

You may not break any records next time you fish for tailwater catfish. But if you employ the right tactics under the right conditions, you're almost sure to catch plenty of eating-sized catfish, and every time you return, there's always the chance you'll tie into a real record breaker. They're out there now swimming in the tailwaters.

Fishing from Shore

Many tailwater anglers fish from shore. Unfortunately, the shore angler faces distinct disadvantages. Pinpointing casts to distant catfish-holding structures is more difficult and current billows your line, dragging your rig out of position. Fighting big fish is more difficult and time-consuming. Anglers may be crowded together, leading to tangles and tussles.

Shore fishing can be productive, however, if you use proper equipment. Use a long rod—a ten- to fourteen-foot surf-casting rod is ideal—to achieve greater distance on your casts. Holding the rod tip high minimizes the amount of line in the water for better bait presentation, and it also lessens your chance of getting tangled with lines of nearby fishermen. Normal spinning and bait-casting reels both work fine, but you'll achieve longer casts with a good heavy-duty spinning reel. Use nothing less than thirty-pound-test line when targeting big catfish.

Carry plenty of rig components, such as sinkers and jigheads. You'll lose many.

Let your rig settle then get it to hold. But don't leave it in one spot more than a few minutes. Move the bait again to be sure it hasn't tumbled into a hole where cats can't find it.

Safety First

Tailwater catfishermen should be aware of safety considerations at all times. When dam gates are opened, sudden rises in water can be dangerous.

Tailwaters have Jekyll-and-Hyde personalities. One minute a tailwater is peaceful, calm, and easygoing. But in the blink of an eye, it can turn into a raging, out-of-control monster that seems intent on your destruction.

Safety should be foremost on your mind whenever fishing a tailwater. Wear a life jacket every minute you're there. Maintain a safe and legal distance from the dam. Avoid anchoring, if possible, and if you do anchor, use a quick-release tie-off that will let you cut loose in a heartbeat. Keep a knife handy just in case.

Learn the warning signals—sirens, flashing lights, etc.—that indicate impending sudden releases from the dam. Keep your motor in top working order. Watch for boulders, inundated wing dikes, and other structures that can cause you to capsize.

Remember, catching a big cat is never worth risking your life or the lives of others.

Mountain Stream Catfishing

Highland streams often harbor impressive populations of catfish.

Despite popular misconceptions, cool, clear mountain streams offer outstanding catfishing. Proof is found in *Fish Arkansas*, a brochure listing the types of fish found in twenty-four of the Natural State's cold- and cool-water streams. All but one of these waters was identified as having healthy populations of channel catfish. All but two have good numbers of flathead catfish. Blue catfish were listed as residents in nine. No other fish, not even trout or smallmouth bass, inhabit more of Arkansas's mountain streams than catfish.

This same situation exists in many states, and the savvy angler can catch plenty of cats when conditions are right. Especially helpful is a knowledge of the rapids, holes, and pools found in most mountain streams and the ways catfish relate to each structure.

The cool, clear waters of mountain streams aren't often considered prime catfishing hotspots, but these waters frequently serve up superb fishing for big flatheads, blues, and channel cats.

Rapids

Rapids, or riffles, form over hard bottoms and are shallower than other spots because water can't erode the hard substrate. Water flow is constricted here, making it move forcefully. You can see rapids because water boils up here creating haystacks and whitecaps.

Holes

Holes form below rapids. The bottom softens here, and the rapids' churning water scours it away, leaving a depression several yards long.

Pools

Below each hole, the current slows. Sediments fall, the downstream end of the hole gets shallower, and a pool forms. Pools have no significant depth changes. They may extend a mile or more depending on bottom composition and river size. But when the water encounters another area of hard bottom, rapids form again, and the sequence starts anew—rapids, hole, pool.

A bobber/drift presentation proves the undoing of many mountain stream cats.

Of these three structures, holes typically harbor the most catfish. Cats travel through rapids and pools when moving and sometimes visit these areas to feed. They seldom stay long, however. Holes, on the other hand, provide depth, current, food, and security. The hole's deepest portion is the den or bedroom area where cats rest out of the current. The upper end is the kitchen or dining room where cats usually feed.

Rocks, logs, and other cover in a hole's deeper upstream end are especially attractive to actively feeding fish. Cats ambush prey from behind these current breaks. Cover objects where current is lighter or water is shallower aren't as likely to hold active catfish.

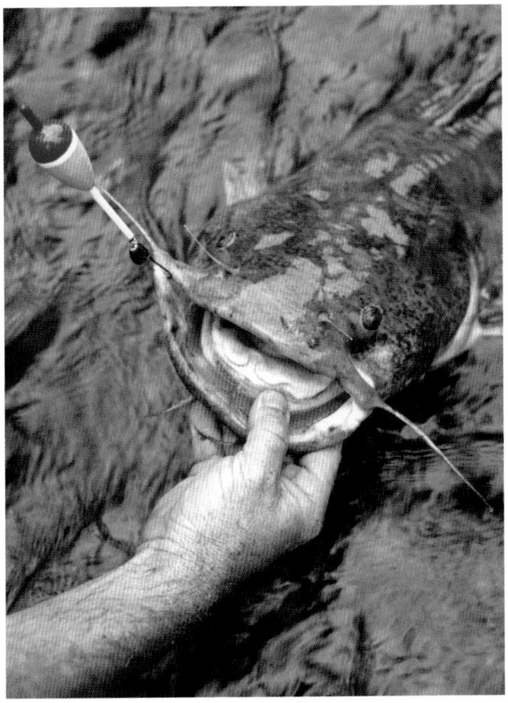

Wade Fishing

One excellent mountain-stream fishing technique is wading and casting to fish-holding structure and cover. If the stream isn't too deep, a bobber/drift presentation works well. Position the bobber so the bait hangs just above the bottom. Add enough weight to hold the bait down, then drift the rig alongside cover and structures. With practice, you'll become adept at steering the bait past holding areas without worrying about hang-ups.

A drift presentation is still appropriate in deeper water, but dispense with the bobber and add just enough lead so the bait still bounces along in the current. To rig, slip an egg sinker on your line, and eighteen inches above the bait, add a barrel swivel to hold the egg sinker in place.

Good bait choices include crayfish, night crawlers, minnows, creek chubs, hellgrammites, grasshoppers, salamanders, and frogs.

Mountain streams are hotbeds for untold numbers of fat sassy catfish. It may seem unusual fishing for cats outside the mosquito-infested bottomlands you normally visit, but it's a change of pace you're sure to enjoy.

Finessing Big-River Cats

One of the country's top cat guides shares a technique for catching cats in flowing water.

If you ever catfish on the Tennessee River in Hardin County, Tennessee, you're liable to run into a charming fellow from Corinth, Mississippi, named Phil "The Little Catman" King. Phil practically lives on the stretch of river between Pickwick and Kentucky lakes. He's a well-known personality in these parts for at least two reasons: 1) he's a nationally renowned catfish guide, often written about, and often seen on TV fishing shows, and 2) he's won more catfishing tournaments than perhaps any man alive, including the World Championship of Catfishing and the Cabela's King Kat Classic.

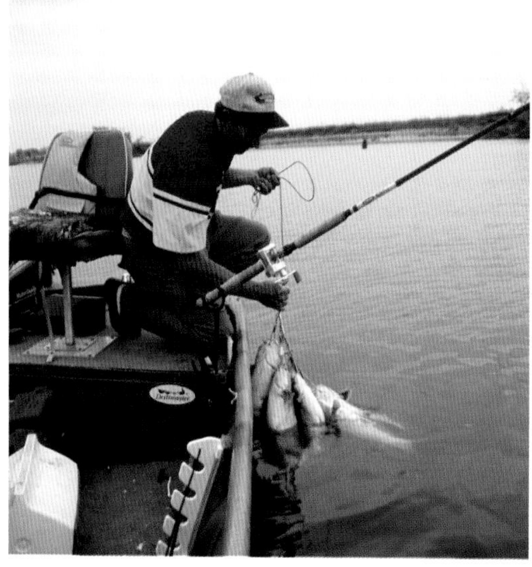

Mississippi catfish guide Phil King uses specialized "finesse" tactics to catch big stringers of river catfish.

I had the pleasure of fishing with Phil and learned a catfishing tactic you could probably apply successfully on almost any big catfish river. It's basically a way of bottom-bouncing baits as you drift, but it's not quite as simple as that description makes it sound. To me, it's a form of "finesse fishing." The angler must develop a keen "feel" for his bait rig to keep in the fish zone without getting hung up.

Rig Right

Let's start with Phil's rigging. This consists of six main components: a three-way swivel, a barrel swivel, a two-ounce bell sinker, two 5/0 Daiichi Circle-Wide Bleeding Bait hooks, and fishing line—sixty-five-pound Berkley Whiplash braid for the main line braid and

sixty-pound Big Game mono off the three-way swivel. The rig is baited with one of two baits: a big bloody chunk of fresh chicken liver or what Phil describes as a "catfish sandwich." The latter is simply the innards of a big skipjack herring sandwiched between two side fillets from the same baitfish.

Presentation

The rig is presented in deep river holes, some dropping below seventy feet. Phil starts at the head of a hole and drifts through after the bait rig has been lowered to the bottom. Most cats hold beside river-bottom timber and rocks, which "telegraph" signals through the braided line to the angler above. The angler must be attentive at all times, raising or lowering the rig with the rod tip so he maintains "feel" with the rig below and keeps it bouncing across the pieces of cover and structures without hanging up.

While drifting, Phil watches a fish finder, looking for signals indicating cats holding near structures below. If he spies good fish that fails to take the bait on the first drift, he may drift through the hole again, targeting those spots that appeared to hold catfish once more.

During the four hours my son Josh and I fished with Phil using this method, we caught scores of blue and channel cats in the five- to twelve-pound range. Bigger specimens eluded us, but

Phil King (right) and the author's son, Josh Sutton, with a nice mess of channel and blue cats caught while "finesse fishing" in the Tennessee River.

Phil has landed blue cats and flatheads up to fifty pounds using this tactic. For the big river angler hoping to catch numbers of cats with an occasional trophy-class fish in the mix, this is a superb technique that's easy to learn.

Wing Dikes and Eddies

On navigable waterways, fishing long rock dikes is the way to success.

The long rock wall jutted from the shore out into the Mississippi River. At the wall's end, the river rolled around on itself to create a huge vortex. It looked like someone had pulled a huge plug from the river bottom and all the water was going down an enormous drain.

We called such maelstroms suckholes when I was a youngster trotlining the river with older relatives. Some call them "whirlpools." James Patterson of Mississippi River Guide Service prefers the term "eddy."

"Drop your bait right at the edge of that eddy," Patterson said, "and free-spool it all the way to the bottom." I did as he suggested, and to my surprise, the big chunk of shad went straight down. The instant the bait touched bottom, before I was quite prepared, something huge grabbed it. And when it did, that something huge nearly snatched the rod from my hands.

Tennessee catfishing guide James Patterson often catches trophy catfish in the swirling waters around Mississippi River wing dams.

I never saw that something huge. It got the best of me, as the big ones often do. I'm quite certain, however, it was a catfish—probably a sizeable blue. And I learned that day that catfish fans who often fish large navigable waterways should study and understand both structures Patterson and I were fishing: wing dikes and eddies.

Wing Dike Facts

The rock walls known as wing dikes are placed in strategic locations to help maintain ship-channel depth and lessen shoreline erosion. They are most numerous in hydropower and navigation dam tailwaters but may be scattered along the entire length of a big river. They fulfill their intended functions by diverting the current. They usually lay perpendicular to shore, and when moving water strikes one, it swirls back on itself. The force of the current then moves outward toward the middle of the river. The water velocity slows, allowing suspended sediments to fall and accumulate on the river bottom.

Inactive catfish typically stay on a wing dike's downstream side lying on the bottom, usually near inshore reaches. Current is minimal here, so rest is possible.

Catfish Positioning on Wing Dikes

Most feeding catfish, especially the more numerous small cats, hold near the river's bottom on a wing dike's upstream side. The reason for this is three-fold. First, water hydraulics here create a "tube" of reduced current near the bottom running the length of the dike. Hungry cats can feed here without using excess energy. Also, this is an abundant food zone with crayfish and mussels in the rocks and shad, herring, and other baitfish holding in the slower cylinder of water. Finally, when the river's high and the wing dike is submerged, catfish can feed on addled or injured forage animals easily captured in the boil-line directly above the rocks and immediately downstream.

You should now understand the basics of wing dike catfishing: to catch lots of eating-sized cats, fish the upstream side. Downstream is rarely as productive.

There is another lesson, however, perhaps even more important: trophy catfish—blues, channels, and flatheads—are best targeted around the eddies near the ends of wing dikes. This I learned from James Patterson, who often fishes around these whirlpools with his clients and who frequently catches monster cats when doing so.

"I don't fish the eddy part of this rotation," Patterson told me the day I hooked something huge. "Instead, I fish the current along the edges. I find that catfish in eddy water are not active. Active cats are along the edges, so that's where I want to anchor and fish."

Baits, Rigs, and Tactics

Like most ardent blue-cat anglers, Patterson relies on two primary baits to entice his quarry. "I use live shad a lot, even though they're hard

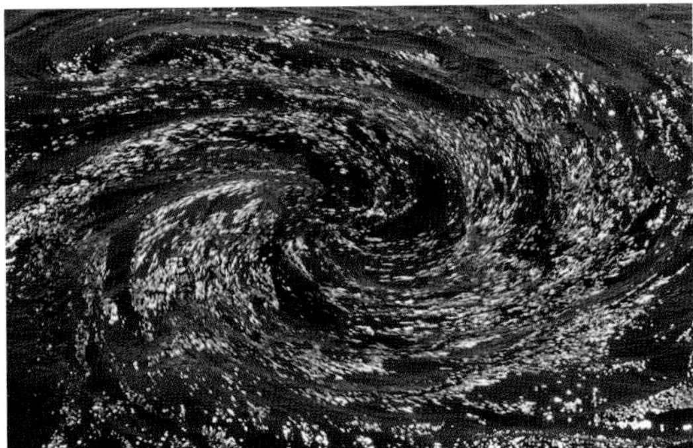

An eddy, or whirlpool, forming at the end of a wing dike. Bait dropped adjacent to this swirling bit of water will sink quickly to the bottom, where it's sure to entice any nearby cat.

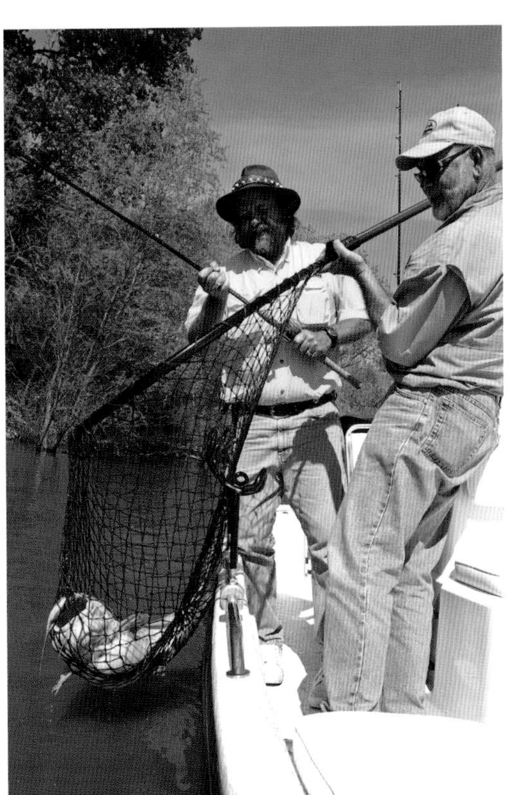

James Patterson (right) nets a nice Mississippi River blue cat author Keith Sutton hooked while fishing near a wing dike.

to find," he says. "Cut skipjack herrings also are good bait."

A simple three-way-swivel rig is Patterson's standard. The two-foot hook leader is tipped with a 3/0 to 7/0 Eagle Claw Kahle hook. The eight-inch weight leader is tied to a three-ounce sinker. His fishing gear consists of "a heavy-action casting rod with a light tip and a lot of butt strength" and a bait-casting reel that holds at least 200 yards of twenty-pound-test line.

"I anchor above the hole I intend to fish," Patterson says, "then cast to the spot and let the reel free-spool until the weight hits bottom. Sometimes I'll have out two hundred feet of line. Blues usually hit hard and quick, so rod holders are necessary if you fish more rods than you can hold."

It would seem that a bait tossed to the edge of one of these huge suckholes would swirl a round and a round. But when done properly, the bait will sink quickly to the bottom and remain stationary. Reposition your rig if necessary to achieve this end, then prepare for the rod-jarring strike that will soon follow if a giant cat is nearby. Often, big cats cruise slowly through a hole waiting for something to jolt their taste buds before they rush in to strike. Allow the bait to sit up to ten minutes, but if there's no bite by then, move and try another eddy hole.

Strikes usually come quick and hard, so use heavy tackle and keep a firm grip on your rod at all times. One moment of inattention could cost you the catfish of lifetime. I learned that lesson the hard way when my "something huge" got away.

Jungle Cats

When cats are hiding in heavy cover, you have to move in with them to enjoy success.

On lakes with little fishing pressure, thick cover doesn't seem to hold any more large catfish than other, more easy-to-fish areas. But on heavily fished lakes, there seems to be a definite correlation between big cats and woody tangles.

There are two primary reasons for this. First, common sense says catfish don't get big by frequenting heavily fished haunts. Most heavyweights get that way by living in out of the way home sites where most anglers don't dare to venture. That's why they haven't already been caught.

Second, big catfish instinctively prefer the protection of heavy cover. Outsized cats are extremely wary and angler-shy, and this contributes to their natural tendency to hide in the most concealed places possible. Dense thickets provide sanctuary from the enemy above.

Jungle cats will still accept an angler's offerings but only on their terms. To be successful, you

When cats are ambushing prey from the thick cover of weed beds and dense timber, the angler may have to use pinpoint fishing tactics to capture his quarry.

must be willing to make a slow, cautious, difficult entry into the flooded jungle.

Jungle Hideouts

Not every patch of thick cover will hold big cats. The best provide easy movement between shallow and deep water. Look for brushpiles, fallen trees, inundated willows and buckbrush, flooded timber, and other dense woody cover along channel drop-offs, underwater humps and holes, the edges of shallow flats, and other fast-breaking structures. Other "jungle" hideouts hold big cats, too, but these are among the best.

One hotspot to investigate is where several trees have washed out and toppled into the water on an outside stream bend. Outside bends usually have deep pockets of water adjacent to a channel break. Add the thick cover provided by branchy underwater treetops, and you have an ideal jungle cat hideout.

Jungle Gear

Heavy line and tackle are a must for this type of fishing. Use at least twenty- to twenty-five-pound-test line and a long stout rod. Strong line is a necessity when hossing big battlewise cats out of these hideaways. You don't want to let a hooked fish fiddle around in the cover. Get it out of there if you can, and let it do its fighting closer to the boat or shore. The long rod gives you a fighting advantage and allows you to better fish dense thickets where casting is virtually impossible.

If you're fishing from a boat, take along a big landing net, too. It's tough getting a giant catfish in a boat under any circumstances, but the right-sized net can help tame your quarry.

Another tip: set your drag just barely below your line's breaking point. You don't want a big brushpile cat peeling off any more line than necessary, or you'll be hung up in an instant.

Jungle Warfare

Now that you're properly armed and on the field of combat, you need to plan the logistics of your attack. Fact is, there's only one way to

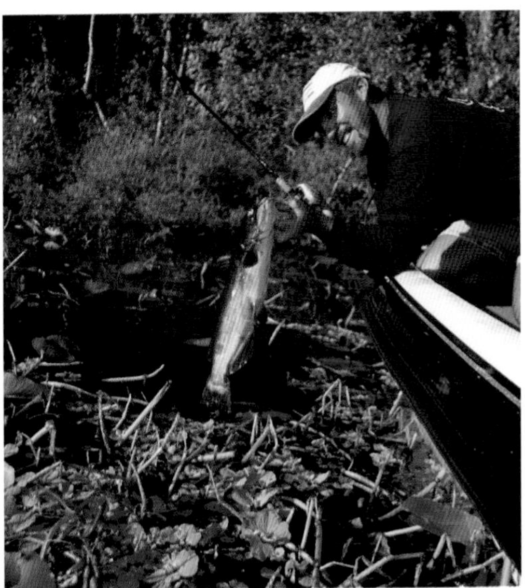

Catfish often bury themselves in thick cover. The angler must move in close and fish his rig in small openings to find success.

go about it: you have to get right in there with them for close-quarters combat.

With a bobber rig, there's less chance of getting snagged beneath the surface. A slip bobber is best because it allows you to reel your entire rig right up to the rod tip. This allows more freedom to work the rig back into cover.

Any standard catfish bait can be used, but for jungle cats, cut shad or carp are hard to beat. Big cats love cutbait, and it won't tangle itself up like live minnows or crawfish. Thread a chunk about two inches square on a 3/0 hook, and unless the current is strong, don't use any weight.

Get within rod's reach of the cover and work slowly and precisely, moving your rig over, under, through, or around the cover until you can ease it down in an opening. You may catch a few nice cats along the edge of the cover but most will be buried in it, striking only when you put the bait right on their nose.

When you do get a strike, react immediately, setting the hook hard and reeling like crazy. You must get a good hookset and pull the fish out of cover before it has time to tie you up. That's why heavy tackle is so important. This battle requires brawn not finesse.

Fishing for jungle cats can be extremely frustrating. You get hung up a lot trying to move your rig into an open pocket. You get hung up when you're in the pocket. Then, if by some miracle you haven't hung yourself up, the cat will do it for you. Only after considerable practice will you overcome these obstacles to your sanity.

The nice thing is, practice makes perfect. And if you stick with it long enough, odds are you'll eventually land one of the biggest catfish you've ever laid eyes on. The safari may exhaust you physically and mentally, but when that fat jungle cat is finally flouncing in the bottom of your boat, you'll know it was worth the extra effort.

Catfish on the Rocks

Rock-covered shores attract catfish searching for meals and spawning sites.

My dictionary defines riprap as "a wall or foundation of broken stones thrown together irregularly." I'd have to go a step further and describe riprap as among the most outstanding yet often overlooked places to catch catfish in a river or lake.

Few other types of shoreline cover hold large numbers of catfish as consistently as does riprap. Put a dozen men on a strange lake and let them all fish different types of structures for one day, and for numbers of fish caught, I'll bet on the guy who picked the riprap. This type of shoreline cover holds catfish year-round.

Targeting the riprapped bank in the background produced this nice Mississippi River blue cat for Oklahoma catfish angler Jeff Williams.

Riprap is a covering of rocks used to reduce shoreline erosion. It provides cover, depth, shade, protection, and food—everything a catfish could desire—making a top fishing area wherever it is found.

Riprap is found on nearly every lake and on many rivers, and when you stop to think about it, you can see why this type of rocky structure is appealing to catfish. One reason is because riprap provides a home for Mr. Whiskers' primary food supplies. Algae grow on the submerged stones. Shad and minnows are attracted to the vegetation. Catfish arrive to eat the baitfish.

Every ten-year-old boy knows that crayfish—a favored forage of cats—thrive under rocks, often in the form of riprap bordering lakes and streams. These rock walls are often the only decent crayfish habitat in an entire lake, and catfish will stack up to feed on these tasty morsels. I've taken cats on riprap with as many as two dozen crayfish in their stomachs.

Another reason riprap provides good catfishing is because the rocks provide good basic habitat structure. There is cover, depth, shade, and protection. Riprap is usually found near deep water since it's most often found around bridges, causeways, or roadways that cross channels or near the dam itself.

Another major plus is that riprap is extensive. Even if you fail to find fish concentrated on a certain spot, you can often cover enough riprap on a river or lake to take home a limit.

Riprap plays a strong role in big-river catfishing simply because there is typically so much of it along the river channel. On the Arkansas River in Arkansas, for instance, there are hundreds of long rock walls known as wing dikes. The US Army Corps of Engineers placed these in strategic locations up and down the McClellan-Kerr Navigation System to help direct water into the main river channel to prevent erosion.

The wing dikes have functioned as they were intended and have also proved to be a boon to the area's summer catfishermen. During June, July, and August, as water temperatures soar, channel, blue, and flathead catfish concentrate along the riprap where there is slight current. Anglers may occasionally take a large trophy catfish along river riprap, but most of these fish weigh ten pounds or fewer.

Tips for Riprap Catfishing

When fishing river riprap for catfish, the first place to begin your search for fish is along the very ends of the rocks. If the catfish aren't there, gradually work your way past other areas along the riprap. Sometimes an unusual feature along the wing dikes will attract and hold a school of catfish.

If you're fishing a long wing dike that is uniform in appearance, look it over, up, and down, keying in on objects or contour changes that distinguish a small section of the wall from its surroundings. Sometimes a tree washed in will be enough to attract catfish. Other times a difference in the rocks will do the trick. Look for spots where big boulders change to smaller rocks. Points, cuts, pipes, and culverts all create something different and may attract catfish.

At the same time you're checking the riprap for these peculiarities, you should check for unusual bottom features with a sonar unit. The alert angler will check closely for a creek channel that borders a wall, submerged humps, a pit, some brush, a submerged roadbed used during the riprap's construction, or some other nuance that might tend to concentrate fish on a structure that may extend for miles.

The author's son, Matt Sutton, brings in a nice channel cat caught on a long stretch of riprapped bank on the Missouri River. The cats were concentrated near the big rock on which Matt stands, one of the few variable structures on an otherwise lookalike stretch of shore.

The rules about fishing the ends of the rocks first and locating unusual features also hold true for riprap on lakes for the same general reasons. Currents and wind-pushed waves washing over the end of a riprap dike create an eddy or calm water zone around the back side of those rocks and at the same time carry food downstream. This is not the case where waves wash straight into the riprap.

While cats don't necessarily hold in this slack-water eddy, they may swim in and out of it, moving over the end of the rocks in the process. Of course, this all depends on current flows and wave force, as well as on the movements of prey items, such as shad. If you've ever observed a school of shad or other baitfish swimming along the rocks, you know they stay in schools that are forever moving. They move up and down the rock walls and around the ends, and catfish often follow.

Bridge riprap can be especially important in lakes. Bridges usually span creeks, rivers, or connecting channels, and the bridge area often represents the deepest water in the area. Fish concentrate near distinctive features such as bridges. This happens as fish are funneled into the narrow section of water where a bridge crosses a lake or reservoir. Also movement between two areas separated by a bridge is restricted to this relatively confined area. Some moving catfish are going to make this area their home or at least remain long enough to feed in the shallows before continuing on. Food is carried through these man-made funnels by current. Catfish take advantage of this and hold out of the flow on the downstream side to check out the selection of groceries washing past.

When fishing bridge riprap, the four corners formed as the riprap bank gives way to the bridge superstructure are always worth a few casts regardless of the presence of other structures. These corners form semi-points that often hold several catfish. The downcurrent points are best, as these are ideal ambush spots for catfish. Cast into the current from a boat stationed on the bridge's downcurrent or downwind side. This allows your bait to move downcurrent in a natural manner.

Under tough windy or post-frontal conditions, bridge riprap may produce catfish when fishing other areas proves fruitless. The feeding habits of bridge-oriented cats seem to be less affected by these conditions than do those of other catfish populations.

During windy weather, bridge riprap excels due to the funnel effect discussed earlier. Wind increases the flow of water and food through the area. Resident catfish react instinctively to the wind and line up to feed on baitfish blown into the rock walls. Also, as the wind throws choppy water on the rocky bank, crayfish are stirred up and become easy pickings for feeding cats. Unless there are safety risks, the riprap angler welcomes a good wind, and so do catfish, especially during hot summer months.

One reason riprap attracts catfish is because it also attracts favored food animals, such as crayfish.

Because bridge-oriented catfish are primarily deep-water residents that move occasionally into the food-filled shallows, weather fronts tend to have less of an adverse effect on them. If the creek or river channel beneath the bridge is fairly deep, catfish can avoid much of the trauma associated with a strong front. Catfish also find shade from harsh post-frontal sunlight around bridge pilings and beneath the superstructure itself. Often by fishing bridge riprap, a catfish angler can avoid most of the post-front doldrums. In any case, bridges and the associated riprap are usually good for a catfish or two under normally adverse conditions.

The Angling Approach

Although catfish fans can and do fish riprap areas from the bank with much success, riprap fishing from a boat allows one to present the bait in a more natural manner. This also enables the angler to work much greater expanses of riprap than would be possible on foot from the shore.

Where's the best place to catfish on a long stretch of lookalike riprap? Look for points in the rocks, areas where big rocks change to smaller rocks, woody cover adjacent the riprap, or anything else that is different from the norm.

The fisherman should position his boat downstream below the end of the rocks and cast upstream. Use only enough weight to keep the bait moving slowly just over the bottom, and allow the bait to come down with the current, following the same natural movement of real food.

Allow the bait to settle near the end of the rocks on some casts and in the eddy zone behind the rocks on others. And if the normal downstream retrieve doesn't produce a fish, cast downcurrent and try retrieving upstream. Just because you don't hook a cat on the downstream retrieve doesn't mean the fish aren't there. Work the rocks carefully to find the best pattern before moving somewhere else.

After working the end of the wing dikes, try making long casts parallel to the rocks, fishing different depths. During the day, catfish will generally hold in deeper water; at night they'll move into the shallows to feed. When the current has swung your line to the end of its arc and it's remaining tight and stationary, allow the bait to stay there for several minutes. Catfish are drawn to food by taste and scent, and moving the bait too soon can lessen your chances of catching fish.

Baits for Riprap

There are as many different baits for catfish as there are catfishermen to use them. Every cat man has his favorite, but some work better than others when fishing riprap.

As mentioned earlier, baitfish and crayfish are at home in this rocky environment, so naturally shad, minnows, and crayfish are the basic bait choices. A three-way rig with the weight and hook on separate lines will save a lot of rerigging. The weights often fall in crevices between rocks, lodging and causing a hang-up. Rig a weight line that's of lesser breaking

Catalpa worms, the larvae of the catalpa sphinx moth, are often gathered from catalpa trees and used by catfishermen targeting riprap catfish.

strength than your main line and hook line, and all you'll lose to a hang-up is your lead.

Some riprap catfishermen use catalpa worms for bait. They're easy to acquire, attractive to catfish, and stay on the hook even in swift water. Night crawlers are always good baits, but when stream fishing, you're apt to catch more drum on them than catfish. Doughbaits don't usually hold to the hook well in current, but sponge baits and dip baits are fantastic for all types of riprap catfishing.

If you're fishing specifically for flatheads, live bait is the only way to go. Small bream, goldfish, or minnows hooked through the lips or behind the dorsal fin can bring smashing strikes. Blue cats seem to prefer cut or whole shad.

Don't overlook artificials for catching catfish. There are many baitfish- and crawfish-imitating crankbaits that will take cats when bounced through the rocks. Deep-diving models work better, as the longer bill helps keep the line from snagging. Riprap catfish also will hit a variety of jigs and spinners.

Riprap offers all the things catfish need for living high on the hog, so it's little wonder you

find so many catfish on the rocks. What is surprising is the number of catfish anglers who overlook riprap as a source of great catfishing. If you're one of those anglers who continues to cruise right past this great structure, stop next time and take a second look at those rocky riprap walls. They may save you a lot of otherwise fishless days.

Cure Bad Habits for Trophy Cats

The catfish may not have lockjaw. It could be the error of your ways that is preventing you from catching them.

"What can I do to catch more trophy catfish?"

Many anglers want a simple answer to that question, but unfortunately, there's rarely one to be found. I've been chasing catfish for decades and have learned that no magic formula ensures success every time we fish for big blues, flatheads, and channel cats.

One thing is certain, though; when we're having an unproductive fishing day, as often as not it's due to our own errors—not because trophy catfish are exceptionally evasive or tight-lipped.

The cure? Do some self-analysis and determine if you're missing fish because of bad habits. This chapter will help you do that.

Bad habit #1: Using the wrong bait.
Remember that kid Mikey in the old Life cereal commercials? His friends try the new breakfast food on this freckle-faced youngster because they say, "He'll eat anything."

Many anglers think catfish are like Mikey. They believe no matter what food is on the table or river bottom, catfish will eat it. In fact, many folks believe catfish behave like underwater vultures, cleaning lake and river bottoms of carrion and garbage. Consequently, they say, it matters not what type of bait you use for catfish, and indeed, the more rotten and smelly the bait, the more likely a big catfish will find and eat it.

To some extent, they're right. Catfish are scavengers and aren't really picky about their food. But this applies primarily to small catfish.

For example, I've caught thousands of channel and blue cats on homemade and commercial stinkbaits. But fish caught using prepared baits are usually fewer than five pounds. Trophy specimens are rarely enticed with our favorite stinkbaits.

Consider flatheads, as well. Small ones will hit prepared baits, crawfish, worms, and other enticements without hesitation. If it's heavyweights you're seeking, however, these baits don't work so well. A meat and potatoes meal for a giant flathead is another fish—a live fish—such as a

Anglers must use the right baits when targeting trophy catfish, or their efforts will fail. For example, a live herring such as this is an ideal bait for a trophy flathead, but dead baits, grocery baits, and commercial baits rarely entice heavyweights of this species.

bullhead, chub, sucker, or sunfish. Trophy flatheads rarely eat anything except live fish.

The bottom line is this, and scientific studies have shown it to be so: a catfish twenty-four inches or longer, regardless of species, sustains itself on a diet comprised almost exclusively of other fish. For flatheads, this means live fish. Trophy blues and channel cats will devour dead baits, too, but even so, the best dead baits are fresh baits. A chunk of rotten, smelly shad or herring won't work nearly as well as a chunk cut from a just-caught baitfish.

Remember these things when fishing. If you want to catch lots of catfish up to twenty-four inches long, almost any bait from chicken liver to worms will work. But if it's trophies you're after, you'll improve your chance of hooking up if you use fresh or live fish baits.

Bad habit #2: Failure to use tactics specific to species and locale.

A catfish is a catfish is a catfish, right? This is another way of saying all catfish are alike, and tactics that work for one species work for all. Many anglers fish as if this were so, but it is not.

The author yanked this nice flathead from its hiding place in dense cover using a live fish bait. Targeting each species of catfish in the right place using the right bait is key to the angler's success.

Each catfish species exhibits behaviors specific to that species. Consequently, we must gear our tactics toward the particular species we hope to catch to enjoy success.

For example, trophy blue cats behave much like striped bass. They feed primarily on shad, herring, and other schooling highly mobile baitfish. Consequently, big blues are more migratory than other cats and more frequently found in open-water habitats.

While big blues and channel cats often congregate in loose schools containing several trophy-class individuals, flatheads are more solitary fish. Rarely will you catch more than one trophy flathead in a single fishing hole. Flatheads are cover lovers, as well, hiding in brush, log piles, and cavities to ambush prey. Channel cats and blues sometimes do this, too, but not as frequently as their big brown cousins.

Flatheads almost always are caught in or near some type of dense cover, while blues and channel cats most often are not.

These are just two examples showing species behavior differences. Space does not permit an in-depth dissertation here. Yet knowing just these things, we can immediately improve our odds for success.

For example, let's say we're fishing a reservoir bristling with sizeable flatheads but few blue cats. If we fish offshore structures, such as river channels and humps—a productive means for busting big blues—we might fish years without catching a trophy catfish because the more abundant flatheads rarely if ever use these habitats. If we focused our efforts on nearshore cover, such as laydowns and drift piles, however, we might quickly find success—if we use live baits—because big flatheads love these spots.

To use another example, let's say we're fishing a big river with healthy populations of all three major catfish species. If the only bait we have is cutbait, and we spend our time fishing near dense shoreline cover, we reduce our chances of catching a trophy fish because flatheads, which prefer live bait, are the predominant species here. If we move offshore, however, and use our fish-finder to locate big fish holding near shad schools around bottom structures, our success rate should improve because this is the realm of trophy-class blues and channel cats, which love cutbait.

The concept I'm trying to get across is simple, really. We must target the predominant species of catfish in each body of water using tactics specific to that species. And to do this, we must learn the specific behavior patterns exhibited by big blue, channel, and flathead catfish. Failure to do so will lead to frustration because trophy cats will be caught by chance and not by design. And when we leave things up to chance, the odds for success rarely fall in our favor.

Anglers should never lose sight of the fact that catfish are easily repelled by things such as insect repellent, gasoline, tobacco, and sunscreen. If even a minute quantity touches the bait, a catfish won't bite.

Bad habit #3: Ignoring the catfish's extraordinary sensory abilities.

This bad habit is one of the most prevalent, yet few anglers realize an inability to catch trophy catfish may be caused by something as commonplace as applying sunscreen or casting a shadow across our fishing hole. Let me explain.

Catfish have turbo-charged senses. Take taste, for example. When it comes to this sense, no creature on earth can compare. A catfish has dense concentrations of taste buds all over its body and not just in the mouth. The densest concentrations are on the gill rakers, so the fish can taste things in the water flowing over the gills. But taste buds cover the outside of the catfish, as well—whiskers, fins, back, belly, sides, and even the tail.

The catfish's olfactory sense is amazingly keen, as well. Without going into a lot of anatomical details, let's just say they can smell some compounds at the incredibly low concentration of one part per ten billion parts of water. That's how acute this sense is. And the sense of taste has a comparable level of acuteness.

These powerful senses enable catfish to thrive in turbid water and various areas where other fish cannot. A catfish can zero in on food even without the benefit of sight, using only the senses of smell and taste.

These sensory abilities also benefit anglers because they help catfish find the angler's bait even in adverse conditions.

What many people don't consider is the fact that catfish also can easily detect things in the water they don't like, and these compounds can be tasted and smelled by catfish even in extremely minute quantities. According to scientists who've studied catfish senses, such turn-offs include gasoline and ingredients found in commonly used products, such as sunscreen, tobacco, and insect repellent. It stands to reason, then, if you apply sunscreen or insect repellent with your hands or accidentally get gas on yourself and later handle bait with your hands, you may be repelling the catfish you're hoping to catch. Your catch rate will improve if you avoid contact with such materials as much as possible.

Other senses can work against anglers, as well. For example, catfish have very good eyesight despite popular misconceptions. And while they do not rely on this sense as much in waters where visibility is limited, it plays a key role in their behavior in waters that are clear.

Did you know, for instance, that catfish will spook when a shadow crosses the water? Biologists learned this while conducting lab experiments that could be fouled up for weeks simply because someone put their hand over the top of an aquarium. This may be of no concern to a catfish angler fishing muddy water because fish in muddy water don't see shadows from above. When fishing clear water, however, you'll rarely catch a cat while fishing beneath your boat or in water upon which you're casting a shadow. That's one reason many catfishermen are more successful at night—no shadows. And it's a good reason to always keep the sun in your face or to your side, not at your back, to avoid casting a shadow on the water you're fishing.

Here's another fact you may not have known. The lateral line and advanced hearing system of a catfish help it detect low-frequency sound vibrations. Creatures scurrying across the bottom, flopping at the surface, swimming through the water, or walking along shore all create low-frequency vibrations catfish can sense. This "vibrational" sense is so keen, some cultures have used catfish for centuries to warn of earthquakes.

This is not a problem for savvy anglers who fish with a measure of stealth. But go stomping along the shore, and you can spook catfish—including big catfish—even when you're many yards away. And the sound of a dropped paddle or sinker is like a warning siren to your quarry.

Knowing these things, you can see why it's very important to be aware of the catfish's extraordinary sensory abilities at all times. If you don't, your catch rate will fall.

Bad habit #4: Fishing only on the bottom. Catfish are well-adapted for feeding on the bottom of rivers, lakes, and ponds, but if you think they never feed at mid-depths or on the surface, you're wrong. Trophy blue and channel cats often suspend at mid-depths to prey on baitfish, such as shad and herring. And at times when frogs are plentiful, for example, big cats will come to the surface to gobble up their dinner. Working a live frog topside is one of the best of all ways to catch a channel cat weighing more than twenty pounds.

If bottom fishing doesn't produce a bite within a reasonable time, watch for surface activity—particularly in summer and near dawn or dusk—that indicates fish are taking their food at the surface, or watch your sonar for suspended fish and use a float rig to present bait at the proper level.

Bad habit #5: Fishing only during summer.

For some reason, many people associate catfishing with summer. In fact, many aficionados restrict their fishing to this season alone. There's nothing wrong with this; lots of trophy cats are caught by anglers during hot weather. Summer, however, is not necessarily the best season for catching heavyweight whiskerfish. Anglers who learn to find and pattern catfish during other seasons often discover the bite is even better when the water and the weather are cooler.

Those who regularly catch trophy blue cats often do so by fishing deep ledges in winter. Normally sedentary flatheads roam and feed ravenously during high water in spring and again in autumn prior to entering a period of winter torpor. Channel cats bite spring, summer, fall, and winter. Ice fishermen often catch them.

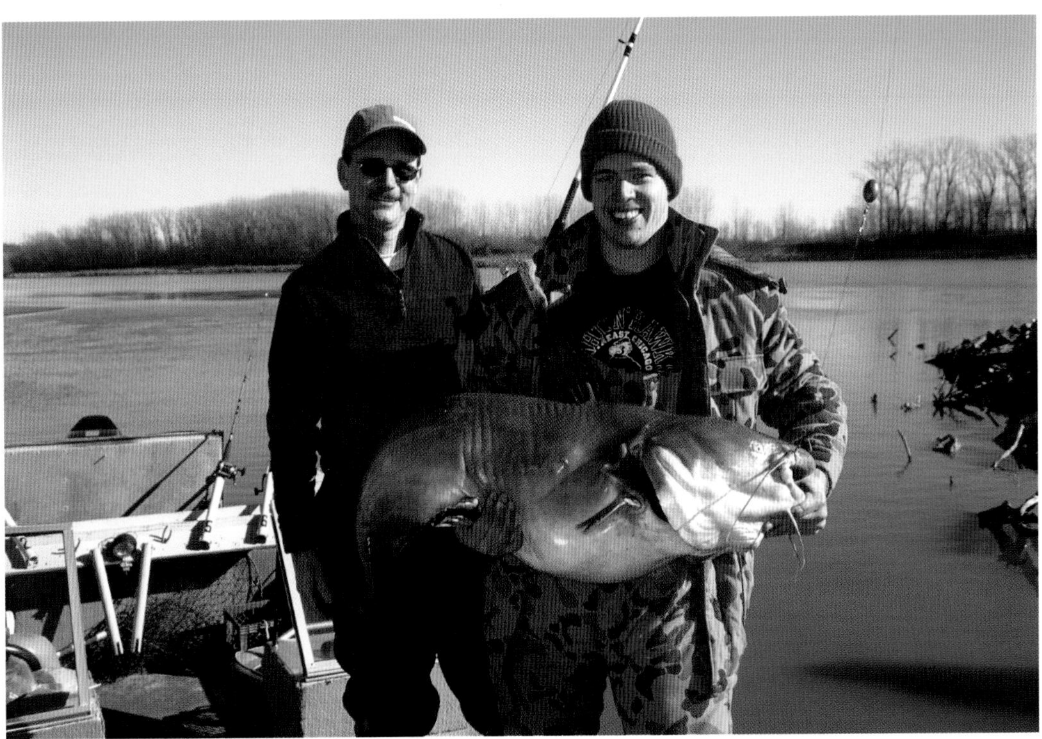

Many anglers associate catfishing with the hot summer months, but other seasons may be more productive for trophy cats such as this big winter blue.

The worst time to fish? During the spawn, which usually peaks in early summer. Egg-laying females and nest-guarding males are in cavities and may not feed at all for a period of days or weeks.

Conclusion

At times, nothing we do can entice a trophy catfish to bite. For reasons we don't fully understand, big fish often become inactive and darn near impossible to catch.

It's important to remember, though, that a poor catch rate may be totally unrelated to the level of catfish activity. Frequently, it's just a result of our own bad habits. To increase the odds of hooking a beefy blue, channel cat, or flathead, examine your tactics now and then, and be sure you're doing everything correctly to the best of your ability. Getting rid of bad habits may be the best way of all to ensure success when you hope to catch a trophy.

More Bad Habits

Using dull hooks buried in bait. Many cat fans don't have problems finding fish, yet they're continually frustrated when they can't hook those that bite. To cure this problem, always fish with sharp, exposed hooks. Run the hook point over a fingernail. Sharp hooks dig in. Those that skate across the nail without catching should be honed or replaced. And instead of burying your hook in bait, leave the barb exposed. Catfish won't notice. More hookups will result.

Using the wrong rig. It's important to learn a variety of rigs and use each when appropriate. A simple egg-sinker rig may work great in a pond but not a river. Drift rigs may be needed when cats are scattered and hard to find. A specialty rig, such as the float-paternoster, is best when fishing large live baits. Learn more rigs, catch more cats.

No sonar. A sonar fish-finder helps pinpoint big catfish on structures and cover you'd otherwise miss. Buy one, learn to use it, and use it often.

Fishing the wrong waters. Trophy catfish seldom come from creeks, ponds, and small lakes. It happens occasionally but not enough to merit your attention. When seeking a true heavyweight, focus your fishing efforts on large rivers and lakes.

Lack of persistence. Persistence is one of the most important qualities of those who frequently catch trophy catfish. Anyone can learn the tactics necessary for catching cats, but to catch trophy fish, you must keep bait in the water where the big ones swim. Learn everything you can about a lake or river where you know those big fish are. Then stay at it, day after day after day, learning more. Catfishermen who do that have the best chance of catching the catfish of a lifetime.

Section VIII

Alternative Tactics

Jug Fishing

You'll be hard-pressed to find a form of catfishing more fun than jug fishing.

"Thar she blows!"

When a big catfish pulls a jug under, the call rings out. The fish isn't as big as Moby Dick, of course, but this is as close to whaling as you can get in a river or lake.

My fishing buddy paddles hurriedly, trying to pull our johnboat alongside the speeding milk jug. The catfish pulling the jug wants no part of this. The jug sounds and then reappears twenty feet away.

My friend moves fast. This time, we reach the jug before it submerges. I swing a big landing net beneath it and bring up a ten-pound channel cat, our third of the afternoon. Before it's unhooked, another jug cuts a wake across the river.

"Thar she blows again!"

For pure country boy fun, nothing equals jug fishing for cats. Decades ago, folks called it "blocking" because blocks of wood were used to float the participants' catfishing rigs. Nowadays, empty milk or soda jugs are more likely to be used. Save a few, tie on some line, add hooks, bait 'em up, and you're ready to jug fish. The only other necessities are a boat, a paddle or trolling motor for pursuing your

Jug fishing is a simple, old-fashioned method of catfishing that can provide long hours of fun and excitement.

quarry, and a big net for landing the cats you hook. You can fish with jugs in any body of water where catfish live from small ponds to big rivers and lakes.

Making Jug Rigs

Any narrow-necked plastic container with a tight-fitting lid can be used. I prefer one- to two-liter soda bottles. When sprayed with fluorescent orange, chartreuse, or black paint, they're easy to see, and most catfish can't hold one under too long. The latter characteristic is important because you want the jug to exhaust the catfish enough that you can more easily net the fish.

I rig each jug with soft Dacron or braided line because it doesn't get as loopy and hard to handle as monofilament. Use fifty-pound-test or more in case you hook a whopper. Tie directly to the jug's handle or neck if you like, but jugs tip up better, signaling strikes, if you attach line to the cap instead. Do this by drilling a small hole through the cap, running the line through the cap from outside to in, and tying to a small metal washer on the inside so the line won't pull back through. Screw the cap back on, and you're ready.

Tie plenty of line to each jug, then lengthen or shorten it as needed. Do this by wrapping line around the jug and securing it with tape or a rubber band or by loosening the washer and stuffing line inside the jug. The latter method is best if you want the jugs to tip up when a cat takes the bait.

For cats up to fifteen pounds, I use one or two 1/0 to 3/0 circle hooks, which usually impale the fish in the corner of the mouth. Two hooks rigged tandem, one above the other, allow you to test different depths. When trophy cats are targeted, I prefer 5/0 or larger circle hooks that

A coating of brightly colored paint improves the visibility of jugs used for floats.

accommodate larger baits. Each hook must be needle sharp.

It's sometimes helpful to tie a bell sinker above or below each hook to hold the bait near bottom and to slow movement of the jugs when it's windy. Add your favorite bait—fish pieces, night crawlers, hot dogs, stinkbait chunks, etc.—then release the jugs several feet apart and let them drift in the breeze or current. Check regulations for jug fishing restrictions before you go, and limit the number of jugs you use so you can properly watch them and be sure none are lost and left to litter the lake or river.

Float your rigs near catfish-attracting structures and cover for more hookups, but always fish several feet away from tree tops and rocks so your jugs won't snag. Follow at a distance so you don't spook fish, but be ready to react the moment you see action.

Ready for Action

Each jug functions like a big fishing bobber. When a catfish bites, the jug stops and bobs. When the bait is swallowed, one of two things happens—the jug zips away across the water or it disappears beneath the surface. This is where the fun really starts.

Move in as fast as you can and try to grab the jug, dip a landing net beneath it, or snag the line with a long pole that has a hook on the end. When using your hands, grab the jug but never the line. If you grab the line, you could get tangled or cut. If you've hooked a small catfish, you probably won't have much trouble. But when a big cat takes the bait, the jug may sound then pop up several yards away time and time again before you get close enough to snare the rig. Spooked catfish may surge away every time you get near. For this reason, it's best to take a buddy each time you go jug fishing. One of you paddles or operates the motor during the pursuit. The other stands ready to capture the fleeing cat. Both wear life jackets, in case of an unexpected spill.

Fishing with Pool Noodles

A modernized method of jug fishing employs floats made from the long, hollow, closed-foam noodles that kids float on in swimming pools. These signal a strike better than regular jugs because when a fish takes your bait, the noodle stands up and waves around.

Cut one five-foot noodle into three twenty-inch floats. Drill a hole through each noodle from one side to the other about four inches from one end. Make the hole large enough to accommodate a piece of plastic drinking straw or metal tubing as long as the noodle is wide. Run the straw or tubing through the hole. This serves as a protective sleeve that keeps your fishing line from cutting through the foam when a fish is on.

Next, cut a four-foot piece of stout fishing line. Run it through the sleeve, and tie the line securely around the noodle. To the line's lower end, tie a three-way swivel. To the swivel's bottom eye, tie another piece of line six feet long. Add a hook and sinker to this. To the other eye of the swivel, tie a two-foot leader line with a hook on the end. Rigged this way, you can fish two baits at different depths, which should increase your catch.

If you're "noodling" at night, add reflective tape around each noodle's top so it shines when a flashlight beam hits it.

When the noodles aren't in use, just wrap the line around each one and plant the barbs of the

Empty plastic bottles aren't the only floats used for jug fishing. Many anglers now use foam pool noodles to make highly effective and inexpensive rigs.

Pool noodle floats can be stored in a milk crate or box until use.

hooks in the foam to keep everything in place. You can place a dozen or more in a plastic crate or big garbage bag for carrying. Then when you get to the lake or river, all you have to do is unroll the lines, bait the hooks, and drop the noodle rigs in the water.

Good baits include night crawlers, minnows, chunk-style commercial baits, and pieces of hot dogs.

Jug fishing is a simple way to catch catfish, tailor-made for children and adults who never grew up. Load up this season and give it a try. For high-level excitement and downright fun, nothing beats jug fishing.

Yo-yo Fishing

For some fast-paced catfishing fun, try this specialized form of limblining.

Billy "Toothpick" Blakley reminded me how much fun playing with yo-yos can be.

We were supposed to be catching the giant bluegills inhabiting Tennessee's Reelfoot Lake. Unfortunately, the bluegills played hard to get. After a long almost-fishless morning, I suggested to Toothpick, who is a fishing guide at Blue Bank Resort, that we do something different.

"How 'bout yo-yos?" he inquired.

"What?" I asked.

"Yo-yos," he said. "Let's go yo-yoing."

Don't misunderstand. Toothpick wasn't talking about walking the dog or doing a sleeper with my Duncan yo-yo. In the South, if a grown man asks you to go yo-yoing, he's not asking you to play with a kid's toy. In this region, adults probably yo-yo a lot more than kids nowadays. The difference is, the kids are playing and the adults are fishing, although there are those who maintain the two are one and the same.

White's Auto-Fisher

In fishing parlance, yo-yo is a nickname for the Automatic Fishing Reel, or Auto-Fisher, a neat little mechanical device patented on July 12, 1949 by John W. White Jr., a native of Arkansas. White had the notion that if a fisherman can

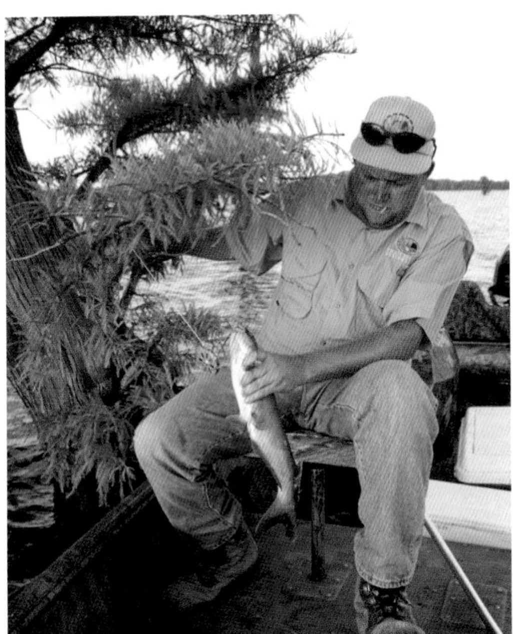

Billy "Toothpick" Blakley brings in a nice channel cat taken on a yo-yo in Tennessee's Reelfoot Lake. The low-hanging branches of cypress trees make ideal anchor points for these automatic fishing devices.

use ten times as many hooks, chances are he can catch ten times as many fish. Multihook trotlines weren't to his liking because they are too restrictive. He preferred to pick several individual hotspots and fish all of them at once, so using individual fishing units was the only answer.

White's original prototype incorporated the spring-loaded end of an old window shade. It consisted of a carbon-steel spring, a galvanized steel reel, a ratchet, and a body to hold it all together. Interestingly, the only important change over the years came when White began painting Auto-Fishers fluorescent orange so they could be spotted more easily at a distance.

The Auto-Fisher's "yo-yo" nickname makes sense when you see one in action. A length of nylon line is stored on the spring-loaded reel. The line runs through a metal ear with a hole in it, and a snap swivel and hook are placed on the line's end. If you pull on the line's end, the reel turns, and line comes out. If you release the line, it snaps back, rewound on the spool by the action of the spring. The line stops rewinding when the swivel becomes seated against the metal ear.

Placing and Setting Yo-yos

Yo-yos usually are hung singly from tree limbs, docks, poles, or other stable objects above the water. The hook is baited first, then line is pulled off the retractable spool, and a catch, or trigger, is set in a notch on the spool to hold the line at the preferred depth. When a fish takes the bait, the catch is released, and the spring tension pulls the line tight. This sets the hook in the fish's mouth. The fish is then fighting the spring, and it is eventually worn down. The

The line on a yo-yo can be lengthened or shortened to suit various fishing situations.

spring tension can be set at hard, medium, or light. The yo-yoer comes around periodically to remove his catch and reset the lines.

With the help of two friends, Toothpick and I set out seventy-five yo-yos. Reelfoot Lake provides an ideal setting for yo-yo fishing thanks to the abundance of cypress trees growing out in the lake. Each cypress has low-hanging branches where the yo-yos can be attached, and because the trees grow in clusters, you can set dozens of yo-yos where they all can be watched.

Yo-yo Baits

Toothpick prefers night crawlers or other earthworms above other baits.

"Small channel cats are abundant in Reelfoot," he told me. "And experience has shown me that worms are as good a bait as any when you're after small cats for the dinner table. You can buy a couple of hundred worms at any bait store for a pretty reasonable price, and that's plenty when you're fishing a few dozen yo-yos."

Select your bait based on the type of catfish you want to catch. Worms are excellent for small channel cats, but equally productive baits include chicken liver, catalpa worms, crawfish, stinkbaits, and minnows. Live fish baits—minnows, goldfish, small sunfish, etc.—are best for flatheads. Blue cats fall for cut shad or herring.

Toothpick and I tied each yo-yo to a branch near the water, baited the hook, then stripped off enough line to keep the baits four feet or so beneath the water. Although the swivels at each line's end were ample to weight the baits we used, some yo-yo fishermen add big split shot or other weights to keep their baits down, particularly when fishing areas with current.

In the cypress groves we fished, baits placed nearest to each tree's trunk produced best. Initially, some yo-yos were placed near the trunk, others at the ends of branches several feet away from the trunk. When we determined that in-close yo-yos were producing more cats, we moved the outer devices closer to the trunks.

Proper Placement and Tracking

"Just because you have a lot of hooks in the water doesn't mean you're going to catch a lot of catfish," Toothpick said. "It's important to place each hook in a spot where catfish are likely to be feeding. Experimenting with different presentations can help you determine the best spots on a particular day, but it's important to learn the specific types of cover and structure catfish prefer in order to be a successful yo-yo fisherman time and time again. If you place your rigs in fishless water, you won't catch fish, simple as that."

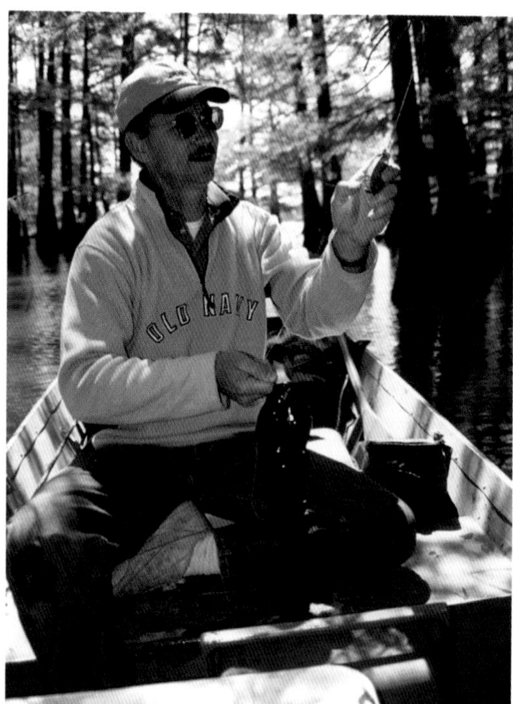

Fishing with yo-yos allows the angler to choose several prime fishing locales and fish them all at once.

At times, you may be able to place and set all your yo-yos before the catfish start biting. But at other times, you'll be setting one out when you hear a catfish fighting the line on another one you already baited. Toothpick and I experienced the latter. Before we had placed all seventy-five of our yo-yos, we had already caught ten nice channel cats.

"It's important to monitor your yo-yos closely in order to avoid exceeding the creel limit," Toothpick says. And always practice selective harvest. Keep smaller cats for eating, and release the big guys to maintain the trophy stock.

The popularity of yo-yos is easy to understand. Many fishermen use them to stock their freezers for the winter at times when the fishing is at its best. Lots of fish can be taken quickly with yo-yos, and sometimes, time is of the essence. Using yo-yos is a good way to gather the makings for a fish fry, especially when only one man is responsible for obtaining the supply.

Fishing with yo-yos is pure unadulterated fun. You can't "walk the dog" with a White's Auto-Fisher, but you can "catch the cat." Try it and see.

Yo-yoing the Right Way

Yo-yos are illegal in some states. In other states, there are numerous restrictions on yo-yo fishing. In my home state of Arkansas, for example, it is illegal to suspend more than one yo-yo from any horizontal line, wire, limb, or support. It also is unlawful to leave yo-yos unattended (out of sight or hearing), except from sunset to sunrise when each yo-yo is clearly marked with the name and address of the user.

Always know your local regulations and abide by them.

There is an effort underway by some irate anglers to have yo-yos banned altogether. This is largely due to a small group of slob fishermen who don't properly attend their yo-yos. An unattended yo-yo can be a hazard to fishermen, and if left unchecked, many fish are hooked and die, a lamentable waste. Yo-yo fishermen can help eliminate the opposition to this enjoyable sport by following regulations, removing their catch as soon as possible, and removing all yo-yos following every outing.

Keeping Track

Keeping track of all the yo-yos you have out is important. Common sense requires it because you don't want to leave a yo-yo unattended where your catch will die and spoil. In some states, the law requires you to set all your yo-yos in a small area so they can be watched constantly.

When I fish with yo-yos, I track those I have out by several methods. First, I try to set all my yo-yos along a straight line course—along a river bank, along the edge of a tree line, etc. That way I don't have to look all over the place for my sets. I follow a straight line from one end of my sets to the other then back again. Each yo-yo is placed in sight of the one before it. And each time I run my yo-yo line, I count the devices to be sure none have been missed.

A splotch of fluorescent paint sprayed on each yo-yo helps immensely when you're trying to spot them, or you can tie a small piece of flagging tape to the end of each branch on which a yo-yo is suspended. When I'm finished fishing, I count my yo-yos again to be sure none are missing. I never leave a yo-yo behind and neither should you.

Yo-yo Tips

- Most successful yo-yoers agree conditions are best in spring when ravenous catfish are more likely to be roaming the shallows.
- Green timber flooded by spring overflows is an especially productive place to fish with yo-yos.
- When fishing waters with few overhanging limbs, carry a hammer and some sixteen-penny nails. Drive nails into stumps and logs—never into live trees—and hang your yo-yos there. Remove the nails when you leave.
- Try tying a yo-yo beneath each jug when jug fishing. You'll get a higher percentage of hook sets, but you'll have to use two-liter jugs or bigger.
- Some yo-yo fishermen prefer lively fish, frogs, or salamanders rigged on short lines so they wiggle and thrash right at the water's surface. Tie to your anchor point, then pull out enough line to keep the baited hook just below the top of the water. This is a deadly setup for attracting hungry catfish.
- When rigged with appropriately sized hooks and baits, yo-yos can be used to catch crappie, bluegills, and other sportfish in addition to catfish. Check local regulations for restrictions.

Make Your Own Trotline

Trotlining is more exciting than you think. Don't knock it till you've tried it.

"I don't understand why anyone would want to trotline for catfish," a friend says. "It can't be very exciting. You run a long line through a hole, bait it, and then just leave it there. You don't even feel the fish bite."

I pointed out to my narrow-minded friend that despite such misconceptions, trotlining is one of the most exciting and time-honored methods of catfishing. No, you don't feel the fish strike. No, you don't experience the bend

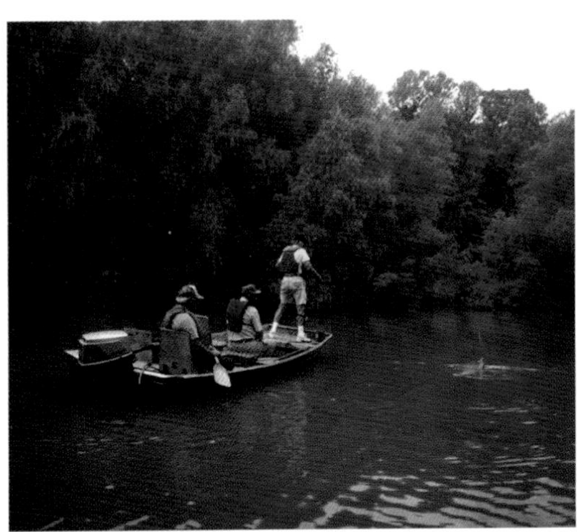

Some anglers can't imagine how trotlining could possibly be fun. But those who enjoy this time-honored method of catfishing say it can be just as exciting as catching a cat on rod and reel.

of the rod over a heavy fish. But trotlining offers its own special brand of excitement.

Adrenaline starts pumping as you paddle to your line. You shine your spotlight through the darkness, and when your marker is spotted, you make your way to one end of the set. Will the line hold any cats? How many will there be? Could this be the time when a monster will surface? The questions nag you as you lift the line and grab it.

You feel vibrations running through the trotline like an electric current. Yes, a cat has been caught—perhaps several cats. Your adrenaline rises even more as you pull your way past the empty hooks toward the one that holds your quarry.

Suddenly the water boils. The way it boils lets you know this is no little fish. To make such a disturbance, its tail must be the size of a Frisbee. You pull your way closer, and the catfish yanks hard against the line, almost ripping it from your hands. Your heart races. Beads of cold sweat run into your eyes.

Suddenly the water erupts, and you must brace yourself with a foot against the gunwale to keep from going in. You hold tight, keeping careful eye on the hooks dangling from the line and wondering all the while if it is possible to bring the monster in. The fish is thrashing the water, soaking you and your fishing partner and letting you know in no uncertain terms that it will not be taken without a fight.

Yes, my friends, trotlining is exciting. It is always exciting because it is shrouded in mystery and expectation. What's out there beneath the inky black surface of the water? What will you find when you lift the line? Sometimes it's nothing more than a few eating-sized cats. But that's OK. That's why you're there in the first place—to gather the makings for a fish fry. Still, you never know for sure what will surface next.

Giant blue cats, flatheads, and channel cats all fall for trotlining tactics. And as you might expect, heavyweight cats are much easier to subdue using the sturdy line and hooks of a trotline than with rod-and-reel outfits, which usually are unsuited for fishing lines heavier than fifty- to eighty-pound-test. Hook a sixty- to seventy-five-pound flathead in heavy cover and fast water, and it'll snap eighty-pound line like sewing thread. Hook it on a trotline made with 200-pound droplines and a 600-pound main line, and you might have a chance to land it.

Homemade Trotlines, Griffin Style

Ready-made trotlines can be purchased at many tackle distributors, or you can make your own like Ralph Griffin of Jonesboro, Arkansas. Like most dyed-in-the-wool trotliners, Ralph custom-makes all his lines, shunning inferior-quality, store-bought trotlines that come prepackaged and ready to fish. He shared with me his simple yet effective method for creating a sturdy and inexpensive trotline.

Ralph Griffin nets a dandy cat caught on a trotline in the Mississippi River. Although trotlines are frowned upon by some in the catfishing fraternity, their use dates back more than a century in this country, and where legal, they provide a fun means for catching numbers of nice cats.

Trotlines have numerous hooks, and several catfish may be caught each time the line is checked. Anglers should keep only the smaller fish they catch and only as many as they need to eat. It's important, as well, to follow special regulations regarding trotlines and to remove all lines after each use so they don't present a hazard to boaters and other anglers.

"For the main line, I prefer #60 tarred nylon seine twine I purchase from Memphis Net & Twine," he said. "The coated line is more durable, and this size is heavy enough to hold big cats yet has the proper diameter for easy rigging."

This line is rated at 558-pound-test and costs about $5 per one-pound spool. "A one-pound spool is adequate to make one twenty- to twenty-five-hook line," Ralph continued. "All the lines I use have twenty-five hooks or less. The overall length of each line is determined by the size of the fishing area I want to cover with it."

To prevent catfish from twisting off, Ralph attaches 1/0 stainless-steel barrel swivels directly to the main line. This is done by doubling a section of the main line between your fingers to form a loop six to eight inches long. Tie an overhand knot in the upper part of the loop to maintain the loop on the main line. Then run the end of the loop through the eye of a swivel and pass it over the end of the swivel. Cinch it tight with the swivel centered in the loop.

Droplines or "stagings"—short lines from which the hooks hang—are attached to the swivels. Ralph makes each one from a piece of #18 nylon line (170-pound-test) cut twelve to sixteen inches long.

"Each piece of line is doubled so the tag ends are together," Ralph instructs, "then you tie an overhand knot where the tag ends are and tighten it. Now, push a piece of this smaller line through the bottom eye of a swivel, pull it through, and loop it back through itself. When you draw it tight, you have a hanging loop of line six to eight inches long where you'll attach a hook."

Ralph prefers 5/0 stainless steel Limerick hooks. "This is just the right size for most of

As a safety precaution, the trotliner often wears a knife on his leg or keeps it in another easily accessible location. Should he somehow become hooked or entangled in the line, the knife might be a lifesaver.

the fish we catch," he notes. "I use pliers to twist each hook slightly, so the barbed end is turned outward from the shank. I believe this increases the number of catfish I hook. The hooks must have large eyes that allow a doubled piece of #18 line to be pushed through them."

Each hook is attached by passing a dropline loop through the front of the hook's eye then looping it down around the hook point. The loop is cinched snug against the hook shank, and you're ready to rig another dropline and another and another until your line is the length you want it. The droplines should be spaced five to six feet apart along the main line.

Number and Placement of Lines

To increase the chance of success, Ralph often uses six or more lines all placed in areas he's scouted to identify as catfish hideouts. I have accompanied him on many days to run his lines. His lines usually stretch from willows and other shoreline anchor points out into the river perpendicular to the current. The end of each is attached to a heavy weight to keep the current from swinging it into the bank. Because the trotlines are usually stretched from shallow water into deep, they cover a variety of water levels.

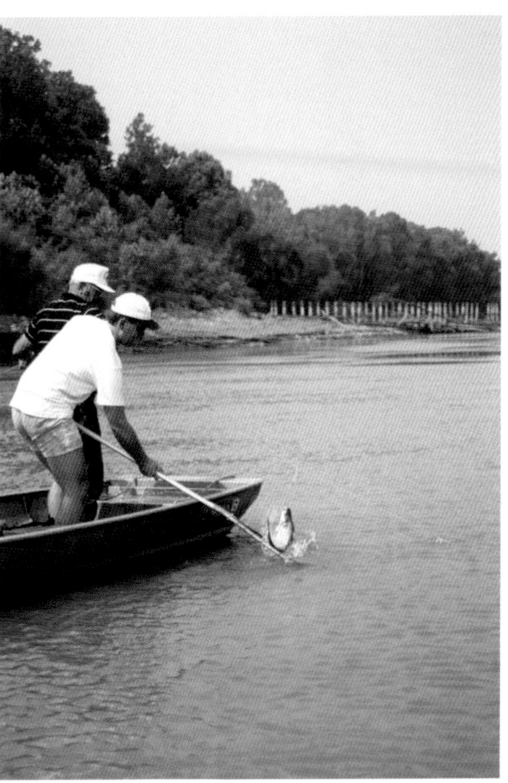

When checking a trotline, it's safer if you have another person to assist you. Dealing with multiple hooks on a weighted line can be dangerous if it's not done properly.

"With the lines set that way," Ralph says, "at least some of the hooks are going to be at the level catfish are feeding. If cats are feeding shallow, most of my catch will be on the shallow end of the lines. If more cats are feeding deep, the opposite will be true."

Ralph baits his lines with live fish. Goldfish or carp are preferred because they remain lively on the hook for extended periods, but shiners are used in a pinch and also produce well.

His tactics and trotlines work. Each year, Ralph catches many cats heavier than thirty pounds. His largest flathead to date was a fifty-seven-pounder and his biggest blue an eighty-four-pound monster.

"That one provided proof positive that the simple trotlines I make will hold the biggest cats," Ralph says proudly. "And they'll work for any catfishermen who puts them to the test."

Trotline Tips

When placing your line in a river or lake, take time to pinpoint prime areas, such as outside bends, tributary mouths, wooded flats, and creek channels where cats are likely to be lurking. Tie the line between two secure anchor points—from one snag to another, for example—then weight it in the middle or at a couple of points along its length to carry it near the bottom. Chunks of shad or skipjack herring probably make the best bait for large blue cats and channels. When fishing for flatheads, large frisky baitfish such as sunfish, goldfish, and carp outperform all else. Run your line every few hours to remove your catch and replenish lost bait.

Use special care when running your lines. Keep a sharp knife handy on your belt or strapped to your leg to cut the line if someone is accidentally hooked. Lines should always be removed when you leave so there's no chance another angler or animal might get tangled in the hooks.

Some say trotlining doesn't qualify as true angling at all. Others call it lazy man's fishing. A few go so far as to declare it unsporting. Nevertheless, trotlining is a traditional and legal method of catfishing in many areas. Done properly by conservation-minded anglers, it seldom hurts a catfish population.

Most of all, trotlining is fun. Before you condemn it, give it a try. You might get hooked.

Step-by-Step Instructions for Making a Trotline

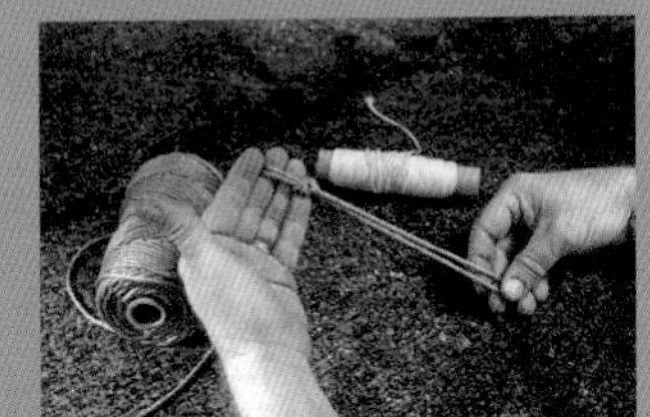

1. Tie an overhand knot in the main line, leaving a six-inch dropper loop. Space the loops at five- to six-foot intervals along the line.

2. Attach a barrel swivel to the dropper by threading the dropper through the eye and back around the swivel.

3. Cut a twelve- to eighteen-inch piece of smaller diameter nylon line, double it, and tie an overhand knot with the tag ends.

4. Push the smaller line through the bottom eye of the swivel and loop it back through itself.

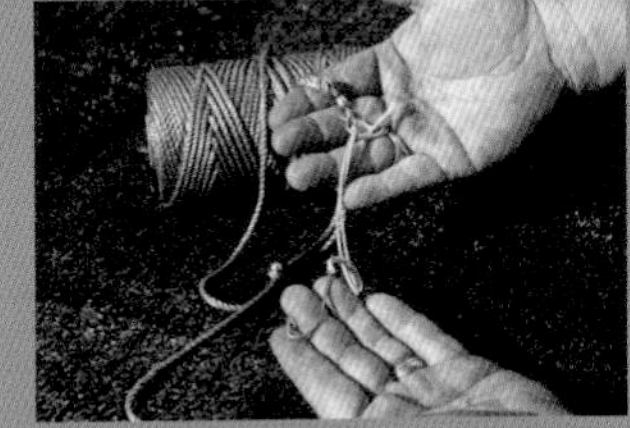

5. Add a hook by pushing the looped end of the smaller line through the hook eye then loop it back around the hook.

6. Finished droplines should be six to nine inches long and tied every five to six feet.

Snagging Cats

Only a hardened few are man enough to be snaggers.

In spring, they gather at the dams, standing shoulder to shoulder on the banks of muddy rivers. They come to fish, but to the uninitiated, their fishing seems foolhardy.

They use no bait. Their rods are extraordinarily long—sometimes more than sixteen feet—unwieldy, heavy. They cast huge weighted treble hooks far into the roiling water then snatch them through the water with hard jerks that jar their bones.

It looks like work. It is.

Cast. Reel. Snatch. Reel. Snatch. Reel. Snatch. Reel. Snatch.

Again. Cast. Reel. Snatch. Reel. Snatch. Reel. Snatch. Reel. Snatch.

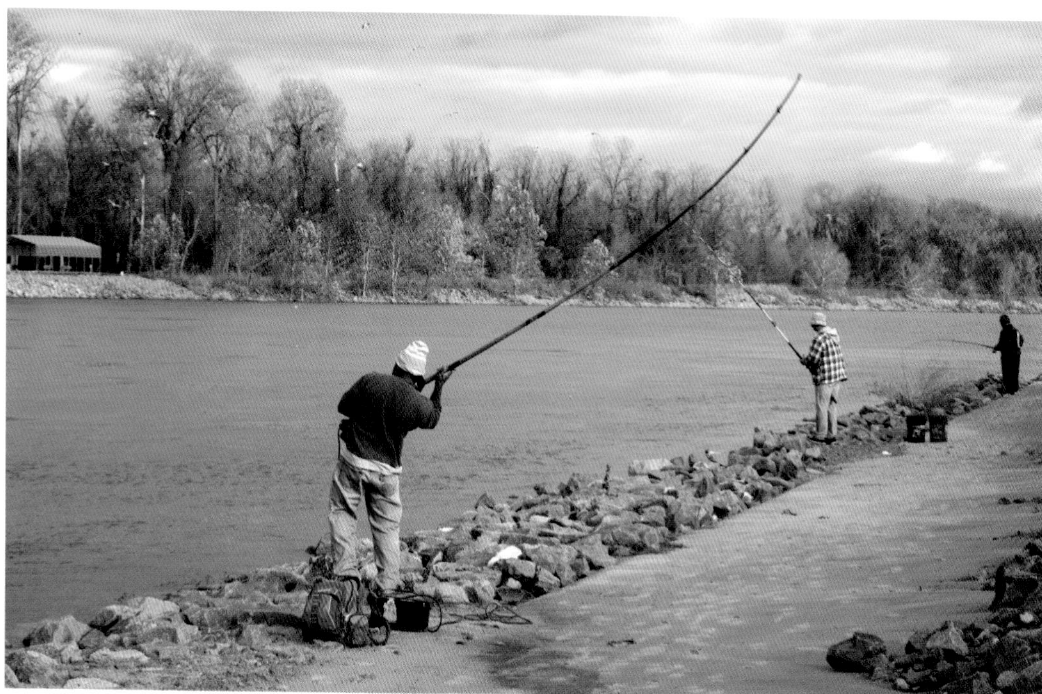

Dam tailwaters often attract crowds of snaggers in late spring and summer as catfish numbers swell when the fish migrate upstream.

They work the water with blind hope. They cannot see the fish they hope to catch. They do not know if the fish are even there. They know they will come though, huge numbers of them, as they have come for centuries, drawn upstream on their instinctual spawning migrations. Perhaps they are there already. Perhaps not. But come they will, sooner or later, in March or April or May or June, and when they stop at those concrete barricades, the snaggers will be there to greet them.

"How ya doing , Ol' Whiskerpuss? I cannot see you, but sometime today, or this week, or this month, after one snatch or ten thousand, my hook will bury in your flesh, and I will fight you and land you and take you home to eat. Until then, I will not be happy, I will not go away."

They are hardened men, these snaggers. You will not find among their ranks the fat, the flabby, or the out of shape. Their muscles are as hard and rippled as ironwood. I have never, in forty years among them, seen a woman in the mix. Nor a single yuppie. Farmers, yes. And carpenters and steel workers and factory laborers and river rats. Hardened individuals accustomed to back-breaking work. No wussies here.

The belly is their one weak spot if their tackle is an indicator, for covering the butt of each long rod is a split rubber ball used to soften the gouging their undersides must take. With each yank, the rod digs, the snagger winces. At day's end, they may be black and blue from breast to groin.

On a good day, if Lady Luck shines upon them, their rod doesn't break, their reel doesn't burn up, if a big cat doesn't spool them off, if the water is just so, the catfish are there, and if all else goes well, maybe, just maybe, they'll have a catfish or two to show for their labor.

Then again, maybe not.

The question taunts as you watch them. Why? Why do this? Why work so hard for so little gain? Why turn a relaxing sport into this form of masochism? Surely catfishing was never meant to be this way.

And so you walk up and ask one flat out, "Why do you do this?" And they reply—the same answer again and again:

"What's it to you?!"

Did I mention hardened? Hardened to the core. To the man.

I became a snagger for a while—had to try it for myself. Stood shoulder to shoulder with the tough guys lining the river banks below a local dam. Threw two eight-ounce snagging hooks with a sixteen-foot surf rod. Learned to cast seventy yards, sometimes more. And learned to stand there, hour after hour, day after day, casting, reeling, snatching, until I blackened my gut with bruises and could not turn the reel handle another revolution.

Once I snagged a catfish. It was, perhaps, the biggest I ever had on rod and reel. Spooled me off in thirty seconds flat. Zzzzzzzzzzz! Pow! That was it. Gone. 200 yards of fifty-pound mono. Never turned its head.

I wept. I quit.

Wussy, they said.

No doubt about it, snagging is a tough way to catch catfish. But in some states where the sport is legal, it appears to be growing in popularity. In my home state of Arkansas, below each of the twelve dams on the Arkansas River you will find on a nice spring day scores of snaggers flailing the water where just a few years before there were none. Why? I cannot say for sure. But if I were to make an educated guess, I would say it has something to do with the extraordinary challenge of it all. In today's world, people are looking for challenges. Skiing down Mount Everest. Jumping motorcycles across canyons. Sky diving. Bungee jumping. Competing in the Iron Man and Iditarod. Pushing the limits of human endurance and sanity.

Snaggers fit the mold. They see something that can't be done by average human standards, and they decide they must do it. And in the doing, they become addicted. Sweat and burning muscles fuel their fires. Doing things the easy way isn't in their nature. And that is why a shade-loving, bank-sitting wussy like me will never be a snagger.

And you? What about you? Think you want to try snagging? I've tried my best to talk you out of it, but no doubt, some of you will be inspired to give it a try. Guys like you never listen.

That being the case, here's the poop on snagging catfish.

Basics

In some parts of the country, the term snagging is seldom used. "Snatching" is a common moniker in many areas, and some folks prefer the term "blind-jerking." Whatever you call it, however, wherever it is done, snagging works along the same basic lines.

A typical snagging rig: 10 ounces of lead and a giant treble hook.

Typical equipment consists of a ten- to sixteen-foot heavy-action saltwater rod, usually a surf rod, and a large-capacity bait-casting or spinning reel spooled with fifty- to 130-pound-test line. Two or three 8/0 to 14/0, needle-sharp treble hooks are tied tandem on the line, and a heavy weight up to twenty ounces is used to sink the hooks in swift tailwaters. Once on the bottom, the rig is jerked through the water until it hits a snag or a fish. Lots of terminal tackle is lost to logs and rocks, thus you will always see wise snaggers with an extra supply of hooks, sinkers, and line.

Snagging rods must be long so the snagger can better control his hooks and weights, which are frequently cast one hundred yards or more to provide greater coverage of the fishing area. Ideally, the snagging rig should move just inches above bottom when jerked by the fisherman—high enough to avoid entanglement with rocks and logs but not too high to miss catfish holding near the bottom. Long rods allow this type of retrieve.

Long rods also allow increased casting distance, which is important when bank fishing as most snaggers do. Snagging is possible from a boat, but unless the craft is extra wide and stable, the snagger's jerky movements can cause an upset. Long rods also provide extra hooksetting and fighting power, additional advantages important in this unusual sport.

Spinning reels seem to be preferred by most snaggers largely because of the increased casting distance they allow. But good bait-casting reels are tougher and provide more cranking power for big cats. The most important qualities regardless of the type you select are durability, large line capacity, and a good drag system. Select a model you're comfortable casting.

Fishing line takes a beating when snagging in cover-strewn waters, so abrasion resistance is an important characteristic. Most snaggers I've encountered use heavy monofilament. Quality brands are relatively inexpensive but offer superb blends of tensile strength, fairly low stretch, and high abrasion resistance. Dacron line also is popular and offers better hooksetting power.

Braided superlines also are gaining favor because their small diameter allows more to be spooled on a reel. Fifty-pound test has the diameter of twenty-five-pound mono, so you can pack more of it on, thus lessening your chance of getting spooled by a giant catfish. Although expensive, these lines have the lowest stretch of any line type, which makes them great for sticking hooks into trophy cats.

Treble hooks for snagging must be constructed of heavy durable wire and should be honed to needle-like sharpness before using and at regular intervals while fishing. Some snaggers use only one hook, but two or three is more typical. These may be tied to short droplines—attached to loop knots on the main line—above a terminal sinker. But most snaggers prefer to tie directly to the main line for more strength and most use specialty "snagging hooks," which are large trebles that have a conical lead weight molded around the shank. The weights on commercial snagging hooks come in a variety of sizes for use under varying conditions.

Snagging can be back-breaking work. Long heavy rods are necessary for snatching the snagging rig through the water, and the angler may make hundreds of snatches for each fish caught. Good physical conditioning is a prerequisite for success.

Done conventionally, snagging is back-breaking sport. There's a long cast to get the rig out in the river, a short delay for the weight to sink, then a violent backward jerk of the rod and quick reeling to recover slack line, another jerk and more rapid reeling, and so forth and so on until the line is reeled in. The angler then makes another cast followed by more jerking and reeling until, hopefully, a hook hits its mark.

Hundreds of casts may be made before a hook connects with a catfish, and there are times when the method is totally unproductive. I've also sat and watched snaggers catch catfish on every cast, including blues and flatheads up to eighty pounds. Timing is everything. When catfish numbers reach their peak in the water being fished, snagging is best.

When the efforts pay off and a catfish is on, there's plenty of exciting, white-knuckle action for the fortunate angler. If the catfish is hooked in the tail as often happens, the battle may be the most action-packed you've ever experienced. If it happens to be a big cat, as well, you're in for a rough and tumble ride.

I've seen many snaggers bury the hook in something solid, what seems like a log, and watched the astonishment on their faces when that log decided to swim away and take their gear with it. Mystery makes snagging fun—the mystery of wondering what will be hooked next. Sometimes it's a big paddlefish, an ancient river wanderer that may exceed one-hundred pounds. Because paddlefish feed exclusively on plankton, snagging is the only reliable means for catching them. Often as not, however, it's a catfish the snagger snags, and even a ten-pounder puts up a whale of a fight when hooked this way.

Places & Times

Most snagging is done in dam tailwaters. There are two primary reasons for this.

First, astounding concentrations of catfish gather in tailwaters when their movements are impeded by dams. And in order to be even modestly effective, snaggers must ply waters where the densest congregations of fish occur. Snaggers fish tailwaters because cats gather there as thickly laid as fence pickets.

The second reason is a matter of legality. In most if not all of the few states where snagging is legal, this activity is restricted entirely to certain portions of various tailwaters. Lakes are off limits as are the main stems of rivers big and small. The snagger has no other choice of waters to fish.

The best season for snagging is spring or early summer. Catfish are drawn to tailwaters this time of year by an urge to procreate. As days grow longer and water warms, cats leave deep wintering holes and begin upstream runs toward spawning areas. Their runs are often stopped short by dams, and as the season progresses, the cats pile up. Some hardcore snaggers ply their favorite waters year-round, and modest numbers of cats may be taken any month. The height of the season, however, coincides with the peak of upstream runs. And if snagging is permitted by law during that time, that's when practitioners should be on the water.

Preparation

The best snaggers I've met have also been the best casters. I've seen some guys who could fire a snagging hook like a cannonball, casting it

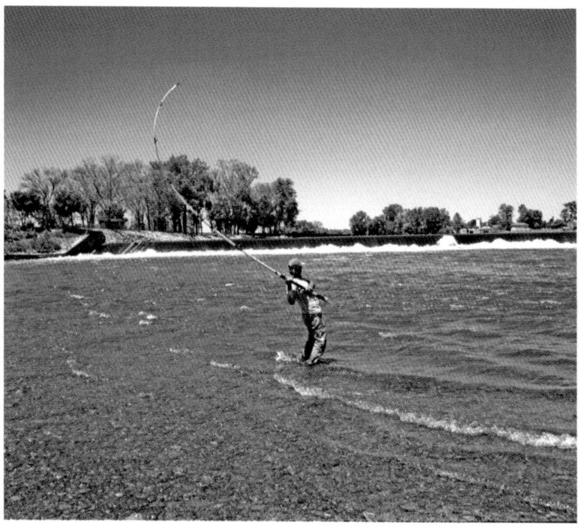

Long casts increase the efficiency of the snagger, and powerful snatches make sure the hook buries in any fish that is struck. Note the tennis ball on the butt of this snagger's rod—added protection for his belly.

well past the mid-reaches of the Arkansas River, a distance of more than eighty yards. And always, they caught the most cats.

The reason long-distance casters are more effective is simple. They spend more time snagging and less time casting, working broad swaths of water on every cast.

With a little practice, you, too, can learn to cast great distances. The key is learning to "load" your rod. On your backswing, you must create a bow in the rod that will catapult your snagging rig when you bring your rod forward. You must also time your casting movements so your line is released at precisely the right moment on the forward swing. As in most things worth doing, practice makes perfect.

Recent Innovations

In Arkansas, many snaggers now use an unusual type of battery-powered reel to lessen

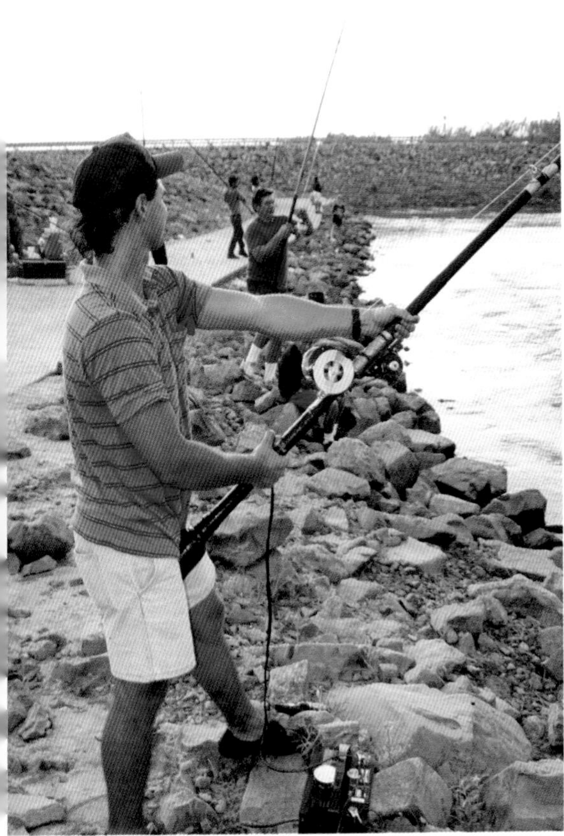

oday's snaggers often use home-tooled ccessories powered by batteries to reduce the oil involved in "blind-jerking" catfish. A push of the utton on the reel's handle brings in slack line, ien the angler jerks again, hoping against hope to ury the hook in a fish he cannot see.

the amount of work required. Constructed from hand-machined parts and connected to a six-volt lawnmower battery, these reels have a button affixed to the rod handle that can be depressed with the angler's thumb. The snagging rig is cast, the angler takes up slack and makes his snatch, then the button is pushed to automatically reel up slack line before the next snatch. No turning of a reel handle is needed, thus the snagger's speed and efficiency are greatly improved.

When these newfangled contraptions first started popping up in Arkansas a few years ago, they caused quite an uproar. People who saw snaggers with large batteries at their feet believed the snaggers might have created some new method of illegal electroshocking. Wildlife officers were barraged by phone calls from folks reporting these apparent law breakers. The devices are so commonplace now, however, that the furor has died down.

In talking with snaggers using the battery-operated reeling systems, I found no reliable source where the equipment could be purchased. Most snaggers, it seems, construct their own rigs in home shops or have friends who help them with tooling and construction. If snagging continues to increase in popularity, however, no doubt some enterprising individual will someday be mass-marketing these innovative rigs.

Conclusion

Before you try snagging, be sure to check local fishing regulations to determine if the practice is legal where you intend to fish. Snagging is illegal in many areas. And where it is legal, numerous restrictions are the rule. All catfishermen have an obligation to know and follow all regulations imposed on their sport. Without these restrictions, our catfishing resources would suffer.

If snagging is legal where you fish or if you're willing to travel somewhere that it is, then perhaps you might want to give it a try. Then again, maybe not. Like I said, this is not a sport for fat, flabby, or out of shape catters. If your idea of a fun outing is kicking back in the shade and taking a nap until a cat bites, snagging isn't likely to tickle your fancy. But if you enjoy a challenge, if sweat and burning muscle fuel your fire, then maybe snagging can provide a new way to liven your days on the water.

Controversy

Snagging remains somewhat—often highly—controversial everywhere it is practiced. It is illegal in many states and restricted to certain seasons, certain waters, certain fish, and certain types of tackle in many others.

Arkansas, a state where snagging long has been practiced, offers a good example of the types of restrictions in effect in many states where snagging is allowed. Here, you may only snag gamefish, including catfish, when fishing from the bank within one hundred yards below a dam. You must keep any gamefish snagged and apply them to your daily limit, and you may not sell them. When snagging, you are limited to one half of the gamefish daily limit, although you may take a full limit of catfish and paddlefish, and once attained, you must cease snagging. Special restrictions apply to certain waters.

There is growing sentiment to stop snagging entirely in some areas where it is practiced. Many people believe it is an unsportsmanlike method for catching fish and that excessive numbers of fish are being harvested.

Studies conducted in areas where snagging is legal and popular do not support these contentions. For example, a survey conducted on two tailwaters on the Coosa River in Alabama found that "snagging catch rates were not excessive." Over a three-month period during the peak spring snagging season, the daily catch by snaggers averaged only about fifty fish. That worked out to less than one fish per hour per snagger. Only five to ten of those fish were catfish, and snaggers had to work several hours for each one caught. Snagging efforts and success dropped drastically during other seasons.

Is snagging unsportsmanlike? In the eyes of many, yes. In the eyes of others, definitely not.

If any practice can be shown to threaten our fish resources, then certainly we have an obligation to restrict that practice. But in areas where it has been studied, snagging catfish does not fit that criterion. It may be a bit different from the norm, but overall, snagging is simply another fun, exciting, legitimate method for harvesting catfish.

Noodling

To increase the excitement quotient on your next catfish trip, try catching 'em with your hands.

I know you will find it hard to believe that an intelligent guy such as me would even consider trying to catch a catfish barehanded while holding my breath underwater. It happened, though. Overwhelmed by a tsunami of beer-induced stupidity one day, I volunteered—yes, volunteered—to try my hand (literally) at noodling. I did so at the encouragement of my father-in-law, who was an ardent noodler for most of his eighty-one years, and my two brother-in-laws, who have been noodlers slightly less than half a century each.

"Folks may call you the dean of catfishing," they said, "but you're not the real dean until you catch a cat barehanded." Thus was I shamed into trying a pastime I had previously considered insane.

We noodled in a forty-acre private lake full of monster catfish, and specifically at a spot dubbed the "Hole-tel." When the lake was constructed in the 1930s, the owner, a man who is said to have loved noodling like some men love gambling or womanizing, created a vast field of concrete holes on the lake bottom in which his beloved whiskerfish could hide and spawn. This allowed him to walk out the front door of his home, wade into the water, and be noodling in less time than it takes to tell it. One of my brothers-in-law became the grandson-in-law of this guy, and pretty soon all my noodling in-laws were visiting the Hole-tel on a regular basis.

And so, on this particular day, I waded out into neck-deep water, took a deep breath, and dove beneath the surface to a hole where my father-in-law had determined a catfish—so he said—was home. Then I reached in.

At this point when you first go noodling, many questions run through your mind. Why am I doing this? Will there be a snake in this hole or a snapping turtle? Do alligators live here? If a catfish is in the hole, will it bite me? How bad will it hurt?

They say big catfish will swallow your entire hand, start spinning, and shred the skin off your arm like a food processor shredding carrots. What will *that* feel like?

Extreme Sport

Catching catfish with your bare hands is an extreme sport by anyone's definition, ranking right up there with bull fighting, skiing Mount Everest, parachuting off waterfalls, and walking tightropes stretched between city skyscrapers. Several terms describe the practice. "Noodling" is almost universal, which is not surprising when you realize this is derived from the word

Author Keith Sutton wages war with a hand-caught blue cat. After his first noodling excursion, he swore he'd never do it again. But he did. Some dummies never learn.

"noodle," meaning a very stupid person—a fool. "Hogging" also is used, as are the synonyms "tickling," "grabbling," "grappling", and "graveling." In Nebraska, they call it "stumping," and in Kentucky, "dogging" is the preferred name.

It's hard to imagine the first brave person who reached underwater and probed a dark hole for dinner. But imagine it we must, for noodling leaves no traces. It is, as one writer describes it, "as ephemeral as some of the boasts it inspires."

Trader-historian James Adair was perhaps the first to leave a written record when, in 1775, he described "a surprising method of fishing under the edges of rocks" among Southern Indians.

> "They pull off their red breeches, or their long slip of Stroud cloth, and wrapping it around their arm, so as to reach the lower part of the palm of their right hand, they dive under the rock where the cat-fish lie to shelter themselves from the scorching beams of the sun, and to watch for prey: as soon as those fierce aquatic animals see that tempting bait, they immediately seize it with the greatest violence, in order to swallow it. Then is the time for the diver to improve the favorable opportunity: he accordingly opens his hand, seizes the voracious fish by his tender parts, hath a sharp struggle with it ... and at last brings it safe ashore."

Seized by the tender parts. I feared that might happen to me instead of the catfish. Nevertheless, I wasn't about to wuss out and look like a big sissy. Holding my breath, I felt blindly for the edge of the hole where the catfish lurked, slid my hand inside, and prayed my father-in-law wasn't pulling a prank on me that involved a snapping turtle or snake.

How to Noodle

Should you be "brave" enough to try noodling yourself, you will have to overcome the natural resistance normal people exhibit when told to stick their hand in a dark hole that might contain God knows what. You then must catch the fish inside.

Keith Sutton poses with the result of his hand-to-jaws combat. Noodling for catfish has become increasingly popular in recent years.

The latter task often is much simpler than the first. When you reach inside the hidey-hole, the occupant, often a male catfish guarding its eggs, goes stark raving mad and bites your hands and fingers with a force similar to that you would feel if you accidentally bashed your fingers with a sledge hammer. All that is required of you is to find a way to surface with the creature in tow ... without losing any digits or integument in the process.

The hole into which you reach may be an old muskrat or beaver burrow, a crevice beneath a rock, a hollow log, or any underwater cavity. Catfish occupy such holes at times year-round but especially during spawning season when laying, guarding, and fanning their eggs.

Most noodlers enter shallow water—never as deep as the noodler is tall—to probe likely catfish hideouts. Sometimes the hole is partially blocked with rocks, small sandbags, or the noodler's body to prevent the catfish's escape. If it is spawning season, however, this is unnecessary. Catfish guarding a nest seldom abandon it. When a hand is inserted, the fish may nip, bite, or if large enough, engulf the noodler's hand. The catfish may spin, causing the sandpaper-like teeth to shred the noodler's skin. For this reason, some noodlers wear gloves, although most believe this hinders the sense of touch necessary for determining the type of creature in the hole, its position, and the best method for grabbing it.

If a catfish attacks, the noodler attempts to grasp it by the mouth or gill cover. If it does not, as often happens outside spawning season, the noodler must make the catfish open its mouth so he can grab it. Wiggling one's fingers may do the trick, or "tickling" the fish

Noodlers catch cats bare-handed by reaching into spawning cavities where the male catfish guards its eggs. A big male may engulf the entire hand when it bites the offending appendage.

under its chin. But sometimes the noodler must rely on feel to find the cat's mouth and forcefully insert his fingers. When a good grip is attained, the noodler attempts to resurface with the quarry.

At this point, the reason for working in shallow water becomes evident. If one cannot quickly stand with mouth and nostrils above the water, he might be in grave danger. Even then, battling a fifty-pound-plus catfish to the surface—and this is often done—may require extraordinary effort.

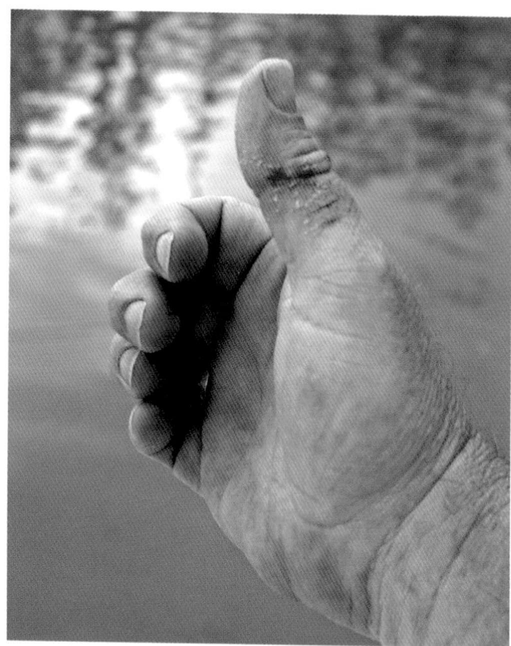

Noodling can be rough on the noodler's digits—the author's thumb after a blue cat chomped down on it.

Dangerous Sport

Check local regulations before noodling. In some states, it's illegal. In others, noodling is permitted but only with restrictions.

One also should consider the many inherent dangers. Crippling injuries can result. Reaching in holes can lead to serious cuts, so up-to-date tetanus shots are a must. If an arm or hand gets stuck or if an exceptionally large cat is tackled, the noodler can drown. Risks are high. Participants should be aware death or serious injury can result.

The closest most folks will come to hand-grabbing catfish is reaching across the table and grabbing a fried fillet off a plate. That's also dangerous but only when you're sharing a table with hungry friends and there's only one fillet left.

Me . . . well, I was stupid enough to try hand-grabbing the old-fashioned way. As I cautiously

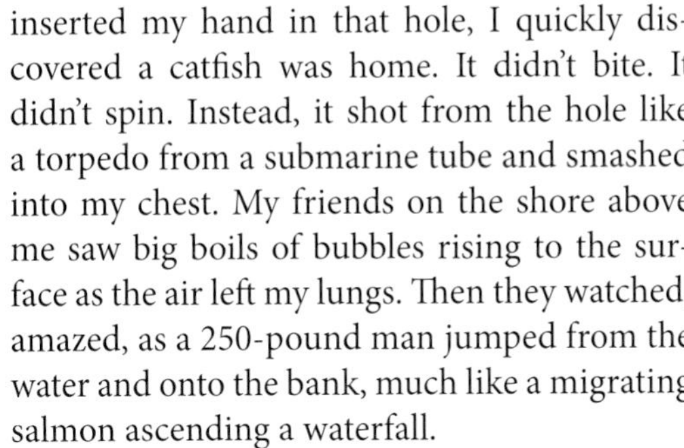

inserted my hand in that hole, I quickly discovered a catfish was home. It didn't bite. It didn't spin. Instead, it shot from the hole like a torpedo from a submarine tube and smashed into my chest. My friends on the shore above me saw big boils of bubbles rising to the surface as the air left my lungs. Then they watched, amazed, as a 250-pound man jumped from the water and onto the bank, much like a migrating salmon ascending a waterfall.

Blood dripped from my arm where the catfish's spines had brushed me.

"What happened?" my father-in-law asked.

"Something bit me," I said, breathlessly. "A snake or a snapping turtle, maybe. I'm finished noodling."

"Dean of catfishing, indeed," my brothers-in-law chortled.

I counted my fingers. Ten. I still had all ten.

My noodling adventure ended then and there.

Section IX

Catfish Conservation

Why Catch and Release?

If you keep all the catfish you catch, it's time to change your ways.

"Catch-and-release catfishing": until recently, that term seemed to be an oxymoron, like "casual sex" and "non-alcoholic beer." Over the past couple of decades, however, more and more catfish anglers have joined the ranks of catch-and-release anglers. New regulations, such as slot limits and length limits, are responsible in some locales. But for the most part, I believe catfish fans, more conservation-minded than ever, have shown voluntary restraint. "Today's releases are tomorrow's trophies" has become the motto of many.

There are good reasons for this, reasons you should consider if you're still among the majority of catfish anglers who keep most of the fish you catch.

First, you're likely to enjoy better fishing for trophy-class catfish if you and your fellow anglers release larger specimens. Big catfish are

A channel cat like this 30-pounder may have grown for years before reaching its trophy potential. Releasing large catfish such as this helps protect stocks of heavyweight fish, thus enhancing trophy-fishing opportunities.

especially vulnerable to overharvest because when trophy-class cats are removed, it takes years to replace them.

Take flatheads for instance. Ten years are required to grow a thirty-pounder, even under the best circumstances. Flatheads exceeding fifty pounds are relatively rare individuals that may be twenty to thirty years old. If you remove a trophy flathead from a river or lake, decades may pass before it is replaced by a fish of comparable size.

Channel and blue catfish populations are similarly affected. Trophy fish are older uncommon fish. Yet many catfish anglers never consider releasing those they catch, especially big ones.

Small cats are much more common than big ones, so if you're fish hungry, keep some smaller ones to eat. There's no hard and fast rule to follow, but I personally draw the line at five pounds. The fillets and steaks I eat come from smaller catfish.

Resist the temptation to keep the heavyweights, and encourage others to do likewise. Shoot some photos, then carefully remove the hook and release the fish back into the water.

Release Right

When you do practice catch and release, be sure to do it right. Catfish are extremely hardy. An individual may live for hours out of the water. But if you expect a cat to survive following release, it's important to handle it properly. Follow these simple tips, and you can greatly increase the chances the fish you turn back will remain healthy and available for you or some other fisherman to catch again.

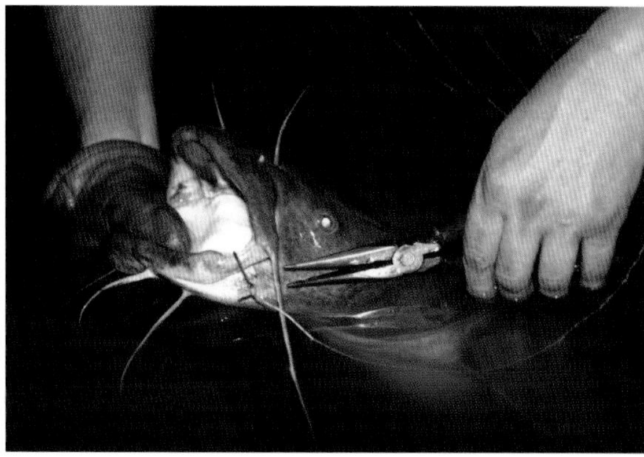

When handling a catfish prior to its release, keep the fish in the water as much as possible while removing the hook.

- Use circle hooks when catfishing. These tend to hook fish in the corner of the mouth, vastly reducing mortality. Barbless circle hooks are even better. If you prefer other styles of hooks, use barbless models if possible or crimp the barbs with pliers.
- If a cat does swallow the hook, don't pull it out. Cut the line as close to the hook as possible, leaving the hook inside the fish.
- Bring the fish to the boat quickly—don't play the fish to total exhaustion while attempting to land it.
- Hold the fish in the water as much as possible when handling it, removing the hook, and preparing it for release. Want photos? Remove the fish briefly, and snap your shots quickly.
- Wet your hands so you don't remove the protective slime coating the fish.
- Use landing nets made with soft small mesh, such as salmon nets. These are easier on the catfish's smooth skin.
- Don't squeeze the fish or put your fingers in its gills. Cradle it in the water and move it

back and forth to oxygenate the gills. When the fish is properly rested, it will swim from your hands.

The Red River Example

The best catfishing I ever enjoyed was on Manitoba's Red River, one of those rare catfish rivers where barbless hooks are required by law. The daily channel cat limit is four, none of which may exceed twenty-four inches. On a three-day fishing trip there, I caught around fifty channel cats, all of which were larger than any channel cat I had previously caught during a lifetime spent pursuing them. The smallest weighed approximately seventeen pounds, the largest approximately thirty-five pounds.

I have often wondered that if a river in Canada, where the growing season is short, can produce such tremendous numbers of trophy catfish, what might a similar river in the United States produce if similar fishing restrictions were placed upon it? If more catfish anglers practiced voluntary catch and release, if more of us push lawmakers to enact reasonable harvest restrictions, perhaps someday we'll have the answer to that question.

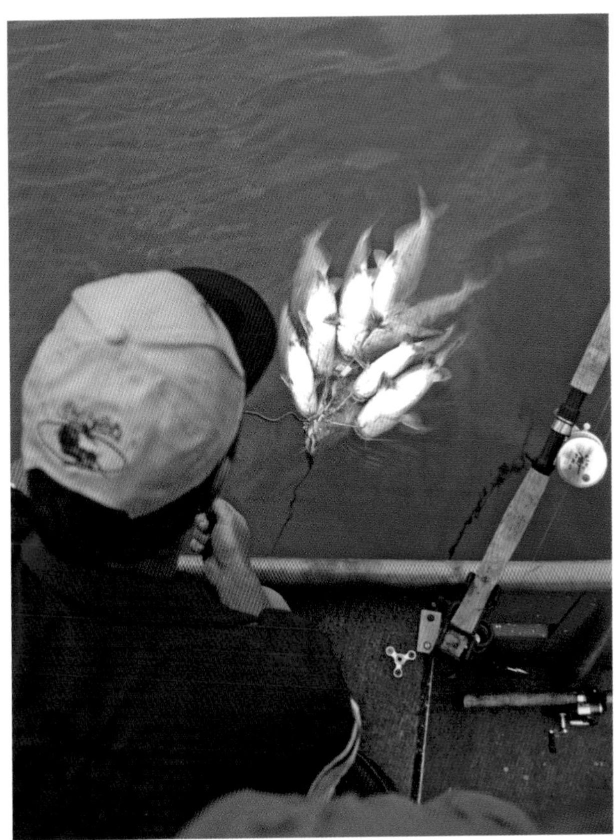

Today's conservation-minded anglers practice restrictive harvest, keeping smaller catfish to eat and releasing trophy specimens to be caught again.

Section X

Eating Catfish

Cats for the Pan

For most catfish anglers, eating the catch is the reason for fishing.

Catfish have been a staple of our cuisine throughout recorded history. Native Americans ate them, as did European explorers and the earliest settlers. In fact, our hankering for delicious catfish has done nothing but grow with catfish now among the most popular American food fishes.

While different types of catfish are very similar in flavor, catfish connoisseurs agree there are distinctive differences that make one species preferable over another for fastidious diners. In some cases, physical differences between species and size classes also necessitate differing means of preparation to facilitate the utmost gustatory enjoyment of the catch.

These things being so, let's look individually at each species and its unique qualities. Knowing the differences will enable you to savor to the fullest these delectable freshwater fishes.

Channel Catfish

Let's begin our discussion with the most popular, most widespread, most abundant member of the family, the channel cat. Everywhere it swims, this species is targeted by a devoted group of anglers who like nothing better than

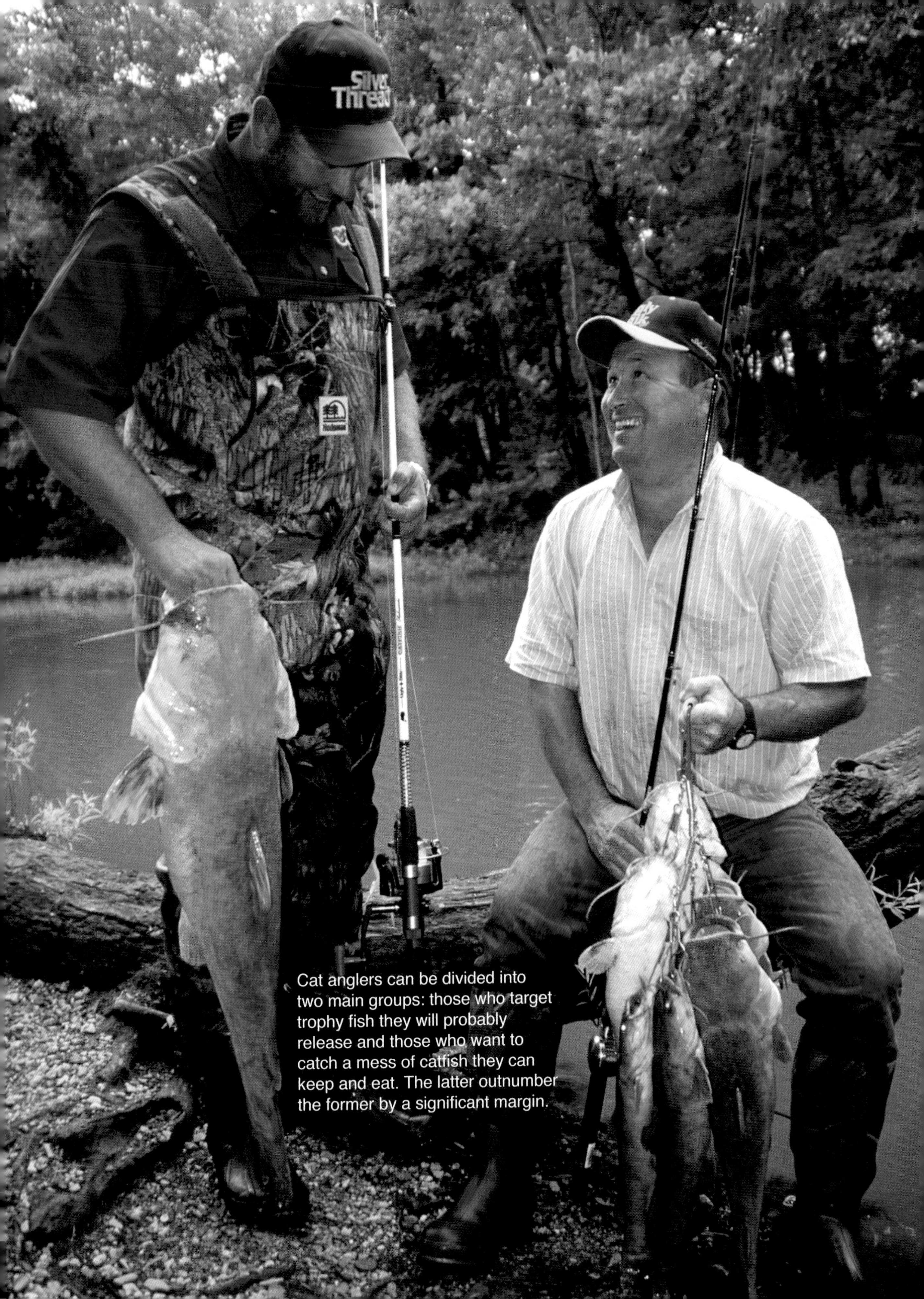

Cat anglers can be divided into two main groups: those who target trophy fish they will probably release and those who want to catch a mess of catfish they can keep and eat. The latter outnumber the former by a significant margin.

catching and eating this whiskered wonder. In states where catfish anglers have been surveyed, fifty to seventy-five percent prefer fishing for channel cats. And when asked to describe the number and size of catfish they preferred to catch and keep, most preferred four five-pound catfish or ten two-pound catfish over one twenty-pounder, a fact I think correlates to the belief that smaller catfish are more flavorful than heavyweights.

Most catfish anglers agree there's nothing tastier than just-caught catfish cooked and eaten by the water where they were caught.

When channel catfish are caught in extremely muddy, hot, or polluted waters, it is likely the flesh will have a poor taste. The same is true with other species of catfish. It is best, therefore, to concentrate fishing efforts where water quality is good and keep the catch alive or on ice until prepared for eating. I love the flaky white meat of all channel cats caught and cared for in this manner, but without doubt, the best tasting channel cats I've eaten were caught from icy cold lakes and ponds in winter and cooked fresh from the water over a campfire.

Blue Catfish

I once bet a friend fifty dollars he couldn't distinguish a fried blue cat fillet from a fried channel cat fillet in a blind taste test. My buddy was constantly saying a fat blue cat was better eating than any channel cat. But with a blindfold on and two plates full of channel cat fillets in front of him to sample (yes, just channel cats), he stated emphatically that plate number one must indeed be blue cat because of its distinctively better flavor. I graciously accepted payment of the wager.

Today's blue cat anglers handle big fish carefully to allow a healthy release. If fish are wanted for eating, smaller ones are kept.

Healthy populations of blue cats usually contain numerous individuals up to ten pounds. Larger older fish are much less common, but in some prime waters, catching several twenty- to forty-pound blues during a few hours is not considered unusual during peak fishing times. Specimens weighing fifty pounds or more are scarce and often difficult to find and catch, but more and more anglers enjoy the challenge of targeting these big hard-hitting trophies.

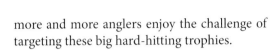

So what about those larger blue cats? Are they good to eat? I am often asked that question and always reply the same. Yes, they are delicious—a fact I confirmed many times in my younger, more ignorant days when I kept and ate every catfish I caught. Now I encourage fellow catfish anglers to practice restrictive harvest. Keep smaller fish to eat and release larger catfish—those that are older and less common—so they continue growing and providing trophy-fishing opportunities. There's no hard and fast rule to follow, but I personally draw the line at five pounds. The fillets and steaks I eat come from smaller, more abundant blue cats. Same with channel cats and flatheads.

Flatheads

When a mess of fish for the dinner table is wanted, the abundance of small flatheads in many waters makes it a cinch to load a cooler with plenty of eaters. And load the coolers we do, for many of us old cat men strongly believe a one- to five-pound flathead has a delectable flavor far superior to other catfish. I cannot say for sure why this should be, but flatheads scavenge much less than their brethren, preferring live foods, such as sunfish and crawdads, to the meals of dead fish or detritus blue and channel cats hastily devour. Perhaps it is this difference in diet that gives flatheads a taste many of us find much sweeter and flavorful. To me, it's like the difference between a fillet basted in butter during cooking and one that is not. The former titillates the taste buds in ways the latter cannot.

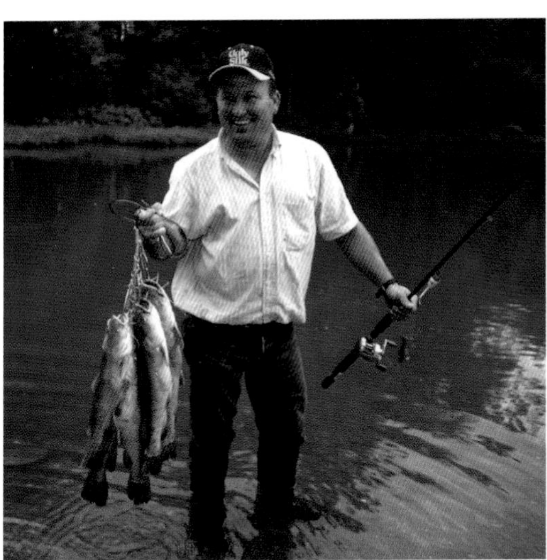

He's smiling because he knows these small flatheads are among the best eating fish in freshwater.

To heighten this savory flavor, one should always do two things when preparing a flathead—or any other catfish for that matter—for cooking. First, before skinning each fish, use a rope or nail to hang it head up from a support above a five-gallon bucket. Then use a knife to cut off the tail where it joins the body. Blood will pour out from a vein in the tail, thus "bleeding out" the fish, an endeavor that produces whiter, better tasting meat. The first time I tasted wild catfish bled in this fashion, I was amazed at the marked improvement in flavor.

Second, after you skin the fish, use a sharp knife to remove all dark red flesh along the fish's sides, particularly along the lateral line. This meat tends to have a strong, disagreeable flavor and contaminants that may be in the water where the catfish was caught tend to concentrate there. Get rid of it and the catfish not only tastes better, it's also healthier to eat.

Bullheads

Some anglers I know throw back all the bullheads they catch, claiming they have soft flesh and a disagreeable taste. Such is often the case when the fish are caught in muddy or polluted water or placed on a stringer to die in warm water. However, if you catch bullheads

Bullheads don't get very big, but a mess of small ones properly cleaned and prepared will provide several delicious meals.

in clean water and immediately place them on ice, they are delicious. Be sure to trim away all dark red meat on the sides, then roll the fillets in seasoned cornmeal and fry golden-brown for an entrée even jaded diners will enjoy.

Recipes for Catfish

For some folks, frying is the only way to cook a cat. There's simply no tastier method of preparation, so why bother with anything else? Case closed.

Truth is, versatility is one of catfish's greatest assets. Serve it fried, smoked, poached, baked, broiled, braised, sautéed, or barbecued. Or combine it with other foods for casseroles or chowders. Catfish can be eaten in a sandwich, a salad, a pizza, or an omelet. You're limited only by your imagination, as you'll see when perusing the many delicious recipes that follow.

The biggest mistake to avoid is overcooking. Catfish is naturally tender and cooks quickly. It's done when it flakes easily with a fork. If you wait for it to float in hot oil, you've probably cooked away the natural moisture that makes catfish so succulent and destroyed much of its unique flavor in the process. When deep-frying, heat the oil to 365 to 370 degrees Fahrenheit—no hotter. The old throw a match in the oil and wait till it lights trick rarely results in the proper frying temperature. Use a cooking thermometer to get it right or a deep-fryer that can be set at the correct heat.

Bon appétit!

Fried Catfish, Arkansas Style

This recipe can be used with any type of catfish and will feed a dozen or more people at your next home fish fry. The hot sauce/milk marinade adds a nice piquant flavor to the catfish without making it spicy hot.

6 pounds catfish steaks and/or fillets
3 (3-oz.) bottles Louisiana hot sauce
12 cups milk
3 cups yellow cornmeal
1 cup flour
2 tablespoons salt
1-1/2 teaspoons cayenne pepper
1-1/2 teaspoons garlic powder
Peanut oil

Marinate catfish one to two hours in a mixture of the hot sauce and milk. Remove fish and drain.

Combine the dry ingredients in a large plastic bag. Add the fish a little at a time and shake to coat.

Cook the fish in two inches of peanut oil in a deep fryer heated to 365 degrees Fahrenheit. Fry until the thickest part of the fish flakes easily with a fork, about five to six minutes. Remove and drain on paper towels. Repeat with remaining fish.

Serves twelve to fifteen.

Quick and Easy Grilled Catfish

This makes a delicious meal when you're in a hurry and cooking for two. Preparation is quick and simple, and the cooking time is just a few minutes. For more dinner guests, just multiply the amount of ingredients.

1 pound catfish fillets
3 tablespoons Worcestershire sauce
2 tablespoons lemon juice
1 clove garlic, crushed
1/2 teaspoon paprika
1/8 teaspoon ground black pepper
6 cherry tomatoes, halved lengthwise (optional)
2 green onions (optional)

Combine Worcestershire sauce, lemon juice, garlic, paprika, and pepper and pour over catfish fillets placed in a single layer in a large baking dish. Marinate in the refrigerator for two hours.

Transfer catfish to a large sheet of heavy-duty aluminum foil. Fold up the sides of the foil to form a rim. Pour the remaining marinade over the catfish. Garnish with tomato halves and green onions.

Grill over medium heat for about five to six minutes or until the catfish flakes easily when tested with a fork at the thickest part.

Serves two.

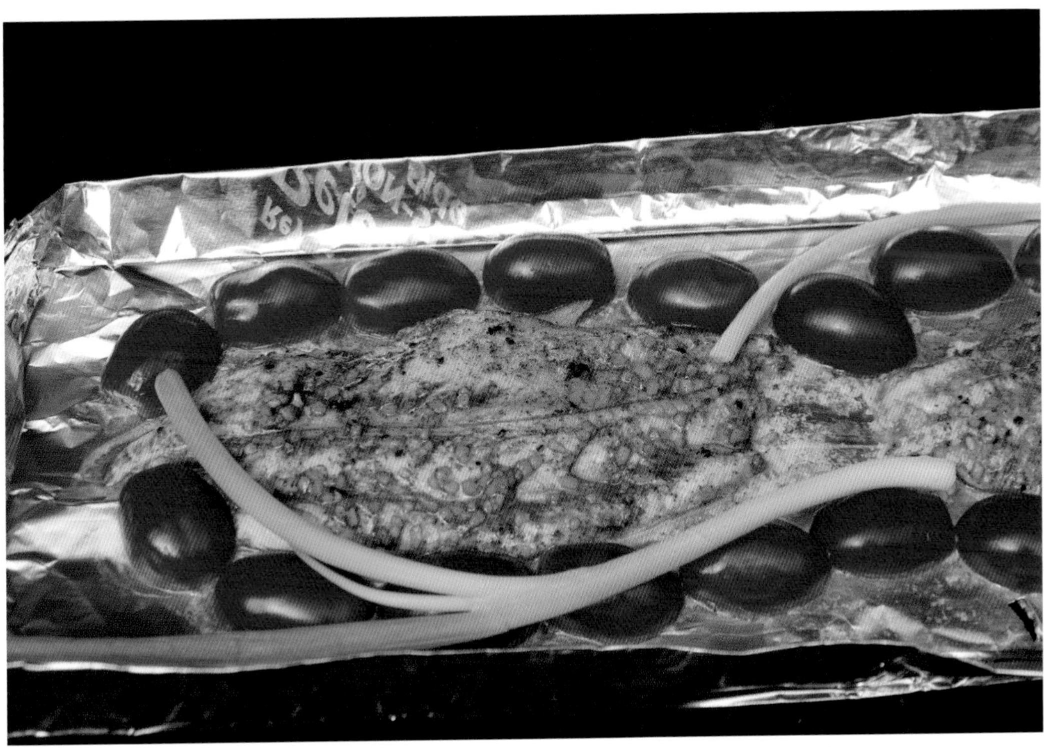

Blackened Catfish with Crawfish Sauce

This Cajun recipe is a real crowd pleaser. You can make it fiery hot by seasoning the fish heavily with the blackening spice and Tony Chachere's Seasoning or use less of these ingredients if you don't want your lips to burn when you eat. Either way, it's delicious!

4 (8-oz.) catfish fillets
Blackening spice (available in the supermarket spice section)
4 tablespoons butter or margarine
2 (10-3/4-oz.) cans condensed cream of shrimp soup
1 soup can half-and-half or milk
1 pound peeled, cooked crawfish tails
1 to 2 tablespoons Tony Chachere's Original Creole Seasoning
Chopped fresh parsley or cilantro for garnish

Season the catfish fillets to taste with the blackening spice. Heat the butter or margarine in a large nonstick skillet until bubbly, then add the catfish one piece at a time and sauté until crispy on the outside. Transfer to a warm plate. Add more butter to the skillet if necessary, and cook the remaining pieces of fish.

While the fish is cooking, prepare the sauce in a nonstick saucepan by combining the remaining ingredients except the garnish and heating over low heat until warmed through, stirring constantly. Do not allow to boil.

Serve the fish hot with a ladle full of sauce poured over each piece. Garnish if desired with chopped parsley or cilantro.

Serves four.

Lime-Broiled Catfish

Here's another delicious, time-saving recipe that makes the most of fresh catfish fillets. If you don't have limes available, lemons can be substituted.

2 pounds catfish fillets
1 cup melted butter or margarine
2 limes
Lemon pepper
Chopped fresh chives for garnish

Pour the hot melted butter in a large bowl, and dip each fish fillet. Transfer the fish to a rectangular pan lined with nonstick aluminum foil. Squeeze one half lime over each piece of fish, and season to taste with lemon pepper.

Place under a preheated broiler and cook six inches from the flame for three to four minutes or until the thickest part of each fillet flakes easily with a fork. Garnish with chives if desired, and serve immediately while the fish is still piping hot.

Serves four.

Cat Cakes with Dijon Sauce

When making these scrumptious fish cakes, adjust the ingredients if necessary to be sure they are moist enough to hold together but not so moist that they fall apart when cooked. And don't mess with the fish cakes when they're in the pan, or they'll break apart. Flip once during cooking. Cook a large batch if you like, then freeze some cakes by placing them on a sheet pan in your freezer for half an hour. Store them in freezer bags, and when you're ready to cook, take out as many as you need and defrost overnight in the refrigerator. They'll be ready to cook the next day.

1/2 cup vegetable oil
1 tablespoon chopped green pepper
4 tablespoons chopped green onion
1 pound catfish fillets, cooked, flaked
1 egg, beaten
1 tablespoon mayonnaise
6 tablespoons dry bread crumbs
1 teaspoon dry mustard
1/4 teaspoon ground black pepper
1/4 teaspoon cayenne pepper
1 teaspoon seasoned salt

Sauté green pepper and green onion in two tablespoons oil until soft. Drain. Mix with remaining ingredients. Chill for at least twenty minutes. Form into patties, and cook in the remaining oil until golden brown on each side. Serve with Dijon sauce.

Dijon Sauce
1/2 cup plain yogurt
3 tablespoons dry mustard
1/4 cup mayonnaise
1 tablespoon chopped green onion
2 tablespoons dill pickle relish
2 tablespoons balsamic vinegar

Mix all ingredients and chill until ready to serve. Serve at room temperature.

Serves four.

Catfish Gumbo

We often use catfish from the freezer to make this favorite on cold fall and winter days when we want something hot to warm our bellies.

½ cup chopped celery
½ cup chopped onion
½ cup chopped green pepper
1 clove garlic, minced
¼ cup vegetable oil
4 cups beef broth
1 (16-oz.) can peeled tomatoes
1 (10 oz.) package frozen sliced okra
2 teaspoons salt
1 teaspoon black pepper
¼ teaspoon thyme
1 bay leaf
Dash Louisiana hot sauce
1 pound catfish fillets
1-1/2 cups hot cooked rice

Cook celery, onion, green pepper, and garlic in oil until tender. Add broth, tomatoes, okra, and seasonings. Cover and simmer thirty minutes. Add catfish after cutting it into one-inch pieces. Cover and simmer fifteen minutes longer or until fish flakes easily. Remove bay leaf. Place a quarter-cup of rice in each of six soup bowls. Fill with gumbo.

Serves six.

Quick Baked Catfish

When time is of the essence, this easy recipe cooks up fast for a tasty dinner that's hard to beat.

2 pounds catfish fillets
½ cup mayonnaise
Bread crumbs
Paprika
Salt
Pepper

Lightly coat fillets with mayonnaise and roll in bread crumbs. Place in a baking dish coated with nonstick cooking spray, and season to taste with paprika, salt, and pepper. Bake in a preheated 450 degree Fahrenheit oven for about twelve minutes or until fish flakes easily when fork-tested.

Serves four to six.

Catfish Po'boys

We love sandwiches, and few are better than this Louisiana-style po'boy. For the best flavor, make it on fresh bread that's crusty on the outside and soft on the inside.

6 fried catfish fillets
6 French rolls
1 cup catsup
3 dashes Tabasco sauce
1 tablespoon prepared mustard
1 tablespoon minced onion
Dill pickles

Cut rolls in half lengthwise, scoop out the soft centers, and place in the oven until hot but not crispy. Combine ketchup, Tabasco, mustard, and onion. Spread the hot rolls with this mixture, then top with catfish, dill pickles, and the top of the roll.

Serves six.

Microwave Catfish, Potato, and Onion Casserole

For a delicious change of pace, whip up one of these quick and easy casseroles, a hearty one-dish meal that can be ready to eat in an hour or less. The cheesy taste makes it a family favorite.

4 medium potatoes
3 medium onions
1/2 cup melted butter
1 to 1-1/2 pounds catfish fillets
1 teaspoon salt
1 teaspoon black pepper
8 oz. sour cream
1 (10-3/4-oz) can cream of mushroom soup
1/2 cup dried bread crumbs
1/2 pound shredded Velveeta cheese
Paprika

Wrap potatoes and onions in plastic wrap and make a small vent hole in the wrap of each. Cook in a microwave oven for twelve minutes. Allow to cool and cut into slices. Lay the slices on all sides of a large square or rectangular baking dish and brush with butter.

Place fish fillets on the bottom of the dish, and season with salt and pepper. Mix the sour cream and mushroom soup and pour over all. Sprinkle on bread crumbs and Velveeta cheese, then season to taste with paprika. Microwave about eighteen minutes on high, then allow to sit about three minutes before serving.

Serves four.

ALSO AVAILABLE

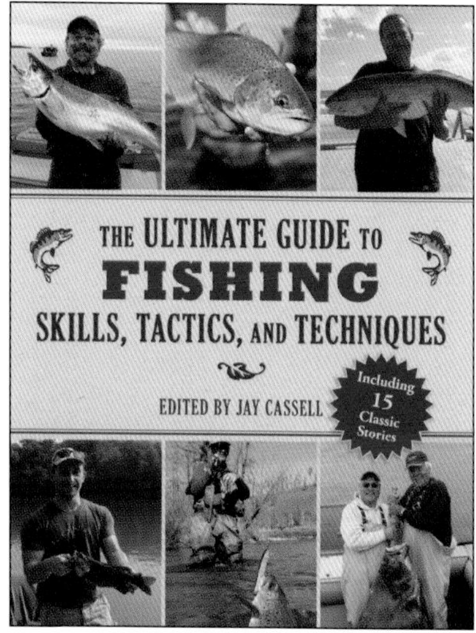

The Ultimate Guide to Fishing Skills, Tactics, and Techniques
A Comprehensive Guide to Catching Bass, Trout, Salmon, Walleyes, Panfish, Saltwater Gamefish, and Much More
Edited by Jay Cassell

With fishing advice from such experts as Bill Dance, Roland Martin, Wade Bourne, Tom Rosenbauer, Kirk Deeter, Charlie Meyer, Conway Bowman, and Lamar Underwood, *The Ultimate Guide to Fishing Skills, Tactics, and Techniques* profiles all of the major gamefish in both fresh and salt water and reveals pro secrets on how to catch them. Learn how Roland Martin entices largemouths with striking lures. Study Bill Dance's twenty tricks for consistently catching bass in thick weed beds or clear, open water. Want to know what Kirk Deeter and Charlie Meyer have learned from their years of fly fishing for trout? How about Lamar Underwood's tools for success? It's all here, divided into sections on bass, trout, walleyes, pike-pickerel-muskellunge, panfish, salmon, steelhead, catfish, ice fishing, and saltwater fishing for easy reference. You'll also find sections on knot tying, boats and boating, comfort and safety on the water, and even delicious recipes for cooking your fresh-caught fish.

This volume also includes a classic reading section featuring stories from such fishing literary legends as Nick Lyons, Ted Leeson, and John Taintor, who remind us what fishing is really all about.

$24.95 Paperback • ISBN 978-1-61608-561-2

ALSO AVAILABLE

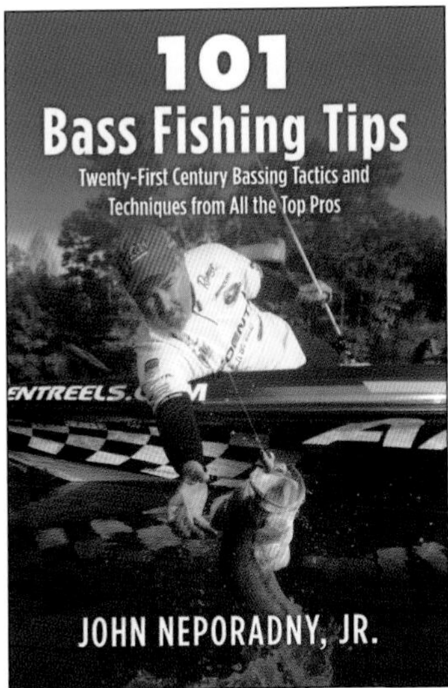

101 Bass Fishing Tips

Twenty-First Century Bassing Tactics and Techniques from All the Top Pros

by John Neporadny, Jr.

John Neporadny is an expert bass fisherman, and he's here to offer his secrets and those of other fishing greats on hooking hawg largemouths in *101 Bass Fishing Tips*. The latest techniques and tactics are revealed in this book full of tips from the top touring pros. The best competitors of the Bassmaster and FLW circuits share their secrets on how to catch largemouth bass throughout the year on various bodies of water.

Learn how to select the right tackle and lures so you can fish just like the pros. Bass fishing's elite anglers also discuss how to find fish on structures such as drop-offs, ledges, points, and flats. They also describe their tricks for coaxing bass out of weeds, bushes, stumps, docks, and other types of cover.

Beginners and advanced anglers alike will discover a treasure trove of valuable information they can apply on their favorite waters to catch America's most popular gamefish. Full of information and great stories, *101 Bass Fishing Tips* is the best guide available to help fishermen land more bass and is a revealing look at the exciting world of professional fishing.

ALSO AVAILABLE

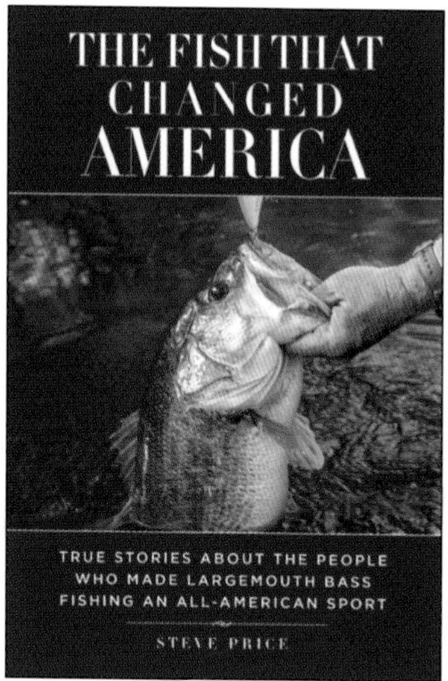

The Fish That Changed America
True Stories about the People Who Made Largemouth Bass Fishing an All-American Sport
by Steve Price

Bass fishing changed from pastime to business in part because of competitive tournaments and the publicity they generated. That publicity, in turn, sparked a demand for more and more information from the tournament fishermen themselves—how they caught bass—so in essence, the sport fed upon itself. Author Steve Price has interviewed dozens of anglers over the past few years, and he fits each of their stories into a complicated puzzle that forms a comprehensive tale of competitive record holders and fishing industry insiders alike.

The Fish That Changed America is not simply about tournament bass fishing, although some of the stories included here do involve competitive anglers. Rather, Price has tried to embrace a wider view of the entire sport and to show how different facets of bass fishing meshed so perfectly at the same time, leading to the state of the industry today. The participants—those who laid the foundation for what all bass anglers today enjoy—tell their own stories of what happened during those not-so-long-ago years. Many of the stories, such as the standing room–only funeral for a famous largemouth bass, touch on far-ranging topics that all anglers will enjoy.

$24.95 Hardcover • ISBN 978-1-62914-558-7

ALSO AVAILABLE

The Orvis Beginner's Guide to Carp Flies
101 Patterns & How and When to Use Them
by Dan C. Frasier

Carp are one of the most widely distributed and abundant fish in North America. Their prodigious size and habit of finning in shallow water make them appear to be easy fly-fishing targets. In reality, most anglers quickly discover that they are extremely difficult to hook on a fly. It takes years to discover how to catch them consistently. The reason? Carp can be very selective about what flies they will take.

This book will help to short-circuit that learning curve. Carp's selectivity can be boiled down to diet. Understanding what they are eating allows the angler to choose and tie a fly that will produce. *The Orvis Beginner's Guide to Carp Flies* walks the fly fisherman through the steps of identifying the most likely food source, illustrating the best patterns that imitate that food, and discussing how to effectively present those flies. With detailed information on tying all of the important carp flies, this book eliminates months of trial and error in your fly selection.

$12.95 Paperback • ISBN 978-1-62914-463-4

ALSO AVAILABLE

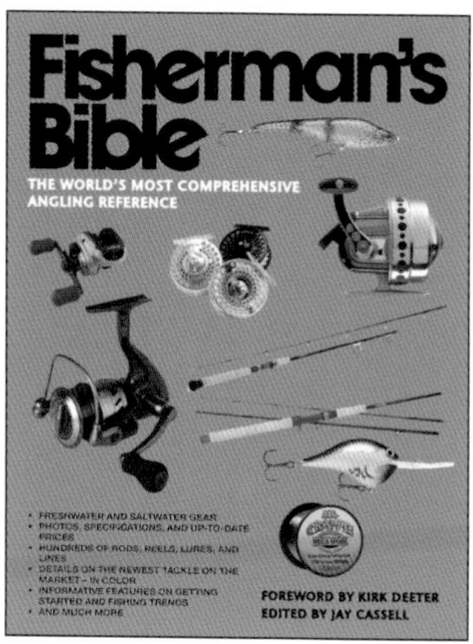

Fisherman's Bible
The World's Most Comprehensive Angling Reference
Edited by Jay Cassell
Foreword by Kirk Deeter

In the tradition of the bestselling *Shooter's Bible*, Skyhorse Publishing presents the *Fisherman's Bible*, the most complete reference guide for new fishing equipment and its specifications. Now, anglers will only need one book to discover all the new gear on the market as well as look up specs on accessories currently in production.

A comprehensive full color feature on new products includes large photographs of every rod, reel, and lure with extensive product details and feature listings. In addition to the latest gear, the *Fisherman's Bible* offers thousands of rods, reels, lures, and lines that have been in production and are currently on the market. All products are divided into fresh water and salt water, and further separated by spin, spincasting, baitcasting, and fly fishing. Nearly every fishing gear manufacturer in the world is included in this unique compendium.

With an introduction highlighting the hottest new products on the market, as well as timely features on such informative topics as new trends in fishing, a beginner's guide to fishing, and what and where to fish: popular species and prevailing methods, the *Fisherman's Bible* is an essential authority for any beginner or experienced angler, wherever he or she may live or choose to fish.

$29.95 Paperback • ISBN 978-1-61608-837-8

ALSO AVAILABLE

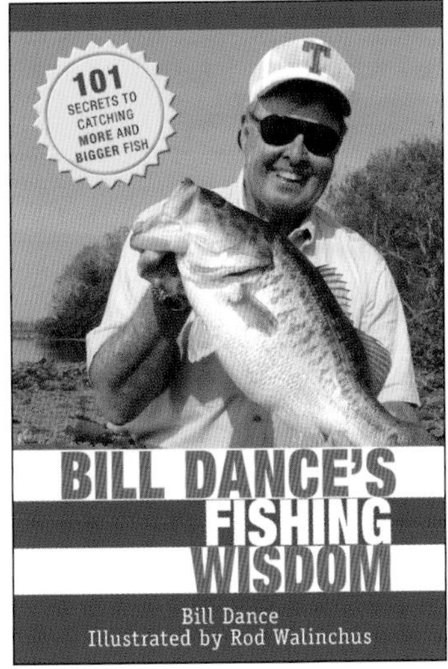

Bill Dance's Fishing Wisdom
101 Secrets to Catching More and Bigger Fish
by Bill Dance
Illustrated by Rod Walinchus

Bill Dance is one of America's best-known fishermen and has more than fifty years of on-water experience. *Bill Dance's Fishing Wisdom* combines his years of experience, knowledge, and wit into 101 tips that are sure to help any freshwater angler catch more and even bigger fish! Bill offers advice that might surprise even the most experienced fisherman, such as the importance of matching your line size to your lure when topwater fishing and how to prevent 75 percent of line failures with better knots. Complete with drawings by Rod Walinchus and color photographs, *Bill Dance's Fishing Wisdom* is key for any fisherman to have in his tackle box, boat, or lake cabin.

$16.95 Hardcover • ISBN 978-1-61608-267-3

ALSO AVAILABLE

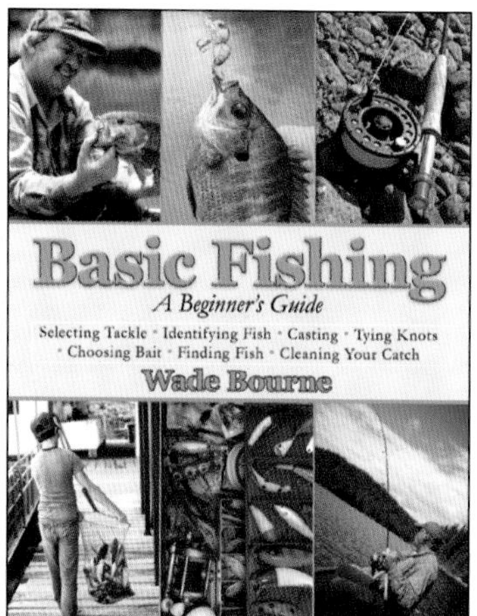

Basic Fishing
A Beginner's Guide
by Wade Bourne

New to fishing and have no idea how to start? With *Basic Fishing*, you'll be an accomplished angler in no time at all. Expert angler and award-winning outdoor writer Wade Bourne has created a step-by-step guide that masterfully breaks down the art of fishing with diagrams, vivid photographs, and lessons on:

- Different types of fishing equipment and how to select the best tackle
- Baiting techniques for artificial and natural baits
- Tips for selecting the best fishing spot
- Handy methods for cooking and cleaning fish

. . . and more!

$12.95 Hardcover • ISBN 978-1-61608-210-9

ALSO AVAILABLE

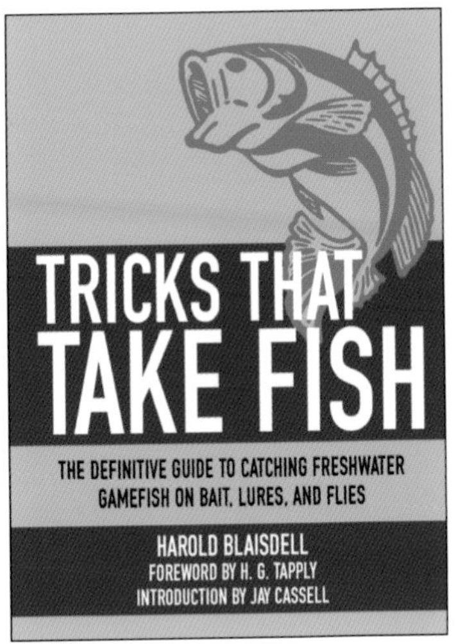

Tricks That Take Fish
The Definitive Guide to Catching Freshwater Gamefish on Bait, Lures, and Flies
by Harold Blaisdell
Foreword by H. G. Tapply
Introduction by Jay Cassell

Seasoned fisherman Harold Blaisdell shares the secrets he's discovered over years of catching trout, bass, salmon, pickerel, pike, and more. You name it, he's caught it. Here you'll find tips for catching trout with worms or minnows, attracting lake salmon with wet flies, making homemade decoys for ice fishing, and much more!